Liberalism and War

Military power is now the main vehicle for regime change. The US army has been used on more than thirty different occasions in the post-Cold War world compared with just ten during the whole of the Cold War era.

Andrew Williams provides a detailed study on liberal thinking over the last century about how wars should be ended, using a vast range of historical archival material from diplomatic, other official and personal papers and situating his study within the debates that have emerged in recent political theory. He examines the main strategies used at the end and in the aftermath of wars by liberal states to consolidate their liberal gains and to prevent the re-occurrence of wars with those states they have fought. He also explores how various strategies: revenge; restitution; reparation; restraint; retribution; reconciliation; and reconstruction, have been used by liberal states not only to defeat their enemies but also transform them.

This book will be of great interest to students and researchers of security studies, liberalism and international relations.

Andrew Williams is Professor of International Relations at the University of Kent at Canterbury and Visiting Professor at the Institut d'Etudes Politiques of the Université de Lille II, France.

The New International Relations

Edited by Barry Buzan

London School of Economics and Richard Little, University of Bristol

The field of international relations has changed dramatically in recent years. This new series will cover the major issues that have emerged and reflect the latest academic thinking in this particular dynamic area.

International Law, Rights and Politics

Developments in Eastern Europe and the CIS

Rein Mullerson

The Logic of Internationalism

Coercion and Accommodation

Kjell Goldmann

Russia and the Idea of Europe

A Study in Identity and International Relations

Iver B. Neumann

The Future of International Relations

Masters in the Making?

Edited by Iver B. Neumann and Ole Wæver

Constructing the World Polity

Essays on International Institutionalization

John Gerard Ruggie

Realism in International Relations and International Political Economy

The Continuing Story of a Death Foretold

Stefano Guzzini

International Relations, Political Theory and the Problem of Order

Beyond International Relations Theory?

N. J. Rengger

War, Peace and World Orders in European History

Edited by Anja V. Hartmann and Beatrice Heuser

European Integration and National Identity

The Challenge of the Nordic States

Edited by Lene Hansen and Ole Wæver

Liberalism and War

The victors and the vanquished

Andrew Williams

Routledge
Taylor & Francis Group

LONDON AND NEW YORK

First published 2006
by Routledge
2 Park Square, Milton Park, Abingdon, Oxon OX14 4RN

Simultaneously published in the USA and Canada
by Routledge
270 Madison Ave, New York, NY 10016

Routledge is an imprint of the Taylor & Francis Group

Transferred to Digital Printing 2005

© 2006 Andrew Williams

Typeset in Baskerville by Taylor & Francis Books

British Library Cataloguing in Publication Data
A catalogue record for this book is available from the British Library

Library of Congress Cataloging in Publication Data
Williams, Andrew J., 1951-
    Liberalism and war : the victors and the vanquished / Andrew Williams.
        p. cm. – (The new international relations)
    Includes bibliographical references and index.
    ISBN 0-415-35980-5 (hardback : alk. paper) 1. Peace-building–History–20th century. 2. Conflict management–International cooperation–History–20th century. 3. Reconciliation–History–20th century. 4. Liberalism–History–20th century. I. Title. II. Series.
    JZ5538.W55 2005
    327.1'72–dc22

                                    2005006718

ISBN10: 0-415-35980-5   ISBN13: 9-78-0-415-35980-1

ISBN10: 0-415-37833-8 (pbk)

Taylor & Francis Group is the Academic Division of T&F Informa plc.

This book is dedicated to the memory of
Miklòs Molnàr (1918–2003)

Contents

Preface

The liberal triumphalism that surfaced across the western world in the early 1990s following the defeat of Soviet communism has given way at the start of the twenty-first century to an extraordinary level of division and heart-searching. As western liberals have struggled to come to terms with the wider non-liberal world, the sense of certainty and supreme self-confidence, which emerged when they watched the Soviet Empire crumble and its ideology wither on the vine, has now largely evaporated. Because the benefits of liberalism so often seem self-evident to liberals, they are prone to ignore their own internal disagreements and the dilemmas and contradictions that have always existed at the heart of liberal thought. Certainly in the aftermath of the Cold War there was a tendency to forget that the emergence of liberal thought is still a relatively recent phenom-enon and that it is very likely that liberalism can only flourish under favourable conditions. As a consequence, the triumphalism that prevailed in the wake of the Cold War now looks not so much overly optimistic as naive. Hopes of operating in a new era characterized by peaceful change waned as western countries have either had to watch from the sidelines both new and unexpected bouts of conflict and the continuation of longstanding violence, or become actively engaged in war. Even more traumatic, liberals have had to come to terms with the fact that the demise of communism has not eliminated opposition to liberalism. On the contrary, liberals have had to acknowledge that there is virulent opposition around the world to some of their core ideals. Under these circumstances, it is perhaps surprising that liberals have failed to close ranks against their opponents. Yet instead of pulling together, liberals have become increasingly aware of their own internal dilemmas and contradictions.

This sensitivity to these problems, however, has arisen not because of the perceived weakness of liberalism, but because of its existing strength. Through-out the twentieth century, liberalism confronted powerful enemies that sub-scribed to conflicting ideologies. It was an era of total war. Under these circumstances, liberals have never been in any doubt that war is a price well worth paying to ensure that liberalism prevails over its enemies. Pacifism has never been part of the liberal creed. There is, however, much less agreement amongst liberals about either the validity of using force to propagate liberalism or what constitutes an appropriate liberal response when anti-liberal forces have been defeated at the end of a war. What do victorious liberals do with the vanquished? And, indeed, who constitute the vanquished? As the West has discovered in the post-Cold War era, there are no easy answers to these questions. Moreover, in many ways, the questions become especially difficult to handle when liberalism is operating so clearly from a position of strength. Many liberals have been deeply shocked by the insistence that civil liberties need to be curtailed in order to contend with the threat posed by terrorism. At the same time, the decision in 2003 to attack Iraq, either to protect liberalism in the west or to promote liberalism in Iraq, is considered by many liberals in the West to be both immoral and illegal. The criticisms would, no doubt, have been made, whatever the circumstances, but it is likely that they would have been much more muted if the West has been more obviously confronted by an existential threat.

In this book, Andrew Williams places the current ferment amongst liberals in a much broader historical context, exploring how liberals have responded to the problems that arose when wars were terminated throughout the course of the twentieth century. Examining the current dilemmas and disagreements in the context of this much longer time period makes it possible for Williams to offer a more nuanced and balanced assessment. The intention is not to provide a comprehensive chronological account of peace making in the twentieth century. Rather the aim is to select appropriate case studies from this era that will reveal how thinking and practices changed during the twentieth century and thereby help to account for the approaches that have been adopted in the post-Cold War era. In other words, Williams is able to show that policy makers are not operating on the basis of a *tabula rasa* but are contributing to a complex and on-going process and debate. Of course, it would be encouraging if it could be shown that policy makers have learned from the past and that the quality of decision making is steadily improving. In practice, such optimism rests on a false assumption, because policy makers have no alternative but to aim at a moving target. The present never replicates the past.

Williams is cautious about anticipating the outcome of current developments but accepts that the attempts to use force to eliminate security threats to the West and at the same time to promote liberalism could prove to be profoundly counterproductive. This double move, however, is at least in part a reflection of dilemmas that are inherent within liberalism. But more optimistically, Williams also acknowledges that reflexivity is an embedded feature of liberalism and so whatever the outcomes of current policies, they will be internalized and have an impact on future thought and practice. It is this factor, according to Williams, that helps to maintain the vibrancy of liberal ideas. This book pulls together a wide range of fascinating historical material in support of this conclusion.

Richard Little
University of Bristol

Acknowledgements

I would like to thank in particular the following individuals who have given me helpful comments on various drafts of this book or whose suggestions have led me down interesting paths: Ruth Abbey, Christopher Cramer, John (A. J. R.) Groom, Ken Kennard, Christian and Carolyn Leffler, Anthony Lentin, Ben Perks, Brian Porter, Bertie Ramcharan, Blair Ruble, Anne Stevens and Peter Wilson as well as the entire Williams family – Jane, Nicholas and Rebecca – who were often used as sounding boards for my more outlandish ideas. My apologies to those I have omitted to thank.

I would also like to thank the archivists and librarians in the many places that I have visited over the years and especially those at the National Archives in Kew, London, the Archives Nationales in Paris, the Library of Congress, and the Seeley Mudd Library at Princeton. Thanks also to the staff of the Carnegie Endowment for International Peace and the United States Institute for Peace in Washington DC, who were very kind in giving me copies of their documentation and putting up with my impertinent questions. As has become customary I would also like to give thanks to Chris and Lois Mitchell and Judy and Neil Garrecht-Williams, who have always extended me a warm welcome in Washington DC and New York respectively.

I would in particular like to thank the Editor of the *Review of International Studies* and Cambridge University Press for giving me permission to reproduce in part my article, '"Reconstruction" Before the Marshall Plan', Vol. 31, July, 2005, pp. 541–58 and Routledge publishers and the Editors of *Diplomacy and Statecraft* for allowing me to reproduce passages from 'Sir John Bradbury and the Reparations Commission, 1920–1925', Vol. 13, No. 3, September 2002, pp. 81–102.

Last, but not least, I would like to thank the man who launched me into this enterprise many years ago, Miklòs Molnàr (1918–2003), my teacher and friend. It is to him that I dedicate this book.

Introduction

Liberalism [might] be regarded as a conspiracy of the intellect against human nature: a true triumph of hope over experience.

John Charmley[1]

Liberal states have always sympathized, or on occasion gone to the aid of, those 'vanquished' by illiberal regimes, especially in the last hundred years. Usually that was with reluctance and after much soul-searching. In the nineteenth century the leader of that century's great liberal state, Lord Palmerston, was able to say that 'we have no eternal allies and no perpetual enemies'[2] and non-intervention even against those states that were deeply abhorred by British liberal opinion were (generally) left alone. But also in the last hundred years the 'Victors' have increasingly been liberal states themselves. They have used war and its aftermath as a means of spreading or confirming an ideology and practice that has become increasingly self-consciously universal in aspiration and impact. This trend has now arguably reached its highest, or 'lowest', point, depending on your view of the actions taken in Iraq since 2003.

For liberal states, so long on the back foot in their dealings with illiberal aggressors, have now taken the offensive in what is often referred to as 'pre-emptive' mode. The President of the greatest liberal state the world has so far seen has declared open season on 'rogue' states, by which he means those who do not agree with the principles underpinning the United States' political, social and economic system. The 'vanquished' have suddenly become those who previously lived by a creed of dictatorship, extreme Marxism, Communism or other ideology deemed dangerous in Washington. The aim of this volume is to show how that happened and to ask what its consequences might be, both for the targets of this new liberal fury and indeed for liberal states and for liberalism itself. Paul Berman calls this new attitude a militant 'liberal American interventionism'.[3] Many older liberals would call it ill-judged, immoral and counter-productive. Much of the discussion in this book might be seen as 'historical', but a central contention is that the present behaviour of the United States has its roots in both liberal philosophical debates but also in the historical experiences of an increasingly self-confident 'West' faced with a series of what have been seen as illiberal enemies. Another key contention is that there is another, possibly 'purer', liberal impulse that we see in the denunciations of the militant liberalism of the current American administration, one that downplays the role of the United States as the defender of 'freedom' but allows for individuals in areas of the world that have suffered persecution from illiberal regimes to rebuild their lives.

We can see the footprints of the new liberal militancy everywhere. In an interview on BBC television on the first anniversary of the attacks on New York of 11 September 2001 James Woolsey, Director of the CIA between 1991 and 1995, made a number of interesting and, in his mind, linked statements. The first was that the Gulf War of 1990–1 had 'never ended'; the second was that in 1918 there had been (by his count) about ten democracies, 80 years or so later the number was just over 100. Other (American) speakers, all with Establishment backgrounds, stressed that the Second World War had created democracy, peace and prosperity in Europe at the end of a long and terrible war. Such a process of war leading to these desirable ends was now necessary elsewhere, in Iraq. The 'unfinished business' of 1991 now needed to be finished and the liberal coalition 'against terror', mainly the United States and its faithful ally the UK, would be at the forefront of this. Another speaker made the analogy of what would happen once this had been done. In crockery shops there are usually signs saying, 'if you break it you own it'. In Iraq, as in Bosnia in the mid-1990s and Afghanistan in the early 2000s, the logic was clear. Wars had to be succeeded by reconstruction, as they had in 1945 and in the 1990s with the old Eastern Bloc. A member of the ultraliberal American Enterprise Institute put it even more succinctly: 'America's revenge' was 'to turn tyrannies into democracies'.[4]

Hence this book is an exploration of the genealogy of that kind of thinking over the last century, particularly, but not exclusively, as expressed in American political discourse and action. Its emphasis is a study of the main strategies used by states that consider themselves to be 'liberal democracies' in the aftermath of wars since about 1900 to try and consolidate their liberal gains and to prevent the re-occurrence of war with those they have been fighting. It may well be, as Plato has often been quoted as saying, that 'only the dead have seen the end of war', but it is a contention of this book that liberal thinkers and latterly liberal states have increasingly come to believe that they can bring about an 'end' to war by the spreading of liberal ideas and practices to those countries that do not yet recognize them as a blueprint for thought and action in international and domestic politics. There have been many liberal thinkers and statesmen who have implicitly or explicitly expressed the belief that the spread of 'liberty' or 'freedom' will bring about an end to war as an acceptable way for states and peoples to resolve their differences.

> If the developments of the last 15 years or so since the end of the Cold War have taught us anything in the study of international relations one lesson must be that ideas really do matter in the elaboration of policy by powerful states. As A. C. Grayling put it succinctly, 'our understanding of the human situation and the choices we make in managing the unruly and difficult complexities of social existence, are founded on ideas – usually, ideas

systematized into theories. Ultimately it is ideas that drive people to peace or war, which shape the systems under which they live and which determine how the world's scarce resources are shared among them. Ideas matter.'[5]

How much more so do they matter when those that believe in them have the ability to destroy the planet, deploy huge military and economic force and can claim a cultural dominance the like of which the world has never seen before? These players are the liberal democracies of the West. In the last 15 years or so liberal democracies have become obsessed with the idea of trying to create a 'stable peace',[6] one that briefly looked possible after the end of the Cold War. The events after the attacks on the World Trade Center on 11 September 2001, the invasion of Afghanistan in 2002, the second war on Iraq in 2003, the constant fear of attacks by Muslim Fundamentalist groups and the ensuing security measures in all liberal democracies have all contributed to a feeling that liberal states and communities of states have to protect themselves against ever more dark and illiberal forces. Many people have put this down to the particularly messianic (even 'fundamentalist') view of the world as encapsulated by the policy-makers around the current President George W. Bush in the aftermath of the first direct attack on the United States' mainland in 2001. But clearly there are strong historical precedents for the kind of thinking being used by the President and his advisors. Is what we are now seeing in the Middle East and elsewhere the apotheosis of a much deeper strain of thought and action in the United States and beyond, or is it the aberration of one over-heated American Administration? This has to be done without reading history backwards, an ever present temptation, so many of the chapters of this book will look at the past use and abuse of liberal impulses over the past 100 years.

The quote from John Charmley at the head of this chapter – 'liberalism [might] be regarded as a conspiracy of the intellect against human nature: a true triumph of hope over experience' was a jibe at President Woodrow Wilson of the United States. Wilson was part of a tradition of American liberalism that has flourished in the twentieth century as that country has emerged from its nineteenth century isolation to become the greatest power on Earth. Several recent books point to the enduring legacy of Wilsonian intervention, Michael Mandelbaum talking of the '[Wilsonian] ideas that conquered the world; peace, democracy and free markets'.[7] Wilson himself was as free with the use of the word 'freedom' as have been all American Presidents, a classic example being his declaration during the Presidential campaign of 1912 that 'I believe that God has planted in us visions of liberty ... that we are chosen and prominently chosen to show the way to the nations of the world how they shall walk in the paths of liberty.'[8] British Prime Minister David Lloyd George was able to marshal the same word to his cause during the First World War: 'Liberty is the sure guarantee of good will among the peoples of the world. Free nations are not eager to make war.'[9] The difference is that whereas Wilson was claiming that the United States was 'chosen' by God to spread this 'freedom', Lloyd George was stating what has become almost a 'law' of international relations – democracies do not go to war with each other – not an exclusive concept.

Wilson's theological certainty and that of many of his successors and predecessors, has often been to the dismay of British 'realists' like Charmley but also to many liberal Americans. Other (also liberal) Western politicians, notably Georges Clemenceau and David Lloyd George at the Paris Peace Conference in 1919, were able to scoff at Wilson's pretensions – 'God has his ten commandments, Wilson his fourteen points – we shall see.'[10] But many other Americans have held similar quasi-messianic views to Wilson. Charmley quotes a recent American Ambassador as saying 'America is a place where freedom dwells ... a beacon in the darkness, an ideal that illuminates the lives of millions ... [who] believe in the ultimate goodness of America, its destiny of greatness'.[11] But before the United States truly stepped on to the world scene similar expressions were heard from British liberal imperialists, as will be described in Chapter 1. One of the main features of the past hundred years has been the passing of the flame of the aspiration to liberal leadership of the world from Great Britain and its Empire to the United States, a process that has rightly been dubbed the 'Special Relationship', even if it is now quite clear who is the dominant partner.[12]

This Wilsonian desire to change the world in America's democratic liberal image has had its most recent proof in the actions of both Democratic and Republican Administrations since the end of the Cold War in the early 1990s. However, the basic liberal impulse has been overlaid by a very strong current of thought in the United States that this time the situation that Americans find themselves in is 'different' – '9/11 has changed the world'. Now the United States must fight not only for the freedom of others, but also to maintain its own. Not to launch pre-emptive strikes on potential enemies would be to ignore a 'clear and present danger', as the CIA puts it. One straw in this wind came from the book by Paul Berman, *Terror and Liberalism*, who pointed out that while previous President Richard Nixon was quite explicit that the war against Iraq of 1991 'will not be a war about democracy', that view was now untenable. Now, says Berman, 'we were facing a totalitarian menace – something akin to fascism ... the entire situation has the look of Europe in 1939, updated to the post-Cold War Middle East'. So '[s]houldn't the Arab world be as forward thinking as other parts of the world? Are Western freedoms only for Westerners? (No one thinks that Middle Eastern oil is only for Middle Easterners).'[13]

Berman is evoking the mobilization of 'liberalism' in a cause which has came to be called 'neo-conservatism', that of an interventionist spreading of the word; Nixon that of an old-fashioned nineteenth-century liberal as well as many that opposed war in the terms of the liberalism of John Stuart Mill, who famously said that 'peoples get the governments they deserve'. Non-intervention was then, and for many liberals is still, the norm. So what we have seen since 1989 is the emergence of a much more militant strain of liberal interventionism, one that sits in uneasy relation to older forms, as is evidenced by Prime Minister Tony Blair's (essentially liberal) Cabinet being split down the middle about how to act in the war on Iraq of 2003. Many American liberals feel uneasy about the war in Iraq, but they are also on the whole in favour of the victory of American arms there, if only to bring their soldiers home. The United States is thus stuck, as is Prime

Minister Blair, on the horns of an exquisite liberal dilemma. To withdraw the troops would be to sanction the victory of illiberal forces, to stay there is to be accused of illiberal actions themselves. The linguistic acrobatics from both sides of the Atlantic about 'weapons of mass destruction' (not found in Iraq) and bringing 'freedom' by blowing up various Iraqi towns or detaining suspects in Guantanamo Bay without trial or even charges being laid, demonstrates that even President Bush is uneasy about the task he has embarked upon and its potentially open-ended implications. The great liberal states now find themselves in the uncomfortable position of being accused of being warmongers for the first time, as will be suggested, in Britain's case, since the Boer War.

Of course this is not the first time that liberal states have felt under attack and have had to correspondingly look to both their defences but also to examine their underlying belief systems. In the twentieth century, in 1914, in 1939 (and many times in the intervening years), during the Cold War and since, there have been a number of occasions on which liberal states have indulged in a frenzy of self-examination and self-criticism. The expression 'why do they hate us so much?', much encountered since '9/11', has been a constant refrain ever since liberal world powers have existed. In the nineteenth century when the great, if imperfect, liberal world power was Britain, many of the British liberal elite asked why Revolutionary and Napoleon's France hated it so, why was Tsarist Russia and other would-be colonial powers so seemingly ignorant of the benefits that the British Empire was bringing to the peoples of Africa and much of South Asia and elsewhere? Many nineteenth-century American, German and even British liberals could understand that Britain was in fact self-seeking, but they still found the opposition to it far more appalling on the whole. In the twentieth century why did the Kaiser and Adolf Hitler seem intent on eliminating all liberal opposition to their plans for European domination. Why did the Soviet Union seem to want to spread its illiberal message across the globe? How could anyone claim that the United States, the twentieth century's great liberal power, could be suspected of imperial ambition when its urge was so clearly to liberate?

The tone of the above sentences is clearly ironic, but much of the outrage is not. The issues this book seeks to elucidate are related to how liberal states feel they should respond once they have defeated the challenges of the illiberal states through war or persuasion (which they have largely succeeded in doing) and trying to prevent their reoccurrence. For what distinguishes liberal states from their illiberal counterparts is that they believe quite sincerely in the creation of a better world and that they are exemplars of what that world should look like. In this, 'neo-conservatives' bear more than a family resemblance to Wilsonian liberals. Even if they are obviously not immune from seeking and holding power, they believe that they are doing this for the common good.

This is also a book that is appearing in a series on international relations (IR) as an academic subject. So how might it be said to fit into that subject's interests and obsessions? I take it as axiomatic that the main reason we study and practise IR is to try and create a world where statesmen will not see war as the instrument of choice for change. As Chris Brown has written, IR itself can be said to have come out of the pursuit of answers to the prevalence of war and to 'address and promote the prospects of peace'. Brown furthermore points out that IR can be seen as having its main roots in a reaction to the horrors of the First World War and as having its roots in the liberal American political science of the nineteenth century, which explains IR's 'Anglo-American leanings', ones which still dominate its institutional structure and 'academic discourse'. Furthermore, again in line with Brown's commentary, 'liberalism' is here seen as being of the mainly 'Anglo-American' variety, based on an elevation of the individual above the state, not, as with many Continental liberals, on the subordination of the individual to the state. In turn this disposition has had a marked influence on the current in IR known as 'Liberal Internationalism', underpins liberal beliefs that a sustained, even permanent, peace is possible and is reflected in the Charter of the United Nations and many other pious declarations, a discussion of which will be developed in Chapter 3.[14]

It will be argued in this book that these 'leanings' are in part at least an inherent dialogue between 'realist' obsessions with power and interest and 'liberal' yearnings after what Immanuel Kant called 'Perpetual Peace' and has often been referred to since as the 'democratic peace',[15] one guaranteed because all the parties to it are democratic liberal states, so that we might see not just a cessation of hostilities but 'an end to all hostilities' and the end 'of all existing reasons for a future war'.[16] The European Union is often used as a perfect model of what such a complex might look like. So in particular this book asks if and how we can create what is often referred to as 'just and lasting peace' after war? It is thus in the tradition of the early fathers of the discipline, as it is liberal in inspiration, universalist in aspiration and holds within it a belief that some sort of largely peaceful international society is not only possible but is in existence in parts of the world, if by no means everywhere. However it is also assumed that we have to be very self-critical in our assumptions about liberal values, to acknowledge that they are open to accusations of hypocrisy and self-justification. The realities of power must not be ignored and it is for power that most wars have been fought.

So what is the approach that should be taken in the following chapters and in the case studies that are embedded within them? It was a *leitmotiv* of my previous book on the conceptualization and implementation of the so-called 'New World Orders' of the twentieth century that history must be taken more seriously as a source of inspiration for IR scholars. That belief seems to have struck quite a chord with some of its readers.[17] This volume aims to continue to develop that insight but to change its form slightly. In this book I want to better thematize the inclusion of both contemporary and primary and secondary historical materials to better show the emergence of what I deem to be areas of reflection and action in dealing with wars and their aftermath. This is somewhat in contrast to the very '*evenémentiel*' approach of the last book, which attempted a fusion of diplomatic history and the history of ideas.[18] This leads in practice to a division of the main themes of the book into areas of action and reflection or what I would term 'mnemonic themes'.

Most of these themes, whether by chance or by historical design, seem to begin with an 'R'. It can be said without much fear of contradiction that many of the basic categories of thinking about how we should seek to end up wars do indeed begin thus – look for example at 'Reparation', 'Restitution', 'Reconciliation', 'Reconstruction', 'Resolution' and even 'Remembrance'. These are words that crop up constantly in the historical record of the last hundred years or more, not to mention the more obvious 'Revenge', 'Retribution', these last two of an older, pre-liberal era, provenance. The central aim of the book is to elucidate how they have evolved as terms and as practices; how they have harboured within them huge contradictions of belief and practice, especially for the liberal leaders of the 'West'; how they have been successful or not in preventing future wars; and how they have interacted (or not) with each other.

The method used will be those of the historian of ideas and of the comparative historian. These two approaches both stress the need to show the contingency of events and ideas in a particular epoch and how they have evolved. As Norman Naimark has observed '[c]omparative history... allow[s] the observer what is structurally the same and what is different in [different] cases and to think about what has changed and what has remained consistent over time'. Naimark's brief is to look at the notion of 'ethnic cleansing', which he stresses has changed considerably in its scope and meaning over the centuries.[19] In this case I am interested in a wide variety of phenomena that have changed in their definition and implementation over time. So for example, the concept of 'reconciliation' of formerly warring parties can be seen as new phenomenon in its recent 'Truth Commission' phase as seen in South Africa, but a much older idea that is embedded in Christian doctrine and practice, among other world views. The 'R's in this book are all forms of mental concept that we often use unquestioningly and a-historically. But of course they have all been embedded differently in different periods of even recent history. The challenge is to show how these different key ideas have assumed different forms in different historical periods and why and how they have merged in the policy practices of liberal states and those they have defeated.

This is not intended to be a definitive study of these 'R's, each of which have an existing and growing literature to which I am in great debt. Neither can it be exhaustive as no one could cover the topics dealt with in this book with such rigour, especially give that publishers have a necessary desire to keep word limits down. I have had to suggest which cases to concentrate on, which literature to privilege, which testimony to privilege. This is a book written with the instincts of the historian for what is significant and not one that aims at being comprehensive. It is hoped that it will stimulate a debate about how to emphasize or de-emphasize how these actors and processes described have interacted with each other over the last century. The choices that I have made in what needs to be highlighted and what can be left unsaid are mine, not necessarily those of my readers. Please feel free to disagree with me in that choice.

Design of the book

This book is clearly about the linkages between the aftermath of war and the making of peace. It has of necessity to be selective in what is examined. Not *all* wars will be subjected to the same level of scrutiny. Hence although Chapters 1 and 2 are dedicated to looking at some of the key liberal thinkers and thinking about how wars should be, or ended, in their historical and therefore evolving, context, a few key episodes have been chosen for their exemplary characteristics. These chapters also mainly, but not exclusively, concentrate on the nineteenth and twentieth centuries as a back-drop and to establish a framework, within which we can examine the more detailed liberal policy options for ending wars in subsequent chapters.

The remaining chapters will look at these liberal policy options, the 'R's, in some detail, again using a wide historical perspective. The first of these (Chapter 3) will look at what is widely seen as the 'cautionary tale' about how liberal states should *not* deal with a vanquished adversary, though the imposition of a 'reparations' regime. Many observers and policy makers working for, especially, the British and American governments before and during the Second World War saw the failure of the Treaty of Versailles summed up in this failed policy, one that was in any case reversed by a resurgent Germany in a way that humiliated the Victors of 1919. The next two chapters, 4 and 5, on 'Reconstruction' show the evolution in parallel and subsequent to the failed reparation option. 'Reconstruction' is still the tool box of choice for dealing with the aftermath of major conflicts, as we are now seeing in Iraq. Understanding its advantages and failures as an option is a crucial element in the conduct of current international politics. So are the other major categories of tools highlighted in Chapters 6 and 7, the attempt to find 'legalistic' solutions in the aftermath of wars, especially those of 'retribution', primarily through War Crimes Tribunals and 'reconciliation' (also often referred to as 'restorative justice'). Chapter 7 will also make some links with another, in many ways younger 'R', that of conflict 'resolution'. It is my belief that this option holds within it enormous promise for bringing a lasting solution to the problems created by war, as can be said to be evidenced by what is now unfolding in Northern Ireland. But ultimately the test of whether we can move to a global system where liberal norms and practices dominate and not those of the 'realist' jungle, will depend on the thinking and practice of the dominant liberal state(s) of the day. In 1900 this was Great Britain, now it is the United States. So the Conclusion will try and assess to what extent we can count on the good sense and understanding of the values and norms that underpin our liberal world order, for that is surely what we have, of the current leaders who claim to speak for us all and they are mainly based in Washington DC.

Sources

Apart from the writings of a number of precursor academic colleagues who have looked in some detail at what happens in the aftermath of wars,[20] the main first source for this book lies in the writings of liberal theorists and practitioners (by which I usually mean policy makers) of international politics. The choice of who 'really mattered' in either category is necessarily subjective and also has changed over time. The choice of which thinkers to analyse can seem bewildering as one of the key attributes of liberal societies is the sheer breadth of reflection that goes on in them, a source of both great strength and also of great seeming weakness. Civil society is by definition an inclusive and ever broadening and self-critical concept. Thus I have tried to use what must be seen as the main source of civil society opinion formation, the liberal (and other) press, both broadsheet and periodical.

Second, I have also used a fair variety of individual and foreign ministry unpublished and published material, especially from the United States and Britain. This I do not believe needs defending as the sources of foreign policy thinking have always originated in such source material. However, the discussion of IR theory and practice has to take into account Brown's assertion that this was developed largely as part of an Anglo–American progression. In many ways non-Anglo–Americans have always felt excluded from the resulting discourse. Those hostile to this, many of them 'critical' theorists or even Marxists, would generally see such intellectual cooperation and its ensuing policy choices as evidence of the emergence of a 'transnational', or even an 'Anglo–American class', one based on shared capitalist aspirations that has, in the words of Inderjeet Parmar, 'develop[ed] international networks – social, economic, ideological and begins the process of creating a transnational capitalist class, over and above the nation-state'. As Parmar indicates, the best recent statement of this can be found in the works of Kees van der Pijl, but also in such writers as Robert Cox, Stephen Gill and Craig Murphy. In their view of the world the drive for American hegemony is at the root of all claims that liberalism is a force for good in the world.[21] Gramscian Marxists like Gill and Cox would also point to the links between this economic and political networking for the emergence of an 'intellectual' hegemony.[22]

That remains to be proven. Parmar dismisses van der Pijl's analysis as 'economistic'. All these Marxist writers can be seen as taking what they wish from the historical record, but then, it could be argued, so do liberals who wish to defend what is being attacked. Parmar is also very critical of van der Pijl's 'absence of [historical] evidence' for many of these claims, but they are widely used in secondary literature and are rarely directly rebutted. I would not wish to deny such critiques completely but certainly hope to present the historical record in a different light.

So, third, I use a variety of 'unofficial' sources, particularly those of what can be termed the liberal 'think tanks' and publications. In the great liberal states, the United States and Britain in particular, these have proliferated since 1919 as a response to what Woodrow Wilson called the 'apotheosis of public opinion'. Alas they are largely untapped sources about liberal thinking in IR, except by historians, much of whose writing is not on IR reading lists.

Fourth, we must not forget the lineage that exists between academic and even what is often referred to in derogatory terms by academics as 'populist' philosophizing.[23] This may often be because such books are read whereas ones like this one are not! So the book will be littered with references to such thinking. The writings of Norman Angell and other so-called 'idealists' were for a long time dismissed in the study of IR. This was largely due to the belief that there had been a 'paradigm shift' away from an earlier generation of 'idealist' thinkers towards a much more 'realist' way of thinking about the world. Liberal thinkers and writers were bundled into the former category. This was clearly nonsense as an increasing number of IR theorists have now realized.[24]

The 'idealists' and the 'realists' were often the same people, or did not see they were in opposition. This was and remains a debate, about what 'ought' to be and what 'is'. The defence of liberal values and the creation of what many see as a global civil society, one based on liberal ideas, is the key focus of this book but also of much thinking in IR in general. All IR theory and indeed much of liberal, realist or whatever thought it might be argued, is about how to create a better world that is simultaneously fair, productive and endowed with meaningful institutions and goals for all its citizens, the pursuit of the Aristotelian 'good', in which a solution to the scourge of recurring war has always figured very largely.

1   The roots of liberalism and the first great liberal century

Let not England forget her precedence of teaching nations how to live.

John Milton, 1643[1]

I detest a man who knows what he knows.

Oliver Wendell Holmes[2]

Introduction: beginnings and ending of wars in thought and practice

The beginnings and endings of wars are totally linked, whatever paradigmatic approach you may take to war itself. War aims have no sense unless you have some idea about what you want the post-war situation to look like. Even in non-democratic societies there is usually some justification for war that is proposed before it is embarked upon. Adolf Hitler's Germany manufactured a 'border incident' with Poland in 1939 that 'insulted' German pride and sovereignty. Saddam Hussein had the clear aim in 1990 of 'restoring' Iraqi sovereignty over its '19th Province'. Both were excused on the basis of the moral authority of the state. The possibility of the 'amoral' war therefore seems to be ruled out even by its most amoral instigators.

But in democratic societies a far greater moral case for war has to be made. Even in August 1939 Chamberlain had real problems persuading the British that the continuous affronts to freedom by the Nazis could not be tolerated after they took yet another people's freedom. As the century wore on liberal democracies found it increasingly necessary to take public opinion with them, as the nature and timing of American involvement in two World Wars can be said to show or Tony Blair's insistence on the 'moral' case for attacking Iraq in 2003. Sometimes this is a post-facto moral and public-pleasing formula, like the necessity of Prime Minster David Lloyd George to build a 'land fit for heroes' in 1918, or President Franklin Delano Roosevelt a 'new world order' in 1945. But increasingly the case has to be made that this will be part of a meliorist project explicitly linked to defending and/or developing liberal democratic practices and ideals. This chapter and the next aim to show how that liberal agenda has developed *ad bellum* and, by extension *post bellum* looking at the evolution of liberal thought and practice in the engaging of, or resistance to, war by liberal states.

A preliminary question for us has to be why we need to think about this at this particular moment? This has been explained by Chris Brown as follows: first, there has been much more concern about 'Real World Events' since the 1970s – and wars in particular. The proliferation of wars in the 1990s and since is added incentive. Second, the question has been re-posed as at whether wars can ever be justly fought, with Michael Walzer's *Just and Unjust Wars* as one particular milestone in this questioning. Thirdly, there has been a restatement of key philosophical ideas (as in John Rawls' *A Theory of Justice*, of 1971), including 'the proposition that social arrangements are unjust unless the inequalities they inevitably involve can be rationally defended' – the principle of 'distributive justice'. There is now a widespread questioning of such questions as 'what obligations do rich states/societies/people have towards poor states/societies/people?'[3] Fourth, there has been a persistent split in liberal ranks between those who believe in what is usually termed a 'communitarian' view of rights, versus a 'cosmopolitan' view that everyone has rights and good liberals elsewhere should therefore defend them. This latter view has coloured recent reflection on the duties of liberal states to intervene or not to intervene if there is an inter-state or even a civil war that is causing widespread suffering to civilian populations. So is there now in the words of Michael Ignatieff, a 'modern conscience' that dictates intervention in the affairs of other states for humanitarian reasons as a norm, not an exception? If so, why is this?[4]

To this we might add that there has been an increasing conflation of the idea that the 'international community', meaning the 'civilised' and 'liberal' states, have a duty to dispense their justice to those who do not yet possess or understand it. This is a view that has arguably seen its greatest development in the thinking of the 'English' school of IR and Hedley Bull's 'Grotian' conception of international community.[5]

But do policy makers think like that? Have they ever done so? The short answer is 'yes' and there is, as this chapter will hope to demonstrate, a long and distinguished tradition of political thought (or what we now call 'normative' thinking in IR), especially of the liberal variety, that has made an impact on policy makers. Policy makers themselves have had many such thoughts as they too are motivated by instincts other than national interest. To assume otherwise is to assume that policy makers are not moral beings, a curious position to take, or that national interest does not have a moral component. Even those most identified as 'realists' would never take such a bold position.

So perhaps we make too much of the great divides of the recent past. Political (or 'normative') theory has not just been invented, it has been re-discovered in the context of the post-Cold War period. In the circumstances of a liberal 'triumph' after the end of the Cold War practitioners as much as theorists of IR have had to look to their laurels on how far they can claim that the actions of liberal states justify their dominance in the international system. When there was no option for the West other than to resist the attempted Soviet claim to global hegemony, there was no need to talk about 'ethics' in foreign policy or to justify the expansion of Western military and other forms of power. That was self-defence.

Now there is a clear need to consolidate the victory of the West by claiming a clear moral high ground. Hence in the West and beyond both practitioners and theorists feel a need to demonstrate how they can justify their victory in terms of the international 'good' of all.

In a fundamental sense the West has always understood this. Wars have long been seen as the culmination of a protest about how a local issue of sovereignty or the moral basis of how a wider international society is organized. The wars of decolonization in the 1950s and 1960s are examples of the former. Even that mainstay of 'realist' thought and practice, 'sovereignty', is not a neutral term, it holds within it a host of moral imperatives – the 'right' or otherwise to nation and state-hood, what Robert Jackson calls the 'moral standing of states'. The World Wars of 1914–18, 1939–45 and the Soviet Bloc versus the West between 1947 and 1989 are the paradigmatic examples of the latter. Sometimes the two overlap, as in the war in the Former Yugoslavia, which pitted the rump Serbia-Montenegro against Bosnia-Herzegovina and Croatia, where the global community felt a clear moral as well as strategic interest. In the circumstances of war it is clear that normative as much as empirical questions are in play here.

As a good empiricist I can accept the notion of 'schools of thought', or even 'paradigms' but with the proviso that we must avoid too strict a demarcation. Most, if not all 'isms' have been described by philosophers like W. B. Gallie and William Connolly as 'essentially contested concepts', especially liberalism. They are messy, open to multiple interpretations and often contradictory. They are also full of 'blind spots' about themselves. They are necessary to give the practitioners of any such theory the feeling that they are being consequential and coherent. To a critic they may not be so at all, and many of the 'mistakes' and 'hypocrisies' that liberals have been accused of are far more ones that can be seen as 'dilemmas'. Problems can be solved, dilemmas by their very nature cannot.

Moreover, philosophers like Jacques Derrida assure us that no element of thought or action can be divorced from any other, that they are all part of an evolving 'text'. In Terry Eagleton's words 'no system of meaning can ever be unshakably founded' and 'every coherent system is forced at certain key points to violate its own logic'.[6] Constructivist and post-modern IR theorists of war and peace make the same links between what they say is the nexus 'war – power – modernity'.[7] The simplified insight of this school of thought is that ideas (like liberalism), political institutions (like the state) and the relationship of means of production and the *Zeitgeist* (as with modernity) mutually determine how ideas are implemented by soldiers and politicians.[8]

This is, of necessity, a summary survey and it relies on a certain number of basic inspirations, particularly the writings of W. B. Gallie, F. H. Hinsley and Michael Doyle, on whom I have drawn a good deal.[9] It is also dogged by the problem of names being given to ideas. It could be argued that 'conservatism' might be a better way of describing what here passes for 'realist' thought. Jennifer Welsh for example points to Edmund Burke as the founder of a particular kind of notion of 'international legitimacy.' Conservatives assume the existence of a society of states with rules about how sovereignty can be conferred, legitimized and transferred.[10] These ideas, which Burke developed looking at the American and French revolution, have had profound effects on not just 'realist' thought but also on liberal thought, as in the discussion about 'humanitarian intervention', very popular since the end of the Cold War.

So this chapter and the next will therefore attempt to trace out the main parameters of (at least some of) the different schools of thought on war and peace and ask what can be said to be 'bedrock' and what can be said to be part of a shared debate. However, the primary concern will be with *liberal* thought as this the overall concern of the volume. This chapter is intended to act as a backdrop to future chapters that will look at the practice of various kinds of statecraft by individual liberal states and by the liberally-inspired international community, as reflected by their signature of the United Nations Charter and other documents of the same ilk, at the end of wars or 'after victory' as Ikenberry puts it.[11]

In general, an attempt will be made to assess the workability of the key ideas put forward, especially by liberals. For example, does democracy bring about peace? Is democracy necessarily a universal category? In particular it will be necessary to ask in this chapter and throughout the book whether the doctrine known as 'liberal internationalism' (LI) and whether LI in its various manifestations can be seen as an expression of 'British–American' liberal values (the French use the epithet 'Anglo-Saxon') and interests? In so doing the chapter will touch on some areas of the liberal canon that are familiar, such as the nineteenth-century liberals Immanuel Kant, Richard Cobden, John Bright and John Stuart Mill and others that can be identified as key liberal thinkers on war and peace. But the main thrust is to show the influence of ideas on policy makers, not just on the theorists themselves. This will mean that inevitably some thinkers and practitioners will be left out but hopefully not forgotten in other parts of the book and in the debate to which it will contribute.

Liberal thought: some generalities

Core beliefs and core dilemmas

What does it mean to be a liberal? John Gray has put it thus:

> Liberalism is *individualist*, in that it asserts the moral primacy of the person against the claims of any other social collectivity; *egalitarian* inasmuch as it confers on all humans the same moral status and denies the relevance to legal or political order of differences in moral worth among human beings; *universalist*, affirming the moral unity of the human species and according secondary importance to specific historical associations and cultural forms; and *meliorist* in its affirmation of the corrigibility and improvability of all social institutions and political arrangements.[12]

In practice this often means that liberals have strong views about morality as a guiding principle in both domestic and international life. As Richard Bellamy puts it, the strand that most people associate with liberalism is what he calls 'ethical liberalism' within which most prominent British liberals can be included (Adam Smith, John Stuart Mill) as well as many continental philosophers like Kant, Hegel and (most of) their respective followers. Their 'philosophical core' is the notion of 'liberty' and the belief that it was possible for all members of any society to benefit from this as individuals. Linked to this is a belief in 'progress', which as Bellamy points out, has 'theological foundations'.[13] The word 'theological' is important because it has often been said that it was the shift from the pursuit of religious unity (by definition across Christendom) to the search for political unity within states or across states in some form of *cosmopolis* that marks the beginning of the modern liberal era of 'civil societies'.[14]

Linked to notions of reason and morality, a bedrock of liberal belief emerged by the end of the nineteenth century that was clear and which differentiated itself from conservative and socialist thought and practice. Liberals have always looked to the carving out of new cultural spaces, to the creation of new senses of possibility. So in the nineteenth and twentieth centuries, science was seen as providing possibility for endless improvement, reflected in the great novelists of the nineteenth century in particular. But, as many have pointed out, this clear normative and practical framework came up against the hard bounds of reality as the market has proved incapable of delivering the kind of liberty, or even progress, that liberals wished to see. Science has proved a huge disappointment, creating as much despair as progress. Equally capitalism, the handmaiden in many liberal eyes of democracy, has of course come in for huge criticism. Take just one example, a comment by American social historian John Dos Passos in 1938 on J. P. Morgan the great American banker:

> Wars and panics on the stock exchange, machine gun fire and arson, bankruptcies, war loans, starvation, lice, cholera and typhus: good growing weather for the House of Morgan.[15]

The seeming defeat of an emerging European liberal consensus in the nineteenth century, for Bellamy 'the era of liberalism',[16] by the events of the First World War highlighted many of its key drawbacks and contradictions, not least the assumption that capitalism would reduce the danger of war between industrial states. Liberalism was forced to review its basic tenets in a very painful way in the inter-war period. An appreciation of this interiorization of the lessons of war is vital for understanding how both 'Anglo-Saxon' and continental European thought, not to mention extra-Western thought, has been in a quandary about the very basis of liberalism's claims to be the philosophy and praxis of equality, universality and amelioration. Hence, ever since its emergence as a coherent philosophical and practical position, liberalism has gone through a bewildering number of debates and broadly speaking polarized into what has come to be known as (for example) the 'liberal–communitarian' debate, one which pits a disparate group of thinkers in what has been deemed an 'ontological' debate about what liberalism means in practice.[17]

However, generalizations about liberalism can be both illuminating and mis-leading. Louis Menand was able to claim with much truth that 'in the nineteenth century liberalism meant a commitment to free markets: in the twentieth century it meant a commitment to individual liberties'. But when he goes on to examine a number of key nineteenth and twentieth century American Liberals – John Dewey (1859–1952) is one such – he finds that such generalizations are also dangerous. Dewey, whom we think of as 'a representative American liberal', neither believed in unfettered free markets or in excessive individualism. Most of his life was spent in the pursuit of getting people to organize for liberal aims – 'he rated solidarity higher than independence'. But where he was an archetypal lib-eral, says Menand, was in his 'opposition to the reproduction of hierarchies – political, social, cultural and even conceptual' and in that sense 'he was probably as liberal a thinker as the United States has produced.'[18]

Also in this vein, there is the dilemma about whether being a liberal also means one is 'middle class', or that ultimate Marxist put-down, 'bourgeois'. The 'middle class' certainly emerged during the same period as the rise of liberal thought; it was the 'base' from which this ideological 'superstructure' emerged, (to put it crudely). The liberal was almost always, in the nineteenth century at least, a man of commerce. As Peter Gay puts it: 'in societies where men of commerce gained great wealth and great reputations alike, middle-class ideologues took their order to be the very repository of civic virtue, destined to exercise power in the state and leadership in high culture.' Gay reminds us that John Stuart Mill described the middle class in 1826 as 'the glory of England'. As he further reminds us, even Marx and Engels praised (in the 1848 *Communist Manifesto*) those they thought were doomed to the dustbin of history:

> The bourgeoisie has subjected the country to the rule of the towns. It has created enormous cities. It has drawn all nations, even the most barbarian, into civilisation and ... rescued a considerable part of the population from the idiocy of rural life.[19]

The liberal intelligentsia of the West still sees itself as the 'repositories of civic virtue, destined to exercise power in the state and leadership in high culture'. Indeed they often define the debates of politics and culture and also their antitheses within these domains. They are, in the Gramscian sense of the word, truly 'hegemonic'.

That these 'hegemons' have exercised a hugely disproportionate role in international as well as national politics can therefore come as no surprise. What is, perhaps, surprising is that in spite of their continual arguments among them-selves they still dominate the debates of politics and culture and combine this with an ability to send vast numbers of young (mainly working class) men and women to war for their ambiguous, and indeed often contradictory, ends.

Seemingly with this in mind, David Williams has suggested that liberalism as a 'political project' is not just 'the production of theoretically justified ends and arrangements'. It has to include a 'sociological and political account of the barriers to achieving those desirable ends and arrangements', it 'involves the use of certain characteristic "techniques of transformation" [and ... it] can only be a project embodied in a political agency'.[20] It has, in other words, no reality without practice.

As Doyle says, there are many 'varieties of liberalism' as expressed in international thought. But the main idea is that 'promoting freedom will bring peace' – governments with a profound respect for individual liberty will exercise 'restraint' and have 'peaceful intentions' in their foreign policy.[21] Liberals believe that the application of the basic tenets of the credo to the practice of international relations, both in terms of how states should relate to other states, will lead to the creation of a better world. This translated in the nineteenth century (and indeed later) into an aversion to intervention unless at all avoidable and also into strong principles about how strong states should relate to other *peoples*. Many of the greatest liberals historically have taken strong stances on both non-intervention and imperialism, as well as about the need for states to co-operate, often to the point of 'uniting' in some way and they can be seen as test points for the differences with 'realist' thinkers and practitioners, by which we often in fact mean 'statist', and 'structuralist', by which we usually mean 'Marxist' or 'socialist'.

Are we not all liberals then? In theory we probably could be said in the West to now accept the basic norms of liberal discourse and action. But that means we also have to come to terms with the inherent contradictions in such stances. To quote but the most obvious: freedom must be constrained in order to continue; how do you protect the weak from the strong? How do you reconcile freedom/equality and order?[22] Equally we could argue that what one generation of liberals has found congenial is condemned by the next as 'Victorian values'. Can you just condemn such ideas as patriotism while denying that it was just such ideals that (arguably) saved great liberal states like Britain in 1940 from ruin? Is not patriotism in a liberal state the defence of liberal values? Hitler was only one of the illiberals who confused liberals' statements with lack of purposeful intent. If used to attack religion it can descend into preposterous claims that Christianity, for example, is only obsessed with sex and that it does not provide support for many liberal views while being quietly and effectively critical of abuses of such freedoms. In other words, liberals can be as intolerant as those they attack.[23]

Liberalism is also a contradictory ideology. Freedom, liberty and other expressions are fraught with difficulty. Whose freedom should we privilege in any given situation, can liberty be untrammelled? And so on. Because it is tolerant and encourages an 'open society' it is also vulnerable to attack by its 'enemies'.[24] This is literally (as in the World Trade Center attacks of 11 September 2001) and metaphorically the case. So we have to be tolerant of difference which can mean tolerating those who are not at all tolerant themselves – fundamentalists or extremists of all kinds. Where does 'tolerance' have to end and 'incitement to hatred' begin? This has particular resonance when we look at how tolerant liberals have been when they perceived their core values as being under threat.

A wider philosophical critique of liberalism must also come from what many would see as its 'ludicrous' over optimism. As one of the great liberals, Kant, put it, in war: '[t]here are dishonourable stratagems. [But] some level of trust in the enemy's way of thinking [*Denkungsart*] must be preserved even in the midst of war, for otherwise no peace can ever be concluded and the hostilities would become a war of extermination.' For Kant that would be inconceivable, for:

> a war of extermination – where the destruction of both parties along with all rights is the result – would permit perpetual peace to occur only in the vast graveyard of humanity as a whole. Thus, such a war, including all means to wage it, must be absolutely prohibited.[25]

But the twentieth century has seen many examples of just such wars arguably, as had the centuries before Kant wrote these words.

As Alain de Botton points out, from Seneca onwards conservative philosophers have believed that it is unwise to have 'dangerously optimistic notions about [what] the world and other people are like'.[26] John Gray seems in his recent books even to criticize what he sees as a quasi-religious belief in progress when he claims there is no evidence that human agency can achieve very much at all. The roots of liberalism are to be found in Judaeo-Christian mysticism, one that does predict a better life. Faced with the realities of environmental degradation, over-population and the other horsemen of the Apocalypse, liberals have no reason to believe they can affect the world for the better. Gray asserts that '[t]he idea of humanity taking charge of its destiny makes sense only if we ascribe consciousness and purpose to the species; but Darwin's discovery was that the species are only currents in the drift of genes. The idea that humanity can shape its future assumes that it is exempt from this truth.' For Gray a better approach is that taken by Eastern mysticism, which teaches an acceptance of the world as it is and to live in harmony with it, not to try and mould it in our own image, which the West has done to disastrous effect for centuries.

As Edward Skidelsky, a critic of this view, has pointed out, this view is conservative in the extreme and directed against liberals and Marxists alike: 'both vainly aspire to remake the world in the image of reason.' But Eastern mysticism has also been of great appeal to 'Nazis and modern management gurus. Gray's approving summary of Taoist doctrine could also stand as the formula of modern totalitarianism.'[27] For Skidelsky, Kant's optimism and humanism thus conveys a far greater solace and credibility.

There can be no definitive answer in this debate, indeed it is one of the 'consolations of philosophy' that we continue to have it. The proof of any philosophy has to be in the eating, and the study of war and peace gives us reason enough to hold contradictory views simultaneously most of the time.

Liberal attitudes to war

As has been mentioned and will be further stressed below, liberals have long taken as a core belief the notion of *non-intervention* in other states' affairs. This is linked to the notion of *tolerance of difference*, a belief taken from both notions of

Christian charity but also from a pragmatic desire to trade and to work through economic tools to reduce tensions and increase integrative processes. Many, if not all, liberals also have a strong streak of disbelief in what they see as extreme ideologies (communism and fascism, but also extreme religious belief) – hence the quote from Oliver Wendell Holmes to Harold Laski in 1930 that heads this chapter: 'I detest a man who knows what he knows.'

The main impetus for this increasing scepticism was, in that case, the First World War, the gap between stated goals and dismal outcomes and the manner of its waging. But Holmes had felt the same about the American Civil War, in which he had fought for the Union and been wounded several times.[28] This scepticism that war can ever achieve its stated beneficial aims also comes out very strongly in the thinking of Woodrow Wilson and nearly all American and British liberals. So another key contradiction can be found in the notion of the 'New World Order', a liberal perspective on global politics and one that has been repeatedly exported by force since 1917 at least. We also see it in the notion of 'humanitarian intervention' one that will be further explored in the next chapter. At what point is the 'moral conscience of mankind', as Walzer puts it, sufficiently shocked to merit intervention in the sovereign affairs of another state? *So is there an overall dilemma that is dominant in liberalism, the moral imperative to act or the moral imperative to stand back?*

This does not mean that liberals, or liberal governments, are necessarily pacifist. As Gilbert Murray, the famous early twentieth-century liberal, put it:

> I start from the profound conviction that what the world needs is peace. There has been too much war and too much of too many things that go with war. ... Before the [Great] war I was a Liberal and I believe now that nothing but the sincere practice of Liberal principles will save European society from imminent revolution and collapse.

He had had no problem in supporting the war against Germany, '... of course I supported the war. I believe it was necessary',[29] but what he did object to was the way that it was waged.

To explain this seeming dichotomy, Martin Ceadel has argued that the nature of opposition to war in the twentieth century necessitates an initial distinction between 'pacifism' and '*pacificism*' (his italics), the first meaning an outright opposition to participation in war, a perfectionist 'moral creed', the second more an 'ethic of responsibility [which] believes in implementing reforms at the political level – rather than waiting for profound changes in men's consciences'.[30] Prior to the Second World War *pacificism* essentially meant some form of 'internationalism', of which Ceadel discerns three main strains. The first of these is a mainstream liberal belief in the innate illogicality of war, as war is linked to atavistic nationalism. This had to be cured by 'improved international contact', essentially economic and cultural, or, if this fails, by diminishing the sovereignty of the state by transferring power to federal or confederal higher bodies. The second puts the causes of war down to capitalism and imperialism and sees some form of socialism as the only answer. A third strand, which Ceadel rightly sees as being strong just before the war, blends the two first strands, seeing war as economically irrational while attributing its encouragement to various capitalist influences and in particular the arms manufacturers.

Pacificism, says Ceadel, was particularly strong in inter-war Britain, but also a feature of the United States and in both countries 'was an integral part of its liberal, protestant political culture'. As has been pointed out, liberalism has strong 'theological' roots. Where nationalism was the dominant feature of political culture, as in Germany and 'where liberalism was too weak to nourish [any form of] pacifism' or in France where such movements were almost exclusively on the Left, it was probably easier to take a 'middle position between submissiveness and Realpolitik', as *pacificists* did in Britain or the USA, when the threat of an expansionist neighbour was not as obvious as it was for France.

We therefore have to ask, against whom can intervention by liberal states be justified? Gerrit Gong has written of the emergence of a clear liberal 'standard of civilization' by about 1905, under which countries and peoples were and are judged to be worthy, or not, of sympathetic treatment by Western liberal states. His first 'standard' has to do with the guarantee of basic rights; the second the existence of a '"civilised" state as an organized political bureaucracy with some efficiency in running the state machinery; [and third an] adhere[nce] to generally accepted international law; [fourth] fulfill[ment] of the obligations of the international system [in diplomacy]' and finally, the state must 'conform ... to the accepted norms and practices of the "civilised" international society' (so against slavery, suttee and polygamy for example).[31]

Liberals fought for all of these in the nineteenth century and this explains, at least partly, the particular appeal of Wilsonian and broader 'Anglo-Saxon' New World Order thinking of 1916–18 in Britain and the United States as it posited a re-ordering of international relations along lines that were already embedded in an existing liberal consciousness. In order for such ideas to spread, the over-arching liberal ideology had also to take root elsewhere. This did not happen until after the Second World War, in Germany, Italy and Japan at least and in each case it was by force of arms.[32]

Many of these states could be termed 'imperialist' and for many American liberals, Empires, as in Woodrow Wilson or Franklin Delano Roosevelt's cases, or Monarchs, as with Tom Paine, were anathema. The United States and Britain had a long-standing difference of opinion about the 'benevolence' of the British Empire but it was rarely seen in the same noxious category as those of Germany or Japan in the 1930s and 1940s or the Soviet Union until 1990. There is an obvious overlap with a hatred of authoritarian regimes, as with Churchill and Roosevelt against the Nazis, or Ronald Reagan against the USSR. Thus there is some liberal disagreement about who are the *main* enemies of mankind, but agreement that such people are 'uncivilized'. The reason is that these categories sum up what liberals most abhor and that attack what they most cherish. Karl Popper's *The Open Society and Its Enemies* (1943) was and is perhaps the best statement of what this is – freedom must be the aim, endless self-criticism/democracy the tool, a pluralistic society the guarantee. Such a society will ultimately be much stronger than its totalitarian enemies. In modern liberal terms it will be extremely tolerant, resistant to hypocrisy, informed by open and clear moral codes, respectful of human rights, distrustful of invasive state intervention in personal life and deeply suspicious of nationalism, patriotism and such appeals to 'tribal' identity.[33]

Liberal internationalism

The main concern of a book like this is the interaction of such ideas with the global international system; on their role in modelling this system and then changing it. 'Liberal Internationalism' (LI) has become the catch-all phrase to describe liberal thinking about war and peace. The expression first came to prominence in the First World War, although it arguably has earlier roots in the critique of domestic liberalism in the writing of J. A. Hobson in the late nineteenth and early twentieth century.[34] It has been closely associated with the thinking and actions of President Woodrow Wilson in the United States, but has also become linked to many 'idealist' writers of the inter-war period who will figure in coming chapters. LI has specific American roots that are both 'progressive' and 'conservative' in that some Americans came to believe that it was either America's moral duty to spread the liberal gospel to the rest of the world (broadly speaking Wilson's position) or that it was in America's interest to do so given its increasing aspiration to world power.

The doctrine of LI has wrought enormous changes in the world since the end of the nineteenth century. It has created a framework of international co-operation and a spreading definition of commonly held norms which do indeed include a purported respect for human rights, non-intervention, anti-imperialism, freedom of commerce and exchange and religious and political tolerance. It has seen off a raft of sanguinary dictatorships in Nazi Europe and the Soviet Union and influenced the moderation of many others, including arguably China. It has also led to the spread of an economic system of capitalism that many (liberals included) would say is deeply divisive to a global political system dominated by one liberal state the United States of America. Its origins can also be traced to the United States. Wilson was a prime publicist of the idea, but he did not give birth to it.

In order to trace where the framework came from and to see where its inherent contradictions still exist, a wide detour into nineteenth-century political thought and practice is necessary. In so doing I will attempt to show how the 'dilemmas' that liberal thought have inevitably produced can be teased out of the main thinkers in the foundational canon upon which liberal statesmen still explicitly or implicitly rely.

Seventeenth and eighteenth century liberal thinkers on peace and war

The search for the origins of any major field of thought is fraught with difficulty. Some might argue that the 'bedrock' of liberalism lies in the late eighteenth century, with the thinking of Adam Smith, who 'gave the Physiocrats' critique of the mercantile system an edge with the argument of an international peace flowing naturally from liberalism' – in other words, no capitalism, no liberalism. Mill wrote that:

> It is commerce which is rapidly rendering war obsolete, by strengthening and multiplying the personal interests which act in natural opposition to it. And it may be said without exaggeration that the great extent and the peace of the world, is the great permanent security for the uninterrupted progress of the ideas, institutions and the character of the human race.[35]

Locke and the 'inconveniences' of life, liberty and property

None the less Locke has come to be seen as one of the key originators of many tenets of the liberal idea. Indeed John Locke could be termed the father of modern liberalism in his descriptions of the state of nature and the application of human reason to the amelioration of humankind and a founder, with Jeremy Bentham, of what Doyle calls 'Liberal institutionalism', the organs of a liberal state. He was working within what could already be identified as a 'political and philosophical space that was both secular and modern' as well as reacting to the political and theological thinkers of his day, like Thomas Hobbes. We should not forget, as Doyle says, that his liberalism was 'revolutionary' in its day even if 'today his ideas seem utterly commonplace ... [Locke's] "life, liberty and property" became Jefferson's "life, liberty and the pursuit of happiness" and the justification of revolt against all manner of tyrants.' The 'State of Nature' was one where such things pertained, a 'State of War' where they do not. In order to assure that the former is the rule, good government must be instituted and the inhabitants of such a state will 'consent to civil society, a commonwealth'. Where good government is not instituted or maintained, rebellion becomes acceptable.[36]

Theodore Menand has pointed out that Locke's provision of the 'philosophical foundation of the Declaration of Independence' does not mean that Locke, or indeed the Founders of the United States, necessarily believed that individuals had the kinds of inherent rights we now associate with each person, in the sense of 'human rights' but rather that he and the Founders believed that '[s]ocieties are composed of autonomous individuals who establish governments in order to protect their natural rights'. The debate that took place between Jefferson and Madison in the *Federalist Papers*, and many times since, shows that the heartland of Western liberalism is not unequivocal in its belief in the primacy of individual rights over those of the community. The 2002 'Patriot' Act carries very strong restraints on the liberty of the individual in the interest of the community. As Menand also points out, the legal history of the United States is littered with such examples and can be summed up in Oliver Wendell Holmes' 'pragmatic' belief in the importance of 'context'. Freedom is not without its limits.[37]

Although it would be invidious to draw too many ahistorical lessons from Locke, we can still try and draw out what was significant for us as the revolutionary nature of liberalism is still with us. It does aim to change the world and has succeeded in that better than any other ideology. His thought has provided many of the key ideas upon which the wider project of liberalism, both national and international, is still based.

In the realm of the international as in the domestic, the 'state of nature' will ensure peace. Wherever the sanctity of life, liberty and property prevail there can be no 'state of war'. A Commonwealth of all nations will be the result for those who cleave to the basic principles of the 'Natural Law of Nations'. They will uphold the law in their domestic setting and be the natural allies of other nations that do likewise. As Doyle puts it they therefore act as 'rational *legal* egoists' bound to abide by the law but also bound to exercise prudent advantage when they doubt that others are upholding the law', and in so doing risking the establishment of a 'state of war'. For Doyle, the inescapable conclusion of this is that states that uphold liberal tenets have the right to intervene in any state that does not: 'any aggressor state that violates the natural rights of states or individual makes itself the target of a just war of defense and even conquest.' The implications for international law and the post-Cold War notion of 'humanitarian intervention' are clear says Doyle, for this doctrine would seemingly justify any action that could be claimed as supporting the principles of life, liberty and property. This goes far further than most international lawyers of today would venture in that it seems to justify pre-emptive war as much as wars of self-defence and also the notion of the individual responsibility of statesmen in the sense now envisaged by the International Criminal Court. Doyle even suggests that Locke gives the perfect basis for going beyond the state of nature for individual states to a wider Commonwealth of states, a world government.[38]

However this is perhaps to read into Locke what he could not have foreseen: the modern international system. Apart from the claims outlined and much developed by Doyle, which are clearly of immense importance, he had little to say about international politics in the sense that we understand it now. It is arguable that his main contribution was to engage in the colonial debates of his day, where he attempted to justify British colonial practice in the new colonies of North America. There the idea that the legitimacy of the state was based on its ability to promote a rational, egalitarian and just political system, or 'Commonwealth', had a very practical application as the incoming British state had to justify its disenfranchisement of the native population. As David Williams has pointed out, Locke's view was that Indians had no inherent right to their land or resources because they had not used that land and resources to best effect and 'uncultivated nature has been left to itself, without the help of letters and discipline and the improvements of arts and sciences'. Williams makes it clear that Locke thus wished to see the improvement of mankind to make the poor 'sober and industrious all their lives after'.[39] For Locke the main purpose of existence was to make men 'better' and if that required colonial coercion, then so be it. The basis of a right to property was that it had to be earned. A similar logic was used by the state of Israel and by Zionist Jewish colonists before and after 1948 to justify the expulsion of Arab 'nomads' from their land so that it could be improved by technologically more advanced settlers. Loche thus justified what to many modern liberals are seemingly very illiberal practices.

Another contributory area of IR that can be pointed to, lies in the inter-relationship between nations in times of war when the attempt to export the 'state of nature' will lead to the ordinary population being caught in the crossfire between governments of whatever hue. In Michael Walzer's words:

> [i]n international society, as in Locke's state of nature, every individual member (every belligerent power) claims the right to enforce the law. The content of this right is the same as it is in domestic society: it is first of all a right of retribution, to punish guilty men and women; it is secondly a right of deterrence, to protect oneself and others against criminal activity.[40]

But as Walzer points out, retribution and deterrence may sit easily with each other in a domestic polity in peacetime in war they do not. It can, in the cases used by Walzer to illustrate his point, lead to innocent people suffering for the fault of others, in this case German prisoners of war shot as a reprisal for the shooting of French civilians. We could enlarge on that by suggesting that liberals have the problem that it is often to make the guilty government of a state suffer for its crimes that the civilians of that state must also be punished, even if they are not guilty, but in many ways also victims of their own government. The logic is clear in many wars that have been waged by liberal states in the last hundred years. We can therefore see that in the foundational thinking of Locke remain many of the dilemmas, or 'inconveniences' that haunt liberal states still.

Immanuel Kant[41]

Immanuel Kant was arguably the greatest of the liberal internationalists. Indeed, according to Chris Brown, 'Kant is the greatest of all theorists of international relations' because he tried to 'put Enlightenment on a sound footing' through an understanding of self and was against Hume's 'antimetaphysics' for 'it is the mind that gives order to nature rather than nature which reveals patterns to the mind'. Pure reason will not do as it cannot explore the moral universe, even if it might conceivably explore that of science.[42]

For Kant the question was how you can act in such a way that you always treat humanity, whether in your own person or in the person of any other, never simply as a 'means, but always at the same time as an end', so we are all 'law mak[ers] of a kingdom of ends'. In other words, for Kant, all politics must be governed by morality to devise 'a constitution allowing the greatest possible freedom in accordance with laws which ensure that the freedom of each can co-exist with the freedom of all others'.[43]

Kant's ideas (followed by generations of liberals) are complex, but are summed up here. Rationality makes us morally responsible for a reasoned approach towards other individuals and peoples. In his *Critique of Pure Reason* and other writings Kant asks us to approach each other with openness as our perception of the world can never be anything more than partial. We do not and cannot know everything, but that puts us under the imperative to find out and to be free.

The Enlightenment produced a number of men (Rousseau, Voltaire, Hume, Kant) who saw themselves as 'global' individuals, even if not all of them were in agreement with Kant as to what that should mean in practice (especially Rousseau). But we can date the development of many key ideas in IR from Kant and these other thinkers. Kant was convinced that the principle objective of man is to grow morally and to put himself in agreement, or reconcile himself, with others, as without this there will only be war. So individuals must unite in a social contract that has at its base the individual. In this last point he disagreed with Rousseau, whose social contract was based on the notion of a *general*, not an *individual* will.

The only book that Kant wrote for a popular audience, *Perpetual Peace* (1797), was an important one not only as a work of political theory, but also as 'a convincing answer to the problem of war [without which] the rest of his moral and political philosophy turns to ashes'[44]. The problem was its inaccessibility to the vast majority of even informed political opinion, so that it has been often quoted as a key inspiration for liberal internationalists. Gallie sees its propagandistic effect as 'a failure, indeed a disaster'.[45] But for Gallie the idea behind it is key to all thought on the subject since. For Kant asks in very concrete terms: 'How can we conceptualise the problem of peace?' (and how can we do this in a world of states)?

Kant's 'Definitive Articles' state that:

- Nations should be republics (he did not say 'democracy') (First Article) and the constitution will be based on the civil rights of individuals within that state
- And be united in a federation of free states (Article 2)
- Everyone has the right to demand hospitality of that state – as a refugee for example, (but only if he behaves peacefully and there is no right of abode necessarily), (Article 3) and 'can be seen as part of a universal state of mankind (*ius cosmopoliticum*).'[46]

These ideas are at the heart of 'liberal internationalism' – into which tradition we can put Mill, Jeremy Bentham, Woodrow Wilson, Franklin Delano Roosevelt, Jean Monnet and the idea of a 'new world order' as well as the idea of one based on a peaceful Europe. In addition, there is embedded within this tradition the idea that free market or at least some form of liberal economics is the cement for all this, as is human rights. This is a cosmopolitan tradition that sees man as the measure of all things.

Kant's impact was supported and accentuated at the beginning of the nineteenth century by the growing commercialization of the world, which Jeremy

Bentham thought would destroy war on its own, an idea that is repeated in the twentieth century with the writings of Joseph Schumpeter whose *Capitalism, Socialism and Democracy* (1950)[47] claimed that capitalism dislikes war and imperialism's unlimited forceful expansion, a theory that he expanded upon in *The Sociology of Imperialisms* (1919), because it does not pay. Schumpter claimed in support of his theory, for example, that British imperialism was not an intrinsic part of Britain's economy. He can thus be seen as another of the originators of the democratic peace argument – but such ideas can also be found in the writings of Norman Angell and virtually all the idealist Liberals of the 1920s and 1930s.

Bentham equally had a moral objection to all war, one not unnaturally based on the principle of utility, and as Cobden in the next century believed, it was illogical in that detracted from trade, the fountain of all prosperity. His *Plan for a Universal and Perpetual Peace* (1786–9) has echoes of Kant within it but a greater emphasis on war's economic illogicality. It is perhaps significant that these thoughts were not published until Cobden's day, in 1843, when they were seen as mainstream liberal thought.[48]

Liberalism and foreign policy, peace and war after Kant

Most states by 1815 had accepted the need for principles of international order, even those that were not democratic. All of them tried (and, for a realist, 'try' still) and reinforce what Andreas Osiander calls the 'structural principles of international society'. These were and are: the number and identity of international actors (states, but also international organizations); their relative status *vis-à-vis* each other; the distribution of population and territories among them and; '[t]he various kinds of institutions or organizations that actors may share among them'.[49] These principles are arguably what the international system has been working out ever since. Liberals have always believed in more integration in thought and deed by the liberal forces of Europe and the world; Marxists in a similar collaboration between socialist leaning peoples. Realists would not see either of these solutions as more than idealistic nonsense, but would accept, as did Bismarck in the nineteenth century, that national self-interest could often include avoiding war and encouraging national cooperation within certain bounds. The current debate on 'what kind of Europe' we want reflects this divide very well.

It is also worth remembering that the main issues of war in nineteenth-century Europe were over nationalism and the effect this would have both on established autocratic Empires in Europe but also over the linked spread of liberalism, which these same autocratic empires saw as a dangerous cancer at the heart of traditional political and social values. The Napoleonic wars had been fought by the autocracies on the basis of a need to defeat both tendencies. The opposition to these autocracies had received an enormous boost from Napoleon's military, legal and cultural successes. Liberal nationalists led the way until the middle of the nineteenth century, although their nationalist ambitions were to some extent hijacked by a revitalized conservatism after the 1848 revolutions.

Until then, many liberals believed that the abolition of monarchy and its replacement by 'nation' as the guiding principle of human organization would lead to the end of war. As Thomas Paine said, until '[m]onarchical sovereignty, the enemy of mankind and source of misery, is abolished and sovereignty is restored to its natural and original place, the nation' there could be no peace. 'Were this the case throughout Europe the cause of war would be taken away.'[50] It was the case that the main threats to peace and security in Europe during the nineteenth and indeed the twentieth centuries were the remaining autocracies, Germany, Russia and Austria–Hungary. Generally speaking nationalism was thus seen as good thing, but it was assumed that this would lead to the end of autocracy, which was often not the case. Few states had constitutions and fewer still were democracies. But the 'self-determination' of peoples was seen as a first step towards a truly democratic and liberal world system and thus encouraged by liberals, even if, as Michael Walzer interprets Mill in *On Liberty* (1859) as putting it:

> We are to treat states as self determining communities ... whether or not their internal political arrangements are free, whether or not the citizens choose their government and openly debate the policies carried out in their name. For self-determination and political freedom are not equivalent terms.[51]

One problem lay in the nature of the 'self' that was being determined, a problem which persists in liberal thinking about, say, Saddam Hussein, or Robert Mugabe's Zimbabwe. Mill shared a widespread eighteenth- and nineteenth-century belief in the need to beware of 'barbarians' – if those who led people to 'freedom' were of such an ilk they could be reprimanded and if necessary intervened against. This was made quite clear in *On Liberty*, as Locke had. The justification for the massive destabilization of the North African Caliphate regimes and many African kingdoms in the nineteenth century by overwhelming force was because they were 'barbarians' indulging in 'barbaric' practices, like slavery. In such circumstances moral impulse and foreign policy were uneasy but inevitable bedfellows, as they have continued to be ever since. Current liberal thinkers and policy makers (Robert Cooper is one that combines both roles) are unrepentant in using Millean language to defend the intervention in Iraq in 2003 on these grounds.

Equally the rise of socialism was predicated on the moral need to create a pan-European (and beyond) fellowship of working people of all societies. The International set up by Karl Marx in 1848 with the rallying cry 'Workers of all lands unite, you have nothing to lose but your chains' in the *Communist Manifesto* assumed that nationhood was another bourgeois snare which would inevitably set working class against working class. The only solution was an organizational structure based on class, above the state and ultimately undermining it. As Francis Wheen points out however, Marx himself recognized the revolutionary power of liberal thought to the point where the *Manifesto* has been recently called 'a lyrical celebration of bourgeois works'. Marx however roundly rejected the liberal notion of enlightened individualistic self-interest, which liberals believed would bring the world to capitalist bliss. For him it could only lead to war and suffering across the planet as imperialism took the dogma to all quarters of the globe. Wheen comments that liberalism has tried 'to create a world after its own image' and has largely succeed in so doing. Even the main street of Beijing now:

> looks eerily like Main Street, USA, with McDonald's, Kentucky Fried Chicken, Haagen-Dazs and Pizza Hut, plus several branches of Chase Manhattan and Citibank in which to deposit the profits. No doubt a Marxist would say that the Chinese are not socialist, but the liberal should surely comment that they are not democrats. Without democracy the Chinese nation is as likely to be manipulated into warlike activity as Germany was in 1914.[52]

What did happen, in terms of the result for the bourgeoisie and the working class alike, was that the rise of the nation state led to warfare being transferred from being the Sport of Kings to being one of civilian war. Both liberals and socialists struggled throughout the nineteenth century to get their views accepted within the court of either national or world public opinion and opposition to war as an instrument of normal state practice only fell into disrepute where liberals and socialists alike succeeded in getting their very different messages across. All that Europe actually got until the First World War was a very realist structure, the Concert of Europe, which to a large extent succeeded in restraining the nation states of Europe, nascent liberal democracies and autocracies alike, in a collective self-interest to largely keep war outside European boundaries by multilateral conferences stopping quarrels turning into wars.[53]

How would wars be? – Thinking in the nineteenth century

The Crimean War, which pitted the French, Turkish and British states against Russia (1854–6) has often been dismissed as an 'abortive and futile episode'. It is seen as minor episode in the British and French Imperial attempts to hold back the tide of Russian expansionism in the Middle East, a side-show of the 'Great Game'. But the contemporary debate was very different. As Olive Anderson puts it, '[a]lmost to the end' of the war and the signature of the Treaty of Paris in 1856, 'contemporaries expected something very different from what actually came to pass. They expected a long and global war, terrible in its scope and divisive in its outcome – devisive not only with regard to power relationships but with regard to the great contemporary issues of liberalism and nationalism'. In England, seen as the home of all progressive thought and increasingly seen as the greatest of the Powers both militarily and economically there was enormous debate on these issues.

Around the middle of the nineteenth century opinion-making in England was remarkably evenly divided between those who judged the present by looking back to the past and those who judged it by looking forward to the future. ... The country was poised between Coleridge's 'Principles of Permanence and Progression', between the 'wisdom of the ancestors' and the march of intellect.

The past was a very fashionable subject during this period and '[p]art at least of the explanation lies in the prestige of modern history as a moral science and its commercial success as a form of literature'. Anderson points out that the Napoleonic Wars which had dominated British military and other forms of thinking for 25 years were central to this success, so that any war was seen through the lenses of that quasi-global experience. But also many looked forward to the triumph of science and technology, in which fields Britain was seen as pre-eminent and certainly far better equipped than the backward Tsarist Empire. For moderate liberals this meant a short war that would reconfirm British leadership against dictators. For socialists it could be the portent of a wave of revolutions (Anderson reminds us that it was in this context that Marx referred to revolution becoming the 'Sixth Power of Europe') as the Tsar's subjects were liberated by French and British guns, celebrated by Marx and later by Edward and Eleanor Aveling, in *The Eastern Question*, 1897. Whatever happened they all 'expected the war to provide a great, almost a portentous event in the history of the world'.[54]

Britain went into the war with many liberals fearing what war would do to a global player like Britain. It had an extensive Empire, but also a 'uniquely industrialized, free trade economy, already closely geared to world trade. How would the workshop of the world fare in what promised to be a world war?'[55] Again Britain had some understanding of what might happen by looking back to the Napoleonic period. The Royal Navy had more or less ensured that Britain could continue to trade and to blockade the enemy states of Europe. It had proved to many people's satisfaction, and not for the last time, that Britain did not 'need' Europe.

The roots of this reflection lay in the increasingly dominant ideology of liberalism. The nineteenth-century liberals were very influenced by both the 'revolutionary rationalism' of Shelley, Coleridge and others influenced by the French Revolution (even if they turned against it) and by the Benthamite idea of utilitarianism, by what must be called a 'scientific' conception of human behaviour. This created what has been called by J. A. Hobson, himself a prominent liberal thinker, a belief and a confidence in 'enlightened self-interest, operating first on the material plane ... [but which] below all immediate appeals to individual self-interest there lay a law of social harmony'. This 'material plane' was especially seen as happening through the expansion of free trade and a generalized non-intervention by governments in the affairs of men, as much as was feasible, 'in the peaceful pursuit of their own material and moral interests.' Associated with this Hobson sees an overwhelming optimism in the future and a degree of 'moral consistency', the hallmarks for many of the classical nineteenth century Victorian liberals.[56]

Cobden and Mill

Richard Cobden was a classic example of this trend, as were John Stuart Mill and John Bright. F. H. Hinsley has associated this movement in ideas with the development of the modern state as a result of and in the aftermath of the French Revolution.[57] Cobden espoused, as did Mill, the notion that non-intervention in the affairs of other states was usually the wisest course, a notion that can be found as far back as Locke. Mill has been quoted as saying that self-determination, a right that all peoples should have, did not necessarily mean that they would create states that were pleasing to liberal states. To hope for this was wildly idealistic. The impetus for freedom in a community is analogous in this scheme of things to the search for virtue in an individual: 'they cannot be set free, as he cannot be made virtuous, by any external force'.

So in purely utilitarian terms, intervention to liberate must fail. If it is of short duration it cannot make an impact, if of long duration it will be self-defeating as it will destroy the very forces for freedom that it hopes to encourage. So if the people cannot become free by their own efforts no amount of outside help will do the job. As Mill says 'peoples get the Governments they deserve'. To take the Millean argument forward a hundred years, Walzer agrees that in the cases of Germany and Japan after the Second World War we might see a case for Mill being wrong, but these he says are not typical and '[t]hey clearly don't arise in every case of domestic tyranny'.[58]

So liberal thinkers like Mill were against using liberal states' superior force, one endowed by democracy and capitalism. But they also saw the development of a growing world-wide interdependence and thought in conformity with the changes 'that have taken place over the entire globe'. This led them to denounce the balance of power and the impediments to trade both within and between countries, as well as war itself. The repeal of the Corn Laws in 1846 showed that he had largely won the intellectual argument over free trade, but not by any means that over non-intervention.[59] Cobden's idiosyncratic view of the world could see no logic in singling out one foreign nation to hate, such as Russia, when Turkey was just as bad. He put this down to the inability of the Englishman 'to do two things at the same time'. For him all illiberal states were as bad as each other, or rather, as his biographer put it, 'prejudice against other nations [w]as ungenerous and puerile'.[60]

For Cobden, war was to be avoided at all costs, as was intervention in the affairs of other states, with disputes to be worked out by constitutional arrangements with other states wherever possible. The problem was always one of 'What next? And next?', the title of one of Cobden's pamphlets in January 1856 concerning the termination of hostilities with Russia. What did war produce other than more war? He also asked how was it possible to defeat a country like Russia that was essentially wedded to the idea of economic self-sufficiency. This in turn should have led, said Cobden, to a seminal shift in the way liberal states looked at notions such as aggression and defence. The only answer, he wrote, was to band together with like-minded liberal states and 'constitute a European bulwark against Russian aggression by means of treaty arrangements which would bring into being a "federation of the States of Europe'". This he believed, as did J. A. Hobson who agreed with him in 1919, would 'prevent any possibility of attack from a common enemy'. Since Hobson and Cobden were advocating doing this with Germany against Russia there was much prescience in their agreement, even if it was alas an idea too soon for its times.[61] Cobden was thus, as will be noted repeatedly, not against war *per se* but against the illogicality of its waging.

The danger was that liberal states in attacking illiberal ones would end up damaging their own interests more than those of the enemy. To read Mill (and Cobden) through Walzer's formulation: what must be done in all cases was 'to recognize and uphold communal autonomy'.[62] This is the kind of thinking that motivated Woodrow Wilson and, indeed, Franklin Delano Roosevelt. They wanted to make a world safe for states. They wanted these states to then band together to defend themselves against aggression in international organizations, to in effect 'pool' their sovereignty, but that did not mean giving up the notion of sovereignty, but rather reinforcing it. Mill and Cobden were thus making an important moral distinction, which Ceadel approvingly quotes Hinsley as saying was based on 'a greater displacement of assumptions about relations between states than any that has taken place in history'.[63]

The decline of British power, 1900–18

When one single Power has come to epitomize the liberal values of its day, as has (for good or ill) the United States today, the fate of that one state is crucial for an understanding of why liberalism can get itself into trouble at the moment of its seeming triumph. The nineteenth century had seen remarkable strategic and economic stability in some ways. British power had kept the peace at sea and liberal regimes' aims had begun to see their fulfilment though a gradual break-up of the old autocratic Empires in Europe. Liberalism seemed to be on a winning streak. Italy and Germany had gained their self-determined independence, after the liberal revolutions of 1848. The hegemony of the City of London had ensured the spread of liberal ideas of free trade and had helped create a kind of Lockean 'Commonwealth' of the bourgeoisie, even if political power was still not over-concentrated in the hands of the people, even of the 'middle classes' in many parts of the world, or indeed of Europe. Autocracies in Russia, Austria–Hungary and Germany still persisted, even if there were real stirrings of democracy even in these places. But the United States was emerging as what even Karl Marx could see was a successful and growing liberal bourgeois capitalist state, a helpful stabilizer and promoter of democracy in the Americas and even a benign restraint on Britain's excessive military ambitions. There was real and growing affection between the increasingly powerful liberal elites of the United States, Britain and Germany. Most significantly what we now call 'globalization' was there in all its main elements by 1914. Most commentators would not have thought it conceivable that Britain and Germany, the two industrial and commercial powerhouses of Europe, could ever go to war. They had far too much to lose. The theories of Jeremy Bentham, and even those of Immanuel Kant, seemed to be on the verge of their full realization.

But even by the middle of the nineteenth century, British success had spawned jealousy. States felt constrained by the dominance of the City. As Eric Hobsbawm has written, the states of Europe by 1850 felt that they could 'take no action, pursue no policy and undertake no war if the House of Rothschild set its face against it'. The financial power of the City and especially of the Rothschilds, was such that 'their financial power was just as vital to the state bureaucracies and the standing armies'.[64]

British self-confidence had also been eroded by the rise of other powers with equally or possibly superior technological and military capacity. This led to the Royal Navy and the City of London being two of the main supporters of the Norman Angell thesis of 1910 that war was 'the Great Illusion'.[65] Part of Angell's concern, as was that of the Royal Navy, was that American and/or German power was growing and might threaten the peace of the oceans, what Britain referred to as the 'Freedom of the Seas'. American Admiral Mahan and Britain's Halford Mackinder had popularized geopolitical theories that were taken by many to mean that there was likely to be a battle over who should dominate what MacKinder called the 'World Island'. The Royal Navy's interest was to make sure that they continued to control the waters round this, for what they saw as evident reasons of imperial interest. One of Angell's sub-texts was to persuade the Germans and Americans that trying to out-build the British navy to reverse this domination was both foolish and unnecessary. The Royal Navy was there for the whole world's good, not just that of London. It is perhaps not surprising that Americans and Germans were suspicious of this logic. But for Britain, increasingly feeling that its liberal credentials were being questioned in Berlin and Washington, it was vital that the British domination of the seas and its vast Empire did not give rise to excessive suspicion and desire on the part of the other powers. War would have been the inevitable result and this would indeed have damaged British interests, whether Britain won the ensuing conflict or not.

The Boer war and Cecil Rhodes' 'end of all wars'

But, as possibly with Iraq today, a single event can be seen as having profoundly shaken this self-belief. It is arguable that this key event to challenge Britain's moral leadership of the liberal world was the Boer War of 1899–1901. Britain's election of a militant imperialist government dominated by Joseph Chamberlain and the imperial actions of Cecil Rhodes (architect of Britain's Southern African policy for many years) and Viscount Alfred Milner (the Proconsul in the Cape) had allowed those who wished to settle the Boer problem in South Africa a chance to get their way.[66] John MacMillan refers to these politicians as 'apostate' from the older Millean beliefs of liberalism.[67] They had metamorphosed into 'Liberal Imperialists' who saw that change as a necessary adaptation to the world that was emerging after the 1880s – one fraught with potential conflict for the British Empire. They had their counterparts in Germany and, to a lesser extent, in France. This led to an increasingly tense situation as rival imperial elites increasingly dominated what had heretofore been a liberal debate. Hegelian notions of *Geist* came surging to the surface and eventually drew up the battle lines for the events of August 1914.

One of the arenas for the new rivalry that was emerging was in Southern Africa, especially between Germany and Britain. So what in 1899 had seemed like a small colonial police action turned into a horrible modern war. The Boers, outnumbered and out-armed, were able to tie down greatly superior British and Empire forces for over two years. The British Government reacted by ever more brutal military and other methods, the most revolting and effective of which was the introduction of the 'concentration camp'. These were not entirely new (the Czars had their equivalent much before and the Spanish in Cuba had implemented similar policies) but they did lead to a succession of imitators, of which the most notorious are the Nazi and Soviet camps later in the century. Richard Evans' recent book on the origins of the Third Reich argues that the main models for Hitler were the German camps that helped to exterminate most of the Herrero people of what is now Namibia between 1904 and 1907. It would appear that these German camps were also the main inspiration for the supporters of *Apartheid* in South Africa.[68] But the point is that these were policies by a liberal state that set itself far higher standards than 'mere' Germans or Russians. Much of the liberal press used the German and Russian political scene as the place to parade its disapproval of illiberal practices.

That these policies were directed against fellow white Europeans rather than the usually more excusable black populations of Africa led to a breach in the liberal establishment in Britain and condemnation from liberals abroad. Benedict Stuchtey's excellent study of liberal opinion and the Boer war makes it plain that Thornton was right to say that Britain experienced 'a loss of moral content, from which it has never completely recovered'. Political liberalism was split by those who saw the need to support England in her hour of war and those, like George Macaulay Trevelyan, H. G. Wells, Sydney and Beatrice Webb and many more mainstream liberals like James Bryce, who condemned the whole action in South Africa.

Stuchtey shows how the events of the war encouraged imperialists in both Britain and Germany, an encouragement that was to have appalling consequences in little more than a decade, but also demoralized liberals within and outside Britain who had always looked to her as a fountain of peaceful action and intention. The Boer war broke all the liberal tenets of how foreign policy should be conducted at once. This was a war of economic and political conquest, it was directed against a small people eking out an existence on a barren veldt, a people wedded to strict moral codes and hard living conditions. In liberal Britain, J. A. Hobson saw it as the basis for his critique of imperialism and poets like Thomas Hardy were scathing of the results of the war for ordinary Englishmen.[69] In Germany the great liberal Theodore Mommsen saw it as souring relations between Germany and Britain for a long while to come.[70] In France there was a predictable backlash for the nationalist right (such as Maurice Barrès and the virulently anti-Semitic Edouard Drumont) but also from French liberals like Gabriel Monod (a founding member of the League of the Rights of Man). Much was made of 'les uniformes maudits des hordes de Kitchener' in the French language *Le cri du Transvaal*.[71]

In the United States the verdict was just as condemnatory, although it must be said that the war also coincided with the United States' own imperial adventure against Spain which netted it Puerto Rico, the Philippines and, arguably, Cuba. The great poet of imperialism, Rudyard Kipling, was delighted that the Americans were at last taking up the 'White Man's Burden'. Kipling enthused that there 'is no place in the world today for worn out nations', like Spain. The Americans were 'on the threshold of ... the White Man's work, the business of introducing a sane and orderly administration into the dark places of the earth'.[72]

Why should these powers and their emerging liberal elites sympathize with a country that professed to stand for the good of all mankind when it was prepared to behave in the venal way it did? This was especially the case when the evidence of British atrocities came out. As a long-term consequence, during the First World War, many Americans saw Britain as the potentially greater enemy of American liberal values than they did the Germans, a tendency that it took a long time to dispel. Another reason for some sympathy was that the Boers were 'backward'. As Arthur Conan Doyle wrote at the time: everything about the Boers was 'of the 17th century ... except their rifles'. But as Piers Brendon pointed out in a review of a recent book on the war 'its [main] lesson was not that of Kipling but of Orwell: it enabled so many imperialists to see what he called "the dirty work of the empire" at close quarters'.[73]

Furthermore, many British liberals would not have found the German criticism of the Boer War out of place. As Keith Robbins has pointed out, James Bryce, one of the greatest of British liberals before 1914, and British Ambassador to the United States between 1907 and 1913:

> had no embedded hostility towards Germany ... Hegelianism was not the same as British Liberalism, but the aim of both was elevating and lofty. Bryce also believed in the existence of 'Teutonic freedom' – a notion shared by many of his academic contemporaries. The concept was never closely defined but it was held to bind Germany and Britain together. ... The United States, the British Empire and Germany were 'natural' friends. Certainly there were differences between them and aspects which each found distasteful in the other, but these were essentially disagreements within the family. In August 1914, the family was broken.[74]

The Boer War and similar imperialist adventures round the globe can unfortunately also be seen as showing up the true potential for liberal hypocrisy. Milner, Rhodes and others had started as liberals before leaving Gladstone for what they saw as his naivety towards 'kaffirs' and the like. It was necessary to teach the inferior races of the world how to behave (hence Kipling's urge to 'take up the

White Man's burden'). This led to the architects of this, such as Milner, often referring to the notion of '*Lebensraum*' for white people. The treaty that ended the Boer War, the Peace of *Vereeniging*, is a curious mixture of liberalism and imperialism, a blend that was seen as natural by Milner, Chamberlain and Rhodes. The main effort was to dilute the Boer's 'Dutchness' by settling 'three men of the British race to two of the Dutch, [after which] the country will be safe and prosperous. If there are three of Dutch to two of British we shall have perpetual difficulty.'[75] A recent author has written that '[t]hey fought for a future union between unequal partners under the British flag, a union in which Afrikaners would be gradually denationalised and swamped by British immigrants'.[76]

In public pronouncements the policy was presented as the best form of 'self-determination', in order to outflank Gladstonian liberals who spoke of sub-jugated peoples like the Boers, 'rightly struggling to be free'. Out of this emerged the notion of 'trusteeship', ironically most pushed in the Treaty of Versailles by General Jan Smuts, military commander of the Boers defeated by the British in 1902. Both he and his new imperial collaborators in South Africa and France had no problem with denying self-determination to 'natives'. Sir Edward Grey, who represented the best of Gladstonian liberalism in the new century summed up the Milner–Rhodes–Kipling axis when he said in 1892 that 'Rhodes is not exactly what you call a Liberal. . . . He has a new version of "one man, one vote" for South Africa, viz., that he, Rhodes, should have a vote, but nobody else should.'[77]

The 'liberal' imperialists wanted to see the realization of Charles Dilke's dream of an Anglo-Saxon world, a *Greater Britain* (the title of his infamous work of 1869) or of Cambridge Regius Professor of Modern History J. R. Seeley's federation of English-speaking peoples, based on what they saw as an obvious English racial superiority. Cecil Rhodes put this at its most stark:

> I contend that we are the first race in the world and that the more of the world we inhabit the better it is for the human race. . . . Added to which, the absorption of the greater part of the world under our rule simply means the end of all wars.

These words, uttered at Oxford to an adoring crowd of undergraduates, some of whom would form Milner's 'kindergarten' to administer South Africa after the Peace of *Vereeinging*, was part and parcel of a *Weltanschauung* that many fascists of the twentieth century would pervert to their own illiberal ends. But for many of the architects of the Boer war they saw the subjugation of Boers and other, lesser, natives as merely the best possible amalgam of imperialism and social reform. They were in effect using the agenda of liberalism in conjunction with the political instincts of imperial conservatism.[78]

A sympathetic biographer has admitted that Milner in particular had a view of the world that in some ways was a pre-echo of Hitler's. The difference was that whereas Hitler had presented German racial superiority as an excuse to grab *Lebensraum* in Eastern Europe for a disciplined and humiliated people,

Milner and Kipling presented English racial superiority to an undisciplined and self-confident British population.[79] To which, it might be added, a British population severely contaminated by liberal and democratic principles which Kipling and the others never ceased to bemoan, although never to seriously challenge. But it is unsurprising that such statements as those by Rhodes should have made an impact on the European extreme right who were looking to redeem themselves in the face of history after the crushing defeat of 1918. If impeccable Englishmen could talk of racial dominance leading to the 'ending of all wars' why should not that racial group be German? Perhaps the British had won the First World War mainly because they had better understood the logic of empire? Milner, Kipling and other imperialists spent much time after the Boer War with lunch clubs called the 'Co-efficients' or the 'Compatriots' which sought better ways of ordering the world along imperial as well as liberal lines.[80] These groups can indeed be seen as the forerunners of the liberal and other 'think tanks' that have had so much influence on British and American foreign policy ever since (see Chapter 2). But whereas they formed part of a lively and balanced civil society, in Germany, Italy and Japan, what would have been seen as quaint or even wild speculation saw its realization in the *Drang Nach Osten*.

Conclusions

The pre-1914 liberal bequest to thinking about war and peace is therefore immense but also contradictory. If there was to be a moral growth of the individual and by extension of individuals in communities, it had to be decided in what kinds of configurations these individuals and communities should exist. If it was to be in states what could be done about states that threatened their neighbours? Should there be an organization for mutual defence as indicated by Kant? Should non-intervention be the norm under nearly all circumstances as, for example, suggested by Cobden and Mill? Oliver Wendell Holmes echoed Cobden exactly in his above quoted letter to Laski of 1930: 'some kind of despotism is at the bottom of seeking for change. I don't care to boss my neighbors and to require them to want something different from what they do – even when, as frequently, I think their wishes more or less suicidal.'[81] For all of these writers a person's fate was essentially one that he or she should work out for themselves, as should a people. Freedom may be a moral imperative, but it is one that should be discovered not imposed. This tradition of moral self-sufficiency is their greatest legacy, one that has been continued by thinkers like Walzer but also one that shines through in many liberals still refusing to accept the idea of intervention by strong states in the affairs of weaker ones, unless and then only sometimes, in the name of an international community, as organized in the United Nations.

Nineteenth century liberals in Britain, the United States and Europe also lived in a century where their basic well-being and security were not seriously under threat. Continental Europe saw the progressive triumph of a series of national projects, all fired by a mixture of Hegelian impulses to see a people's self-fulfilment and liberalism to free the individual.[82] There were no credible challenges to this dual ideological hegemony until 1914, even from socialism and the end of the 'family' that had been nineteenth-century Europe. In the twentieth century many dictators looked at liberal societies seemingly at odds with themselves and assumed that they had 'gone soft', as Hitler did about Britain the 1930s. What was arguably being observed was not 'softness' but the necessary working out of contradictory opinions before the last resort, war, was undertaken. We can also find other liberals, notably Locke, to whom the idea of non-intervention would not have been such an anathema – it was an 'inconvenience' that needed to be resolved. Presidents Woodrow Wilson, Franklin Delano Roosevelt and even the two George Bushes would under most circumstances find common cause with Mill and Cobden, at least on the issue of intervention, but all would also accept that freedom had to be exported at the barrel of a gun if it was necessary to defend a liberal heartland, whether that be Britain or the United States, or indeed Europe as a whole. But Kant had also not fully appreciated that liberal democratic states would not necessarily band together in the face of an attack on one or more of their number. The twentieth century saw a number of examples of this, notably in 1914–18 and 1939–45. In both cases it took a near defeat of democracy before the United States was persuaded to join in the collective security effort to save liberal principles.

Then as now the balance had to be kept, but in liberal societies that would inevitably mean a variety of opinions about which side of that balance had to be tipped. Many nineteenth-century liberals would have been astonished to see the rise of private actors and a transnational mobility which has arguably done much to damage the power of communities to regulate and rule themselves. They therefore wanted interdependence but may have balked at 'globalization' as it has arguably displaced authority in democracies away from elected parliaments and into the boardrooms of multinational companies. This has in turn displaced allegiance for many people from their state and even their 'people' to an abstract entity, global capitalism. This is perhaps the greatest dilemma facing liberal thought after the end of the nineteenth century, one that has not been fully resolved today.[83]

The next chapter will extend this thinking by looking at some of the main thinkers and practitioners of the twentieth century.

2 Twentieth-century liberalism and thinking about war and peace, 1918 to the present

War is our scourge: yet war has made us wise/And fighting for our freedom, we are free

Siegfried Sassoon, 1915[1]

[M]odern internationalists are no longer mere non-interventionists, for the same reason that modern Radicals are no longer philosophic individualists.

J.A. Hobson[2]

Introduction

Whereas peaceful relations had characterized the nineteenth century more than any previous one, at least in Europe itself, the twentieth was the century of 'total war' when the full implications of peoples organized as nations with the power of industry and technology bore their full fruit. Liberal thinking and practice had to adapt themselves to a totally new situation and were forced into a sharp realization that 'progress' was a double edged sword. The 'proto-globalization' or 'interdependence' fostered by Britain in the nineteenth century under its (largely) benevolent dominance was to see itself unhinged by the First World War and then re-adapted, first as the 'West' after 1945, and then as a doctrine of 'spheres of stability' pitted against 'rogue states' in the post-Cold War period by an increasingly powerful and 'imperial' United States. Many of the justifications for such an expansion of its power can and could have been taken straight out of Locke's or Mill's writing on war and peace outlined in the last chapter. There may be 'inconsistencies', in Locke's words, in the coercive nature of Anglo-American liberalism for much of the twentieth-century, but it has the merit of self-belief. Many (but by no means all) American leaders have claimed that they have a morally superior claim to equate what is right for peace with what is right for the United States, much as many leaders in Britain did before 1900. The 'city on the hill' is now one that looks far wider from its shores than before 1914. The question has to be whether this is *hubris* that will turn, as it did for Britain, into *nemesis*?

The twentieth-century has also been very different from its predecessor in other significant ways, as many historians, like Eric Hobsbawm, have written of the 'short Twentieth Century' one that starts in the trenches of the Western Front and ends with the collapse of the Berlin Wall, encompassing the most trying moment for liberal hegemony and its triumph.[3] Richard Vinen has pointed out that claiming it was 'short' or not is to assume that 1914 is the starting point and is to make assumptions about the 'bourgeois arcadia' in which many were supposed to live, when in fact very few did. Any history will have to be selective in its choice of focus or 'structure', but, as even Vinen admits, '[m]uch writing on twentieth-century Europe is marked by an aching nostalgia for the period before 1914'.[4] Nostalgia was thus for the 'strange death of liberal England' as George Dangerfield put it, indeed for that of liberal Europe, and for the 'prevailing meliorist myth', in Paul Fussell's celebrated term, that had faded away. As Siegfried Sassoon reflected in middle age, in 1914 'no one could have been more unaware that he was in for one of the most unrestful epochs in human history, and that the next twenty years would be a cemetery for the civilized illusions of the nineteenth century'.[5] It cannot be forgotten that the First World War happened at the end of the longest period of sustained peace in the history of Europe to that date. Peace and the corresponding possibility of what we would now call 'globalized' economic practices were seen by 1914 as the natural birthright of the global citizen. But it was to disappear for much of the next century. The question that a liberal would have to ask though is, was that peace a *democratic* peace or was it an artificial one, doomed to fail?

This chapter is broken down, as its predecessor, into a number of historical snapshots: the period of the First World War; the aftermath of that war; the Second World War and the post-war period, and, finally; the period after the Cold War up to about the end of the century. This chapter will complete the backdrop for the elaboration of liberal policy that has been evolving since 1900. It will in particular track the fortunes of liberal ideas and of liberal states in their attempts to channel thinking about war and peace in the twentieth-century from the First World War until the 'humanitarian intervention' of the 1990s. There will also be a brief discussion of the challenges the 'neo-conservatism' poses for liberalism as a whole in the period after the election of George W. Bush in 2001, and the subsequent wars in which his Presidency has been involved in Afghanistan and Iraq.

The vectors of thinking about liberalism in peace and war after 1918

If it is to be maintained that IR, and particularly its response to the questions of war and peace, is an 'Anglo-American' enterprise, there is clearly a need to show how that can be traced through the main vectors of policy making. The two great innovations in this area that we can clearly identify are the international organization (IO) and the liberal think tank.

International institutions

Since at least the time of Kant, there has been a liberal belief in the ability of the international community of nations to organize the planet in its own image. This belief is often referred to as 'liberal internationalism', which can be seen as a key plank of 'Anglo-Saxon' ideas that have come to be institutionalized in the 'West' and more widely though the IOs. This has sometimes been resented by other states, with the French view as particularly striking. During the First World War when the idea of a 'League of Nations' was being discussed, the French set up a 'Commission Bourgeois' (named so after its Chairman Leon Bourgeois). Littered through the deliberations of this body are references to the dominance of liberal thinking of the American kind, or 'faithful to the Anglo-Saxon tradition' as one senior French Quai d'Orsay official put it in the 1920s.[6]

But there was, and has been ever since, frustration by these very same 'Anglo-Saxons' with the way the IOs have worked since 1919. The League of Nations was sidelined by the British and indeed all of the powers in the inter-war period. There are similar examples of visceral distrust of the United Nations from that organization's inception, from the implementation of the Marshall Plan in 1947 (see Chapter 4), through to the attack on Kosovo in 1999, or in the 2002–3 arguments about whether to go to war with Iraq. The Anglo-Saxon liberal states have seemed far more ready to bypass the UN than those illiberal states who normally would not be seen in such a distinct light, like Russia and China. American and British politicians and policy makers have wanted to make use of these bodies for the furthering of what they see as the natural interests of mankind, which 'naturally' conflate with liberal values. It might be argued that the liberal elites in Washington and London have now tired of their own creation. In the aftermath of the war in Iraq a clear split has developed between those in Washington who see the task of the democratic powers of standing by 'the world's newest democracies', a view that sees the wars in the former Yugoslavia, Afghanistan and Iraq as evidencing the 'spread of freedom across the world'. In contrast to this the worried Secretary General of the United Nations, Kofi Annan, has spoken of the 'rule of law [being] at risk around the world'.[7]

All shades of opinion in the past hundred years seem to agree that there has to be a very dramatic change in the relationship between states and peoples in order to arrive at a 'stable' peace – one where 'neither side considers employing force, or even making a threat of force, in any dispute, even serious disputes' and that there needs to be a radical rethink of the way that humans relate to and between each other in settled communities.[8] Another way of putting it is that in order to have a 'positive peace' there has to be created 'a social and political ordering of society that is generally accepted as just'. So whatever this may be seen as being (and there are many different definitions of 'just') it is 'certainly a far more complex affair than war.'[9]

The example that is often quoted is the change in the relationship that has come about in the case of Western Europe. Hundreds of years of war have been transformed to the cooperation on all levels of the European Union. James Goodby claims that to have this there has had to be agreement on a variety of key issues: common values 'almost certainly democratic values ... a similar sense of identity or self-image, transparency and some denationalizing of defense establishments, and a reasonably healthy economy'.[10] But in order to get to this situation many wars were fought, ended and started again. Fifty years ago the words of Marshall Foch in 1919 might have seemed more apposite than any claims of a future of peace; surely this was just another 'twenty years truce'? The aim is therefore is peace, but a *stable* peace, 'laid in principles purely pacific' as Edmund Burke wrote in 1775.[11]

Liberal think tanks[12]

When liberally-inspired IOs have failed or not been seen as sufficiently ardent in their development of liberal ideas and policies, liberal think tanks have usually filled the gap. They are new to the twentieth-century and reflect both the complexity of the international system of the last hundred years and also the complexity of the moral and political dilemmas faced by liberal states. The nineteenth century had its intellectual commentators, the twentieth has seen, in Woodrow Wilson's words, the 'apotheosis of public opinion', one which has required a much more sophisticated framework for working out liberal foreign policy dilemmas. If the nineteenth century was characterized by a meeting of the social elites, 'the aristocracies' of Europe and beyond, that of the twentieth has increasingly been defined by the meeting of elites of a different kind, ones more wedded to meritocratic advancement through the accumulation of capital and influence over democratic polities. So if, in the words of Walter Bagehot, 'nations touch at their summits',[13] the vector for that 'touching' has undergone significant changes in the last 100 years.

Some liberal think tanks, notably the Carnegie Foundation for International Peace ('Carnegie') (1910) and the (liberal imperialist) Round Table (1910) in Britain, just pre-date the First World War. Both produced (and still produce) journals that have had varying degrees of impact on the policy process, in both cases significant until the Second World War at least.[14] The key liberal think tanks such as the Royal Institute of International Affairs ('Chatham House') and the Council on Foreign Relations (CFR) emerged out of the Treaty of Versailles from vast, and previously unheard of array of 'experts' that had been marshalled by the British, the Americans, and to a much lesser extent the French, and had in so doing given birth to a new transatlantic elite that was scornful of the way the peace was finally settled in a revengeful way. These people were also to make up the ranks of IR academia, with the first British Chairs at the universities of Aberystwyth, and the London School of Economics, both of which were held at various times by Versailles veterans like E. H Carr, Alfred Zimmern and Philip Noel-Baker. In the United States many of these policy makers now returned to their university posts or helped set up think tanks.

In a study of the relationship between the CFR and Chatham House in the 1930s, Inderjeet Parmar stresses that these institutions, supposedly, or rather mythically, set themselves up as 'idealist' bastions of 'liberal internationalism'. They were also, if not mainly, 'practical, utilitarian, power-conscious, and in the service of either America's projected rise to globalism or the maintenance, in one form or another, of Britain's global position'.[15] They were also tied together by many intellectual, even 'civilizational' bonds, of which Parmar singles out 'scientism', a quasi-positivist belief that the 'truth' could be found by dint of proper research; 'elitism', the belief that they could and must lead public opinion, and; 'religiosity' with both sets of elites having deep religious convictions, both linked to 'Anglo-Saxonism and the cult of manliness' in a kind of 'muscular Christianity'.

Parmar points out that both Chatham House and the CFR had a membership drawn from 'discontented junior officials/advisers who felt [that the] growing importance of public opinion required "enlightenment"'. They embodied a group of elite thinkers, predominantly from Ivy League universities on the American side of the Atlantic (63 per cent) and from Oxbridge and public schools in Britain (74 per cent and 84 per cent respectively) with strong links to their respective civil services and governments. Academia and the law were well represented and drawn from all political parties. In brief, they represented the foreign policy elite of Britain and the United States.[16]

We might therefore see the CFR, Carnegie and Chatham House as housing elite representatives of a nineteenth-century culture that were to hand over the reins of foreign policy making in the Second World War to a new bureaucratic elite within government. This elite was not impressed by the German idealism of a Kant or Hegel, it was indeed very dismissive of what it saw as having brought about 'militarism'. If it had an 'idealist' side it was more akin to and reflected in the increasingly dominant 'logical positivist' philosophy of the Vienna School. Wittgenstein had taken Cambridge by storm; he and Karl Popper were to become the gurus of this generation who wanted to find scientific cures for international society's ills.[17] In the Post-War Planning of the Second World War, the CFR, Chatham House and the Carnegie played a crucial role as well as many of those who were disgusted by the Treaty of Versailles on both sides of the Atlantic. They have been succeeded in the post-Second World War period by many imitators, some of whom will be referred to in coming chapters.

Were these think tanks merely expressions of Anglo-American interest, an interest they were prepared to foist on the rest of the world in the name of liberal internationalism without any due regard to the wishes of the local inhabitants? Are they not *still* willing to do this, as has been asserted by many on the left? In Bosnia, Kosovo, Afghanistan and Iraq, Britain and the United States stand 'shoulder to shoulder' on most issues of war and peace. Writers as diverse as John Kampfner and Noam Chomsky have made this point repeatedly. Kampfner points to 'Blair's' Wars' as the product of exactly the kind of 'muscular Christianity' and belief that they hold the key to the 'truth' that inspired the early denizens of Chatham House. In a 1997 speech he quotes Blair as saying: 'century upon century it has been the destiny of Britain to lead other nations. That should not be a destiny that is part of our history. It should be part of our future. We are a leader of nations or nothing.' Although Blair has made the move from 'humanitarian warrior' in his early years as Prime Minister to the more 'hounded' or even 'damaged warrior', Kampfner shows how Blair is a true product of a liberal vision of the world that requires military intervention to promote values in which liberals fervently believe.[18]

Chomsky is more extreme in his criticism, often linking American with British efforts in war zones (most notably the Middle East) and pointing to Britain as 'America's loyal subsidiary' in the common interest of securing markets and dominating local elites.[19] That there are close links between the two states is undeniable (see 'The Special Relationship') as is the evidence that their elites have at least since 1919 worked very closely on elaborating intellectual frameworks for IR. But it has not always been thus in terms of policy. The United States was at logger-heads with Britain for most of the period until 1941, and there were severe tensions, at times verging on open hostility. It was only with the Second World War and Britain's desperate need for American aid and military support that it could be argued that its 'subsidiary' essentially began to tow the American liberal line. Even after this, as with Suez in 1956 and during the Vietnam War, there were huge differences of approach. What is clear is that in terms of ideal world orders, liberal, capitalist and democratic, the two states' liberal elites have long seen eye to eye. Where they have disagreed is on how this ideal framework should be expanded and maintained.[20]

But the main question has to be why did they grow at this particular moment? Liberals had noticed the inexorable rise of violence in war against civilians after 1900 in Europe. The rise of the liberal think tank; received a huge boost in this observation. The best example was in the 1913 Carnegie report 'To Inquire into the Causes and Conduct of the two Balkan Wars' that had started in 1910 and continued for some years, involving Greece, Bulgaria and Serbia in various geo-metries.[21] The report provided a detailed and in places graphic description of the history of the area, the motivations and actions of the parties and the economic and human costs. Such wars had previously taken place, waged by Europeans, but only in the imperial 'Scramble for Africa' after the Treaty of Berlin of 1874. Atrocities in these wars can be noted in profusion, especially in South West Africa, but these were either not reported or glossed over in general, even excused in the name of civilizational necessity.

The Carnegie report had a very impressive role of authors, most notably Henry Noel Brailsford, who went on to become a key figure in the British Inde-pendent Labour Party and the Lib–Lab pacts that emerged as the Labour Party. He was one of the few real foreign policy experts of his day that had travelled widely in the Balkans before the First World War, and his *Macedonia* of 1906 can still be read with great profit. Other contributors included the Russian liberal and historian Paul Milyukov, who was a prominent member of the Provisional Gov-ernment of 1917 in Russia. Its contents are in parts dry analysis of military expenditures, in places as horrific as Johan von Grimmelshausen. One particu-larly harrowing section of convincing (as there was no propaganda benefit to be derived) evidence that is quoted is from soldiers' letters (Serbian, Greek and Bulgarian) back to their families from the front. One, from a Greek soldier, reads:

Dear Mother, I send you my greetings. I am in good health ... We have to – such is the order – burn the villages, massacre the young, only sparing the aged and children. But we are hungry ... With greeting,

Your son, Jean Lihoudis.[22]

In 1993 this report was reprinted by the Carnegie Commission, with a foreword by George Kennan, the purpose of which publication was to demonstrate how little the behaviour of Balkan nationalists had changed since 1913. As Kennan pointed out: 'the commissioners of 1913 were almost alone in their effort to bring to the attention of the world the truly alarming aspects of Balkan violence. Today they would have had a host of collaborators in such an effort.'[23] This was the first and arguably the most significant of such reports, ones that we now take for granted. This in turn shows the vital importance of such think tanks in forming our current liberal consciousness.

In 1913 the authors hoped that they would provoke a change in the way Western governments behaved as well as those in the Balkans. They saw this as an integrated problem. One example of this is where D'Estournelles de Constant wrote in the Introduction:

> The real struggle in the Balkans, as in Europe and America, is not between oppressors and oppressed. It is between two policies, the policy of armaments and that of progress. One day the force of progress triumphs, but the next the policy of rousing the passions and jealousies that lead to armaments and war, gets the upper hand.

The real culprits in 1913 were not seen as 'the Balkan peoples. . . . Do not let us condemn the victims.' For the Report's authors the real culprits were those who declare that 'war is inevitable, and by making it so, asserting that they are powerless to prevent it'.[24]

During the coming war, many French political figures looked back to the first organizational attempts to create institutions for peace, and particularly the Treaties of Westphalia and Vienna, but also to the Concert of Europe and the Hague Agreements of 1899 and 1907. Senator Gabriel Hanotaux called the Hague meetings 'les premiers battements du coeur de l'humanité.' This required, in the words of Aristide Briand in 1916, future joint architect with American Senator Kellogg of the 'Pact to Outlaw War' of 1928, a peace 'basée sur le *droit international* et garantie par des *sanctions* contre laquel aucun pays ne pourra se dresser'[25] (his italics). But they were to be disappointed in the 'Anglo-Saxon' peace that was the war's first result.

Liberal thinking about the causes and solutions to world wars, 1914–20

The last chapter finished with a consideration of the anguish caused to liberals by the Boer War. But the Boer War was alas to be but a preliminary skirmish for the trials of liberalism to come after 1914. Virtually all liberals greeted the First World War with dismay. It showed up the fallacy of the idea that science and morality would go hand in hand to keep the peace and promote progress. The nature of warfare had outstripped liberals' understanding of how to control it.[26]

Michael Howard started his famous series of lectures published as *War and the Liberal Conscience* with a description of the bewilderment of the great liberal George Macaulay Trevelyan at the events of 1914–18. He had been 'perhaps the last of the great Victorian liberals' who had seen Britain's great moral crusade of the last 200 years as the 'era when Englishmen burst the bonds of monarchical tyranny' and then went on to encourage the rise of nations so that the 'people of Europe ... came to share the blessings of freedom and nationhood in their turn'. This was all supposed to lead to peace across Europe, instead of which it had led to war. Howard reports him railing to an acquaintance that: 'I do not understand the age we live in, and what I do not understand I do not like.' H. G. Wells was another who publicly expressed his confusion. After a trip to the Italian Front in 1916 he commented:

> If I were to be tied down to one word for my impression of this war, I should say that this war is *Queer* [sic]. It is not like anything in a really waking world, but like something in a dream. It hasn't exactly that clearness of light against darkness or of good against ill. But it has the quality of wholesome instinct struggling under a nightmare. The world is not really awake.

Wells rightly saw the emergence of a Nietzschean cult of 'nationalities and ... strange loyalties and .... Irrational creeds and ceremonies' but he also found refuge in that he felt sure that:

> the time draws near when mankind will awake and the dreams fade away, and then there will be no nationality in the world but humanity, and no king, no emperor, nor leader, but the one God of mankind. This is my faith. I am as certain of it as I was in 1900 that men would presently fly.[27]

But, as Howard points out, it was not that Trevelyan (or indeed Wells) had any problem with the notion of war itself – which 'for him was the very stuff of history, and he found no difficulty in reconciling it with his liberalism'.[28]

This was the liberal *pacificistic* feeling about war, a belief that war should be a last resort, but that ultimately it was better than tyranny, the true root cause of all war. So as Howard points out, George was able to support the war against Germany, while his brother Charles Trevelyan was a prominent member of the Union of Democratic Control, led by E. D. Morel, who led opposition to the war. Their fraternal differences hinged on who or what they thought to 'blame' for the war and hence how it might be resolved and hopefully not repeated.

Equally, over the Atlantic, John Dewey could say that 'I have been a thorough and complete sympathizer with the part played by this country in this war and I have wished to see the resources of this country used for its successful prosecution'.[29] On the other hand, his friend Jane Addams, a key influence on Wilson according to his biographer Thomas J. Knock, was convinced that the war was wrong, and said so on many occasions.[30]

This ambivalence is revealing about what Howard calls the 'liberal conscience', driven by a belief that the world is neither unalterable, as conservatives see it, nor that it is determined by 'historical processes which [men] may understand but which they are powerless to control'.[31] Liberal thinking is the richest repository of reflection on the causes and cures for war and the First World War was the greatest challenge that this belief system encountered at the very height of its power at the end of the nineteenth century. Such thinking has continued ever since, and the First World War has proved its resilience in being the bedrock on how that thinking has developed. As the recently celebrated eightieth anniversary of the Treaty of Versailles demonstrated, the debate over what caused the war and how it ended is still very vibrant and instructive and has, rightly or wrongly, informed judgements about many wars since.

One early twentieth-century liberal thinker that had made a huge impact on liberal thinking about peace and war was of course J. A. Hobson. His writing on imperialism had an impact well beyond Britain and had influenced virtually every liberal, and indeed many non-liberal, thinker of his generation and the next, including, most famously, Lenin. A great admirer of Cobden's ideas on non-intervention, Hobson blamed imperialism for converting what should have been in a Cobdenite world 'friendly competition into cut-throat hostility'. From 1870 on, the 'hustle for foreign markets [led to] powerfully organised trades, especially in the textile and metal industries beg[an] to strengthen their hold upon their governments, so as to secure tariffs for the protection of the home market and diplomatic aid for winning foreign markets'. This was compounded (and made 'far more important and less predictable') by huge increases in overseas investment and the implanting of white colonists to protect and gather in the fruits of this investment. These investments are controlled by fewer and fewer more powerful men, so that:

> [f]oreign policy was thus destined more and more to come under the secret or open control of powerful financial groups. ... Obstructive governments must be bullied, competitors from other leading countries must be kept out ... foreign lives and property must be protected against mob violence or official injustice.

This had been the logic behind the bullying of China throughout the nineteenth century. But for Hobson what really mattered was that only some kinds of governments would allow such narrow interests to dictate national action. It is still the idea behind many demands for intervention when capitalist interests are threatened in the third world today.

Hobson saw that liberalism had moved on since Cobden's day: '[m]odern internationalists are no longer mere non-interventionists, for the same reason that modern Radicals are no longer philosophic individualists'. The state must not be seen as the *necessary* enemy, but the condition 'for the liberative and creative service of the State are summed up in the word: "democracy". ... Democracy alone can make the modern growth of the state compatible with individual liberty.'[32] In effect Hobson was re-defining Kant and Cobden in the modern age. His formulation had the important feature of rejecting the idea that social reform at the international and national level had to be linked to imperial design, as Milner and the advocates of Anglo-Saxon racial superiority implied. Hobson was thus at least, if not the, key inspiration for a generation of future liberals (and what came to be known as Lib–Labs) who congregated within a revitalized liberal wing of British politics known to posterity as the Labour Party. The breaches shown by the split into 'Liberal Unionist' and 'Gladstonian Liberal' over the Boer War, was the death knell of the British liberal consensus, one whose demise was hastened by the First World War.[33]

Wilsonian liberalism and the making of a lasting peace

The official, as opposed to the philosophical, liberal reaction to the events of 1914–18 took in some of these ideas. The classic liberal definition of the reasons for the outbreak of the First World War as well as the basis for ending it and, hopefully, any further wars like it, can be found in President Woodrow Wilson's Fourteen Points of January 1918. Wilson was quite clear that Germany was mostly to blame for the First World War, but he was not convinced that it was solely to blame. The Fourteen Points were a loose catalogue that identified key specific problems, such as the need for the self-determination of certain peoples of Europe, but they also held critiques on a structural level of what was wrong with the international system itself.

Wilson drew much of his intellectual inspiration from the evolving belief in (chiefly) the Democratic Party in what had become known as 'Progressive Internationalism'. This was virulently anti-imperialist in the tradition of Thomas Paine (and therefore deeply suspicious of British imperialism) but also deeply committed to national and international social reform, one of the key claimed aims of the British imperialists.[34] His thinking undoubtedly had deep roots in Presbyterian (even Covenanter) 'Christian doctrine' and his main 'intellectual activity' in a competent if not glittering academic career 'was the pursuit of more perfect government at all levels'.[35] The Fourteen Points drew heavily on these ideas and were very similar to the calls for open diplomacy by British liberals.

The one key area where Wilson and Hobson intersected was in the desire to reduce imperial contests. Many of the Points are directed to the freeing of trade (Point III), the 'Freedom of the Seas' (Point II), an idea that Cobden had also espoused and decolonization (Point V).[36] They were vague enough to make most statesmen, soldiers and civilian commentators alike feel that their particular belief in what had started the war was being described, but specific enough to enable all those groups to see how their plan to end it could be accommodated. Otherwise the acceptance by the German High Command, as well as the Allies of them as a basis for a negotiated peace is incomprehensible.

But the key to changing of international politics lay in the first of the Points, which called for 'open covenants, openly arrived at'. As early as 1912, one of the greatest liberal commentators on British foreign policy of the last century, E. D. Morel, had summed up the need for Anglo–German understanding and reconciliation:

> I believe that the greatest national interest of the British people is at this moment, and will continue increasingly to be, the establishment and maintenance of friendly relations with Germany; a full and frank examination by responsible statesmen in both countries of the national problems peculiar to each in their relations with one another, leading to an appreciation of their respective national necessities, and to a mutual adjustment of the same with the sacrifice neither of honour, not prestige, nor legitimate needs on either side.

Like Angell, Morel did not believe that war between the two countries was in any way inevitable, but it would require that the two states deal openly and frankly with each other. Furthermore he believed that the man who formally declared war on Germany in 1914, Sir Edward Grey, the British Liberal Foreign Secretary between 1906 and 1915, had deliberately misled both the British people and the Germans over pre-war rivalry, especially about Morocco over which war had nearly broken out in 1910.

For Morel the way in which the crisis had been defused, that of secret bilateral diplomacy, had created the peril in the first place. This 'Secret Diplomacy and the "Balance of Power"' had caused the World War and '[w]e are now in the presence of the utter failure of the old-fashioned methods of safeguarding peace by preparing for war.'[37] The paper cover of the 1915 edition has a man blindfolded with the words 'Secret Diplomacy' stumbling over the cliff of war. Morel worked closely with Charles Trevelyan in pushing this unpopular view during the whole of the war and was imprisoned under the Defence of the Realm Act (DORA) for so doing. His analysis was none the less to be a powerful influence on the final assessment of the war that emerged in the calmer period of the 1920s. It was also to have a profound effect on the idea that diplomacy must be openly conducted in order both to prevent misunderstanding and to provide transparency that public opinion could judge.

However those who would normally have been sympathetic to Morel's high moral tone did not universally accept it. In reply to this attack on British foreign policy, Gilbert Murray, also a liberal, concluded that Sir Edward Grey had in fact made very few mistakes in his dealings with what turned out to be the foe.[38] For the reviewer of his book on Grey, the problem was that Germany had never made its intentions clear, 'allowing a fog of anxiety to cover relations between the two states'. Britain had made 'repeatedly offered guarantees of friendship and a naval truce', and all that Germany wanted, in Prime Minister Asquith's words was 'a free hand when it selected the opportunity, to overbear, to dominate, the European world.'

These two passages illustrate the liberal dilemma of wanting states to understand the 'illogicality' of war while accepting that not all states have equal moral worth. Murray, and other prominent liberals like James Bryce, agreed in principle with Morel's desire to find better ways to conduct foreign affairs, ones that would be based on moral arguments as much as on *realpolitik*. In 1910 Norman Angell had pointed to this liberal mindset, or what Howard refers to as the 'liberal conscience', one that can be said to permeate British, American and other liberal states' foreign policies to this day.

In 2003 Michael Mandelbaum, a long-time admirer of President Wilson, declared in the title of a book that Wilson's were 'the ideas that conquered the world: Peace, Democracy and Free Markets ...' and that they still do in our century. For Michael Mandelbaum what we have seen in the 1990s is evidence that the 'world ha[s] passed this way before, in fact three times before. The aftermath of the Cold War was the last stage of a recurring historical pattern'.[39] Even for those who are ambivalent about his legacy for United States foreign policy, Wilson's impact has been enormous. Henry Kissinger called him one side of the 'hinge' of American foreign policy since 1917 – the other was Theodore Roosevelt.[40]

Mandelbaum is surely right that much of the liberal internationalist policy agenda still sees its roots in these three big ideas. The question is whether they have really taken root as Wilson intended them to? At the time it did not look so obvious or simple. In 1917 Wilson had been in tune with his public opinion that the United States would enter the war only on the basis of there being a peace without indemnities. In this task he called mainly on liberal thinkers and the emerging think tanks for his inspiration and ideas about how the post-war organizational structures should be planned. Wilson was urged by Angell in October 1917 to 'emphas[ize] the formulation of new principles rather then the collection of factual information' in Wilson's thinking about how the war should be ended. Thinking should not be 'dominated by lawyers', even if this proved a vain hope. The resulting American preparatory mechanism, 'The Inquiry' was dominated by liberal academics and thinkers.[41] The result was that American preparation for the negotiations and Wilson's initial positions in Paris were very schematic, but also very liberal and innovative.

What Wilson tried to introduce, initially through the Fourteen Points of 1918, was the notion that 'blame' for a war should not be solely vested with the vanquished state but with the system itself. This necessitated a new kind of international thinking said Wilson and his followers, one that allowed for both reconciliation between previous enemies and for the establishment of mechanisms that would prevent future wars by allowing for a just and equitable discussion of how peace should be designed to ensure that the 'us and them' motivation for war was eliminated.

The equivalent British preparations were much more based on the use of very detailed documents on specific issues and based on principles of long established British national interest.[42] Hence Wilson's 'Inquiry' and the British 'Blue Books' aimed at putting flesh on very basic bones. In the Second World War this process was taken to far greater lengths. The 1941–5 'Post-War Planning' that took place in the United States and Britain was of a hugely different order of magnitude to that which had occurred in 1914–18. The lesson had been learnt in Washington that in order to properly win the war the peace had to be properly planned too. Hence by the end of the twentieth-century, as in Bosnia, Kosovo (but perhaps not, interestingly, in Iraq), almost as much preparation for peace was made as were military preparations for war.[43]

David Lloyd George, the British Liberal Prime Minster, has often been blamed for derailing Wilson's grand design. But although he has often been cast in the guise of a cynical and ultimately nationalist politician, Lloyd George was in many respects a classical Victorian idealist liberal in the same mould as Trevelyan. He was seen in 1916 as the only possible replacement for the (Liberal) aristocrat Herbert Asquith. Randolph Churchill is reported by Lloyd George's biographer, Michael G. Fry, to have told his son Winston that before 1914 'all save you two are pygmies'. Lloyd George was a direct inheritor of the 'humanitarianism and radical dissent as funnelled through Gladstone', a Liberal who hated war, who was no jingo imperialist and stressed the need for Britain to exert 'moral' leadership in the world. His was certainly a muscular *Christian* liberalism, as is evidenced by his dislike of the Turks, a trait which he shared with many other liberals, including Gladstone. But he was an advocate of multlateralism, a firm believer in free trade and the idea of a European concert of powers to keep the peace.[44]

So Lloyd George did not repudiate the Fourteen Points. For him they were the 'moral background'. Even for the arch-realist Sir Maurice Hankey, the Secretary to the Big Four and to the British Cabinet for over 20 years, he saw the Fourteen Points as a crucial reference document. Huge hopes were put in American leadership and ideas. In the words of Margaret Macmillan, 'the whole world was turning to the United States . . .'.[45] But the British and the French had developed much clearer practical ideas of what they wished to see after the war, and those ideas were defined by civil servants or politicians unaffected by American liberal ideals. The result was that there was a mismatch between Wilson's liberal rhetoric and the resulting document, the Treaty of Versailles, which bore all the hallmarks of British national and imperial interest and a French intransigence grounded in a real fear for their future security. In such circumstances lateral liberal thinking was not going to have much of a chance, 'moral background' or not.

The failure of 'self-determination'

It was also the case that what might be seen as Wilson's big liberal ideas were full of internal contradictions, seen at the time and many times since. The really big ideas were those of 'open covenants openly arrived at' (discussed above, page 48), economic freedom and self-determination. The first two had a solid pedigree and pre-war heritage and had been discussed widely during the war itself by the UDC and other groups who influenced Wilson and, to a far lesser extent, public opinion. The third was in harmony with much of the spirit of national awakening of the nineteenth century, but had arguably been tainted by the end of that century by a quasi-imperial or even racially motivated idea of *blut und boden* in its European manifestations. The clearest demonstration of this came in Germany where the initial democratic and open impulses of the revolutions of 1848 had been transformed into the obscurantist and irredentist ideas of the German right and, ultimately, were to be transformed into the mystical Aryan nationalism of Adolf Hitler. As British liberalism developed its imperial drive so did much of the nationalism of *Mittleuropa*. In any case none of the benefits of liberal innovation were to be offered to extra-European peoples, not even the Chinese.[46]

Self-determination was thus a tradition with a twin edge. Wilson assumed that to free the countries of the Austro-Hungarian and German Empires to find their national destiny would automatically prompt them along the paths of democracy and peace. The inter-war period was to show that this was far from the case and the paths along which they were largely prompted were those of irredentism (Hungary, Germany, Yugoslavia) or exclusive nationalism. Only Czechoslovakia seemed to have developed a genuinely democratic and inclusive structure and political ethos and that to some extent made it one of Hitler's main targets. But it was arguably the small states that were supposed to benefit their peoples and the cause of peace. Macmillan records the American Military Attaché at Versailles, Tasker Bliss as:

> predicting another thirty years of war in Europe. The 'submerged nations' are coming to the surface and as soon as they appear, they fly at somebody's throat. They are like mosquitoes – vicious from the moment of their birth.[47]

As an eponymous CIA agent put it in the 1980s, 'small states are a damned nuisance'.

The failure of disarmament and measures to abolish war

It should not be forgotten that for the United States, Britain, and many other states, such as Japan, much of the diplomatic effort of the inter-war period was spent on trying to ban the notion of war itself and in developing its corollary, disarmament. There were innumerable attempts to curb the naval armaments of the powers, especially Britain, partly in the interests of equity and partly in the supposed interest of a collective security regime that it was hoped the League of Nations would implement. Not all of these initiatives were failures, in that British naval forces were reduced by the Washington Naval Treaties of 1921 and 1930, to the benefit of the Japanese and American navies. The main failure was that of the League 1932 Disarmament Conference, which broke up in acrimony in 1934 having been in preparation since 1924, mainly due to German intransigence.

In spite of this evident failure, American think tanks were still claiming as a central assumption in the early years of the Second World War that 'after the present wars there will be a disposition, shared by belligerents and important neutrals alike to carry out a progressive and general program for the limitation of armaments by agreement among the nations'. It was felt that arms races were obviously the result of 'political tension' between states and that 'a political settlement must precede a program of arms limitation'. The CFR felt, at least until Pearl Harbor, that the United States would be willing to cooperate with that process even 'though it may not participate in the political or territorial phases of a peace settlement'.[48] What that might mean in practice was dependent in turn on how the war turned out, with victory for either side, or some form of stalemate or social revolution.

The failure of the League of Nations

The most obvious of these failures was that of the post-Great War international organization that was supposed to ensure peace and stability. The League of Nations had tried to come to grips with the problems of collective security by aspiring to be the locus where the powers and the smaller states alike defined aggression and took action collectively against it. This was linked to great efforts to outlaw war, and especially the General Treaty on the Renunciation of War of 1928, usually known as the Kellogg–Briand Pact. The net result had been to persuade many politicians and academic observers alike that relying in any way on international law to adjudicate or define disputes between states was pointless and dangerous, and that only power could be relied upon. Hence 'realism' was born as a perceived antidote to 'idealism' within academe, a binary distinction that still persists today in the more simplistic of textbooks.[49]

Not all have agreed with this condemnatory judgement of the League, especially those who had worked for it. Arthur Sweetzer, who had worked tirelessly within the League Secretariat and outside it, and been involved in many of the truly innovative ideas such as the reconstruction of Austria after 1919 (see Chapter 4), saw the League as having been 'a laboratory' within which 'can be found and analysed all the forces which contribute to fulfilling, and inversely, to negating, mankind's age-old desire for peace'. His view was not that the League had itself 'failed' but that 'a second world war ... [broke] ... out in a vacuum of defeatism and neglect ... [and] its lessons were largely blocked out'.

His explanation for this was partly due to the personalities of those who planned the New World Order. So for him:

> [s]ome of the leaders were new and did not want to hear of efforts that had 'failed', others were tired or made cynical by the war; all had their eyes on the future rather than the past ... almost by tacit agreement the world's statesmen chose to start off anew rather than pick up where they had left off. Yet ... often without realizing it, and sometimes while positively denying it, the architects of the new world organization came out exactly where the architects of the previous one had come out, when they agreed on a voluntary association of sovereign states, far greater in size than the League but with much the same form of organization and not greatly different constitutional power.[50]

While we can agree with Sweetzer that the continuities between the League and the UN were much greater than many others saw at the time or since, as in the expansion of the most successful section of the League, its economic and social activities and that these specialized agencies still do the same kinds of things 'from the status of women to disarmament'. He was also right in saying that 'the same problems and activities that we see in the United Nations ... debates on aggression and use of force, universality of membership, national sovereignty, regionalism and the like' were still being discussed.[51]

There were also clear differences. After 1945 the Security Council gave the Big Five seeming executive control over the main activities of the new organization; the power of the General Assembly was much reduced thereby and the Secretary General had much more potential power than the Director General of the League. They were also being discussed in a radically different context, during the war with all the great powers involved in the final settlement, which had not been the case in 1919, and since 1945 in the context of a Cold War. These contextual differences attenuated both the positive effects of the UN's role, in reducing aggression and inter-state violence and also gave it a new role, one that would emerge in the 1950s in 'peacekeeping', a role that the League had never undertaken.

What had happened was that the liberal internationalism that had inspired the League of Nations (LON) had never been allowed to have its full rein in the implementation of the Treaty of Versailles. As will be described in Chapter 3 the conflict over reparations and debt had rumbled on all through the 1920s until the policy's sheer unworkability and Hitler's rise to power had led to the ignominious abandonment of the former and after the latter had damaged any possibility of real collaboration between the democracies by sapping their will to trust each other. It would be accurate to say that liberal internationalism had been reinforced in the UN Charter. The Kellogg–Briand Pact's essential ideas reappeared in Article 2, paragraphs 3 and 4 and in Article 51.[52] So although the UN was used as its predecessor's architects had wanted to some extent, it was in effect regional power alliances like the Warsaw Pact and NATO or 'coalitions of the willing' that kept the peace in the period 1948–90, and arguably still do. The Security Council has once again been sidestepped in the bombing of Kosovo by NATO in 1999 and Iraq in 2003, and the Security Council has since 1990 in effect delegated responsibility for most enforcement actions, as in the Gulf War of 1990–1 and many more instances since. But the underlying rationale in all these actions has been a proclaimed (or self-proclaimed) liberal internationalism.

So we could argue in line with Sweetzer that the UN indeed does continue the tradition of liberal internationalism of the LON with not too huge a difference of emphasis. What we could also assert is that the reason why the post-war settlement in 1945 was more prone to work was that the area where it was allowed to, the West, was given a *tabula rasa* in terms of economic burden, and indeed given a huge helping hand with the Marshall Plan. The failures of Versailles, which were mainly economic, were indeed learnt. The Charter also introduced a more 'realist' set of fail-safe devices if the will of the intrinsically liberal and peace-loving populace was indeed to be overruled by a 'madman'. It might be argued that these devices have seen their usefulness since the end of the Cold War in facing up to Saddam Hussein of Iraq and Slobodan Milosovic of Serbia, among others. However we could also suggest that the realist corrective to liberal internationalism still holds. It can never be assumed that international solidarity and understanding will overrule a perceived national interest, even in liberal democratic societies. The most that can be said is to reiterate what was said in the earlier discussion of democratic peace theory. On the whole democracies do not go to war with one another as it is seen as antithetical to their basic political principles and to their fundamental economic interests.

Liberalism and the challenge of the 1930s and 1940s – idealism or realism?

Wilson and the UDC represent the high point of nineteenth-century classical liberalism. They were not prophets of what was to come in the period after 1918. The world of the 1920s and 1930s was one where liberalism was under constant and unrelenting attack. The globalized international liberal system of 1914 had been destroyed in the trenches and it was not put back into place after the Allied victory of 1918. As Karl Polanyi pointed out in 1939, where previously there had been a unified and reasonably open economic system underpinned by a belief in the stabilizing power of the Pound Sterling there was now competitive devaluation, where there had been the real basis for free trade now there was protectionism and where there had been relative freedom of movement there were now strict border controls.[53] Politically emerging democracy was replaced by emerging dictatorship, to which the democracies had only the response of a weak appeasement. Domestic politics in the democracies saw weak governments under constant attack from their own and external extremes. The rise of Fascist Italy, Nazi Germany, Imperial Japan and the Soviet Union were the news stories of the day. There was no liberal triumph, more of a rout, only stopped precariously at the gates of Cairo and (ironically) Stalingrad in late 1942. Virtually every element of the late nineteenth-century liberal freedom was under attack and stayed so until the early 1940s.

It should not be imagined, as it is tempting to do in the light of the rise of Hitler, that European liberals had felt that their cause was a lost one. Swiss liberal William Rappard said in 1930 that a Martian could conclude that Europe had become 'Americanized' in that, unlike in 1914, 'nearly half the states of Europe [are] organized as republics [and that] ... the form of more or less absolute monarchical government which was characteristic of central, eastern and southern Europe before the War, has absolutely disappeared'. This was a 'certain result of the great conflagration'. So for him 'all the vanquished were monarchies and all, but two exceptions, became republics'. The results that we can remember most, economic nationalism and its attendant fascism, were largely glossed over. He noted that trade had increased by 27 per cent over 1914 levels, the distribution of wealth had 'impoverish[ed] the middle classes and improv[ed] the lot of the manual laborers [and that this] has on the whole, I believe, tended towards greater social equality'. As 'for the relations of the United States to Europe, [they] have become both more intimate and less exclusive, as have so many other relations in the post-war world'.[54]

This optimism also showed the dilemmas, pointed to by Richard Bellamy, of trying to export a tradition to countries that were not ready for it, as Europe clearly was not in 1930. Liberal thinking had emerged in the particular circumstances of seventeenth- and nineteenth-century Britain, which is why we tend to associate liberalism so strongly with Locke, Mill and other British liberals. For Bellamy:

> [m]ost continental liberals were Anglophiles. But the establishment of liberal regimes, notwithstanding a modernizing economy and society, proved harder on the continent that in Britain, forcing these [continental] theorists to investigate more fully than their English (if not their Scottish) counterparts the social and cultural preconditions of liberal institutions.[55]

To export this idea to societies that had not had the same historical experience was always going to be, and still is, a problem.

So we have to ask whether there is really such a distinction to be made about liberal internationalism, often equated with idealism or utopianism, being superseded by realism as many would aver, after the Second World War? Can we just dismiss the acceptance of a 'moral background' by Lloyd George as a camouflage for naked pursuit of national interest? Was this just liberal hypocrisy? Does that mean that morality can play no role in foreign policy? George Kennan certainly believed so[56] as did most realist writers of the 1940s like Morgenthau, even if we have to see that judgement in the light of Chamberlain's appeals to 'morality' in 1938 over Munich. It was also due to a rejection of British imperialism by US elites, including the organs of the CFR. But this is to misinterpret the appeal of liberal ideological background for Western politicians since at least 1919. Their 'national interest' can be seen as having its roots in the defence of liberal interests.

Brown has neatly explained this seeming dilemma in the context of the 1930s when liberalism was under its most severe attack in over a hundred years, at least partly because of its perceived hypocrisy after 1919. The re-definition of liberal internationalism by Carr in *The Twenty Years Crisis* of 1939 as 'utopianism' or 'idealism' by others reflected a belief that liberal internationalism did not sufficiently account for man's capacity for evil. Rather than war being a phenomenon thrust upon an unwilling population by Machiavellian and militaristic rulers, the general population did not necessarily dislike, or even actually liked, war, and was not especially motivated by calls for international brotherhood in such organizations as the League of Nations, an organization that in any case embodied the interests of a few victor nations. As Brown writes, 'the power of words here is very great – the way in which "realism", a political doctrine which might be right or wrong, becomes associated with "realistic", which is a quality of judgement most people want to possess, is critically important in its success.' Brown also makes the telling point that the 1930s were not a normal period in modern history:

> [t]o put the matter bluntly, we must hope that it was rather unusual for the leaders of two of the most powerful countries in the world – Germany and the USSR – to be certifiable madmen ... judging a set of ideas by their capacity to cope with a Hitler or a Stalin seems to set far too high a standard.

So realism is not a competing theory for liberal internationalism, it is a critique of the latter's view of human nature and a suggestion that the central concern of IR is about '*states* pursuing *interests* defined in terms of *power*'.[57] It could be said to have no more evidence that it embodies any laws of IR than liberal internationalism itself. Both theories are in effect a set of assertions about 'human nature'. In any case the argument cannot be proved one way or the other except by some definitive judgement about what 'human nature' really is.

As Angell wrote in 1947, '[i]n warfare today the idea of solemnly telling your enemy that you are going to hit him has gone completely out of fashion. It belongs to the day of the despised diplomat with his striped pants, wearing his old school tie'.[58] So civilization he said must be defended by 'power' – but for Angell, that was only a stop-gap. For him civilization was the defence of ideas and of social justice, and for Angell that must be through the collaboration of the United States and Britain with Russia in a New World Order based on International Organizations, a vision that had not changed much since the 1920s for him.

Liberal thinking in the Second World War and after

The defeat of Nazi Germany in any case did much to restore the tarnished 1930s vision of a liberalism tainted by compromise, appeasement and confusion. As a recent book on the history of genocide in the twentieth-century makes plain '[g]enocide is the most imaginable affront to the liberal sensibility and the Whiggish belief in the inevitability of progress'.[59] But at least the liberal West had triumphed over the seeming efficiency and invulnerability of National Socialism. Many now gradually abandoned the 'fellow travelling' of the pre-war period, although by no means all as the Soviet Union still appealed to Marxists and others sick of what they saw as bourgeois values in the heady sexual and cultural liberation of post-war Paris and New York. Equally, as Bellamy has pointed out, many of the great books of the 1940s and early 1950s reflected liberal reactions to authoritarianism – he quotes Friederich Hayek's *Road to Serfdom* (1944), Karl Popper's *The Open Society and its Enemies* (1945), Albert Camus' *The Rebel* (1951) as well as J. L. Talmon's *The Origins of Totalitarian Democracy* (1952).[60] To this could be added the growing oeuvre of Hannah Arendt and many others. Liberalism was making a more than tentative come-back even if it was socialism that still dominated intellectual discourse. Hayek commented in 1949 that '[t]he intellectual revival of liberalism is already under way in many parts of the world. Will it be in time?'[61]

As the 1940s wore on more and more evidence started to emerge of the full horrors of the regimes in Nazi Germany, Imperial Japan and even fascist Italy. The great wartime ally of the West, Soviet Russia, own crimes started to emerge, especially after the publication of Richard Crossman's *The God that Failed* (1949) and George Orwell's literary condemnation of all dictatorships of left and right in *Animal Farm* (1945) and *Nineteen Eighty-four* (1948). The Gulag was slowly investigated and found to have been just as awful as Hitler's equivalent. Of course since the end of the Cold War much more has been discovered and none of it to the glory of regimes based on class warfare. The details of those horrors are still emerging, with a huge flurry of books on Soviet horrors since the opening of the KGB archives in the brief post-Soviet Spring of the early 1990s.[62] Hence the Cold War and its aftermath stimulated much liberal thinking. It laid the roots of the individualism and the revulsion against collectivist ideologies of the 1980s into which politicians like President Ronald Reagan and Prime Minister Margaret Thatcher were able to tap to such good electoral effect.

Stephen Krasner is right to feel that the settlement after the Second World War was entirely dictated by the wishes of the victors (mainly the United States and the Soviet Union), but, as in 1815 and 1919, to 'encourage political regimes that were consonant with their own preferences'.[63] The problem was that these types of regime were incompatible, which led to the division of the world into two blocs, only resolved by the end of the Cold War in 1990. This in turn has led to the main 'preferences' of the liberal powers led by United States being the main building block of any contemporary peace treaty, and especially to the insistence on the importance of human rights and democracy in the (broadly) American definition of the term. Sovereignty could thus either be seen as having been undermined by successive peace treaties since 1648 or, alternatively, that the principle that the victor always dictates the terms to the vanquished has merely been reaffirmed.

In IR one of the main features of the development of liberal thinking post-1945 hinged around the idea of creating what have much more recently been called 'zones of peace', where democracy would be able to flourish in its political and economic forms, even if we should more properly call this a form of social democracy, but one with deep liberal roots. Inherent in this were the statements by victorious liberal politicians like Wilson and Roosevelt that there would now be a 'New World Order', one based on declaratory principles of democracy, peace, economic well being and an end to exploitation. The declaration of the Fourteen Points by Wilson had been one such declaration. The Atlantic Charter of 1941 had been another. Both stated a belief in open covenants (or open diplomacy): economic integration through the spread of free markets, and a global multilateral security organisation that would look after the weak as well as the interests of the strong.

The problem was that the first time offering of such principles had proved illusory. Now it was necessary to put teeth where there had previously been only empty promises. A taste of this comes in Churchill's musing about the Atlantic Charter in early 1944. His secretary Sir John Colville records Churchill as saying that although Germany had 'no claim by right' to the principles of the Charter (as Lloyd George had said earlier about Germany's claim over the Fourteen Points), 'I foresee that after the war is over the Germans will make the same play with alleged breaches of the Charter as they did after the last war with repudiation of the Fourteen Points'.[64]

Indeed it could be claimed that at Yalta in 1945 the Allies did breach a large number of the clauses of the Charter, although only the Soviet Union finally kept to these breaches. The Cold War was, in part at least, based on a repudiation of the harsher clauses of the Yalta Accord by the liberal Allies in the interests of a liberal (re)construction of Europe. After 1919 it could just as easily be argued that the Allies stood and watched as Europe burned and tore itself apart (to some extent in the name of self-determination). This time round there could be no such observation without action. As the veteran South African politician Jan Smuts said to Churchill just after the above recorded conversation 'you must speak the language of the Old Testament to describe what is happening in Europe today'.[65] The next day he told Churchill that they ought to rather read the New Testament, 'not so much for the theology, which was out of date, but for the psychology'. What was lacking in 1919 was the political will to do anything about Europe's destruction. In 1945 both ends of Europe had a militant desire to build a New Jerusalem. Unfortunately they were different town plans.

It could also be claimed that after 1945 liberalism in a sense happened by default. In his 1939 classic *The Great Transformation*, Karl Polanyi had claimed that the liberal economic and political system that prevailed until 1914 had been defeated in the 1930s. It had to be replaced by what might be called the 'global New Deal' now on offer from the United States, much more social engineering than *laissez faire*, not the creation of a 'liberal' mindset. Roosevelt and the PWP planners, and even more so the Europeans, wanted to temper liberalism in its worst social excesses by marrying social stability to economic growth. Planning was the buzzword, not economic liberty. But liberalism with a social purpose was a compromise that all except ultra-liberals like Hayek could accept. His 'Road to Serfdom' was to be social democracy, which Ruggie calls the 'compromise of embedded liberalism'.[66] The key figure in this was Keynes, whose managed capitalism was the key policy pursued across the whole of Europe and indeed the United States until the 1970s and the arrival of a more fundamentalist (or old-fashioned, depending on your view) liberalism of Margaret Thatcher and Ronald Reagan. Only then were the global restraints set in place by national governments and international organizations alike slowly deconstructed. Indeed it has been argued that 'globalization' is still less advanced now than it was in 1914.[67]

Europe

As has been pointed out, the Fourteen Points had had an Achilles heel, and that was the notion of self-determination. As Wilson's Secretary of State, and others, had seen in 1919 this was a Pandora's Box that once opened, could not be shut again, and the results of which no one could foresee. By 1945 liberal commentators on both sides of the Atlantic had realized the limits of relying on the self-determination impulse to bring about liberal political outcomes. The American Government had tried as part of its 'Post-War Planning' process to sound out the smaller countries of Europe as to what kind of Europe they would like after the war. It was discovered that all, bar practically none, would prefer some form of union to the status-quo ante of 1939 (or pre the *Anschluss*). They were still threatening to behave like Tasker Bliss's 'mosquitoes' of 1919. The American and the British answer was generally to call for a United Europe. This was both for reasons of *Realpolitik*, as the Americans had no desire to come and sort out Europe's wars for a third time, and partly for reasons of liberal belief. Wilson's self-determination was taken further than Wilson had dared in 1919 and also in another sense, jettisoned altogether.

One area of extension can be seen in the discussions in early 1945 among the powers and in the columns of the liberal press in the United States of a tentative suggestion of extending the principle of self-determination to the peoples of Empires, and particularly those of the British and French Empires. We know that Roosevelt had such an intention, as it was stated quite explicitly in the Atlantic Charter of 1941. Even if in the conditions of the Grand Alliance such a suggestion had to be delicately put in public, in the private discussions between the United States and Britain the *quid pro quo* of financial and economic support in return for a dismantling of the Empire was clearly put.[68]

Another extension of thinking was in the new context of a devastated Europe. The new *mot a clef* was to be integration. The self-determined Europe of 1919 was widely seen as the problem and no longer the solution. A typical editorial in the last year of the Second World War period in the liberal *New Republic* stated that:

> [t]he first thing to note is that excessive nationalism, in any country at any time, is an unmitigated curse and should be fought with all the weapons at our command. ... We should work towards a Europe in which the peoples of the various countries emphasize what they have in common and not their differences.[69]

As another *New Republic* editorial of the same period put it, this new Europe would be made up of states that were 'democratic ... left of center ... modernized as rapidly as possible' and that 'the United States should be the political and economic helpmate in this'.[70] This was the direct precursor of the developing idea of 'reconstruction' to which Chapters 4 and 5 of this book are devoted. It can even be argued that reconstruction has its intellectual origins in the export of American military and ideological power. Furthermore it could be argued that greatest liberal experiment of all time, to reconstruct a whole area of the world was and has been the creation of a united Europe.

The official 'intra-European' story is that Europe was a miracle of self-creation: French Prime Minister Robert Schuman and Jean Monnet its initial architects, and the Coal and Steel Treaty of 18 April 1951 its first act. This in turn led to the setting up of the High Authority of the European Community of Coal and Steel, and subsequently to the Council of Ministers and the European Court of Justice. This in turn led to the first elements of a Common Market and then to the Treaty of Rome in 1956 and other organizations like EURATOM from 1958 on.[71]

The first president of the High Authority (HA) was Monnet. At its inauguration in the Hotel de Ville in Luxemburg on 10 August 1952, the Luxemburg Minister of Foreign Affairs, Joseph Beck, announced that the HA was 'superior to the nation even if the nation is not diminished ... [b]ecause, as has been rightly said, for the sake of peace, the national must be guaranteed by the international, but the international is superior to the national'. This was the answer to 'national egoism'.[72] In his own speech Monnet also talked of the supranational nature of the HA, this was the first 'transfer of sovereignty' in the history of Europe. It was also a clear liberal message – it was 'indissolubly linked to international trade. Our Community will contribute to regulating the problems of trade that are present in the world'.[73]

It is true that in 1945 Social Democrats and conservative liberals alike in France, Germany, Italy and elsewhere were convinced that the only way to save themselves a third time from the scourge of war was in some form of United Europe. Monnet (often referred to as the 'Father of Europe') put it even more succinctly: 'de la solution du problème européen depend la vie de la France.'[74] Alan Milward therefore argues that the nation state in Europe was 'saved' by the process of economic integration, so that the nation state has in no way been 'eroded' by the process towards union. In other words, European Union post-1945 was based on the self-interest of the European states. A classic theory by Walter Lipgens posits that the European Union emerged from indigenous resistance movements and federal movements like Britain's Federal Union.[75]

However in most, if not all, cases these drew on existing federalist theories and practices, themselves largely drawn from the American experience.[76] In what is probably the greatest work of its kind of the period, Clarence Streit's *Union Now*, there was a clear call for the liberal states of the West to in effect merge to form the basis of a liberal international order. The most developed theory in Britain, one that went even beyond this to talk of 'World Government' was that of David Mitrany. His book of 1943, *A Working Peace System*, foresaw the emergence of world or at least regional government based first of all on the 'low politics' of functional cooperation being transformed into cooperation at the level of 'high politics', as now seems to have happened with the emergence of the EU.[77]

Mitrany's ideas can maybe now be seen as having been prophetic but they seemed premature at the time to many liberals. Gilbert Murray was typical in seeing problems ahead in 1944. In a letter to Robert Cecil he wrote that 'Russia is a savage unknown quantity; America is out for economic domination; it is impossible for Europe to recover from the hatred and dissension produced by German atrocities, the Russian atrocities [and many more]'. Cecil's reply bought him back to liberal optimism: 'My dear Jeremiah, All you say is only too true but it doesn't bother me very much because I see no other possible course open to us except to support the United Nations Organisation with all our power.' In a later letter Cecil added in that a 'European Regional Council under the United Nations would also be necessary ... [b]ut it must avoid too ambitious a start or it will excite jealousy'.[78] But by 1946 he was toying with the Churchillian idea of a 'United Europe', as were most British liberals, both to bring Europe within the ambit of the United Nations ideal of a global democratic peace and also to restrain the United States.[79]

However there is a large body of thought, ranging from the liberal to the Marxist, that argues that it was American power, not centrally the Europeans themselves, who made the European democratic peace possible. In a brilliant analysis of the political and strategic thinking of Roosevelt, George Kennan and Dean Acheson, arguably the three main architects of the post-Second World War world, John Lamberton Harper argues that there was a consensus of a broad sector of American opinion by the 1940s that there had to be a solution to the:

> European Question. For Americans, by and large, that question has been how to protect the rest of the world – or at least their own political and social experiment – from Europe's destructiveness, if not necessarily to save Europe from itself. This has led to a lasting ambivalence ... on the one hand, to try to continue circumscribing the autonomy of the European powers and maintaining the degree of tutelage over European affairs to which it has become accustomed; on the other, to foster greater European initiative and self-reliance, come what may ... [B]ut a basic doubt remains: left to their own devices, will the Europeans act in their own best interest and those of the United States?

If proof were required that this is still an 'ambivalence' it suffices to look at the European–American divisions over Iraq in 2003.[80]

Liberal institutionalist IR theorists like Robert Keohane have stressed the need for early leadership in any institutional framework and indeed the need to maintain that leadership. Geir Lundestad takes this argument even further and argues, first, that '[t]he United States promoted the integration of Western Europe, rather strongly until the mid-1960s, [although] less strongly after that'. Second, he goes as far as to argue that the United States has continued ever since 1945 to act as an 'imperial' power in Europe. This was for purely self-interested reasons: 'it did not pursue its pro-integrationist policy primarily for the sake of Western Europeans', but rather because '[t]wice in the Twentieth-century [the United States] had intervened to prevent Europe from being dominated by a hostile power'. So to stop this happening a third time the United States had to remain. Later in the book Lundestad develops the thesis that integration was also the cheapest option for the United States' own security – cheapest in lives and in money. So although Lundestad leaves the 'empire' in lower case and inverted commas he points to many elements of at least 'predominance'.[81] Lundestad thus serves as one pole of a scholarly spectrum of opinion about what created the new Europe. What cannot be denied even by those hostile to the idea of an American (or 'Anglo-Saxon') – led Europe, is that Germany (and Japan) have served as the basic exemplar of 'civilian power' since 1945. Both Germany and Japan have been far more important as economic giants and as military pygmies than they had been for much of their previous existence as nation states.[82]

So while it would be foolish to deny that the environment in which this became possible was not largely provided by the sticks and carrots of American diplomacy, military might and capital, it would be crass to deny that there was also an Atlanticist and domestic European drive for new forms of liberal practice and thought that is in retrospect remarkable. The creation of a United Europe is a clear example of how the self-interest of liberal powers like Britain and the United States can and has been allied to the necessity of finding alternative frameworks for international practice though liberal international theory writ large. There is no necessary dichotomy between the notion of power and the implementation of liberal theory. Indeed there are constant reminders that the two go hand in hand. This has been amply demonstrated since the end of the Cold War.

Liberalism, realism and IR post-1990: 'humanitarian intervention'[83]

Liberalism in confusion or triumph?

In an introduction to a slim publication by the Foreign Policy Centre and Demos, two key liberal-minded British think tanks of the 1990s, Mark Leonard and Tom Bentley considered that:

> [W]e have not found a name to describe the era we are living in, still less to understand how it might work. George Bush's triumphant declaration of a new world order in 1990 soon gave way to a widespread sense of disorder, fuelled by ethnic warfare, resurgent nationalism and disintegration. The end of the nation state, global corporate rule and a clash of civilisations have all been predicted. ... The level of analytical confusion has reached the point where the American journal *Foreign Policy* has offered a cash prize to anyone who can invent a new term to encapsulate the age.[84]

Robert Cooper largely confirms this analysis in the main text of this pamphlet and underlines it by saying that the problem is that many states have now in effect ceased to exist, they have reverted to the 'pre-modern'. But for him what is unlike the last time such a clear distinction last existed between the ultra (or even 'post'- and the pre-) modern there is a big difference:

> What is different today is that the imperial urge is dead in the countries most capable of imperialism ... [g]overning people, especially potentially hostile people, is a burden. No one today wants to pay the costs of saving distant countries from ruin. The pre-modern world exists, as it were, in a different time zone: here, as in the ancient world the choice is again between empire

or chaos. And today, because in the post-war Cold War world none of us sees the use of empires, we have chosen chaos.[85]

In terms of liberal philosophy and practice, in the post-Cold War period the greatest single event was the publication of Francis Fukuyama's article 'The End of History and the Last Man' in 1989. This article, then over-expanded into a 1992 book of the same name, became notorious for its claim that the collapse of the Soviet Union showed the 'total exhaustion of viable systematic alternatives to Western liberalism'.[86] The then recent history of the globe did indeed seem to confirm much of what he wrote. Many previously dictatorial Third, and even 'Second', World states in Latin America, Africa, Eastern Europe and elsewhere had espoused at least the discourse of capitalism and democratic liberalism. Samuel Huntington at that period also wrote about the 'Third Wave' of demo-cratization (1993), very unlike his later claim of the impending 'Clash of Civilizations' (1996).

Unfortunately, the idea that liberals are complacent, arrogant and triumphant has stuck in the minds of many in its heartland and, most significantly, in those areas of the World that feel most aggrieved by its material wealth and what they perceive as its hypocrisy and cultural and spiritual aridity.

The thesis thus also seemed to gloss over one of the many insights that Marx had about capitalism. Capitalism is not only a form of production; it is the basis for the superstructure of society, its cultural and political norms. Justin Rosenberg's critique of what he terms the 'Empire of Civil Society' portrays the 'market', even 'economics' as a form of social dominance far removed from notions of real 'democracy'.[87] Whether we take that argument to heart, even good liberals have to accept that a society cannot be transformed from an agricultural to an industrial or service based society without profoundly shaking its values. Capitalism can also not persuade those that believe in the prophets of previously eternal truths as varied as the Buddha, Mohammed and Jesus Christ that Mammon and his representative on Earth the Multinational Company might be a better bet for eternal salvation. And most significantly it pushes people into searching for other, often older and more spiritually rewarding forms of belief in clan, people or in more fundamentalist religious belief. Has liberal capitalism created a 'world without meaning' or one in which there are too many? Whichever is the answer their natural enemy may turn out to be the liberal forces that liberated them to think thus in the first place.[88] Fukuyama recognized this himself in his writings, the 'last man' of the title of his most famous book or his subsequent bemoaning about the need for 'social capital' in Western and other societies.[89]

Both this triumphalism and perceived hypocrisy comes out very strongly in liberal politicians' statements about their interactions with the rest of the world. Since 1990 the liberal idea that foreign policy must ultimately be designed around moral ends, and if possible always means, has become part of the language of international politics. Western liberal states have played a major role in defining this, not without some major criticism, especially when the terms 'human rights foreign policy' or 'an ethical foreign policy' were coined in liberal Britain in the late 1990s. The terms may have been greeted with ribald comments but it is in fact part of a long tradition of liberal foreign policy going back to Cobden and Mill. However, what they mean in practice is no less loaded with dilemmas than in their own century.

Liberalism as practice in IR after 1990

For the other key expression of the post-war liberal in foreign policy is 'humanitarian intervention', the term most used in the implementation of an 'ethical' foreign policy by liberal states and by the 'international community'. The essence of this is that under certain circumstances it is legitimate for the international community to intervene in the internal affairs of sovereign states. The questions that this poses are to what extent it should be allowed as an exception to the rule of sovereignty and non-intervention, itself a key liberal tenet. Another is what are the motives and how effective is the practice, one that has been seen in the Middle East (Iraq), Africa (Somalia, Rwanda, Sierra Leone for example), and in the Former Yugoslavia (Bosnia, Kosovo). There are hard and soft versions of the doctrine, the first usually called 'solidarism' that urges a cosmopolitan response to an objectively horrible situation. As we have remarked, conservative or 'realist' thinkers see humanitarian intervention as usually wrong and misguided as it damages the basic norm of the international system.[90] But of course, until recently, so did liberals, although the idea could be said to date back to the liberation of Greece from the Ottoman Empire in 1827.

In the years before 1990 the expression humanitarian intervention was not one that slipped easily off the tongues of most liberals. Mill and Cobden's logic still held – intervention could not bring freedom as that had to come from within the individual or the community itself. Walzer uses Millean logic when he wrote in 1977[91] that:

> The list of oppressive governments, the list of massacred peoples, is frighteningly long. Though an event like the Nazi holocaust is without precedent in human history, murder on a smaller scale is so common as to be almost ordinary. On the other hand – or perhaps for this reason – clear examples of what is called 'humanitarian intervention' are very rare.

In fact Walzer could name only two before the period when he was writing and the reason was simple, because '[h]umanitarian intervention is justified when it is a response to acts "that shock the moral conscience of mankind." The old-fashioned language seems to me exactly right.' He did not add the Gulf War of 1991 to his list in the 1992 edition.[92] But since then a host of actions, mainly by Western European and North American liberal democracies, have been launched under precisely that label. Why is this?

Many critics of humanitarian intervention have asserted that it is merely imperialism reworked, a theme to which we will return in subsequent pages. John

Pilger dismisses it as the 'latest [expression] to satisfy the criterion of doing what you like where you like, as long as you are strong enough'.[93]

What has been referred to as 'Post-Settlement Peacebuilding'[94] has been very much remarked upon since the end of the Cold War and has seen its main post Cold War statements in the UN's *Agenda For Peace* of 1992, 1995 and in the Brahimi Report of 1999. Both of these reports aims to find ways to avoid the worst of post-conflict effects such as those in Bosnia and Kosovo on populations, to effect 'structural' changes, for the creation of a 'positive' peace and to try and prevent a relapse into war. This Miall, Ramsbottam and Woodhouse call 'Clausewitz in reverse' – 'the continuation of the politics of war into the ensuing peace' to create armistices that will bring about cooperation between previously warring factions. Many would now argue that we are now seeing the emergence of 'new' kind of warfare to which liberalism has not many answers.

Mary Kaldor, the originator of the 'new' war term, has taken this argument further. Her argument is that a 'new type of organized violence has appeared ... which is one aspect of the current globalized era' – hence 'new wars'. These wars blur the boundary between war ('violence between states') and 'organized crime'. They also involve large-scale violations of human rights. They are post-modern, even to the extent that they can take place in cyber-space. They also are a feature of a much more 'inter-connected world' where the state is less important and firms' economics are more important than politics and 'a power vacuum which is typical of transition period in world affairs' has emerged involving a 'myriad of transnational connections'.[95] So violence has become less the preserve of the state, less extreme, but potentially more vicious (because more 'private', like by warlords); and more connected to problems of 'identity' (economic exclusion, religious belief) rather than to geo-political or ideological goals. These wars tend to hark back to some, often imaginary, golden past where the 'people' were all together. They are anti-cosmopolitan and are seen as being fought to preserve a community, and hence their perpetrators will not use customary cost-benefit analysis. Theirs is a 'holy' struggle.

Moreover it might be said that the main liberal bastion against war, the international organizations, are themselves under threat from rogue Western states. Simon Chesterman argues that the Charter of the United Nations is a clear statement that force should not be used unilaterally; yet it has been increasingly in the 1990s, most often in the name of the United Nations. This has meant that Article 2(4) that underpins this norm of non-intervention has had to be modified in practice so that certain regimes are seen as 'illegitimate', so that they lose the right of sovereignty and protection against the use of force. Chesterman further argues that these actions have led to a decline in the credibility of the Security Council as the sole arbiter of the use of force in the international sphere, yet has been used to claim the revitalization of this body since 1990 through the use of the doctrine. In Kosovo he argues that the use of unilateral force by one section of the international community (the NATO Alliance) severely undermined that claim and is in particular damaging to the ideal of having a norm that is applicable in law under all circumstances, or not. This point was of course also made by Russia and China, Security Council members who voted against the NATO intervention Kosovo in 1999.[96]

So one could be forgiven for thinking that HI is a doctrine practised mainly, if not exclusively, by the United States. One Brookings/Carnegie publication of the late 1990s with the title Intervention has as its sub-title *The Use of American Military Force in the Post Cold War World*.[97] But HI is also a doctrine that can include measures well short of force. The European Union is a major contributor to HI initiatives but prides itself in being a 'civilian power' that projects its influence through the 'humanitarian' side of the HI equation. In Bosnia, Kosovo and Afghanistan in the 1990s we saw the emergence of a division of labour – the United States dropped the bombs and the EU made the peace, a view tempered by the Iraq experience. The events in New York of 11 September 2001 have also played their role in accentuating the feeling that the United States is using the liberal belief that HI is both morally good and beneficial to its recipients for its own ends.

But that would be to deny the genuine universal revulsion against terrorism. Again, the domestic debate over the rights and ethics of reactions to terrorism is being discussed in tandem with an international action to stop it spreading. The problem of 'weak states' is no longer one that can be ignored when those weak states harbour groups that would destroy the heartland of the international liberal order.

Conclusion: is there a distinctively liberal view of the world?

So, in the words of Siegfried Sassoon at the head of this chapter, has war made us 'wise' or 'free'? Liberalism is certainly the ideology that emerges strengthened most obviously by the events of the twentieth-century. Its enemies, Islamic fundamentalism, communism and socialism, all look distinctly enfeebled, if one asks the question that Stalin posed of the Roman Catholic Church: 'how many divisions has the Pope?' Yet liberalism is yet again going through one of it periodic paroxysms of self-doubt, this time galvanized not by a world war between states but by the ever-present threat of a world war waged by terrorists without a country, or even a proper 'base', for as my readers will know 'Al-Qaeda' means the 'base' in Arabic.

The beginning of the 1990s saw liberalism developing into a much more muscular ideology and practice than had been seen since the end of the nineteenth century. The lights that Sir Edward Grey saw 'going out all over Europe' in August 1914 seemed to have been relit. This was the period of the 'End of History', the unravelling of all the alternatives to liberal thinking. Equally the criticism of liberalism was much more virulent than it had been for a long time. It had not seemed worthwhile attacking a tired old dogma from the 1960s right until the advent of Prime Minister Margaret Thatcher in the UK and President Ronald Reagan in the United States. These two political figures signalled the re-emergence of a new liberal, some would say 'libertarian', drive in Western politics that saw the end of the idea that government must involve itself in grandiose projects and interference in the economic domains normally controlled by independent entrepreneurs, often in the name of 'Keynesianism'. It is in this sense that H. W. Brands wrote of the 'Strange Death of American Liberalism', a conscious evocation of Dangerfield's famous text of 1935 on Britain.[98] The left's criticisms of policies ranging from privatization through to military expansionism seemed to be silenced when the USSR agreed to end the Cold War and embarked upon privatization.

But the Academy in the liberal states, stuck in the previous mind-set of a Keynesian liberal compromise on economics and *Ostpolitik* or *détente* with the Eastern Bloc, was furious and rapidly started to point to the contradictions inherent in these developments. What about those who slipped through the net of the new enterprise culture? What about the poor of the Third World who could not benefit from 'export-led growth'? None the less the older national and international institutions of social re-distributive justice, which represented a certain kind of left-wing liberal social democracy like 'Old Labour' and the UNCTAD gave way to the new centre-right ideas and practices of 'New Labour' and the transatlantic 'Third Way' domestically, and internationally, to revamped capitalist organizations like the IMF, World Bank and the new World Trade Organization, the apotheosis of Friederich Hayek and Milton Freedman.

Domestic and foreign policy once again merged in a new triumph of liberal hegemony in terms of both ideas and practice. In foreign policy the new essential discourse was that of an 'ethical' foreign policy, the promotion of human rights and the over-arching principle of humanitarian intervention to defeat tyrants and protect oppressed populations. In many ways this looked like the apotheosis of the thinking of Woodrow Wilson, the CFR and the liberal commentators of the previous hundred years. The national interests of the great liberal powers, and especially that of the United States, were becoming seen as the global interest.

What broader lessons can we draw from the historical legacy of liberalism in the last hundred years to counter this new sense of liberal triumph? In general terms the auguries of history do not bode well. The twentieth-century started with the great liberal Power of the day, Great Britain, experiencing a sense of inner crisis both about the stability of its own strength and in deep division over the liberal credentials that it, and outsiders, believed gave it legitimacy as a power. The twentieth-century ended with the now dominant liberal power, the United States, experiencing some of the same worries. In both 1900 and 1999 it would have been difficult to foresee a coming precipitate decline. But in 1900 Britain such a decline had been on the cards ever since the Great Depression of the 1870s when it became apparent that newly emerging states like Germany and the United States were beginning to threaten Britain's financial, economic and military hegemony. The Royal Navy still looked like the greatest weapon the world had ever seen but others were catching up fast and the technological gap that had given Britain so many of its victories was ebbing fast.

Since the 1970s there has been discussion of the end of American hegemony, not least from (liberal) Americans like Robert Keohane. This has been based on the same mix of fears about economic, military and moral dominance. China is mentioned frequently as the 'next hegemon', Islamic Fundamentalism is often quoted as a potential ideological replacement for liberalism in the developing world (three-quarters of the global population). Some, like Christopher Coker, talk about the 'decline of the West' to explain how the United States is losing its ontological grip on its Allies. The Athenian imperial influence that arguably gave the United States its particular moral force has now been eroded to the point where it must either use its Roman power (carrier groups and the like) or rely on the few close allies left to it, ironically with Britain and its ex-(white) Commonwealth as the clear 'follower'. Even those who have arguably most benefited from American power, Germany, France and Belgium, are ready to abandon it in its hour of need. But maybe we could argue that the divided reaction from the West to the Iraq crisis of 2002–4 is not so much the end of the American world order of 1945 as the apotheosis of it? There is now a genuine debate of moral equals about how to deal with 'rogue' states like Iraq. There is not the slightest chance of the West going to war with itself over this issue, just an honest disagreement about how to deal with renegades.

Liberalism in the United States sees particular ambivalence about its need to defend either country and liberty on one hand or individual rights on the other. The widely used epithet 'Pinko-liberal' is often used by Americans to attack those who espouse what they see as soft attitudes to crime, social delinquency, war or whatever while at the same time in effect defending the right of the utterer. The debate in the United States, as in Britain is not so much a fight between left and right as between different *styles* of liberalism. The 'neo-conservatives' are as adamant in their defence of Lockean principles of liberty as are 'softer' liberals. The views of one of the key 'neo-cons', Richard Perle, interviewed on the eve of President Bush's state visit to London in the aftermath of the Iraq war in November 2003 were summed up in the following terms:

> In Europe, neo-conservatism is shorthand for a unilateralist and crude abuse of American power. Yet its philosophy is rooted in traditions of liberal idealism, dating back to Woodrow Wilson. It was later honed in the era of President Ronald Reagan as he faced down the Soviet Union.

Perle proclaimed himself infuriated by the attempt to 'demonize. The closest equivalent of the neo-conservatives would be classical liberals: people who believe the blessings of freedom should be made widely available. There is nothing warmongering about that.'[99] Other commentators, such as Alex Callinicos, on the neo-con phenomenon beg to differ as to its 'blessings'.[100] But there is no doubt that neo-cons themselves might like the view expressed in a *Daily Telegraph* column about the killing of Theo van Gogh (a film-maker) by an Islamic fanatic in Amsterdam, that 'neo-cons are liberals who got real'.[101]

The American neo-con right has taken upon itself the ideas of the more traditional American LI type liberals and is now bent on exporting 'American [liberal] values' across the globe. Naturally the explanation of why – to defend the United States or to spread 'freedom' – varies, but the result is the same. Conservative internationalism of the President [Teddy] Roosevelt variety has now merged in fact with the liberal internationalism of the President [Franklin Delano] Roosevelt variety. This debate has now gripped the entire West, but it is again a liberal debate about how to defend both core values and physical well-being. Equally, a militant spreader of 'freedom' like President Bush may well feel that the UN has been too slow in rallying to his call for liberation, but the implications for the Wilsonian drama of a united global community working for what the Carnegie and others would have called in the 1920s and 1930s 'world peace through law' or in the 2000s 'the rule of law' cannot be denied. UN Secretary General Kofi Annan has declared the war in Iraq 'illegal' as it was not approved by the Security Council, a body set up, largely, by the liberal United States, to ensure that such a rule is respected. Might we therefore see this as a family quarrel *among* liberals of various complexions, not a fundamental falling out within the tribe? The argument since the advent of the modern welfare state has always been about how much should be left to the market and how much to government domestically and how much liberal states should intervene in the affairs of illiberal states internationally.

Angell's *The Great Illusion* was the key text of the period of Britain's internal doubt before the physical blow of the two world wars, but the moral blow was the self-inflicted hubris of the Boer War. In 1994–5 few doubted that the United States had been right to intervene in Bosnia for humanitarian reasons, but there were grave doubts about its intervention in Kosovo, and even more about its proposed intervention in Iraq in 2002–3. At the time of writing that dilemma has not been fully played out, but the condemnations of hypocrisy and the attacks on the United States' liberal credentials are as severe now as were the condemnation of Britain in 1900.

This was no liberal intervention it was claimed, it is colonialism or about resources ('oil for blood') or even about imperial pique – as President George Bush's father had not finished toppling a dictator in 1991, his son should finish the job. The parallels of history must never be taken too literally, but the evidence of division within liberal Western elites is the same now as it was then. Once again it is Germany and France that are most outraged, once again the Anglo-Saxon powers are denigrating these reactions as the moanings of a frustrated European power. And once again there is the emergence of more or less articulate centres of alternative hegemonic discourse in the Islamic world, and even within the West itself. The left may be down but it is not out. Liberalism ignored Theodor Mommsen in 1901, it would be wise not to ignore German Chancellor Gerhard Schroeder, French President Jacques Chirac and other critics of the war in Iraq now. In many ways the same mistakes seem to be being made. The muscular liberal civilizing influence of Britain became utterly uncompromising as it grew in self-confidence. Is the United States now making the same error of judgement?

3   Reparations

[C]compensation will be paid by Germany and for all damage done to the civilian population of the Allies and their property by the aggression of Germany by land, by sea and from the air.

Lansing, Note 5, November 1918

The sooner the idea of victor and vanquished passed away the better it would be for economic reconstruction. One half of Europe must not go on dominating and penalizing the other half.

Sir William Goode, *The Times*, 12 December 1924

Introduction[1]

The first major policy option pursued by liberal states in the twentieth century that we will explore is one that might be said to be an example of how *not* to propagate liberal ideas. The nature of words changes with historical circumstance, but few have had the resonance of reparation. The policy has been blamed for destroying economies, even for the outbreak of the Second World War. If the Treaty of Versailles of 1919 that ended the First World War has come in for general opprobrium the reparations clauses have received far worse. They provoked anger, dismay and the desire for revenge. Such is the importance of that debate that this chapter is intended to engage in a consideration of the imposition of reparations as key policy instruments in the settlement of wars in the early twentieth century, taking the discussion up to the late 1940s. It will centrally consider some of the surrounding ideas of the debate on the instrument and try and suggest what might be the wider lessons of the (liberal) victor's attempt to extract reparations from the (generally illiberal) vanquished in the aftermath of war.

This is not a debate that stopped in the 1920s as seems sometimes to be the impression one gets in reading accounts of such classic anti-reparations texts as John Maynard Keynes' *Economic Consequences of the Peace* (1920), although we can still read that and its sequel *A Revision of the Treaty* (1921) with profit today. It is worth remembering that the United Nations demanded reparation, albeit in a limited form, from Iraq in 1990–1 and from Germany in 1939–45. Some form of Reparation was suggested in the case of African slavery at the 2001 United Nations World Conference Against Racism in Durban, South Africa, in August–September 2001. But the discussion of reparations since the end of the Cold War has assumed a different tenor, much more to do with restitution for moral damage done to groups and individuals, often many years after the purported events, as in the case of slavery.

The roots of the contemporary idea of reparation/restitution can none the less be found in the earlier debate before the beginning of the Cold War. Here it will be suggested that the basic itinerary of 'reparation' has been to inherit the notion of indemnity in 1919, and to be gradually transformed into the idea of reconstruction in the 1930s and 1940s and then to revert somewhat to the original idea of indemnity in the 1990s. The idea of reparation must therefore be seen as but one layer of a matrioschka doll of policy options that have been deployed by the victors of the great wars of this century against the vanquished. One of the lasting results of the debate about reparations in the 1920s is that imposing economic demands on a defeated state is now seen with deep suspicion as they have a clear tendency to affect the populace at large of a target state and not just the 'guilty' parties within it. In this way reparations can be seen as a counterpart of thinking on war crimes.

It will be suggested that the main lesson of this is that the emergence of the 'individual' has gone in tandem with the emergence of the notion of reparation and other policy options tried by liberal states after wars. This emergence is in effect a product of the rise of public opinion in foreign policy. Its ramifications do go way beyond the personal however. In recent cases where reparation has been sought, it is clearly the case that compensation for, say, an Allied Prisoner of War who was tortured by the Japanese on the Burma Railway, affects Anglo–Japanese relations. The refusal of the Japanese Government to pay such compensation can therefore have a direct effect on many other aspects of bilateral relations. The chapter will thus try and show how reparation became something much wider than compensation, and also how this request for such compensation can often stand in the way of the development of peaceful relations between states and societies.

Reparations and the study of international relations

The policy option of reparation has been much neglected in recent international history and IR scholarship, in major contrast to the debate in the period before 1939 when the term dominated virtually anything written about IR and in the 1970s when the idea was much studied by international historians. The explanations of why this is so vary, but undoubtedly they have to do, first, with the extremely technical nature of the discussions that always take place over a number of years among the victors to settle upon a payment figure and to enforce payment upon the vanquished. Second, recent neglect also reflects the more contemporary obsession with alternative features of the inter-war period that has attracted the historians and theorists gaze.[2] We are now much more interested and much more excited about features of the inter-war period that seemed to be leading somewhere, such as the Soviet Union, or to the creation of a unified Europe, or the echoes of the inter-war period for the debate on idealism and realism for example.[3] But for a time, and even as late as the 1970s, they did provoke a great deal of scholarship, a mere tithe of which could be considered fully in a chapter of this length such is its extent.

International lawyers have not given up their interest in the subject and for good reason. For example, Ian Brownie's work on state responsibility traces the emergence of reparation as a context for dealing with 'guilty' states to the early eighteenth century, as with Vattell's 1758 *Le Droit des Gens*, as part of an overall way of bringing the issue of state responsibility 'out of the clouds and expos[ing it] to more technical and analytical treatment'. Here reparation was seen in the 'concept of reparation for an injury'. Brownlie later defines reparation as 'all measures which a claimant may expect to be taken by a respondent state: payment of compensation (or restitution), an apology, the punishment of the individuals responsible, the taking of steps to prevent a recurrence of the breach of duty, and any other forms of satisfaction'.[4] This all-encompassing definition has been used in its various forms to justify not only reparations against Germany in the 1920s, but also against Germany after the Second World War and in other cases since. The linking of the notions of reparation and compensation is thus of early date.

However it has never been clear that states could claim reparation for damage to *themselves*, and one of the greatest authorities on the subject of legal responsibility, Parry, claimed as recently as 1956 that 'the evidence for the existence of the right of a state to recover monetary reparation in respect of a wrong to itself directly or exclusively, as distinct from a wrong to it via its national or *protégé*, is in effect non-existent. States have not habitually claimed damages from one another – except on behalf of their nationals.'[5]

The main concern here is to ask why such a policy, seemingly innocuous in the sense that it was presented as a plea for justice, came to be so vilified and in the mind of some to be blamed as a major cause of the rise of Hitler, the economic collapse of the 1920s and 1930s, of economic nationalism, and ultimately as the cause of the world's most terrible conflict, the Second World War?

Reparations, 1914–19

In Chapter 2 the main liberal writings on war during the First World War were outlined and their influence on President Woodrow Wilson indicated. His Fourteen Points speech of January 1918 was a clear demand that diplomacy had to be conducted differently in future, along with an endorsement of new rights for peoples ('self-determination') and some blunt demands that the Allies mend their ways in their conduct of future economic and political policy towards the rest of the world. As we have seen, these were all demands that can be found throughout Anglo–American liberal writings before and during the First World War. There had been moves by 1918 to set up a League of Nations based on liberal principles and some indication that the peace would be based on the Fourteen Points. The Germans claimed that it was this liberal-minded adversary for whom they had agreed to lay down their arms.

Wilson had carried American public opinion with him for the early part of American involvement. Until American casualties started to rise in the early part of 1918 the voice of 'revenge' was correspondingly absent. However, by the time Wilson went to Europe in late November 1918 many voices in America, and particularly in the newly conservative isolationist Republican Senate, had arisen to demand a much more illiberal punitive peace, a 'peace of unconditional surrender', partly because by the end of 1918 American casualties were very much higher.[6] This newly hardened attitude demanded that Germany be made to pay for a substantial part of the costs of the war, a demand not even mentioned in the Fourteen Points. The conservatives continued to make progress throughout the discussions in Paris and Wilson was continually pressured both by his Allies and from the other side of the Atlantic to tone down, or even to eliminate, any of the original liberal impulses with which he had arrived for the negotiations. The Versailles Treaty of May 1919 was thus a triumph of conservative, indeed of 'realist', thinking. It had very little of the liberal idealism that Wilson is usually said to have envisaged, with the exception of the inclusion of the Covenant of the League of Nations as the first part of the Treaty, a Treaty which the Senate was still to reject on the grounds that it committed the United States to go to war for the League.

Two issues among many others stand out as illustrating how the Treaty betrayed liberal ideals: the principle of racial equality and that of how to compensate the losers in the war among the civilian population who would have the most to say about the peace. The first was an issue that the Japanese wanted very much to be considered in the Treaty discussions as a way of removing the taint of racial prejudice that had always split the emergent 'Comity of Nations' (as it was called) and which would inevitably stop the emergence of what was later to be called the West (but was not so called at the time). Wilson refused to allow a racial equality clause in the Treaty on the grounds that it would upset the voters of the west of the United States who had a long-standing fear of being 'swamped' by 'yellow races', principally the Japanese and Chinese, even though the latter were largely responsible for building the first railroad out of California towards the East, thus ensuring the state's future prosperity.

The second issue was the according of pensions to those who had suffered in the attacks on Northern France by German forces. The 'Pre-Armistice Agreement' signed by Secretary of State Lansing with Germany on behalf of the Allied Governments on 5 November 1918 was worded, to Germany's reluctant satisfaction, as a promise to make good *material* damage: 'compensation will be paid by Germany for all damage done to the civilian population of the Allies and their property by the aggression of Germany by land, sea and from the air.'[7] However, once the Treaty discussions got under way this was re-interpreted by the French and British delegations to mean the payment of peacetime pensions to all civilian and military personnel who could be said to have suffered from German action.

The net result was to increase the Reparations bill by a huge amount, a subterfuge that did much to embitter Germany in the subsequent period. It was a use of liberal logic in the service of a very old-fashioned idea of revenge, and seen as such.

There was a corresponding revulsion at the Treaty among both American and British liberal public opinion. Moreover, in the United States the seeming defeat of liberal values in the Treaty was compounded by a growing unease about the suppression of 'Bolshevism' in the United States, where American socialists were being hounded, and in Russia where American, British and French expeditionary forces were to be sent. Raymond Robins was reported as saying that 'you can't put down ideas with bayonets'. In the week that the Treaty was signed *The Nation*, a left-leaning liberal publication reported that the annual meeting of the American Academy of Political and Social Science reflected an 'evident undercurrent of uneasiness owing to the antithesis between the ideals which this country represents abroad and the conditions at home'.[8]

However the public mood and that of official America was not consonant with liberal tolerance. This was even less the case in Britain and France.

The logic of imposing reparations on Germany in 1919[9]

In his autobiographical *The Truth About The Peace Treaties*, not published until 1938 and in a very different climate to that prevailing in 1919, British Prime Minister Lloyd George claimed that there were both historical precedents and moral justification for presenting Germany with a reparations bill after the war. He alleged that: '[t]he Germans on their part had been conducting a similar enquiry as to the methods by which, in the event of victory, they could extract an indemnity from their defeated foes.' For him, the justification for reparations lay in the 'fundamental' fact that 'the Central Powers were the aggressors has been established beyond a doubt. ... If the Central Powers were not primarily responsible for the War, the *basis* of reparations disappears' [my emphasis]. There was thus a 'legal case' for reparations.

> The liability to pay compensation for damage by a wrongdoer, and the payment by a defeated suitor of the costs incurred in a vindication of justice are among the integral principles of law in every civilised community. States are not immune from the application of that elementary doctrine of jurisprudence.[10]

So for Lloyd George:

> [a] critical attitude towards the exacting of reparations after a war has been dictated by an undefined and unacknowledged feeling that war is part of the legitimate business of States and that it cannot be treated as a tort. ... This frame of mind has ... [for largely party political reasons] ... been adopted by sections which make a special profession of inculcating the criminality of all wars.

But, he added, '[w]hy should States and their responsible directors be the only corporations to escape responsibility for their injurious acts', especially when those acts are '"criminal"'. . . It would be an entirely new doctrine that nations who make war upon other nations should not be held responsible for the consequences'. This was because '[a]s far as principles of right are concerned, States must abide by the rules of justice which they impose on their own citizens'.

For Lloyd George indemnities have always been demanded by victors in wars. In the old days it was 'ruder and more summary' and in the form of 'pillage, loot and in annexation of territory'. As one of the British delegates specializing in the reparation question, Lord Sumner, had pointed out at Paris, there had been precedents for indemnities in cash. In 1815, 700 million francs had been exacted by the Allies from France; in 1849 Sardinia had paid Austria 75 million francs; and in 1866 'Prussia imposed upon Austria an indemnity of 40 million thalers' and 'considerable sums upon several German states'. All of these payments had been to cover costs of the wars.

However there had been a new departure in 1871, when after the Franco–Prussian war, 'Prussia imposed upon France an infamous indemnity which exceeded considerably the costs of the war. . . . The practice was thus established by the Central Powers that the victor might impose upon the vanquished the payment of the costs incurred by him in the war and something beyond in the nature of exemplary damages.'

The British Government had accepted that principle on 9 November 1914, in a speech by Prime Minister Raymond Asquith: 'We shall never sheath the sword . . . *until Belgium recovers in full measure all and more than all that she has sacrificed*' (Lloyd George, italics). This was reinforced in the clauses of the Treaty of London of 1915 when Italy was promised an indemnity, and further developed in 1916 when it became apparent that, although much of the damage to France was as a result of the war's activities, 'a great deal of the damage was deliberate', in effect part of a policy by Germany to eliminate France as an industrial rival. At the Paris Conference in 1916 it was therefore decided to demand reparation for this.[11] This was reinforced by the British Government's realization early in the war that Britain would face, in Foreign Secretary Arthur Balfour's estimation, 'bankruptcy' or at least major indebtedness for the foreseeable future.[12] Indemnity had in effect become reparation by 1919, a form of indemnity with exemplary damages intended to punish the perpetrator and rebuild the victim of the crime.

Planning for the post-war period among the Allies during the war itself as a whole has of course been noted to have been less than coherent.[13] Since then the whole question of reparations after 1919, or as Lloyd George put it in 1938, '[i]ts origin, its justification, the views of the Government about it. . . . has been completely overlaid by a muddy sediment of denunciation', especially about the role of Lloyd George himself in the policy.[14] Others apart from Lloyd George have also been blamed for the shortcomings of the policy, notably the British representatives at the Paris Peace Conference on the Reparations issue, Lords Cunliffe and Sumner, called by Keynes 'the Terrible Twins' and by James Headlam-Morley as 'the two bad men of the Conference'.[15]

One explanation of the seeming 'muddiness' is because reparation as a policy was used and abused by all sides to stigmatise the policy as supremely moral or immoral.[16] Lloyd George and Clemenceau belong clearly to the first camp, Wilson and Keynes to the second. The former had to justify action to their respective angry public opinions, often using a quasi-religious language (in Lloyd George's case) and an appeal to legal 'justice' in Clemenceau's. Both Lloyd George and Clemenceau were populist politicians with a strong sense of moral virtue. Their opponents, Wilson and Keynes, were what might be termed intellectual meritocrats. They believed they could direct public opinion through reason. Initially they failed but it must be said that the public view on the wiseness of reparations as a policy rapidly veered towards a Keynesian view, especially in Britain.

Liberal thinking about reparations 1918–19

So how did liberal opinion initially view reparations as a policy? In the United States *The New Republic* could see no advantage in using what had often been referred to as the practices of the 'Hun' in dealing with a defeated Germany. In an article entitled 'Reparation: Not Indemnities' the *New Republic* pleaded that:

> [t]he indemnity is Germany's idea, not ours. We do not want crippled or tributary nations anywhere in the world. We are not preparing for future wars, but mean to put an end to wars, and, most of all, we want to end the vile practice of charging the whole cost of the war upon the vanquished, practice that breeds war, since it promises immunity from financial burdens to the successful combatant.

So the *New Republic* could see a logic in reparation: '[t]he indemnity is Germany's ideal ... [b]ut we demand reparation – quite a different thing.' It was 'different' because it was:

> reparation not for war, for we have made war ourselves ... but reparation for the things that we would not do in war, and that no nation cherishing its honour would do. Launching invasion on neutral soil ... thrusting aside the poor safeguards thrown by the conventional laws of war around life and property at sea; these are acts of a nature deserving special penalties. Reparation for such acts differs radically from the indemnity exacted by right of conquest. It is not only compatible with the new order of international affairs: it is essential for the stability of that order.[17]

As the 'Lansing Note' reproduced at the head of this chapter also indicates, the United States believed that 'compensation will be paid by Germany for *all* damage done to the civilian population' was entirely within the boundaries of Wilson's address of 8 January 1918 (the Fourteen Points). Lansing's Note was delivered to Germany before the Armistice on 5 November 1918. In short, the logic of officialdom summed up by Lloyd George was broadly speaking consonant with liberal thinking, at least in the United States. The problem was to emerge in the implementation of the policy.

Keynes' denunciation of the final version of the Treaty as a 'Carthaginian Peace' has come to sum up liberal opposition to the Treaty as a whole and the reparations clauses in particular. His criticism had a particular resonance as he was the primary British representative in Paris from the Treasury, from which he resigned very shortly after the signature of the Treaty, and put a good deal of subsequent time and effort into denouncing it, and especially its Reparations clauses.[18] He gave birth to an orthodoxy, bitterly resented even to this day in some quarters, that, first, the French were blameworthy for their intransigence in face of what Keynes saw as the economic and political illogicality of reparations as a category of political usefulness after wars; and second, that the United States should have taken its responsibilities seriously as the major creditor nation and stood up to both French 'stupidity' and for a global cancellation of debt.[19]

The problems that reparations caused for the victors in 1919

The disadvantages of reparations for the vanquished are only too obvious. What is also clear is that they were and are very disadvantageous to the victor. One key factor identified in the aftermath of the First World War is what might be called the 'false security' effect. Many of the new states of Europe, and many of the old ones, like Belgium, assumed that reparations would rebuild their economies and allow them to stay independent.[20] What they did in reality was to create a false sense of independence, as they were now tied in to the enemy state's economy far more strongly then had been the case as they relied upon it for economic supplies. Yet most of them pursued an ever more virulent policy of economic nationalism, to free themselves from the erstwhile imperial state (as with Austria or Hungary) or to foster infant industries. Not only did this impede their postwar reconstruction (see also Chapter 4) but it also destabilized the very order that the Treaty of Versailles was supposed to uphold by fragmenting the European economy into many smaller pieces.[21]

After 1919 the domestic British advantages and disadvantages of reparations as policy were rapidly apparent, and a *melée* of self-justification, attack and counter-attack developed, one that persisted throughout the inter-war period. Lloyd George has been blamed for not seeing the disadvantages far earlier than 1938, when his above analysis was penned, many would say far too belated in its self-justification. But in the atmosphere of revenge that had prevailed in 1919 he argued that he had been the voice of reason, for the alternative to demanding reparation might have been far worse:

> There must not be an army of occupation, a large army of occupation, kept in Germany indefinitely in order to hold the country down. That simply means keeping hundreds of thousands of young men from this country occupying Germany, maybe for a generation, maybe for more, withdrawing

them from industry, whilst at the same time you would have to keep an Army in order to maintain your Empire. That would be bad business. Besides, it would simply provoke fresh conflict, fresh wars, and instead of coming to an end of war we would simply be manufacturing fresh wars.

Equally there must be no dumping of 'sweated goods' by way of payment as this will put the local (victor's) men out of work.[22]

Perhaps the greatest danger, one that was to some extent apparent immediately, was that of rampant inflation in both the creditor and debtor nations. The complicated process of paying off wartime debts between the Allies was bad enough (France paying Britain and America; Britain paying America; Russia refusing to pay anyone). One of the keenest arguments between France and America before the war even ended was that America's demands on France were causing an inflation of the French note supply, although this started to reverse as more and more American troops flooded into France in the last months before the Armistice. As Keynes, who reported this back to London, also explained the Americans were 'inclined to be hard on us [the British] in the details of financial arrangements'.[23]

This boded ill for the Peace Conference itself and, indeed, although Keynes had good personal relations with at least some of the Americans (notably Norman Davis, appointed by Wilson as United States Treasury Commissioner in Europe in January 1919)[24] there was a quasi-permanent non-meeting of minds between the British and Americans which was to persist until the end of the main business of the Reparation Commission in 1925. The American refusal to link Allied debts (over which it had absolute control as the sole creditor) and reparation (over which the French would not give ground) led to any sensible discussion about how to resolve the financial impasse of the 1920s being crushed between a rock and a hard place and beginning the steady decline of Britain to a huge debtor of the United States. This had very important consequences for the establishment of any global order in the post-war period.

British differences with the United States and France over reparations

It was also born out of the continuing humiliation heaped on Britain by both its erstwhile American and French Allies in the 1920s and 1930s. Even during the war the British, and Keynes in particular, felt put upon in this way. The main forum within which the process of American loans and purchases was orchestrated was the Inter-Ally Council for War Purchases, chaired by an American, Amos T. Crosby (Special US Commissioner of Finance in Europe) whom Keynes (the British Representative on the Council) clearly despised. The French and Americans both talked a great deal and 'we, who are terribly bored and exasperated by the whole business, only join in when we can help it. The upshot of this is that a great deal of steam has been blown off and Crosby has persuaded himself that it is he who is really directing the war.[25]

Officially the United States' delegation in Paris had also been very disappointed in the way the reparation idea had been implemented. In particular they felt duty bound not to link reparation (and the excessive French demand in particular) with the Allied debt question. They felt bound to this by the Fourteen Points and other statements by Wilson, on which basis Germany claimed to have surrendered.[26] Keynes had been informed, strictly it appears off the record, by Paul Cravath, the US Representative on Reparations at the Paris Peace Conference, but 'on which he spoke to me most hotly (and quite definitely) mainly that we were honourably engaged not to ask for the general costs of the war, but only for reparation, which, however widely interpreted, could not cover general costs'.[27]

The Americans had denied from February 1919 on that this in effect meant that they were in some way soft on the Germans. The main legal spokesman for the United States on reparations as the Peace Conference, John Foster Dulles, had assured the President that they were aware of the 'enormity of the crime which Germany has committed'. Neither were they denying that the United States had enormous debts that Germany should be responsible for: '[f]or we too have our war debt. In magnitude it is comparable to that of any other nation, and it constitutes a fearful burden, which is absorbing, and for many years will absorb, the greater part of the nation's income.' Where the United States differed from France and Britain was 'that we demand of Germany, as a condition of peace, all of that reparation, *but only that* [my italics] stipulated for by a fair construction of the agreement with Germany as to what the terms of the peace should be'. So for Dulles this included 'complete repayment to Belgium of the damage to her. ... It further means that the enemy is liable for damage resulting from such miscellaneous illegal acts as the deportation of civilians, attacks on undefended towns, sinkings of merchant vessels, and other illegal acts.' But there was no mention of the war pension which took up so much of the French and British demands and which in effect gave Germany an open-ended commitment to pay reparations far into the future. This memo is memorable not only for its differences with the other states present at the Conference, but also because Dulles kept it in his personal papers long after. It clearly had the importance of a dreadful lesson for Dulles that must not be forgotten.[28]

In addition, Keynes had said, up to the end of 1919 privately, then very publicly, that demands for reparation from Germany could only be counter-productive for the Allies. So apparently the Americans agreed with his analysis. But they could not agree to link the discussions on reparation and that on Allied debts to each other in public. In effect the United States Treasury vetoed the linkage or even discussion of it in Paris, in spite of the fact that France also wanted the issues linked.[29] It might therefore be said that the US refusal to do so provoked the French to be even more insistent on getting their money out of Germany. Keynes' 'plan' was thus to try and establish this linkage through the meetings of a small 'confidential' committee that suggested the United States lending more money to both Britain and France to tide them over the financial chaos in which they found themselves. But the Americans 'do not really intend to do anything' reported Keynes to the Head of the Treasury, Sir John Bradbury. Neither could the French back down a jot on their demands for reparations. Upon this dual refusal by the Americans and French to take his ideas seriously, Keynes withdrew from Paris, in spite of pleas from Chancellor of the Exchequer Sir Austen Chamberlain and Bradbury that he not do so.[30]

Even historians who take a dim view of British (and especially Keynesian) revisionist views on the Treaty and the reparations question, like Stephen Schuker, acknowledge that the logic of Keynes' position was reasonable, no matter how 'tendentious' his 'tracts' may have been. In Schuker's words:

> German reparations represented only one part of the problem of international indebtedness resulting from the war. . . . It was virtually impossible to find a single formula according to which indebtedness of such diverse character could be equitably adjusted. Nevertheless, while war debts originated separately and rested on a moral basis different from reparations, as a practical matter it appeared difficult to the European nations to settle one issue without the other.[31]

The Treaty envisaged a Reparation Commission (Article 233) and this Commission was empowered to ascertain Germany's ability to pay (Art. 234). The sum required would be notified to the German Government by May 1921. Bradbury was chosen to serve as the only British Representative on the Reparations Commission, which convened in early 1920. The final Reparations bill was in the end a difficult compromise thrashed out by Bradbury and the French delegation and led to the Reparation Commission Report of 26 October 1921 laying out what Germany should pay by way of reparations.

Given the absence of the Americans from the League of Nations, and their only having observer status on the Reparation Commission, the relationship between the French and the British was crucial. There is clear evidence of perpetual tension. The French attitude in 1919 can be summed up as 'Germany will pay'. The French reaction to Keynes' *Economic Consequences of The Peace* of 1920 and *The Revision of the Treaty* (1921) – Schuker's 'tracts' – was essentially that they did not believe that Keynes could possibly understand their position. He was, in the words of François Crouzet, '*horrifié, mais non engagé*'. Even if there was a measure of intellectual agreement with him, even in 1920, it was just too early for this to be stated publicly. The French also believed that Germany could pay and should do so, a view that has many followers even today.

The final bill, '*le résultat d'un compromis pénible*', in the words of French Premier Raymond Poincaré, between Dubois, the main French nedegotiator, and Bradbury[32] was judged to be 225 milliard gold marks, reduced after much argument by the Supreme Allied Council in May 1921 to 132 milliard gold marks. Keynes commented that this bill was 'a compromise between the French and British representatives, the latter of whom, Sir John Bradbury, endeavoured to fix the figure at 104 milliards, and defended this adjudication with skilful and even passionate advocacy'.[33] Later on Keynes footnoted that 'the figure of 104 milliards, attributed by Monsieur Poincaré to . . . Bradbury, is probably the nearest we shall get to a strictly impartial assessment'.[34]

But the relationship between the French and British just got more *pénible* as the 1920s wore on. The main problem was that the French in effect had a built in majority on the Commission. The French Chairman had a casting vote and there were only four voting members (Italy, France, Belgium and Britain). As David Hubback comments in the letters he has edited by John Fischer Williams (British Legal Adviser to the Commission) 'the French were bound to win unless their normal supporters, the Belgians, deserted them'. Hubback also points out that only two of the nine members of the Commission were in any way qualified to talk of the complicated financial matters in hand, and of these Bradbury was by far the most experienced. His frustration cannot be underestimated.[35]

Bradbury shared Keynes' insistence on a linkage of Allied debt and reparation. As he put it to then Chancellor of The Exchequer, Sir Robert Horne, in September 1922, without such a 'comprehensive settlement' there was very little real hope of a lasting peace.[36] The immediate crisis that this joint problem provoked was the crash of the mark in Germany, which he and most in Britain put down to the French intransigence over German reparation payments. Bradbury predicted financial collapse in Germany and that this would 'be destructive to all hopes of obtaining reparation, either in cash or kind, for many years to come, if not for ever'. This he predicted could lead to a 'break-up of economic and social order in Germany'. But possibly his most monumental suggestion was the Reparation Commission should itself be transferred to Berlin: 'the interests of Germany and Germany's creditors are, in my opinion, on a long-sighted view, identical.'[37]

In a letter of May 1923 Bradbury to the then Prime Minister, Stanley Baldwin, reiterated that he had:

> always held that no workman-like or permanent settlement of European troubles can be secured except by agreement between Great Britain and France, and that if the organisms like the Reparation Commission are to serve any useful purpose, it must be as fora for the interchange of ideas and the arrangement of compromises – not as mechanical instruments for enabling one Power to over-ride another.

Hence he was convinced that 'an understanding must be reached between the British and French Governments that the practice of taking majority decisions, which is becoming a matter of almost daily routine, should be discontinued'.[38]

It also must be said that the British delegates, Bradbury included (and of course Keynes), had far more sympathy for the German position than they did for the French and that every Gallic explosion was seen as further proof of the French Government's stupidity and recklessness. But Bradbury certainly denied that this had ever made him less than sympathetic to the French point of view: 'I am confident that if I have ever deviated from my instructions, it has been in the direction of concession and compromise, rather than of excessive rigidity.'[39]

The net result was that the three erstwhile Allies could not agree on what was probably the single most contentious issue in international politics of the early 1920s. It soured the peace and made cooperation on virtually every other issue difficult, with the main and most drastic impact being felt in the lack of economic cooperation well into the 1930s. This is the true point of the charge that the Treaty of Versailles in some ways 'caused' the Second World War. By making economic issues into such a crisis it spoiled any possible cooperation in other issue areas, including how to deal with the dictatorships that flourished on the resulting economic chaos that resulted from that non-cooperation. The lessons were not lost on the United States, as we will see below.

Reparations as an issue in the 1920s

American and British liberals in general were appalled by the imposition of reparations, especially in the light of Keynes's two volumes. Among liberals there was a general and great approval for Keynes calling the Treaty a 'Carthaginian Peace'. A typical reaction can be found in American liberal Frank A. Vanderlip's 1923 *What Next in Europe?*, when he pointed out that the logic of using the French indemnity example (of 1871) to justify huge payments from Germany in 1919 was incoherent. In 1871 the indemnity was small, the war (and hence the destruction and loss of life) and area affected was small compared to 1914–18; France had extensive overseas holdings that it could use to pay off Germany (unlike Germany in 1919 which was broke) and there were active financial markets in which to raise the money (unlike in 1919); there would not be a lump sum to pay but (according to Vanderlip) 'a continuing obligation that, if carried out, will lay a heavy hand upon the lives of her youngest children'. France had colonies and an intact merchant marine, Germany had lost hers; Germany must raise the cash though trade where trade has collapsed and markets had been closed off (26 per cent tariffs erected by Czechs, Swiss, Swedes, Dutch, etc.). Hence the Versailles bill must be paid by printing money – whence came hyper-inflation as the German Government could not raise capital in markets because of its huge budget deficit, whereas the French bill was paid by raising private capital. Hence 'Germany is headed towards financial ruin'.[40]

The problems of American isolationism

In contradiction to the oft-held view that the United States withdrew into isolation, it is fairer to say that after the First World War the United States withdrew from the League of Nations but not from Europe. The American-backed Dawes Plan, which was implemented in late 1924 in effect re-wrote the Treaty of Versailles' financial clauses by rescheduling the German reparation debt and being followed up by a series of other debt rescheduling activities, notably that of the French in early 1925. It was preceded by a German demand for a moratorium on the German reparation debt repayments in the wake of the Ruhr crisis of 1923 and increasing signs of internal anarchy in Germany itself.[41]

This in turn led to the setting up of a 'Committees of Experts' who examined how the whole question of reparation might be rethought and ultimately to the London Conference of 1924 and to the Dawes Plan. The question has to be as to why the United States did not go much further in the 1920s and help sort out the problems of Europe by revising the Treaty of Versailles by abolishing Allied debt and thus ending the French need for reparations?

Michael Hogan, the American neo-corporatist historian, has asserted that future President Herbert Hoover (in particular) stressed the need for international cooperation in a 'new associative order' that had a domestic mix of 'private self-regulation by [private sector business] groups [with] government [having] a positive role to play' but which did not dominate. This also applied to the international economy, for 'Republicans waged a sustained campaign against European proposals to supplement the market with public planning or private cartels'. In particular Hogan Hoover, and his Republican colleagues, tried to 'assert ... the primacy of economics over politics, and sought to resolve outstanding issues by technocorporative formulations' – including reparations. This 'building the new order' meant, says Hogan, 'overcoming resistance in Europe, where most leaders were trying to shift the financial burden of the war to the backs of their neighbors'. The Americans therefore sought to use their financial muscle to 'pressure ... the Europeans to fund war debts, reduce reparations and reform finances'. According to Hogan, this was done with the help of the British and in the teeth of French opposition.[42]

Even if this seems a hopelessly rosy view of the period, which included such events as the French invasion of the Ruhr in 1923, described by Charles Maier as 'seali[ing] the failure of the old liberal center at political and economic reconstruction',[43] as Hogan points out this dream failed because the 'associationalism' did not materialize as hoped, and it needed Roosevelt to push the US further down Hoover's desired road by forcing business into partnership with the state. It also failed because of the 1929 crash. Roosevelt succeeded in marshalling business opinion behind a 'conservative version of Keynesian theory', which became more evident before, during and after the Second World War. This was at the root of the Marshall Plan thinking, or as Hogan puts it:

> The American Marshall Planners, like the Republicans before them, tried to transform political problems into technical ones that were solvable, they said, when old European ways of conducting business and old habits of class conflict gave way to American methods of scientific management and corporative collaboration.[44]

From reparation to reconstruction

Commentary at the time saw the entire Dawes Plan as being in large measure an idea that started with Bradbury's proposals to the Reparation Commission in 1922. Sir William Goode, who made this comment in a 'No More War' Congress on 'Finance and Debts' in December 1924 also added that 'the general situation had been much improved by the London Conference of last Summer' (which drew up the Dawes Plan). He added that '[t]he sooner the idea of victor and vanquished passed away the better it would be for economic reconstruction. One half of Europe must not go on dominating and penalizing the other half'.[45] The idea was clearly inspired by Bradbury and Keynes' ideas on revising the Treaty of Versailles. Indemnity had given way to reparation in 1919, and this was slowly giving way to the idea of reconstruction. We could argue that in so doing he was prepared to forgive Germany too easily and to put at risk the Allied relationships of the war years, especially with France and arguably with the United States.

However the inescapable conclusion is that Bradbury saw clearly that demanding a country pay its debts when it felt aggrieved and was unlikely to do so in any case except by recourse to war, if then, it was likely to store up uncountable problems for the future. He was thus trying to provide the intellectual leadership that the United States was not to show until Roosevelt became President. Perhaps if Bradbury, and not the French, had been listened to more carefully by the United States in 1922–4 the Second World War would have lost at least one of its major causes. He and Keynes can thus be remembered as one of the key British architects of the destruction of the idea of reparation and its eventual quasi-replacement by reconstruction as the main way to deal with vanquished states.

Reparations during and after the Second World War

As we have seen in our discussion of liberalism, the economic and political agendas of liberalism must be seen in tandem. The way in which reparation then actually becomes reconstruction needs some close examination. The end of this chapter will show how reparation is finally seemingly ditched by liberal policy makers and replaced by reconstruction. The way in which that latter actually becomes institutionalized will be examined in Chapters 4 and 5.

At first sight it might be said that whatever the musings of thinkers in Washington and London, the 'Lessons of Versailles' were seemingly not totally learnt even by the time of the 'Big Three' (the United States, Britain and the Soviet Union) conference of Yalta and Potsdam in 1945 (where France also participated). There were clauses written into both agreements demanding reparations from Germany.[46] As will be seen below, the main issues at Yalta and Potsdam were the future of Germany, the future of Eastern Europe and the idea of a revitalized world order through the United Nations. It was only when the Soviet Union fell out with its Western Allies, over both European and extra-European issues (notably in Greece, Iran and then Korea) that the Cold War really started. Until then opinions about the implementation (or not) of reparations as part of peace settlement served as a touchstone of differing Allied attitudes to creating lasting peace as they had in 1919. So we need to show how a seeming adherence to the principle that reparations should again be imposed by the victors on the vanquished is not anywhere near as clear cut as it seems.

The debate about reparations in the United States, 1939–45

Michael Hogan has claimed that there were clear 'lines of continuity in American policy between the first and second postwar eras'. This included the idea that European economic integration would tie Germany into such a system as the US wanted to encourage, which allied to the NATO Treaty, would solve Germany's recovery and France's security needs, would keep the USSR out.[47] Hogan says that his thesis can be summed up in the words of Robert Hall of the US Treasury: 'the Americans want an integrated Europe looking like the United States of America – "God's own country"',[48] a view that is shared by many other writers, as outlined in Chapter 2, and one that depended on economic and political interchange on a scale hitherto unseen in Europe.

Washington's key idea for the post-war settlement in 1940s was therefore not to avoid a repeat of the mistakes of the Treaty of Versailles but rather to create a truly liberal world order that would be inoculated against militarism and war.[49] The United States saw the economic causes of war as primordial, whereas for the Russians (and the French) peace and security was not dependent on such 'secondary matters' as Soviet representative Andrei Gromyko was to put it in the Dumbarton Woods discussions to set up the United Nations in 1944.

One of the clearest expressions of the United States' fears about a replay of 1919 can be found in a Memorandum by Oscar Cox, one of Roosevelt's Adviser Harry Hopkins' staff, on the need for a United States 'commitment to use force to secure the peace' of 16 August 1944. Cox said it was necessary to get round the problem that a peace treaty might include, as it had in 1919, things that the United States found acceptable and things that it did not: 'It has been orthodox to think of the Treaty of Peace as one document. As a matter of fact most peace treaties dealt with completely disparate problems.' Cox was well aware of the main point that had sunk American participation in the League of Nations and which had in part led to the imposition of the ruinous reparation policy by Britain and France. The way round this was the introduction of an American veto over the use of force by its successor the United Nations. It was also necessary to separate out the 'demilitarization and the control of the war-making power of the enemy ... from those provisions of the treaty dealing with restitution or reparations for war damage'. It might indeed be a good idea not to have a treaty at all as they were 'not legally required' even if 'for political reasons it might in some cases be wise to have Congressional action or ratification by the Senate'. Reparation could thus be hived off into a different agreement that would not then poison the main deal that needed to be done.[50]

Broadly speaking the American process of 'Post-War Planning' that designed what has been called Roosevelt's New World Order had come to see the causes of peace as well as the causes of war as having their foundations in the right or the wrong sort of economic organization. Ex-President Herbert Hoover's 'New Approaches to a Lasting Peace' of 1943,[51] was typical in saying that the problem was that the League of Nations had 'became an agency for maintaining the status quo'. In Hoover's view a substitute must be found for change through war, for '[i]f we fail to provide peaceful and orderly methods of change, war becomes the inevitable solvent'. In another piece of 1944 Hoover also put emphasis on 'sound economic policies' as the foundation for a 'lasting peace' and praised what the League did in this field of 'international co-operation'. But he also advocated the 'importance of direct dealings between states in handling economic and social questions rather than counting on the intervention of an outside body'.[52]

There was general approval in the Congress for such economic joint action in the United States whereas there was not for joining a security body (as had also been the case in 1919) and it had been widely suggested that they could join the economic but not the security organization.[53] This kind of thinking was widespread in American foreign policy circles throughout the war. For example, the 'Plan of Work' for Post War Planning (PWP) drawn up by one of the main planners within the State Department, Leo Pasvolsky, in 1941 is full of discussion about the past – 'the future must be built on the past' – and about basing peace upon 'principles' that acknowledge the 'lessons which may be deduced from that failure'. Economic failure was always at the top of such lists.[54]

In parallel thinking about reparations the Council on Foreign Relations (CFR) was organized as the most influential voice of liberal commentary within the PWP process. The CFR's exhaustive survey of the 'Preliminary Peace Aims of Eastern European Nations' (the most affected by Germany after all) states that there was agreement, except from Hungary, that: 'Germany should be forced to restore in so far as possible all property taken from occupied territories, and should be forced to pay reparations in kind over a short period for damage done to occupied countries'.

This was of course a big shift from the attitudes of these countries in 1919. As either beneficiaries or targets of reparation demands these were the states that had the most extensive experience of their effects. The emphasis, with minor exceptions, in these sessions of the CFR was all on reconstruction, and this was to be long-term, regional and continental, not on reparation. The CFR's work was extended in a fuller document with a digest of the opinions of 'European Nations' as '[a]ll the representatives consulted considered that the central need in reconstruction is the establishment of a post-war order which will provide general peace and security', and especially establishment of the 'democratic principle'; 'the inauguration of a greater degree of co-operation among nations' and; 'international collaboration in dealing with domestic and international economic problems'.[55] The rationale for this was essentially because 'it was anticipated by most of the representatives that their countries would be able to secure restitution of much confiscated property, and considerable reparations in kind from Germany/Russia [*sic*]'. However, 'it was recognised that this will be completely inadequate to serve as a basis for economic revival'. Loans would be essential, from Britain and the United States and 'perhaps an international agency'.[56] In other words the countries who would most need reparation or some other form of economic help after the war were aware that they could not count on Germany to provide it no matter how much they resented the damage done by Germany. The fact that these countries' representatives were meeting in exile under the auspices of an American think tank, and in Washington, also clearly had an effect.

The Americans had, none the less, reasons to fear a repeat of Versailles on other fronts. For all of these exiled governments, the main problem seemed to be 'frontiers' and here considerable demands seemed to be being made – largely on the basis of restitution, especially by Germany, of land taken since 1937. This suggested many potential problems for the future. The Czechs, for example, said that the Sudeten Germans could have their own administration, but that they must accept a renewed Czechoslovak authority – in fact they were expelled en masse in 1945, thus re-inaugurating a debate about a possible return that has reverberated ever since. It is also ironic that the Hungarian exception to the general rule on rejecting, or at least downplaying, reparations as a useful post-war tool should have existed. Hungary was the central European country most affected by the imposition of reparations in 1919 and had to be saved from them by the Reparation Commission in order for them to be able to reconstruct their economy in the early 1920s (see Chapter 4).

There were powerful voices in all the Allied countries calling for a repeat of the reparations imposed on Germany in 1919. The Labour Party Minister for Economic Warfare in the first Churchill Cabinet in 1940, Hugh Dalton,[57] was very anti-German and took the view, in the words of his biographer Ben Pimlott, that 'after the war the Allies should interfere drastically in the German economy. . . [and] continued to regard the emasculation of Germany as a matter of the utmost importance'. His views, which were outlined in a memorandum of August 1942 on reparations, were influential in the setting up of the Committee on Reparations and Economic Security (The Malkin Committee).[58] This committee made much the same suggestions as the Morgenthau Plan in the United States – a break up of Germany, albeit temporary.

Keynes was on this committee and had spoken against the de-industrialization of Germany. He was also reported by Harry Dexter White to Morgenthau as saying that he 'was heartily in agreement with our view of the desirability of dismembering Germany and as to the relative unimportance of reparations'.[59] But Keynes wanted to 'normalise Germany' says his biographer Robert Skidelsky 'not to destroy its means of livelihood', a vital position for him to take given his intellectual reputation (especially on the reparations issue) and current power as main British economic negotiator with the United States until 1945. Only Lord Cherwell stood out against this position in Cabinet and then from the point of view of wanting to steal Germany's export markets, not a point of view likely to go down well in Washington given Roosevelt's' views on free trade expressed in the Atlantic Charter of 1941.[60]

France and Russia were in any case a far more worrying threat to United States' hopes to reduce the role of reparations during the Second World War. The United Nations Declaration of 5 January 1943 about the restitution of property led the Russians and French in particular to retain a fondness for the ideas of reparation and restitution. So the State Department was aware that 'some demand for reparations will almost certainly be made in the peace settlement'. They were also aware that reparations were also linked to the question of 'war guilt . . . although this point is little discussed because of the controversy over the "war guilt clause" in the reparation articles of the Versailles Treaty'.[61]

Before the conference at Yalta in 1945 this kind of thinking had also become embedded within wider liberal thinking about reparations. The *New Republic* opined just before the Yalta conference that:

> In regard to reparations, the Allies confront a familiar dilemma. It is almost impossible to transfer reparations in cash across frontiers. Capitalist countries don't want reparations in kind, which compete with the products of their own industries. Even Soviet Russia might well hesitate to accept large amounts of reparations in kind, the production of which might build up flourishing industries in a defeated enemy.[62]

Continued Russian admiration for reparations

Unfortunately the Russians were not to agree, as they had already made clear in discussions about the future of the UN (at Dumbarton Oaks in August 1944) that they saw the UN as primarily a peace and security organization, not an economic one – the two should be kept separate they said. So they had interpreted the 'failure' of the League in quite a different manner to the Americans and British. For the Russians the League of Nations had proved that international economic concerns could not be really significant. Soviet representative Andrei Gromyko claimed that the public in general had the impression that the League had constantly under consideration important matters relating to peace and security when in reality it was usually engaged only in consideration of 'secondary matters'. Later on in the Dumbarton Oaks talks Gromyko made this more starkly plain when he said that 'even ideal accomplishment in the economic field cannot in itself prevent aggression. To this there was expression of general agreement.'[63]

At that point Pasvolsky had interjected that, on the contrary, the 'Americans have come to link economic and political co-operation and that they are willing to go much further in international co-operation in each field when they believe that action of each such type is facilitating successful effort of the other type'. This he had admitted 'is a rather new phenomenon in the United States which has developed since the last war and particularly since the depression ... economic co-operation ... in itself is in part a basis for the preservation of peace'. Hence the United States favoured an Economic and Social Council (ECOSOC) and a Security Council under 'one tent' (as then Secretary of State Edward Stettinius put it) of the UN. Gromyko retorted that it would be difficult to separate the two and a 'separate agency, or ... several separate agencies' would be needed, which is what in the end happened. These battle lines meant that during the Cold War the ECOSOC was able to undertake action in the economic field when the United Nations was paralysed at the security level. It is thus yet another irony of the Cold War that the existence of ECOSOC showed that the original American principle that economic activity can help protect from war or contribute to resolving existing conflict flourished whereas the Soviet principle of the importance of security was relegated to peacekeeping until the late 1980s.

Yalta, Potsdam and the reparation issue

In 1945, Marc Trachtenberg rightly states that there could have been a 'spheres of influence peace'. The Soviet Union, the United States and Britain (the Big Three) had fought and won a war as an alliance. There was every expectation in all these countries among most of the leaderships, and especially in The United States and Soviet Union, that that Alliance could be converted into a mutually acceptable peace. Trachtenberg makes the case that in 1945 the Big Three were not dominated by opposing ideological, military and economic considerations, that they did not have a desire for a further round of war, that they were quite evenly balanced in the theatres of war, and that they largely agreed with what they had decided at Yalta and then at Potsdam in February and July of 1945. 'Indeed', says Trachtenberg, 'looking back, it is hard to understand why there was serious risk of armed conflict during that period'. Especially the leaderships of the Soviet Union and the United States were perfectly capable of carving up Europe between them into spheres of influence, they were 'attuned to power realities' and each side 'would have a free hand in the area that it dominated, and on that basis the two sides would be able to get along with each other in the future'.[64]

Roosevelt misread Soviet intentions and their understanding of what had taken place between the Allies up to Yalta. In practice, says Trachtenberg, the Soviet Union wanted total control within its sphere of influence, and this meant, for example, a 'Poland that [the Soviet Union] could control – a country ruled by Communists and run as a police state'. Moreover the Soviet Union had some good reasons to believe that its main Allies would not object in any serious fashion to its behaviour. As Trachtenberg says, this was not an area of the world for any of the Allies where self-determination was the key issue, as for Stalin the whole of Eastern Europe had after all been in effect decided by the infamous 'percentage agreement' of 1944 where Churchill and Stalin had agreed who should dominate which Eastern European country, a judgement with which Trachtenberg and most other historians of the Cold War concur. [65]

The 'Declaration on Liberated Europe' of 1945 was therefore interpreted differently by the Russians and the Americans. Both thought they had gained what they wanted and that the 'details' could be worked out later. What Kissinger calls the 'hinge' of American foreign policy was thus kept intact. The Wilsonians could point to the upholding of American moral integrity, the 'National Interest' or 'realist' camp could claim that no excessively unrealistic demands would be made on American resources in the future. As I and others have pointed out elsewhere, Roosevelt worked in such a way as to leave 'detail' to after the war, while during it he defined general principles. The Russians would, in Soviet Foreign Minister Molotov's account of Stalin's words 'do it our own way later'. James F. Byrnes, the Secretary of State in Roosevelt's last few months and President Truman's for his first year in office, could therefore say that the Declaration fulfilled all The United States' commitments to its Polish-American voters while leaving the real Poles to the whims of Stalin and Molotov 'later'.[66]

As we have seen, the United States did not want to impose reparations on Germany. They were thought to have been a major cause of the Second World War and they had by Potsdam become convinced that the Keynesian logic of creating wealth rather than confiscating it was better than the mercantilistic logic of reparations. The Russians were surprised. As Gromyko recalled in his *Memoirs*:

> Stalin and the rest of the Soviet delegation wondered what Roosevelt and Churchill were thinking when they discussed that question. Roosevelt only wanted to admit the possibility of some nominal compensation; he could not name a sum. Churchill was not willing to concede even a symbolic gesture of reparations towards the USSR.

Stalin and Gromyko decided that the Americans and British had decided in advance to downplay the issue, undoubtedly correctly.[67] What the Russians had not understood, and Gromyko seemed not to understand as late as 1989, was why they took that stance.

At the Yalta and Potsdam conferences in 1945, it was assumed by the Americans that German reparations would play some part in financing reconstruction, along with UNRRA credits, and the establishment of the IMF, the IBRD, EX-IM Bank and so forth. At Yalta in particular there was an emphasis on a punitive treatment of Germany, as exemplified by Roosevelt's seeming support for the Morgenthau Plan of 1944 that would have reduced Germany to an agricultural and dismembered state. But the Morgenthau Plan was dropped after Roosevelt's death shortly after Yalta in April 1945 and there is some evidence that it had been dropped in effect even before it.[68] It certainly had by the time of the Potsdam Conference in late July 1945. Reparations had been replaced by what was called the 'first charge principle ... by which German imports rather than reparation payments would have first claim on current German production', thus encouraging German production and helping countries that needed reconstruction help. This was also helped by a 1946 'level-of-industry plan' which was supposed to get Germany going again.[69]

The need for reconstruction, not reparation, in 1945

So what went wrong? The essential problem over Germany was about the kind of state that was going to be allowed to emerge. The zonal system, where each ally (the Big Three plus France) would govern in a defined area, was agreed at Yalta and confirmed at Potsdam. The understanding in 1945 was that there would be a joint Control Commission that would coordinate activity in the four zones. The main problem was how much of a *unit* Germany was to be.

The Soviet Union kept to its original plan of running its zone as it saw fit, which was with scant kindness to the local population. The results were predictably brutal.[70] It also went ahead in squeezing as much reparation out of the part of Germany that it dominated and while there was little friction between the Allies this was not a real problem. Trachtenberg puts it bluntly:

> It was clear by the time the [Potsdam] conference convened that the Soviets were stripping the Eastern zone of everything of value that could be carted off. Whole factories were being dismantled and prepared for shipment back to Russia. The Soviet conception of 'war booty' or 'war trophies' was so broad that it allowed them to carry off practically everything they wanted from their zone.[71]

James Bacque quotes Soviet Ambassador to London Ivan Maisky telling Churchill that the USSR removed $10 billion ($200 billion in 2000 dollars) of its own estimate of a possible $20 billion.[72]

So at Potsdam an attempt was made to decide on the overall policy of the extraction of reparation, mainly because all wanted a clear definition of the relationship of the Allies in Germany. If one side was to behave in a very harsh way did not that mean the others should as well? Alternatively it meant that the Allies would each have to be given a free hand in their own zones in the hope that 'good fences would make good neighbours'. The overall 'fence' was that divided Eastern from Western Europe, with the dividing line in Germany the exact replica of this. The overall contention could therefore be said to have been that the separate relationships of the erstwhile Allies need not be bitter. Truman had even said at Potsdam that he had become 'Russophile as most of us were' and indeed he even liked 'the little son of a bitch' [Stalin].[73]

But as Trachtenberg says '[t]he Cold War did not develop out of a conflict over Eastern Europe' but rather out of the Western allies' increasing alarm about Soviet pressure elsewhere, especially in Iran and the Middle East in general. This was seen in London and Washington as a breach of the spirit of the 'spheres of influence' peace. Stalin himself had decided that he could put pressure on the weaker of the two main Western Allies. Stalin had some reason to believe that the Americans would not help the British out. After all the Americans had often expressed dislike of the British Empire in forceful terms and the Americans did not seem to have any real interest in Turkey or Iran. When the Russians refused to leave Iran in 1946 and put pressure on the Straights controlled by Turkey, Truman's attitude to Russia hardened and by 1946 he 'was ultimately willing to risk war with Russia'. The March 1946 'Iron Curtain' speech by Churchill in Fulton, Missouri is often spoken of as the key moment when Truman's attitude shifted, but there had been a gradual conversion after Potsdam. The result was the policy of 'containment', in fact adopted even before the term was coined, certainly well before the rationale for the policy was developed by George Kennan.[74]

The implications for Germany were the division of the state into two parts until the reunification process began in 1989. Germany became a laboratory for a different kind of post-war settlement, one inspired by a rejection of what was seen as Russian bad faith and a desire to consolidate a front against Soviet power in Europe. It could also be said that the British and Americans and French had by mid-1945 also decided that they wanted to show the world that a democratic solution to Germany's problems would prevent the next war. The Western Allies were in effect starting to implement a liberal policy of creating the institutions and practices of liberal democracy though reconstruction, whereas the Russians were implementing a policy of reparation and revenge. The Western policy developed over the next few years, with the Marshall Plan, into a much more structured form of policy, while the Russians continued to extract as much revenge and reparation as they could.[75]

The counter logic of the Marshall Plan

Although the Marshall Plan of 1947 will be discussed in more detail in Chapter 4, it had a very important relationship to the wider debate on reparations. In the economic circumstances of 1945 it now seems clear that American logic of rejecting the notion of reparations was correct. As Hogan, among others, has pointed out, it was proving even more difficult to get European recovery going than in 1919. One reason was the relative level of destruction. On every possible indicator, Europe was in a frightful mess. German coal production in 1934–8 had been an average of 159 million tonnes. By 1946 it was only up to 66 million. Even Britain's production was less in 1946 (193 million tonnes) than it had been in 1934–8 (average of 230 million tonnes).[76] Coal was to form the focus of reconstruction plans for Europe as the setting up of the European Coal and Steel Community, the forerunner of the European Economic Community, demonstrates.

Hogan reminds us that nine billion US dollars had already been given in reconstruction aid by the United States by the beginning of 1947, in sharp contrast with the period after the First World War. American fears of Russian and even French intervention to extract reparation and thus risk a repeat of 1919 and the 1920s in general was real. The essential immediate threat was that the USSR was exploiting bad feelings between Germans and Allied forces of occupation. The American Commander in Germany, General Clay, responded by stopping reparation payments from the American US zone in May 1946, and demanded Allied cooperation on economic unification, which he largely got from the British, if not from the French.[77]

In March–April 1947 at the Moscow Foreign Ministers Conference, the French and the USSR combined to demand more reparations and annexations. They also did so in the discussions of the Byrnes Plan and the Marshall Plan in early 1948, the French still talking about 'dismantling factories ... without delay, so that the Inter Allied Agency for Reparations can effectuate their dividing up among the different states that are to be beneficiaries'. They complained that the British and Americans seemed to be 'keeping 400,000 machine tools in the bi-zone (the US and British sectors) more than was necessary for existing industrial needs' and wanted 300,000 of these transferred to the Agency.[78]

The United States and Britain were furious, having by this time made German reconstruction a main plank of their emerging Cold War policy. Herbert Hoover published a report in March 1947[79] which recommended raising restraints on Germany, reviving German industry, and leaving the Ruhr and the Saar region with Germany. This was not universally admired but showed that a new approach was sorely needed.[80]

Hogan argues that such problems led to renewed discussion in the United States about how European integration might help to solve the seemingly endless problem of how to get the Europeans to understand that the end of a major war on the Continent need not necessarily be what we now call a 'zero-sum game' – what Germany loses, Russia and France and others must necessarily gain. The line up of these who wanted this to happen is impressive – Walt Rostow, Secretary of State Dean Acheson, future Secretary of State under President Eisenhower Dulles, Senators Fulbright, Vandenberg, and Dewey, as well as National Security Advisor George Kennan and many others. All thought the Ruhr had to play a key role in this, as General George Marshall said in Moscow in March 1947. It would remain part of Germany. Marshall wanted 'a European solution in a Europe which includes Germany' – the Ruhr would be part of this shared Europe.[81] It must be said that by early 1948 (at the same time that they were complaining about reparations) the French were also talking of an 'international regime for the Ruhr "for the reconstruction of the whole of Europe and to assure their use for peaceful purposes"'.[82]

So for Hogan, the Marshall Plan 'rested squarely on an American conviction that European economic recovery was essential to the long term interests of the United States': strategically (to ensure the preservation of US access to European resources, filling a power vacuum and creating a Balance of Power); economically (to help create an open international economy based on liberal capitalism) and; politically (to control German nationalism, and to reconcile Germany's recovery and French security interests). It was based on 'economic assumptions [that] grew fundamentally out of the American experience at home, where a large internal economy integrated by free-market forces and central institutions of coordination and control seemed to have laid the groundwork for a new era of economic growth and stability'.[83] These themes will be expanded upon in Chapter 4 on the 'R' that came to replace reparation, that of reconstruction.

Conclusions: the end of reparations or their rebirth?

It should not be imagined that the winning of the Cold War by the essentially liberal West led ineluctably to the abolition of a policy that had united them in their opposition to more punitive economic ways to end wars, of which reparations is the most obvious example. One reason for this is that many states did and do not share the Keynesian view that reparations are wrong under practically all circumstances. We could nuance this Western view by saying that much opinion in the West in more recent times does not *per se* disagree with restitution, an older idea than reparation itself as Lloyd George had pointed out in 1932. But they do not agree, on the whole, with reparation, which as was stressed earlier in the chapter, sees itself as a form of punishment with 'exemplary damages'. This may be partly due to historical amnesia and the feeling that the 'democratic peace' will ensure that that there is no replay of 1919. None the less the examples of what happened after the Iran–Iraq war of 1982–8 and even more so the example of what has happened since the end of the Gulf War of 1991 are very instructive as to the corrosive effects of an unresolved reparation issue between states. It also shows that such categories of action as restitution and reparation can easily become confused and can be used by the target (in both cases here Iraq) to justify defiance of seemingly universal condemnation and to claim that an injustice has been perpetrated on it. This is not merely a semantic disagreement over a see-mingly technical issue, but one that has profound political and other con-sequences, as was found in 1919–39. In particular the association of the United Nations with this policy and its failure might be seen as having uncomfortable parallels with what happened to the League in the inter-war period.

The idea that we will encounter in later chapters, that there must be repara-tion for *historical* wrongs, is also firmly back on the agenda. It was most notably reborn in the idea of reparations for the slave trade at the United Nations World Conference Against Racism in Durban, South Africa in 2001. The instigators of the idea are both from the 'North', led by some African Americans who believe that their economic and social lot in the modern United States has been severely compromised by the experiences of their forebears until the 1860s, and also by politicians in the 'South' who wish to blame the Imperial powers for the position they find themselves is due to neo- or post-colonial realities. This idea has spread to the point where the former Dictator of Haiti, Jean-Bertrand Aristide, demanded £16 billion from France for the period when Haiti was colonized until fighting for its independence in 1804, making Haiti the oldest independent black state. It is unlikely that any French court would agree with the idea and the French Govern-ment has already rejected it.[84] It could be argued that it is also a shifting of blame for the commission of present wrongs by corrupt Third World elites on to past gen-erations of colonial oppressors. It is also, and perhaps more importantly, an extension of the liberal idea of legalism with all the contradictions inherent in that.

Elazar Barkan expresses a widely held and somewhat disingenuous belief that 'the Allies in 1945 did not impose reparations upon Germany'. The Russians certainly did and we still accept the importance of the idea as a possible tool in the arsenal of ending wars. But Barkan is right to say that the lessons of Versailles were largely learnt by the Western Allies and that '[t]his introduced a novel fac-tor into international relations: rather than hold to a moral right to exploit enemy resources, as had been done previously, the victor underscored future reconciliation and assisted its defeated enemies to re-establish themselves'.[85] The resulting change in practice was for the morally wrong state, in the case of Sec-ond World War, Germany, to give restitution to the victims of the crimes com-mitted by the Nazis.

Reparations were a touchstone for great power relations throughout the inter-war period. They were technically very difficult and not really understood even by most politicians who agreed with them. They were the 'Schleswig Holstein question' of the early twentieth century. Reparations in the inter-war years revealed the bankruptcy of any form of real cooperation to bring about a 'better' world. Keynes's importance in bringing this to the attention of the world cannot be underestimated. His excoriation of all the Allied statesmen, and especially the Americans (whom he described as 'broken reeds') made such a profound impression that those who have tried to rehabilitate the 'bad men' of the Conference will often admit that they have an almost impossible task. Whether it is right to go on to say that appeasement in the 1930s was as a direct result and also a moral consequence of the failure of reparations is much harder to uphold and many now agree that appeasement was a necessary evil given the previous disarray of the erstwhile Allies, especially over reparations.[86]

The link was already being made in 1923 between the damaging effect of reparation on the norm that was to replace it, that of reconstruction after 1945. In his 'Notes on the Reparation Settlement' of 1922 Bradbury said he believed that the French had both financial and political 'impulses towards settlement'. Financially the French Government had to pay for 'reconstruction, and to meet this expenditure it is essential that she should be able to turn her indemnity claim into cash'. Politically the situation was that 'there are many countries whose interests would be advanced if the whole indemnity arrangements were to fall through, and the longer a settlement is postponed the more France will find herself isolated in her desire to secure reparation. On the other hand if France can succeed in embodying a scheme of reparation into the general plan of financial reconstruction the whole world will become parties to the reparation settlement'.[87] This chance did occur at the Genoa Conference of 1922, a meeting between Germany, Russia and the Allied states that will be discussed in Chapter 4. But as we will see there the reconstruction of Europe did not take place until 1945 onwards, perhaps the greatest missed opportunity of the twentieth century and one that doomed the world to war in 1939.

Reparations was a policy that it is right to see as having been a failure and replaced with others, such as reconstruction. But as we shall see this, in its own turn, has not proved to be the totally unmitigated panacea that it undoubtedly was in the post-Second World war period in Europe.

4 Reconstruction until the Marshall Plan

[I]f punitive economic measures are to be taken against the vanquished, they should be clearly differentiated from reparations for reconstruction purposes.[1]

Crane Brinton 1942

History apparently repeats itself in some part.[2]

Oscar Cox to Harry Hopkins, 1942

Introduction

We have grown familiar in recent times with speeches by American Presidents about 'reconstruction', a concept that has become a central part of the currency of contemporary IR. Yet the liberal idea that you should defeat your enemy and then re-build his economy in order to make the vanquished state and society see the future in a less militaristic way is one that has only developed since the First World War. It is certainly the case that after previous wars, such as those against revolutionary France, it was seen as essential to bring the reprobate defeated state back into the society of nations. Talleyrand was given equal billing with Britain, Russia and Prussia at the discussion that led to the Treaty of Vienna in 1815. But to actually reconstruct a defeated enemy is a more modern concept. And, as was shown in the last chapter, the discrediting of reparation as a tool to prevent future wars was beginning to lead to the changed logic of 'reconstruction'.

Inherent to the logic of the democratic peace is the need to create democratic states, accountable to their own citizens and to the international community. In the Cold War period this meant the creation of democracies by the Western powers in their own sphere of influence, as with Germany and Japan after 1945. In the post-Cold War period it has in practice meant intervention by the Western powers, as in Kosovo, or by the wider international community, as in Somalia, Bosnia, Afghanistan and Iraq. This of course raises many questions of how or who defines the rights of a democratic group of states to intervene where they feel such democracy does not exist and needs to be created, a process that usually passes under the name of 'humanitarian intervention'.

This chapter will therefore first map out the evolution of the term 'reconstruction' historically until 1947. It will be argued that it has its origins in the

American Civil War term of 'reconstruction', and that there have been certain crucial changes in the idea over the period of the next hundred years or so that have made what was always a strongly liberal strategy of terminating wars in a way that is intended to prevent future wars into something more, a policy to firmly entrench liberal values and institutions world-wide.

The genealogy of reconstruction

We can see the intellectual and practical origins of the modern meaning of reconstruction in the rebuilding of the South after the defeat of the Confederacy in 1865. The programme of reconstruction embarked upon by the victorious Union of course led to accusations of Northern businessmen acting as 'carpet-baggers' exploiting the federal contracts to their own ends. Christopher Cramer has rightly pointed out that this was an example of 'reconstruction [as] a form of revolution from above'.[3] In the aftermath of the Boer War we will see that reconstruction became a synonym for assimilation or even imperialism. Such accusations are now commonplace in the according of such reconstruction contracts after civil and international wars since 1991. The contradictions of such a policy therefore have a certain continuity. This continuity derives from the widespread understanding that neither reconstruction nor even 'development', are simply technical feats'.[4] They are a conscious attempt to create a liberal peace in a war-torn area. We should not be surprised that the locally defeated elites, who may not be 'liberal', fight back by hitting at the process.

However in the twentieth century and since, wars have become more and more destructive, it is undeniable that the need for reconstruction has potentially been that much greater. This did not mean that everyone, even in the liberal establishments of the West, has always seen the necessity or good sense in reconstructing the economy of a defeated party. After 1919 there was an attempt by the League of Nations to help the devastated economies of the Axis back on to their feet and a contradictory simultaneous attempt to make them 'pay for the war', as was stressed in the chapter on reparations. As in that chapter, we can see much of the transition from reparation to reconstruction in the observance of the consequences of the former.

None the less, the Morgenthau Plan of 1944 envisaged the total destruction of Germany as an industrial state even after much soul searching about reparations and the 'mistakes' of the Treaty of Versailles. This was only modified after 1946 when it became apparent that the Soviet Union was not going to be a true ally in the peace as it had been in the war. Hence the examples of the reaction of the international community to the First and Second World Wars form a basic backbone around which the chapter is built.

Economic reconstruction before the First World War

The main aim of all foreign policy before the First World War, in all the Chancelleries of Europe and beyond, was to create a world in which the individual national interest of the Powers was best served. This in practice led to various attempts at Concert and cooperation, but exclusively at the level of state structures, if one exempts the timid efforts at functional cooperation in the nineteenth century.[5] Maintenance of the balance of power was seen as a minimum requirement by most statesmen, to be maintained by force if necessary, as was the case in the Crimean War. Economics was seen as the handmaiden of the war effort and all the states that eventually made up the main protagonists in the First World War tried to develop policies that would help them become *Wehrwirtsschaften*.

There was, at least in Britain, the Great Power for most of the nineteenth century, a growing awareness of the importance of maintaining trade and what Olive Anderson calls 'preserving British imports from dislocation [to] keep the British economy unimpaired', as in the Crimean War.[6] It had been appreciated during the Napoleonic Wars that the British economy could suffer greatly from economic attack, but also that it could flourish with the defence of a strong navy that kept the seas open. It might be said that this was the origin of the British perception that the world was a far bigger oyster than Europe where trade was concerned. From this slowly emerged the idea that trade could help the cause of peace, and free traders like Richard Cobden were strong non-interventionists and *pacific-ists* in the Ceadel usage of the term (see Chapter 1), in that they abhorred militarism and crusaders in almost equal measure.

For war was seen by British liberals as almost entirely destructive, commerce as the essence of positive thinking and action, and while 'war could ruin trade, it was powerless to promote it'. It also led them in the nineteenth century into believing that peace could be brought about by the arbitration of disputes and a concert of nations, which in some cases amounted to a federal union of European states, a tradition that stretched back to Immanuel Kant and Jeremy Bentham.[7] This was also in reaction to the increased violence of war and its consequently much greater destructive potential.[8] But most significantly for our purposes, nineteenth-century liberals also believed, and believe, that commerce had a far more profound effect than war in improving states and peoples with them, Cobden's 'peaceful penetration'. America was for him the proof of this. As Spain and Portugal had conquered by commerce, so had Holland, then Great Britain, and now too would the United States.[9] Like de Tocqueville, Cobden saw the future as belonging to the United States and Russia, and there are no doubts that his sympathies lay with the former, a commonplace among liberals for the whole period until at least 1917.

By the time of the turn of the century there was a growing view among British liberals that war was very bad not just for business and trade, but that the aims of war could actually be achieved much better by economic means. Many in military, and especially in naval circles, in Britain were beginning to agree, as was so strongly evidenced by best-selling books such as Angell's *The Great Illusion* of 1910, that there was a growing realization that the potentially catastrophic economic damage that would be done to all sides in a war might well have a corollary in economic renewal or repair after a war. Angell's main point was 'that international finance has become so interdependent and so interwoven with trade' that war cannot result in economic advantage. This was in effect a reworking of the Cobdenite idea of war and peace and also a 'statement of a thesis still revolutionary, one that had to face up to a much stronger and older current still running, that of Hegel's "will to power"'.[10]

However much liberal thinking about economics and war came to dominate strategic thinking in Britain, this was not the case in Germany, for example, where the lessons of the nineteenth century were learnt differently. There Listian doctrines of national self-reliance de-emphasized the role of trade in favour of what would now be called 'infant industry' arguments. There were of course German liberals who espoused a more Anglo-Saxon approach, such as Theodore Mommsen, but they were not the dominant coterie around the Kaiser who not only famously 'set down' his pilot Bismarck[11] but also his policy of accommodating fallen enemies, as Bismarck had done with Austria after 1866 and even with France after 1871. The next war for Germany would be to create a commercial empire bent to the wishes of the German Emperor, not one based on liberal principles of free trade. The Kaiser's fleet was to enforce this idea and to end the 'freedom of the seas' policy espoused by liberals in London. German liberals were essentially swept along by the patriotic fervour of the time and lost intellectual contact with their Anglo-Saxon contemporaries, a dislocation many of them, and especially the Jews among them, came to bitterly regret.[12]

For the more conservatively minded in all the imperial states the notion of reconstruction came to mean an embedding of British/German/Italian/French power more firmly in the territory that been dominated. So the erstwhile liberals, Viscount Milner, Joseph Chamberlain *et al.*, who were responsible for the Boer War saw reconstruction, as was seen in Chapter 1, as the settling of large numbers of British farmers on the Transvaal and Orange River colonies to 'anglicise the country districts'. Milner's 'Kindergarten' was a body of bright young administrators recruited to 'reconstruct' the Boer territories to make them fit into the new British South Africa. It is ironic that the Boers largely succeeded in reconstructing British liberal ideas to make them accept separate development (apartheid) in the Union of South Africa with the resulting destruction of many liberal hopes there for the next eighty years.[13] This 'liberal imperialism' shows the dilemmas of liberal reconstruction at their most stark. In effect it advocated a separate development of not only the peoples of South Africa but was also linked to the separation of the world into rival trading blocs, a move known in Britain as 'Tariff Reform' that was to prove one of the main building blocks of economic nationalism and thus be one major cause of the Second World War.

So for British liberal thinkers ultimately the guarantee of peace was to come with the spread of the principles of political and economic liberty, and for many, like Cobden, that meant looking to the United States as its main exemplar. This at least partly explains the obsessive desire of many liberals during the First World War to have the Americans fight on the side of the European allies against Germany, and also the desire to involve American liberal principles in the peace settlement. This settlement was supposed to be non-annexationist, and politically and economically liberal. This seemed confirmed by Wilson's Fourteen Points and was reflected in the beliefs of British liberals who had either opposed or supported the war effort.

Reconstruction from 1914 to the Treaty of Versailles

From the armistice to the treaty: liberals against the 'cult of irrationality'

In previous chapters much has been said about the influence of Wilson's Fourteen Points on the main clauses of the Treaty of Versailles. What is striking in American liberal thinking about the post-war settlement is how much emphasis was put on economic issues in general. John Dewey wrote a series of articles before and immediately after the Armistice in which he spoke up against the 'cult of irrationality' that thought the war could be won by military means alone. This was an 'obnoxious intellectual influence' that was poisoning American public life by seeing enemies all around, and leading to 'domestic suppression and suspicion' and not only creating an 'irrational submissiveness among the cowardly [and] cultivat[ing] an irrational rebelliousness in others'.[14] The reactions to which he referred were those of the American state clamping down on rational thought about the Russian Revolution, but also about sensible ways to end the hostilities in general.

For many Americans, Russia was giving perhaps the most important lesson that had to be learnt. Before 1914 the United States had slowly developed an interest in Russia, a country seen by many Americans as being rather like their own before the civilizing influence of democracy, as well as a place which held immense potential economic interest for American entrepreneurial flair.[15] Before, during and after the Paris Peace Conference, Russia loomed as large or larger in the American liberal perspective as the end of the war itself. The debate had several facets. American liberals believed that it could be learnt from and also cajoled back into line by economic carrots. In November 1918, just before the Armistice, *The New Republic* was most concerned that all Americans understood that

> [t]errible as the political situation is [in Russia], the economic situation of Russia is much more terrible and infinitely more significant. The political situation will not improve and cannot improve with the anarchy and chaos prevailing if the economic life of the country is done away with.

Intervention was therefore not the way, but economic help in reconstruction was. Moreover this was entirely in the self-interest of the United States, for 'the most deplorable result of Allied withdrawal from Russia is the propaganda there is left entirely to the Germans and the anti-Ally Russians'. They also saw a deeper lesson: 'Russia cannot be conquered. But it can easily be won over. Economic assistance is the best and, probably, the only means of winning Russia over.' It was also the main test case of the Allies' ability to do it: 'in this great struggle for establishing peace upon principles of right and justice, President Wilson will need the moral support of the whole world.'[16] Russia was thus being seen as a test case for the reconstruction that American liberals saw as increasingly desirable. It was also a test case for American liberal courage against Dewey's 'cult of irrationality'.

Other aspects of American public life were also explicitly linked to the reconstruction question. Many commentators noted that politics began and ended in the United States not with the big international picture but in pork-barrel politics, as Norman Hapgood noted just after the Armistice. In the end liberals and conservatives alike would have to take up the challenge to ensure the 'industrial freedom and security that radical and clear-minded conservatives deem indispensable'. It had to be 'based ultimately on the all-round building up of the individual'. Now was the time to do it 'before the public hardens into its customary inertia'.[17]

In another article in *New Republic*, 'The Meaning of Reconstruction' was developed along similar lines. The danger was that it would just come to mean 'let us make money and have a good time', the logic of the carpet-bagger. But it did mean a 'reorganization of private enterprise' in order to remove the 'uncertainties of tomorrow; bread ... [and other necessities, which are] ... enemies of democracies as dangerous as the Kaiser ever was'.[18] Liberals in the United States thus hoped to see a change as dramatic in the United States itself as Wilson was hoping to achieve in the world of international politics. This was reconstruction of not only economies but of men's minds.

Economic reconstruction after 1919: 'colossal practical problems'

By the time the Peace Conference opened in Paris, there was a growing feeling in Allied and Axis countries alike that the war had shown that a controlled and centralized economy was the best way to conduct a war. For example, Fritz Stern has shown Germany could not have fought beyond 1915 had it not been for the organizational and scientific genius of Fritz Haber.[19] So one main lesson that was seen as having been learnt from the war in the context of reconstruction was that the organizational power that the state had demonstrated during the war could be carried on into the peace. The other was that there was no clear agreement on how this energy could be so translated. For many, reconstruction meant *domestic* reconstruction, best summed up by Lloyd George as the creation of a 'land fit for heroes'.[20] In the context of 1919, in the words of the great League of Nations advocate Lord Robert Cecil, this also meant the 'dissatisfaction with the hardships which the period of reconstruction necessarily brought with it', and the term was therefore tainted by association. Lloyd George's first Cabinet after the Khaki Election of 1918 had been called the 'Reconstruction Cabinet'. To convert from a wartime economy to one of peace had always previously meant large number of de-mobbed soldiers swelling the labour market, forcing down wages and causing in Cecil's words 'a good deal of political and industrial unrest'.[21]

The outpouring of books on the subject in the last part of the war and in the early years of the peace was widely noted but so was the difficulty in agreeing on the 'underlying principles included in the necessary reconstruction rather than the peculiarities in the given situations'.[22] One book review in *The Nation* reported that 'books of the most varied quality continue to pour from the presses to meet the demand everywhere for information and guidance in the era of reconstruction which the world is facing'.[23]

The types of book being produced reflected a wide variety of obsessions, by no means all of them liberal. Those who explicitly picked up on the liberal agenda of the War were not in the majority, but the influence of the war itself was ubiquitous. The domestic agenda dominated. *The Nation* noted that 'perhaps the most fundamental of reconstruction problems is the attitude that the government is to take toward economic organization and activity'. Others wrote of the 'The Vision for Which We Fought', and often stressed the need for 'a reconstruction which shall be no less comprehensively and intelligently guided than was the war itself. ... We must mobilize for peace as we mobilized for war. Above all else we must mobilize our intelligence.' This emphasis is the dominant one, with relatively few picking up on what might be called an 'internationalist' need but all on the bewildering vastness of the task. The best that could be said for a liberal inspiration was that Cecil Fairfield Lowell evoked the 'part which liberal thought is prepared to take in these leads in shaping the political and economic policies of the coming age'. But no answer is given and *The Nation* was forced to fall back on the plea that 'what the world stands in need of today is a work that will really link up the idealism of a bygone age with the colossal practical problems of an urgent present'.[24]

After Versailles: the need for 'large vision'

It turned out that one of the main lessons that were learnt by many as a result of the First World War paradoxically damaged the cause of liberalism almost beyond repair. Central planning became one of the key economic ideas of the inter-war period, epitomized by the Five Year Plans in the Soviet Union and similar constructs in Nazi Germany and elsewhere. Even liberals like Angell had to accept that economic efficiency had to be bought at the cost of more government intervention. John Maynard Keynes was converted to 'national planning' by the mid-1930s. The 'New Deal' in the United States was a colossal exercise in planning. *The Great Illusion* of 1910 was followed by Karl Polanyi's *The Great Transformation* in 1939,[25] a book that comprehensively disagreed with the idea that the 'invisible hand' of classical liberalism could ever be seen again. Even the Conservative Harold Macmillan was convinced by the need for 'planning', for the basis for any such reconstruction had to limit the excesses of the 'financial "pirate" and the industrial "buccaneer"' and 'speculation'.[26]

But by the mid-1930s there was a growing awareness that national reconstruction was linked to the problems engendered by the breakdown of international conferences (notably the World Economic Conference of 1933). The only solution for many of the centre ground of American and British liberal political life (which encompassed much of the left and right) was economic planning on a national, but also now international, level. In Britain this was epitomized by the rise of the PEP (Political and Economic Planning) pressure group that bought together Treasury luminaries like Basil Blackett and many academic and government economists and political figures.[27]

For the corollary of the breakdown of international cooperation was that the open, interdependent world that liberals had seen emerge in the nineteenth century, with its central features of a self-regulating monetary and commercial system (free trade) was progressively being replaced by a system of economic nationalism. This was either that of individual countries, like the United States after the Smoot Hawley legislation of 1929, or the Imperial Preference of the British Empire after 1932, or the Schachtian (as in Hjalmar Schacht, Reich Minister for the Economy under Hitler) principles of protection and autarky.[28] It was genuinely believed, even by the great liberal economist John Maynard Keynes by the late 1930s,[29] that Government intervention in the economy was an acceptance that there was no more even a potential liberal global economic system that could be called upon to restrain the warlike nations. So centrally planned 'efficiency' either had to be pursued to prepare the democracies for the war that was to come or it had to be pursued to keep the proletariat in work to stop them becoming either fascists or Bolsheviks.

Many articles of unfinished business also remained between the major erstwhile liberal Allies. The French and the British had a major falling-out over reparations, the subject of the last chapter. This also affected the Anglo–American relationship, but the focus there was on more power-related matters. The United States in particular was annoyed with Britain's persistent refusal to dismantle its control of the Seas. The United States increasingly felt that Britain's monopoly of the ability and the self-perceived right of blockade was dangerous and outdated. This led to a long debate between the British and American governments, to which the Japanese became associated in the 1930s, about what was know as 'Freedom of the Seas'. One of Woodrow Wilson's explicit war aims in the 1918 Fourteen Points was to make the seas free for all, a grievance that had rankled with the United States ever since the British had left America. The reluctance of the British to go along with this led to serious discussion in the CFR and Chatham House about the likelihood of an Anglo-American war in the 1920s: '[a]n Anglo-American war is neither "unthinkable" nor "inevitable"', and; the 'feasibility of settling Anglo-American disputes by means other than violence must be considered'.[30] This also led to the signature of the Washington Treaties in 1921 and 1930 after which Britain's 'Three Power Standard', whereby its navy was as big as the next two put together, was consigned to the dustbin of history.[31] As James Byrne wrote to Hamilton Fish Armstrong of the Council on Foreign Relations in 1928,

> [I]f a state defies the League in certain ways, the rest of the League will do certain things which may be war or certain things which they may not call war like an economic blockade which, however, will, whether called war or not, be accompanied by sea action which goes with war, seizing vessels of neutrals.[32]

This did not mean that liberals did not try to pursue what they felt could be pursued of a liberal global agenda. As a contemporary commentator observed:

> [I]t is a paradox that at the same time that the nations are cultivating their own independence, the field of international action has widened. The actual carrying out of the terms of the Treaty of Versailles necessitated a great amount of joint action [by all nations]. ... The principal organ for the set-tlement of more purely economic questions has, however, been the League of Nations and the associated International Labour Organization.[33]

The activities of the League of Nations (LON) can be seen as the first major incursion into what we would now call 'post-conflict peace building'.

Part of the Versailles Treaty apparatus that might have provided a real reconstruction mechanism was the Supreme Economic Council (SEC) set up during the Paris peace negotiations on 8 February 1919 by Wilson. In its early form it had discussed the blockade of Germany and started thinking about aid to Russia, ably organized by Herbert Hoover in the Supreme Council of Supply and Relief. There were a bewildering array of 60 committees on economic mat-ters (or 'Inter-Allied Councils'), of which Hoover sat on 40 and chaired six.[34] The SEC was later lauded by Stannard Baker as an initiative which 'for a brief time [gave] a kind of economic government, the greatest experiment ever made in the correlation, control and direction in time of peace, of international trade and finance'.[35] Hoover himself was seen as understanding 'better than any other liv-ing being the political consequences of mass starvation'.[36] He was to show this understanding in his leadership after the Conference of the American Relief Administration (ARA), which saved millions of Russian lives through its famine relief work.

But it also showed that the bureaucracy could be stifling, a feeling that is echoed throughout the early 1920s and has remained a problem ever since in any major international initiative. Even the SEC was seen as being too large (about 30 people) and 'ill-equipped to handle the many details involved in most matters or even to decide the general policies for legions of problems that were necessarily the specialities of highly trained experts'.[37] The above-mentioned committees on which Hoover and others sat led, in the words of Thomas A. Bailey, to 'indescribable confusion and disorganization'.[38]

By October 1919 the Council had made tentative steps to foster international cooperation in the re-building of Europe. A memorandum of February 1920 stated that the economists, politicians and financiers that made it up wanted to see countries with a healthy balance of payments lending to those who hadn't. But the first meeting to implement this had the British delegate, Crawford, saying that his country had not yet decided what needed to be done. The Belgians and Italians felt that something should be done immediately given the dire situation in which they found themselves. All of them were worried what would happen if the United States did not participate. The analysis was clear. The war had gravely disrupted all the European economies; it had led to rapid inflation and general discontent, even though the Council's delegates thought this 'normal' after a war. Moreover there was still no real peace as war continued to rage in the East, especially in Russia. The remedies they all agreed were to stimulate production and facilitate as much trade as possible. However the fiscal and other solutions they came up with had the opposite effect. All the states present agreed that deflation was necessary to restrain inflation, balance budgets, consolidate debt and reduce monetary circulation. The only 'new' money was to come in the form of reparations from Germany and, hopefully, loans from the United States. As was stressed in Chapter 3, this was to come at enormous cost in dissention among the Allies and resentment from the former Axis powers.[39]

The French have long stood accused by the British of being the main stumbling block to the reconstruction of Europe after 1919, largely due to the writings of Keynes. Perhaps it would be fairer to say that France felt that the blueprint for recovery was written into the Treaty, one that had after all been signed by all parties. The Americans could reasonably be said to have withdrawn not on economic grounds but because of the Senate's refusal to accept the jurisdiction of the League of Nations over America's war powers. The Quai d'Orsay saw the general measures that needed to be taken in simple terms. According to Articles 16 (1) to (3) in the case of 'recalcitrant' states all that was necessary was a rupture of trade links and of links with individuals in the state concerned and a trade embargo. They would take control of the Sarre to ensure good supplies of coal and iron, and with Britain of German colonies. There was no emphasis on 'carrots' for the French, only on the 'stick'. Moreover they were convinced that this was all they could rely upon. There were no British or American proposals that they could discern that would do any better. In the words of a French diplomat: 'les Allies n'ont pris aucun engagement d'entreaide économique et financière qui puissent actuellement servir de base à une conversation entre Gouvernments. Il y a eu simplement, à divers reprises, de bonnes paroles echanges, sur lesquelles on ne peut faire fond.'[40]

The Americans just found this infuriating in the extreme. Future President Herbert Hoover was reported as saying in July 1920 that Europe was just 'lazy' and not getting down to work. He advocated a business-led approach to reconstruction, and demonstrated what he meant in the most concrete of ways by being the Head of the American Relief Administration (ARA), which sent huge amounts of famine relief to Russia between 1921 and 1923. For Hoover the state had to stand ready to support its own businessmen in order to be able to help others – what Michael Hogan and others have referred to as the 'corporate state'. He, then and later, had little patience with the idea of international organizations carrying out such tasks as reconstruction; a tradition that persists in the Republican Party to this day (and beyond it in the tradition known as 'neo-conservatism'). As Secretary for Commerce between 1921 and 1928 (after which he became President) Hoover wielded enormous economic and political power in the United States. And he in effect was the main director of American foreign policy, especially towards Russia.[41]

In Britain Keynes' *Economic Consequences of the Peace* had emerged and was accusing Lloyd George of having been 'crushed' by Clemenceau. Large sections of the text were circulated to the staff of the Quai d'Orsay. The French had hoped that German reparations would restart the European economy, and they clearly had not, but this had not convinced the French that the British had done anything either, merely pursuing a 'politique à la fois tres hardie et tres egoiste'.[42] This bitterness between the three main Allies meant that any real progress on economic issues was quasi-impossible.

By 1922 there was a realization that the state of the European economy was so bad that drastic measures were needed to try and do something about it, even if what need to be done about it lacked any real consensus. As *The Nation* had said in the above mentioned book review of 1919, '[r]econstruction is, of course, a matter of laws and offices and statistics and other coldly practical things. But it is also a matter of ideals, and the greatest calamity that could befall would be the failure of our political and industrial leaders to be inspired in the coming years by large vision.'[43] Outside the League of Nations the most impressive attempt was the Conference at Genoa of 1922 orchestrated by Liberal British Prime Minister David Lloyd George. Lloyd George was convinced that the only way to restart European trade after the Great War was to bring back the 'pariah states' of Europe, the Soviet Union and Germany, into the 'comity of nations' and to exchange such re-admission and the promise of financial help for promises of good behaviour in the future. The Conference's plans, which were explicitly intended both to find a plan to reconstruct Europe and to bring back into the system the 'pariah states' of Germany and Bolshevik Russia, was an effort which failed dismally, and contributed to Lloyd George's loss of office later in the year. Every other attempt at global reconstruction in the inter-war years foundered on the growing economic nationalism of the main states and paralysed efforts by the liberal democracies to contain or roll back totalitarianism.

So was reconstruction in 1919–22 a failure?

It would be easy to put together the confusion surrounding the SEC's stumbling attempts to start the reconstruction of Europe with the divisions of the Allies over economic matters and say that reconstruction in the immediate post-First World War period was a dismal failure. That would not be entirely wrong. For unlike in 1945 there was no consensus about what the attitude to a continent-wide proposal for reconstruction should be and no state to give a lead in how it must be done. The SEC and the Genoa conference achieved few if any of their aims. The debate that developed pitted the war-enhanced economic liberalism of the United States against the more *dirigiste* instincts of Lloyd George, who has been characterized as a 'Keynesian before Keynes' in his attempts at Genoa to revitalize European trade. It also encountered the enhanced nationalistic fervour of many small and larger European states, many of which had just been put in the position of being able to erect trade barriers where none had exited previously, as across the whole of the former Hapsburg Empire and parts of the erstwhile Russian Empire.

The disagreements and economic nationalism encountered at Genoa are in stark contrast with what happened at the Bretton Woods Conference in 1944. There President Roosevelt was more than happy to start the process that eventually led to vast amounts of capital being raised to help European states, victors and losers, back on to their feet. He was also prepared to put huge pressure, even on his ally Britain, to force the 'Schachtian' (Keynes' word) members of the Treasury to commit to a multilateral open trading system that potentially included all states. In contrast the Americans refused to even attend at Genoa given the presence of a Bolshevik Russian contingent.[44] Not only would they not talk to the Russians to give any hint of a recognition to a state that had reneged on its debts to the United States, they were also convinced that the British were plotting in secret with the Russians to steal a march on their international markets. Such was the nature of the poisonous atmosphere that pervaded Anglo-American relations during much of the 1920s and 1930s. In effect the United States forced Britain into accepting its version of a new international economic order in 1945 after many years of distrust and even active mutual dislike.[45] So while the League of Nations tried to find a role but was not being allowed to have one by any of the major players, the Genoa Conference thus merely served to display the total disarray in which the victors stood on the question of reconstruction.[46]

Equally the divisions which existed over the other parts of the economic equation, especially debt and reparations described in Chapter 3, were bound to impede any plans to get Europe going. Keynes analysis of the folly of reparations can be supplemented by the folly of trying to reconstruct while simultaneously cutting back on the budgets necessary to provide the cash to do so, and deflating the economies of the countries that would have to be the main donors. This in turn restricted the growth of trade and made it ever more difficult for the defeated Axis powers and the victors alike to climb out of their economic morass. The 'fault' could be equally divided among those who refused to take part in the subsequent attempts to reconstruct Europe, that is to say the Americans, and those who were forced to stay but lacked the intellectual or practical skills to have a real 'vision' of what needed to be done. This is the target for Keynes in his various books on the Treaty. It explains why he played such a determinate role in the next big round of reconstruction after a war, in 1941–6. The point made by Cecil Fairfield Lowell that the liberal states had to show intelligence and vision had been proved right. They had not and the result was a brooding chaos that served as the seed-bed for a new conflict.

But the important fact is that the novel idea of 'reconstruction' had taken root. One of the first Professors of IR, Philip Noel-Baker, complained that the expression was:

> often used without any clear concept of what is meant. It is a new addition to post-war vocabulary and like many new things it is used indiscriminately and vaguely thought to mean everything that helps the return to the good old days when all were prosperous before the war.

Noel-Baker sought to pin down the concept more clearly to two major elements – the: restoration of pre-war efficiency [and] ... reconstruction of the economic mechanisms of manufacture, credit, purchase and sale, transport ...' This translated, he said, into a necessary involvement of 'citizens of the countries involved ... [plus] government action ... [plus] international action by governments working together – this is the real experiment.[47]

To this might be added the fact that there were now powerful liberal voices calling for reconstruction to be used as a tool for peace. The *Manchester Guardian* ran a long series during the Genoa Conference, edited by John Maynard Keynes. It was contributed to by a huge array of liberal intellectual, financiers and economists, printed in five languages and intended to create a debate about general post-war economic policy in Europe. This was to serve as a prototype for Keynes and the American liberals under Roosevelt's wartime Administration of a New Deal for Europe. But in 1922 it was truly 'a missed opportunity'.[48]

The League of Nations and reconstruction

On the other hand the fact that Lloyd George and Keynes' views appear to have been premature does not mean that the problems of reconstruction simply evaporated. The very same states that had lauded the break-up of the Empires, and especially those that had received the dubious (economically at least) honour of sovereignty, quickly came to realize that they could not go it alone without cooperation from their neighbours, ones that might have been erstwhile dominators or enemies.

Austria – the first case of international 'reconstruction'

The Treaties of St Germain and Trianon had imposed crippling reparation payments and left both Austria and Hungary as states that were barely economically viable due to the loss of their hinterland and the burden of reparation payments. Vienna in particular was a huge bureaucratic centre of an empire that no longer existed. Unemployment and poverty, even starvation, were widespread as it lost its sources of food. The surrounding states initially allied to prevent the restoration of a Hapsburg monarchy, thus ensuring quasi-isolation. As Cecil put it, 'Austria went on gradually sinking lower and lower in the morass'. He also pointed out that Austria was not a very prominent concern of the Allies so that when its plight was finally considered by the Supreme Allied Council in August 1922 it came up last on the agenda and the League was told to do something as the Allies could provide no money at all.[49] In other words the issue was seen as having been ditched as the League was not at the time, or indeed later, given much credence as a problem-solving institution by the Allied Powers.

Cecil's memory was slightly deceiving him even if the general implication of his comments was correct. The question of Austria was first seriously raised at a conference held in London in March 1921 chaired by British Foreign Secretary Austen Chamberlain. It was realized that something had to be done 'in such a way as to ensure for Austria a practical economic life for the future'.[50] The League attempted to correct this situation by sending a fact-finding economic mission to coordinate a resurrection of the economic integration of the area in the interests of all. This effort, directed by Arthur Salter, which included the future Secretary General of the League of Nations, Joseph Avenol, necessitated what may have been the first in depth analysis of a state's financial and economic problems by an international organization. The findings of the Commission were significant for the whole Versailles settlement, as they argued that without a twenty-year suspension of reparation payments there was no hope of Austria being able to resurrect itself. They also suggested very orthodox economic policies aimed at stabilizing the currency and the balance of payments. The hope was to make Austria once again into the financial 'metropolis' it had been in the days of the Empire, serving the whole area as a centre for financial services.[51] This implied a measure of political control by the League to ensure the establishment of a more balanced economy. It implied a form of financial protectorate status for Austria, the first time that such a thing had been attempted with the appointment of a High Commissioner appointed by the League and one that was later used in Germany and other countries after the Second World War and in the Balkans today.

For the League itself it presented a chance to prove what it could do – in Noel-Baker's words: 'this is a real piece of reconstruction: it is almost the only thing in the world since the war, that is on an important scale, both economically reconstructive and international in character'.[52] It was followed by other important actions, most notably in Hungary. This need not detain us, as it was a case rather like Austria's, except that Hungary was a largely agrarian economy that was self-sufficient in food, which Austria was not. It led to the same result, that of a suspension of reparation payments, which it is important to note was agreed by the skillful actions of Sir John Bradbury, British Representative to the Reparation Commission, and to some extent over the wishes of the French delegation. The leadership role of Britain in this case, from the London Conference of 1921 onwards, was very significant, analogous to that of the United States in 1945 (see below).

Greek refugee settlement, 1923

The other 'reconstruction' case that begs our attention at this period is that of the repatriation of ethnic Greeks expelled from Anatolia in 1922–3 after the war with Turkey that culminated in the Treaty of Lausanne. This was also brokered by the British Government by Lord Curzon who complained bitterly of the 'interminable tedium of Lausanne' and by the significant contribution of the Bank of England to the financial settlement. The Treaty 'require[d] members of the Greek Orthodox Church established in Turkey to emigrate to Greece and Moslems established in Greece to emigrate to Turkey'. About one million Greeks had fled to the coast of Anatolia in 1922 pursued by the victorious armies of Kemal Ataturk. Many were killed in Smyrna in one of the most notorious massacres of the period. Some of the final total of about 1.5 million were helped by Frijdthof Nansen and his Refugee Settlement Commission under the auspices of the League, some by the Mixed Exchange Commission set up under the Treaty. All were destitute and needed money and resources to make a new life in Thrace. The Bank of England was the main guarantor of the £3–6 million pounds needed, supporting the Bank of Greece (at a factor of roughly 39 in current terms a sum of £117–234 million). The final report was happy to report that '[t]he settlement scheme is the third of the important reconstruction tasks undertaken by the League'. This was largely seen as complex financial and logistical exercise, not a moral one.[53]

There were some rumblings within the League mechanism about the moral implications of the resettlement schemes. Nansen's Commission was the main source of this disquiet. Nansen dealt with the real consequences of 1.4 million people descending on a country of only 5 million. Charles P. Howland, who chaired the Greek Refugee Settlement Commission, was adamant:

> On the humanitarian side imagination cannot compass the event. Only those can make the effort of understanding who have seen destitution, misery, disease and death in all their possible forms, and the scale of this disaster was so unprecedented as to demand even from such persons a new vision.

They feared for the future of Greece itself which 'has witnessed the collapse of Hellenism beyond the seas and mountains', even if Greece was now more homogeneous than ever before. But they also feared for the future of the whole world if such an event was to become the norm.[54]

This was the first time that an international organization and a state (Britain) had bankrolled ethnic cleansing. In the documents of the time no moral problem was expressed although the British Government was split down the middle over its attitude to the Greek exodus for reasons of *realpolitik* , Lloyd George advocating a military expedition that led to the Chanak Crisis of November 1922, which was one of the contributory factors in his political downfall (along with Genoa) later that year. The idea of ethnic cleansing had thus been given an official imprimatur and it was a technique used by the Russians in Germany, as well as by the Czechs against the Sudeten Germans in 1945, also to no huge international clamour. In all these cases the victims were the losers in a war widely seen as being of their own making.

So it can be said that the League did pass the tests of reconstruction it was given in Austria, Hungary and Greece. In the first of these cases it is difficult to see that the League could do anything to alleviate the hyper-inflation of 1923 or claim any credit for the subsequent parlous stabilization. The League did not succeed in getting the reparations bill reduced, as that was negotiated by American bankers Dawes (in 1924) and Young (in 1929). Hitler finally abolished the problem by refusing to pay any more of the bill in 1933. Perhaps if this ineluctable result had been carried out by a democratic German Government encouraged by the Allies far earlier, Hitler would not have been able to claim the credit for that and much else of the final revision of the Treaty of Versailles. The League did realize that its most important achievements were in the economic and social spheres, as the Bruce Report of 1939 pointed out, but by then such policies alone, even if they had been far more extensive, were not enough to stop the onset of war.

The build up to the Marshall Plan – thinking on reconstruction, 1942–6

We would be wrong to assume that what became the Marshall Plan sprang ready formed out of the ashes of the Second World War. During the war the main effort was directed to winning, as it had been in 1914–18. There were clear problems in allowing civilians engaged in reconstruction to wander over a battlefield. But there was also a concerted attempt within the Post War Planning sections of the State Department to both better conceptualize and better institutionalize reconstruction efforts after the war had ended. In effect, as a number of writers have pointed out, the Marshall Plan has an interesting 'pre-history'.[55] The most important point is that in this war the winning of it was not just seen by the liberal coalition of states that became the 'Western' part of 'United Nations' – essentially the United States and, less willingly, Britain, as being fought for military ends or by military means. This war was seen as having had its roots in economic causes. The debate about reparation outlined in Chapter 3 holds all these arguments within it. This war was seen in Washington and London as one not just of national reconstruction, but one of a global variety.

The need for international organization

This was best summed up in the nexus of activity that included the Bretton Woods organization, and the United Nations' new functional agencies. As early as 1942 there were weighty memoranda being produced for the President by Treasury Secretary Henry Morgenthau's staff which stated that after the war:

> we shall be faced with three inescapable problems: to prevent the disruption of foreign exchanges and the collapse of the monetary and credit systems; to assure the restoration of foreign trade; and to supply the huge volume of capital that will be needed virtually throughout the world for reconstruction, for relief and for economic recovery. If we are to avoid drifting from the peace table into a period of chaotic competition, monetary disorders, depressions, political disruption, and finally into new wars within as well as among nations, we must be equipped to grapple with these three problems.[55]

The machinery suggested was for a 'United and Associated Nations Stabilization Fund [later called the International Monetary Fund – IMF] and a Bank for Reconstruction and Development [IBRD or World Bank]', which eventually were set up at Bretton Woods in 1944.

The *New Republic* trumpeted in early 1945 that it was a case of 'Bretton Woods or economic warfare'.[57] There could be no compromises on reconstruction as there had been in 1919 – now America must take its global responsibilities seriously. Equally the liberal establishment was terrified of a renewed wave of isolationism and recession in the United States, and a repeat of the 1930s once the beneficial economic effects of war had receded. Roosevelt's Secretary of State Cordell Hull had expressed his fear to Secretary of State for War Henry Stimson at the same time as the above mentioned Morgenthau Memorandum on the IBRD – 'it is going to be a very difficult job after the terrific strain of this war to prevent an equally strong reaction in the direction of "no further efforts" and "life as normal"'.[58] The IMF and the IBRD had to work internationally so that there would not be a severe depression in the United States itself.[59] This could only be achieved by opening up the world's markets to American goods, and the first step in this was arm-in-arm with the British as the inventors of such ideas. It was enlightened self-interest at its most stark. That this coincided with British (and even French desires) for the United States to not run away as it had after the First World War made reconstruction as an idea and as a practice into a kind of vital cement for the new world that was hopefully to emerge from the ashes of the old. But it cannot be claimed that this consensus just appeared, it was the result of a long process of thinking. Liberal and conservative internationalists had to fight hard for the principle of American leadership to be accepted.

There was in particular an attempt in Washington to try and understand the seeming continued French and Russian attraction for the reparation tool which was seen by many in the United States as having caused the Second World War and to try and devise means of weaning them off it. But they also recognized that the Soviet Union did not share this belief so a long process of attempted diplomatic pressure was applied, that ultimately failed as was seen earlier.

But France was different. It was weak and enfeebled, indeed occupied until 1944 and thus much more pliable. Its intentions were not clear in Washington however and there was some open hostility to France in general in the White House and sections of the State Department.[60]

The CFR, which was closely involved in this thinking, received a particularly interesting memorandum to its Peace Aims Group from Crane Brinton, the author of the celebrated *Anatomy of Revolution* (of 1938 and many subsequent editions) and one of the top American experts on France in November 1942. In this he pointed to the fragility of French political life and the need to discover what the French *want* after the war. In particular what are their views about the treatment of Germany and what 'punitive measures do the French favor: Dismemberment . . .? Loss of territory? Trial of war criminals? Reparations?' as well as their views (obviously linked in Brinton's mind) on 'international collaboration' and 'economic reconstruction'.[61]

The United States was right to fear that the French, were they given the chance, might demand a settlement as punitive as Versailles.[62] France would demand reparations from Germany after the war ('their slice of the melon'), especially if other states did. De Gaulle was cited in Brinton's document as having said '"that France will come out of it [the war] intact as regards everything that belongs to her, credited with all that she has lost." And a few French economists and publicists have expressed a belief that France should receive reparations', added Brinton. If such demands were to be made and to be substantial and of long duration 'elaborate guarantees will probably be required to enforce collection. In this case the employment of force would have to be envisaged'.

To avoid this, the document suggested six proposals. First, it was assumed that France will ask for reparations: 'some curbing of reparation demands may be effected by territorial adjustments, as for example the giving to France of the Saar Basin,' as had happened in 1919. This indeed proved to be the case. Second, it was assumed that there would be limitations based on 'the *creditors' willingness to receive and to consume nationally* [*sic* underlining] what the debtors can deliver without creating conditions unfavorable to the interests of the victors. One of France's chief demands will probably be for deliveries of coal.' Third, these payments should be 'liquidated within a relatively short time, perhaps ten years. The formula here might be for payments until physical production in occupied countries had reached pre-war levels [6 or 7 years after the First World War]. In order to place emphasis upon this aspect of the case the term *reparations* might be entirely dropped and in its *place funds for reconstruction* employed' [*sic* underlining]. Fourth, this would lead to a 'Commission for Reconstruction Funds . . . to study and manage the entire reparations settlement.' Fifth, reparations and war debts would have to be linked. This was a vital point for the Americans, for as we have seen these debts were seen as having been part of the same problem as that of reparations in the 1920s. Sixth, 'if punitive economic measures are to be taken against the vanquished, they should be clearly differentiated from reparations for reconstruction purposes'.[63]

This is one of the clearest indications of American thinking before the end of the Second World War about the links between debt, reparation, reconstruction and even other issues such as war crimes tribunals, dealt with in subsequent chapters. But whereas with the French the Americans had enormous leverage, they were also aware that such thinking was not appreciated by the USSR. So the Americans understood that some reference to reparations had to be included in the Yalta Settlement and other before it in deference (mainly) to Soviet wishes.

OFRRO and UNRRA, 1942–6

But they could also decide what was to happen in Western Europe, well beyond the reach of Soviet power. The State Department thus set up in early 1942 the Office of Foreign Relief and Rehabilitation (OFRRO) with a staff of 150 in 1943, which became subsumed into the United Nations Relief and Rehabilitation Administration (UNRRA) from February 1943 on. As with the case of reparations all parts of the United States Government were concerned that they should not repeat the mistakes of 1919, especially as regarded bringing along American public opinion and the Congress. There had been objections within the United

States to the Americans helping in the reconstruction of Europe. As Oscar Cox wrote to Harry Hopkins in December 1942: 'history apparently repeats itself in some part.'[64] Roosevelt was keen that this should not happen again.

UNRRA was administered by Governor Herbert H. Lehman of New York, a close confidant of President Roosevelt. Lehman reported directly to Roosevelt and to Secretary of State Cordell Hull, and he was given a very loose initial remit of coordinating all Federal agencies dealing with rehabilitation both within the State Department and outside it, including with the Allies.[65] We would now call him the 'Rehabilitation and Relief Czar'.

Lehman's role in UNRRA was thus a vital link in the development of the whole concept of reconstruction. Lehman was the beneficiary of thousands of letters giving him the vivid details of Nazi persecution of the Jews and others, especially after the opening up of the concentration camps in 1945. He saw the horrors of conditions in Europe for himself as early as late 1944, and as he put it after talking to the Queen of the Netherlands in November, 'the Queen seemed very sad'.[66] Lehman came to be identified personally as 'one who has such a keen interest in the rehabilitation of the destitute and broken peoples of Europe'.[67] There were over 215,000 Jews in France, Belgium and Holland alone that had been displaced by the war, and hundreds of thousands more across Europe.[68] The tally for other nations was much higher.

UNRRA developed particularly during the latter part of 1944 and into 1945 in the wake of the Allied Armies in Western Europe where it had a European Regional Office, but also to some extent in Eastern Europe. Its biggest operation was in China. At its peak in June 1946 staff numbers rose to 12,893 after which period it started to slowly hand over control of relief and rehabilitation to the United Nations and was wound down by June 1947.[69] Its budget in 1943 was put at \$1.8 – 2 billion of which 90 per cent would be spent on goods and supplies, much of which it was hoped in Washington would be of United States' provenance, but much of which in practice had to be locally generated. A full half of this was to go to China.[70]

However it is difficult to underestimate the newness and scope of this new organization. For once the official hype is not an exaggeration:

> Launched in the midst of war, and expending to global proportions at a time when invaded and disrupted countries were just beginning to emerge from a state of near chaos, UNRRA was compelled to establish its organization on an extremely flexible basis to meet rapidly changing conditions, and to place major emphasis on decentralization of responsibilities and functions.

This was truly 'a pioneer international agency' with an 'almost complete lack of precedent'.[71] But it was very aware that it could not do everything expected of it.

American, British and French thinking about reconstruction, 1943–4

In Britain during the war the idea of reconstruction again essentially meant *national* reconstruction, with some emphasis being put on a revitalized League of

Nations, or the United Nations after 1944. The British were very worried about a replay of 1918 when the Americans had left Europe to its own devices.[72] The French, and notably Jean Monnet, architect of the first French 'Plan', saw reconstruction as part of a wider desire to bring about European unity from their Algiers exile on, as early as 1943. They also worried about the lack of British involvement of 'civil servants serving the public interest' in Stafford Cripps' British reconstruction working parties and the emphasis on employers and trade unionists. Monnet was worried that the British would use this to return to 'an equilibrium under the shelter of protectionist measures'. Monnet was paradoxically in fact more an advocate of a top-down capitalist reconstruction policy; he wanted in effect to force France to become capitalist. In addition, France did not have a reliable statistical service, a basis for British Keynesian thinking until the INSEE was set up after the war, and Keynesianism also did not really take root in France before the 1960s, and was not centrally taught until then at the *Ecole Nationale d'Administration*, the home of the French elite.[73]

Even more than after the First World War there was a feeling as the war came to an end in Britain that this time there must be a recompense for the sufferings of the world. As Sir William Beveridge put it in 1944 in *Full Employment in a Free Society* there must be a peace that is 'assured and lasting, that men of all nations shall be able in future to live without war and without fear of war'. But for Beveridge the necessary corollary of this was that they 'should be able to work and that they should have an income sufficient for honourable subsistence and maintenance of any dependents when for any reason he or she is unable to work'.[74] This went far further than the concept of a 'land fit for heroes' of Lloyd George's dreams in 1918. It was duplicated as a wish in all the Allied states, admittedly in different ways. The French had their 'Plan', the Rooseveltian 'New Deal' was already in place and in Soviet Russia there was a clear commitment to work for all. The Americans, the French and the British thus again interpreted reconstruction to suit their own national predilections.

Lehman made two important visits to Britain in 1943 and 1944, also meeting French representatives on both occasions. His main purpose of these early contacts was to convert his Allies to a more American way of doing things. Lehman even attended a session of a Committee of the British War Cabinet on 14 April 1943 as well as having extensive further discussions with the British military and civilian authorities. These meetings were the relief equivalent of the meetings between Roosevelt and Churchill on strategic matters. At that War Cabinet Committee Lehman prefaced his remarks by saying that 'the purpose of his visit to London was largely educational', to find out what the British could do to help and to ascertain what the local American and British authorities thought ought to be done after the war in Europe and to prepare the ground for what was to become UNRRA being discussed by Secretary of State Cordell Hull.[75] The minutes of a preliminary meeting even referred to 'what Governor Lehman described as rehabilitation'.[76]

The meetings were not without difficulty. The British and American military and political establishments were very wary of this new development. Even

Lehman admitted that although 'he could envisage the link between UNRRA and OFRRO [he] found it less easy to foresee the liaison between [the] United Nations and United Kingdom organization'. He was also well aware of the difficulties of actually delivering aid on the ground, as the North African experience of 1943 had shown, the first time that Allied forces had delivered help in a concrete way. At this point there was little inter-Allied coordination of any kind on the issue but an 'Inter-Allied Committee' had been set up.[77] This was later to be confirmed as the European Advisory Commission (EAC) after the Moscow Inter-Allied Conference of October 1943, as was UNRRA. The EAC was chaired by US Ambassador to London John Winant, and is generally assessed to have not been a huge success and to have fallen victim to the infighting between the Allies that developed as the Red Army occupied large areas of Eastern Europe.[78]

The idea of both new initiatives was to coordinate the liberation of Europe so that the continent could be bought back to a stable economic and political existence as rapidly and as coherently as possible. The Americans even initially seem to have wanted the EAC to be the basis of a new pan-European entity, but that was never to be in the increasing tensions of the early Cold War. UNRRA still stands as the main concrete realization of this period. The logic underlying it from Lehman (and by extension Roosevelt's and Hull's) was because '[i]t was felt that if relief was brought to the devastated countries in the wake of the armies of liberation, this would shorten the war, and help to bring about stability after the war'.[79]

But it was never an easy process. There were turf wars between different parts of the American governmental structure as well as between the Allies and there were grave problems of supply and authorization for funds that had to be cleared through a sceptical Congress. The British Treasury for example wanted UNRRA to be given a very subsidiary role to that of British agencies. The Treasury was 'inclined to think that the function of UNRRA should be limited to that of determination of requirements' and some vague over-sight of distribution in the recipient countries. Lehman then 'raised the question about the administrative practicability of UNRRA exercising any real control over distribution in liberated areas if supplies are to go directly in the name of the supplying nation to the recipient country'.[80] The whole idea of an international organization beyond the control of national governments was as much worry to national bureaucrats in 1943 as it had been in the 1920s.

In early 1943 the British and American armies themselves found it difficult to coordinate what they called a 'civilian relief programme' although there were moves to do so in time for the 'next continental operation' (i.e. D-Day).[81] After D-Day, the American military was in effect instructed to help UNRRA, and did so with efficiency and in Lehman's words 'cordiall[y]' but with the military having 'special reservations'. One telling exchange between Lehman, Lehman's main British counterpart Sir Frederick Leith Ross[82] and a number of American and British Generals outlined an 'unfortunate incident' in Luxemburg when an UNRRA Medical Liaison Officer had circumvented procedure and upset the 'Military authorities' there. Leith-Ross had '[r]eceived a somewhat different version of the incident, but agreed that UNRRA's representatives would work closer with the military authorities in any area in which they are located'.[83]

These 'special reservations' applied to all British governmental agencies as well. Lehman was told by Sir William Bovenschen, Permanent Under-Secretary for War, of the absolute 'necessity of military support and backing if we are to procure supplies for the civilian population in liberated areas'. This was underlined as it was not possible to say how long the military would have to remain in control of any given area and that the War Office 'had been thinking of straight military administration throughout the period of occupation'.[84] The Ministry of Food was equally desirous of retaining control, this time through a previously established 'Combined Board mechanism for Anglo American allocation of foodstuffs'. In the end Lehman had to content himself with asking that UNRRA 'should serve as the central channel for the submission of total requirements for the civilian economy of all the liberated areas'. This worked for a curious reason – one Ministry of Food official 'was very taken with the idea of UNRRA serving as a claimant before some other world supply agency, which he clearly visualised as being controlled on an Anglo-American basis'. It was this 'Anglo-American basis' that really appealed in other words. But as the discussion evolved it became clear why – 'he clearly wants us to make the provision as an Anglo-American combine rather than giving the other countries access to world markets in the immediate post-war period'.[85] To some in London therefore, UNRRA was seen as a convenient excuse for a transatlantic stitch up of post-war trade. But for the wider liberal agenda of free trade, one being pushed by Cordell Hull since the mid-1930s, it was a carrot that would reinforce the evolving agenda of the Bretton Woods organizations.

The first key theme to emerge from these discussions which essentially conceptualized what was to become the biggest reconstruction effort in history was therefore that the military and state authorities (both British and American) disliked the idea of any kind of civilian or non-governmental agency involvement in what was a war zone and that they also wanted to retain as much Anglo–American control as they could. In British eyes this can be seen as maintaining as much as possible of British influence over the Americans and also to maintain the increasingly threadbare Imperial Preference that had been the trading equivalent of Empire. UNRRA had the opposite advantage for the United States of tying Britain into its new vision of a world without trade barriers, it was not intended to particularly include anyone else at this point. The 'UN' in UNRRA was to be minimized as much as possible as far as the British and Americans were concerned. It got even worse with Lehman describing to Winant by November 1944 'the extremely critical attitude of His Majesty's Government'.[86] Lehman had much persuading to do as have all his successors in such posts in subsequent wartime situations with many other governments including, and perhaps now especially, that of the United States.

The second key theme that emerges from this is the feeling that the British and the Americans were the best parties to collaborate on any kind of rehabilitation activities – the French were not trusted. This is partly derived from a generalized distrust of the Free French in Washington (Roosevelt's dislike of De Gaulle was legendary). There was also the problem that the British were themselves short of food even though Leith-Ross thought that 'the British may have to be prepared to reduce their food reserves and their diet a bit further if the reoccupied areas are to be fed'.[87] There was also the problem of French pride which translated into them not wanting UNRRA interfering on French soil. As early as November 1944 Lehman was told by the French Ambassador to London René Massigli that:

> [T]he French Government can handle everything itself, and that it did not need any special assistance from UNRRA. . . . He added that when a man is weak his pride frequently will not permit him to accept assistance. He needs to stand on his own feet. On the other hand, when a man is strong he will accept the cooperation of his friends.[88]

The liberal press in Washington almost seems to have confirmed French worries at this period of the war – 'Lend-Lease' to France (an extension of the same scheme to Britain) after D-Day was seen as a key reconstruction aid by the *New Republic*,[89] mainly because it would allow the French to supply American armies in Europe. This nexus of attitudes might serve as a warning to all such endeavours to 'help'.

A third key lesson from this was that there was a difference of emphasis on the motivation of different kinds of actors within the reconstruction process. There was a potential central contradiction, as occurred in general between the Americans on one side, who favoured much more decentralized organs and their Allies on the other who were leaning towards ever more nationalization and central control. This was the tendency that Hayek deplored in the *Road to Serfdom*, even if many liberals on both sides of the Atlantic saw his diagnosis as 'seeing hobgoblins under every bed'.[90] The liberal establishment in London and Washington were not yet ready for the kind of anti-statism of the liberals of the 1990s. At this point it really was believed that a global 'New Deal' was possible. But it would certainly be true to say that the European Allies favoured the role of the state more than did Americans. 'The key factor in UNRRA's organizational ability is decentralization', as Lehman had put it; and that Americans resented the role of the International Organizations when it was seen as impinging on American national interest, as the League of Nations had been in 1920 and virtually every international agency has been since.

Within the US Senate there was strong resistance to UNRRA. A letter from Dewey Anderson to Lehman of March 1945 talks of those in Congress 'whom have shown their hostility towards UNRRA. I have the feeling that some of the able men are gathering material which will give you a mighty tough shredding in the months ahead'.[91] The main American opposition was 'nationalist' and from food suppliers who wanted aid to be seen as coming from American sources. Opposition to the UN in the United States tended to come from the smaller business classes, who resented any idea of a strong central state control and even more so of that of foreign international structures. Opposition to such bodies as UNRRA then and now also comes from the Army, and the military establishment in general, who resented the involvement of foreign entities in its decision-making processes. This was probably again not helped by the support given to the Plan by British socialists like Foreign Secretary Ernest Bevin who described UNRRA as 'that great organisation, whose contribution to world recovery will receive its just place in history'.[92]

The Republican Party had generally led this charge, as they did in the 1920s, in the 1940s and now in the early twenty-first century. In the period between 1920 and 1945 the key figure was Herbert Hoover whose vision of American dominance was far more based on the need to cater for the interests of American corporate capitalism than those of the state, even the American state. But the view expressed by the Truman Administration when UNRRA was closed down in 1946 that 'the gravy train has gone around for the last time' is still widespread when United States tax dollars are spent by international organizations.[93] In 1945 this first United Nations agency had to be sold as a buttress to American national interest and trade and it was in that way that it survived as it did. But it must not be forgotten that the United States also closed it down in 1946 when it was seen as having fulfilled that narrow purpose.

Such feeling emerges from a populist and small business consensus that can be seen to have had its origins in the rejection of Wilsonian and Rooseveltian internationalism. But it also illustrates the need for IOs in the process. Republican and corporatist opposition to reconstruction efforts eventually led to compromises based on practical considerations. So the United States Army was the main distributor of aid in Europe until 1945, and UNRRA's activity was necessarily limited while fighting was taking place, as is the case in Iraq today. But at some point the Army has to give way to civilian bodies. The question is always going to be about the timing and manner of any such hand-over. Lehman's and UNRRA's line to counter such criticism was always that the main aim was '[h]elping people to help themselves, which underlies the programme'.[94] He worked tirelessly with all of UNRRA's detractors and it unlikely that UNRRA would have been given the time of day in London, Paris or beyond had it not been for Roosevelt's personal imprimatur. Each such operation has to have a Lehman fighting its corner in Washington DC and, given the current overwhelming economic and military hegemony of the United States, this is now ultimately far more important than what the rest of the world thinks.

The Marshall Plan[95]

The sheer audacity of the Marshall Plan (more properly titled the 'European Recovery Program') is still astonishing. It envisaged disbursing $6–$7 billion a year for three years to reconstruct Europe's devastated infrastructure and industry. This is the equivalent in today's dollars of $60–$70 billion (a factor of 10 to allow for inflation) per annum. By way of comparison the Washington agreement of the early 1990s envisaged giving the former Soviet Union $20 billion in financial help to make it capitalist. Its clear aim was the promotion of European integration to avoid the problems of reparation that were discussed at length in Chapter 3. Although Marshall's speech of 5 June 1947 announced that aid did not carry an explicit *quid pro quo* for European integration, others both assumed and insisted in practice that it did – especially George Kennan and Charles E. Bohlen. Neither was it intended, initially at least, to exclude the USSR.[96]

The defeat of Germany and Japan at the end of the Second World War was a clear victory for liberal ideas of freedom and democracy, at least in what became the West and the key player in terms of planning and resources was the United States. But if Europe and the world were to be reconstructed after the war then the question was how, and on whose terms?[97] In Europe many feared that the United States would do as it had in 1919 and leave Europe to sort out its own problems of reconstruction. There was widespread recognition among British liberals in particular that the United States had to be the 'keystone of world prosperity' and that 'if we fail to handle our affairs intelligently we may drag down the world structure, as we did in 1931'.[98] The British had noted from early on the reticence in some quarters for the United States to stay in Europe after hostilities ceased. A 1943 Chatham House report on Congress stated baldly that '[t]he belief that the United States, in its own interest, should take the lead in promoting economic progress everywhere, was vigorously championed by Mr Wallace [Roosevelt's Vice President], whose speeches gave rise to widely divergent reactions'.[99]

The great historian of the Marshall Plan, Michael Hogan, view is also that the American commitment to European reconstruction was not clear before the end of the war. Certainly the finally implemented plan of 1948 was by no means seen as likely until the Cold War began. From his perspective of 1947, before the Marshall Plan was inaugurated by the Foreign Assistance Act in the Spring of 1948, most American attention was concentrated on British plans to create a 'Middle Kingdom' made up of Western Europe and the British Commonwealth. The Anglo–French Treaty of Dunkirk of 1947 can be seen in this context for example. As seen from Washington, Britain was thereby trying to distance itself and proximate Europe from the United States and the Soviet Union.

It is thus hardly surprising that Britain was looking to reconstruct some sort of alliance system that would allow for American absence, even though it was quite clear that this would prove difficult. Hogan is thus right to say that 1947 was the date for real interest being shown in European integration within the American political elite across the board. It is difficult to disagree with his statement that: 'the Marshall Plan can be seen as a logical extension of domestic- and foreign-policy developments going back to the first American effort to reconstruct war-torn Europe [in 1919]'. It was the onset of the Cold War that in a real sense 'activated' American thinking on Europe. Kennan put it characteristically – the Marshall Plan 'finally broke through the confusion of wartime pro-Sovietism, wishful thinking, anglophobia and self-righteous punitivism . . . and placed us on what was, and for six years remained, a constructive and sensible path'. This 'path' was a long term commitment to Western Europe for reasons, mainly, of clearly perceived American national interest. It is not at all obvious that the United States would not have left a defeated Germany (and a humbled France) to their own devices had the Soviet Union not frightened President Truman into tying the notions of 'reconstruction' and 'Cold War' together, a link made in the title of a recent book on Germany in the period 1948–61.[100]

But it was not universally admired. The same corporatist interest that had emphasized the need for American led and run international programmes was hostile to US taxpayers' dollars being used by foreigners, and was present in The Marshall Aid discussions. Former President Hoover led this opposition. Governor Lehman complained that 'Mr Hoover's statement yesterday [to the Congressional committee discussing the Plan] was certainly anything but helpful and I am afraid that he may serve as the rallying point for those who oppose the Plan'.[101] The same people who had objected to UNRRA within the United States now objected to what some saw as its successor. What changed their mind, and arguably changed all United States thinking about reconstruction, was the fear of Soviet expansionism. Marshall Aid was sold to a sceptical Congress as being a key part of 'creat[ing] a stable and productive Europe, whose economic and security needs would be tied together by market forces and liberalized trade, and guided by strong supranational organizations' but also serving wider American aims of stemming the tide of Communism.

Recent scholarship by Sami Abouzahr indicates that The United States was even willing to sink its differences with the French in order to encourage them to stand up to communism in Indochina. French Prime Minister Georges Bidault recognized that Marshall Aid would help him to 'avoid the abandonment of French positions [in Indochina]'. Abouzahr has found that by the Battle of Dien Bien Phu in 1954 'the US was financing 80% of the French war effort' and the money provided by Marshall Aid was also in effect propping up the shaky French political system of the Fourth Republic. Ironically the support for France in Indochina failed completely and may have damaged the cementing of France's recovery after 1945. If France had been allowed to lose Indochina well before 1954, it may well have had a better reconstruction than it in fact did have.[102]

Neither was the Marshall Plan universally admired by British or American liberals. Although Gilbert Murray by early 1947 was sure that Western Europe had to be strengthened against 'the aggressive display of Russia', Robert Cecil was sure that 'when you speak of strengthening West Europe to resist Russia are you not on very dangerous ground? How can you persuade Soviet minds that such a policy is not anti-Russian? Indeed it is. ... The Americans seem to be having one of their fits of hysteria'. Equally he was convinced that 'reconstruction' would not work in Europe '[b]ecause Europe never has been either a Political or Economic whole. ... It looks to me as if all this might work out as into scrapping the United Nations in favour of a new Alliance, based primarily on Western Europe – which seems madness.'[103]

The Marshall Plan certainly excluded the Eastern part of Europe by making the Soviet Union feel excluded from its aims. Western historians of the Cold War like Melvyn P. Leffler and Eastern historians like Mikhail Narinskii now agree that Marshall's intention was that 'the east European countries would take part in the rehabilitation programme on the condition that they alter their almost exclusive pro-Soviet economic orientation in favour of broad European integration'. Moscow could not accept this so the Plan signalled 'the failure of peace in Europe' until 1990.[104]

Conclusions

The end of the Second World War saw the most important episode of thinking about, and acting out the idea and practice of reconstruction. It is the base on which all else in the field is still built. But it must also be remembered that the idea and the practice in all the major cases we have studied after 1918 in this chapter were historically located. There is no one discourse of reconstruction any more than there is one for reparation or any of our other 'r's. None the less there is a certain evolution, with some lessons being learnt and others forgotten. This Conclusion will aim to sum up what the main ones were by 1948 or so.

If an examination is being made of the results of the war on liberal thinking the record after 1945 is obviously mixed. There was a surge of interest in socialistic ideas such as planning, which was famously attacked by Friedrich Hayek in his *Road to Serfdom*. But many believed that the war had shown that the route to follow was a much more involved state, led by Keynesian principles of state intervention to stimulate demand. Liberal capitalism had barely survived the 1930s. The main impulse in Britain was for social justice and employment, not for what were seen as a return to the vagaries of the free market and the oppressing power of 'cartels'. On the other hand, in the West there was revulsion about extreme ideology, be it from left or right. The Hitlerian *Neueordnung* had been a disaster for all those who experienced it. As Mark Mazower has put it: '[f]ascism became the first major ideology to suffer conclusive defeat at the hands of the history it claimed to have mastered'. As a corollary, '[p]eople re-discovered democracy's quiet virtues – that space it left for privacy, the individual and the family'.[105] They re-discovered the delights of liberalism.

Reconstruction, 1950–90

The Cold War froze the notion of reconstruction in the way that it froze much else. The Marshall Plan has provided a paradigm for all post-1945 reconstruction efforts until 1990 and has been evoked since whenever 'reconstruction' is mentioned. It assumed the need to keep sovereignty intact, although in practice it created client states for the West on all continents, tying Western Europe firmly into an Atlanticist orbit from which it is only now tentatively starting to emerge. It was also copied by the USSR whose satellites have either ceased to exist as they were, such as Ethiopia – now divided off from Eritrea, or have effectively ceased to be independent, or whom have been forced to compromise in some way (Vietnam, Libya) or are/were 'rogue states' (Iraq, North Korea). On both sides of the Iron Curtain, aid was given in return for military favours (a classic example being the Cubans in Angola, Ethiopia and Mozambique). But we can assert with a fair degree of assuredness that the real apotheosis of the idea after 1948 has been seen since the end of the Cold War, the focus of the next chapter.

Leadership

The key dilemma after all reconstructions efforts has been, and will continue to be, the question of leadership. In 1919 American commentators saw Wilson going to Paris because 'European statesmen will need the help of the new world in order to restore the balance of the old'. Had the Paris Peace Conference been held in Washington instead of Paris maybe the world would have had a Washington Peace Conference more akin to the Second World War conferences at Bretton Woods and San Francisco. The United States was able to disown the Versailles Treaty not only because Wilson had not got his way over it but because it did not feel the ownership necessary to sell the idea to American public opinion. A contemporary liberal complaint about the Treaty still makes for interesting reading:

> A hundred years from now the young American citizen will study the policy and read the utterances of President Wilson, and his heart will glow with the feeling that in her third time of trial America again gave proof not only of material greatness but of moral grandeur. He will not know that an obscene clamour arose in these great days, demanding that the civil population of a vanquished state be left to perish in famine and anarchy.[106]

In 1918 the main enduring memory in the United States of reconstruction was still that of the Civil War. As Menand has pointed out the majority of the American elite of 1918 had cut its political teeth on the lessons of that war and its aftermath, not that of 1914–18. Cramer suggests that the reconstruction effort after 1865 may even have created, in the radical republicanism of Thaddeus Stevens, a 'populism that was both aggressive and idealistic. It was aggressive insofar as was a project to destroy the power and institutions of the southern elites. Otherwise reactionary southern interests might overwhelm the north and win the peace' He pursues this point by suggesting that 'perhaps American expansionism, carried forth by a coalition of material political interests and sustained by an ideology of progressive democratisation and freedom, has its kernel in the North's republican reconstruction zeal towards the South.' But Cramer realizes that this dream stayed as just that for the nineteenth and much of the twentieth century. The South did remerge as an 'unreconstructed' [my word] and underdeveloped part of the United States and stayed that way, economically and politically, until the late twentieth century. But reconstruction became part of the American miscellany that was then, as now, 'fiercely contested' as idea and as practice.[107]

So the main point about the development of the notion of reconstruction in the period until 1948 must be that it had to overcome the stigma of both extremes of the historical and ideological divide. From the left came the criticism that reconstruction was little better than carpet-bagging: a cover for exploitation. From the right came the accusation identified by Oscar Cox that it was not enough to just appeal to arguments such as 'general humanitarian appeal [or] [i]t is our Christian duty' or even to practical appeal ('it will prevent the spread of bolshevism'). Defenders of reconstruction as a policy option would also have to get round the arguments that '[t]here are more pressing problems at home' and the 'Don Quixote' argument that this was sheer sentimentalism and the United States was 'attempting an impossible task'.[108] As the next chapter will demonstrate this is still the problem today. Leadership in reconstruction efforts will always be difficult to exercise in a liberal state.

5 Reconstruction after the Marshall Plan

There is no country in the world that the United States cannot destroy on its own. There is also no country in the world that the United States can reconstruct on its own.

Tom Freedman, BBC News, 19 November 2003

The most expensive of reconstructions is cheaper than the cheapest of wars.

President Bill Clinton on Kosovo, 1999

Introduction

The above quotations illustrate what had become clear in the era immediately after the Second World War – the United States has become, and remains, the country most identified with the idea that economic, political and even ideological reconstruction is the way to embed liberal ideas in a defeated illiberal state. To be sure, the nature of reconstruction as an idea has developed in significant ways since the end of the Marshall Plan. Often that has to do with the changing nature of the domestic liberal polities that have indulged in the practice. But it is difficult to disagree with the view of that great admirer of Woodrow Wilson's ideas, Michael Mandelbaum, that 'this is the stage of reconstruction', the apotheosis of Wilson's ideal of a world where liberal ideas could conquer the world and put an end to war.[1]

But there is a less warm hearted interpretation of the developments of the past decade or so since the end of the Soviet Union. In the post-Cold War period, holding out the possibility of future reconstruction has become a popular way of encouraging the population of a country (Iraq and Serbia are good examples in the 1990s and since) to overthrow their rulers in return for which they will get lots of aid, and without which they will only get more destruction. It is a form of economic statecraft, a stick as much as a carrot. Equally, the targets have been non-Western and illiberal states like the Former Yugoslavia (FRY), Cuba, North Korea, Iraq, all 'rogue states' in the definition of the United States and most of the liberal West. Can we therefore not see current reconstruction attempts as a form of (perhaps enlightened) liberal imperialism?

One obvious link between the era of Wilson and that of George W. Bush lies in the growing curve of American power over the last 90 years or so. And one way in which reconstruction has become an increasingly vital part of the world system is the way that it has become increasingly linked into what Eliot Cohen calls 'the American way of war'.[2] Reconstruction has become the buzzword of the American liberal world order. This chapter will examine how this norm has been used in thinking about post-Cold War conflicts.

Implicitly linked to this is the developing agenda that has moved from a concentration on the state as the key actor to that of the need to make the world safe for capitalism, free trade and flows of capital, the kind of agenda that dominated British liberal thinking of the nineteenth century and that has been taken up by the United States in the latter part of the twentieth. It has always also had within it a notion of the primacy of individual human rights, but this is an agenda that can really be seen to have flowered only since the end of the Cold War. A recent very illuminating example of this thinking emerged from an interview with Chris Patten, the EU's Commissioner for External Affairs: '[t]o put it at its simplest, countries that make good neighbours, the countries that are best to do business with, the countries that are easiest to invest in, are those that treat their citizens most decently'. Also key to this contemporary liberal thinking is the question of 'morality', by which is meant in essence the consideration of human rights at the top of any foreign policy agenda. As Patten put it in his characteristic and refreshingly pungent style, 'it is bilge to think that expedience and morality in the conduct of foreign policy are in different corners'.[3] A nineteenth-century liberal would have agreed with this, but principally to then affirm that expedience would often have to be the primary consideration, there being so many breaches of morality it was necessary to deal with. The key liberal dilemma has always been to decide when intervention will work, and how it should be attempted given the restraints of reality.

The chapter will therefore examine a number of fundamental themes related to reconstruction that have remained from previous eras or emerged in the years since the Marshall Plan. Until 1990 the world was arguably the same as it had been in 1950, but there is widespread belief that wars, and therefore the post-war aspirations of the victors, have been changed by the twin phenomena of declining state power and globalization. I will therefore look at some of the major examples of reconstruction after 1991, and especially that of the Former Soviet Union, the Former Yugoslavia, Afghanistan and Iraq.

The changing meaning of the term reconstruction

We can also point to a developing belief that if there is to be a lasting peace there must also be an acceptance by the defeated party that they must change their ways and become liberals not just in the political but also in the economic sense. This has marked a shift in liberal thinking from that prevailing in the early to mid-nineteenth century to that prevailing after the First World War and more generally in the twentieth century. In effect there was a shift from the

Cobdenite and Millean view that non-intervention was the norm that must be followed under most, if not all, circumstances, to a Wilsonian and Rooseveltian liberal view that intervention was sometimes necessary if it meant that you could induce long term political change in a recalcitrant war-like country by economic means. To end a war has come to mean not only the defeat of one party, but also the *transformation* of that party. The fact that the victor has generally been a liberal state or a combination of them has in recent times meant that this transformation must be towards accepting the rules of liberal practice.

But it is also important to stress the continuing themes of reconstruction. As we have seen in our historical 'snapshots' there was already before 1945 a huge debate about, and a contrast, between one state/IO delivery of reconstruction and private/public sector delivery. This has only increased in recent times but it has always been there. What is striking is how the historical experience of reconstruction has become part of a developing discourse about it. In the 2003 war in Iraq officials in the United States Government constantly made reference to the experience of reconstruction in Germany and Japan after the Second World War. For example, in the aftermath of the war, when American casualties in the reconstruction phase began to exceed those in the 'war' itself, Secretary of Defense Donald Rumsfeld used many explicit analogies, as in his dismissal of American casualties as very similar to those that had been caused by the remnants of the Nazi forces after Germany's defeat in 1945. President Bush was said to have spent some time reading a book entitled *The Conquerors* about the American pacification of Germany in 1945.[4] This tendency to make such comparisons has been attacked by historians as both inaccurate and a-historical, but it is important as it illustrates a perceived need by key Western political figures to hang their more controversial actions on the hat-stand of an unimpeachable moral past.[5]

It should be noted that the term reconstruction that I use here has become more common in recent years, although current expressions which cover the same area include 'post-conflict rehabilitation' or 'peace building'. Reconstruction remains the term of choice, but they all essentially have the same practical meaning, even if the main term has naturally evolved in a new historical context. Roger McGinty has even introduced the concept of the 'pre-war reconstruction of post-war Iraq'. For him reconstruction now 'aims to deal simultaneously with the direct effects of the conflict and with latent development issues'.[6]

So it can be asserted that liberal states, often organized within the UN (but not exclusively as the current Iraq episode shows), plan the post-war situation both during and after a war with a clear idea in mind. They wish to reconstruct the country in question along what can only be termed 'liberal' lines and the models they draw on are those that were described in the last chapter. The meaning of reconstruction has thus evolved from one of the reconstruction of economies along the lines desired by the local political elites to one that makes it quite clear that this reconstruction must be 'structurally sound'. This in turn means it must be along the lines approved by the largely Western economists that dominate the private financial and capital markets and the international financial institutions alike.

As McGinty points out the post-1989 situation has led to modifications about the way that reconstruction is viewed. The first of these harks back to one of the elements that were discussed in the previous chapter of this book. The military machine does not want peacekeepers or humanitarian workers wandering around on the field of battle when fighting is still going on, a key concern about UNRRA as we saw. Second, with the 'new' wars that we are now experiencing, the media has highlighted the problems of shattered infrastructure, etc. in which such workers have to operate, even if McGinty is right to say that there is nothing much 'new' about such damage. Indeed, even at its worst, Sarajevo in 1994 was never as bad as Berlin or Dresden in 1945. What has changed is the presence of the media to point out the full horrors of war's aftermath. Third, most of the post-war reconstructions now take place against the background of 'ethnic' war. Finally, and this really is 'new', the presence of large numbers of unofficial NGOs working alongside the United Nations has led to much thinking about how the IOs can usefully work with the NGO community.[7] McGinty also points to what we might call an emerging paradigm within the IOs that 'the constituent parts of humanitarian assistance (relief, reintegration, reconstruction, etc.) should be viewed as a totality, 'co-existing synergistically', rather than as a liner progression, and that contexts are 'inherently contextual'.[8] To put it more simply, are liberal states *prepared during the war for the reconstruction that will come after it?*

This was also true of the UNRRA period, so it might be argued that we have evolution within an already existing set of concepts and practices rather than radical disjuncture. The choice of case studies embedded within this chapter is intended to show that evolution from a relatively neutral economic mind-set to one that is more overtly liberal capitalist. The contradictions of this became most apparent in the treatment of the post-Soviet economies, and especially Russia, whose economic and political trajectory since 1991 are probably the greatest test to which the notion of post-conflict reconstruction has ever been subjected. But it also collides most strongly with the belief systems in place in some of the most recent examples of reconstruction, notably in Afghanistan and Iraq, where at the time of writing there is clear and persistent opposition to such efforts on ideological as much as practical grounds. As Terry Eagleton has said '"[w]hat everybody knows without knowing it" is not a bad definition of ideology', a culture-based concept 'tend[ing] to appeal to custom not reason'.[9] Many in the Middle East see reconstruction as an ideology of Western intervention, even imperialism. And one of the main objections that Islamic (but also nationalist) militants in these areas have is to what is perceived as an over-emphasis on individuals and on capitalist practices. In short, the bearers of reconstruction are seen not only as Infidels but also as interlopers.

As we have seen, the language of reconstruction has always been redolent of both political liberal agendas and liberal economic reform. However since the end of the Cold War this has become more explicit. Hence a 2003 review of reconstruction accepts that the reconstruction agenda is often accompanied by, and interacts with, the agendas of economic and political reform, but it follows this by talking of 'national' actors [who] find themselves affected by changes in public spending, relative process and market opportunities.[10]

'Reform' in the new context of the post Cold War era usually means the creation of liberal capitalist institutions and this requires the resettlement of refugees and the demobilization of erstwhile enemy troops, in a delicate 'chicken and egg' relationship. Which should come first, or how should they be 'sequenced'? As Tony Addison says, IGOs from the UN (UNHCR, etc.) have to try and carry out the reconstruction agenda, which he defines as 'building peace and securing political ability', as well as shoring up the state and 'rebuilding basic economic and social infrastructure' before other IGOs, like the World Bank, move in to carry out the 'reform' programme.[11] But, as he points out, the two processes cannot necessarily always be in this sequence.

For much of the debate on reconstruction in the post 1990 period has hinged around the concept of 'value for money'. If the powerful liberal states of the West are to maximize their 'victory' in the Cold War how can they ensure that the money, materiel and men (most peacekeepers are men although that is changing fast) are well used in their collective interest and in the interests of those they are trying to help? In many ways this debate is often the same as that over 'aid'. Conservatives will often agree with P. J. O'Rourke's dismissal of the UN and NGOs 'shovelling money out of the back of a truck'.[12] Liberals would agree that much of the so-called 'aid' does not in fact get to its destination. In the 1990s the International Community pledged more than $100 billion in reconstruction aid donated from Cambodia, through much of Africa (Eritrea, Ethiopia, Rwanda and South Africa) to Bosnia and Kosovo. Not all of it arrived, except as 'good intentions'.[13]

So is the problem one of 'failed states'? Some writers have even talked of 'zones of turbulence'[14] to describe vast areas of the globe where the basic rules of 'civility' no longer run riot. They exist both within states (like in parts of South Africa) or across whole areas of continents, like the Great Lakes of Central Africa where at least five states (Burundi, Namibia, Rwanda, Uganda and Zimbabwe) are involved in the predation of one ex-Belgian colony (the Democratic Republic of Congo, formerly Zaire).

Whatever the context, and these contexts are now far more complicated then they were even in 1945, even if the war has 'ended' (usually since 1990 a civil war), there is an imperative need to rebuild infrastructure (bridges, roads, schools, etc.) and institutions. This latter is necessary to rebuild the norms that make a society tick and embedding them in what would now be called rules of 'human rights' and more broadly the rule of law. As in the past actions have to be taken by national governments and IOs (UN, EU) as well as by NGOs, a more recent development. In these circumstances Mary Kaldor says that 'reconstruction is both a pre-war and a post-war strategy, aimed at prevention and at cure'. Hence:

reconstruction has to mean, first and foremost, the rebuilding of political authorities, even if only at the local level, and the reconstruction of civil society in the sense both of law and order and of providing the conditions in which alternative political grouping can mobilise.

This requires what Kaldor calls a 'focus . . . on zones of civility so that they can act as models encouraging similar initiatives in other places'. She admits this is a tall order, as it requires demobilizing an economy based on war, the creation of jobs, education and public services and economic activity. It is hard to do but '[i]n so far as reconstruction is a strategy for peace it has to provide economic security and hope for the future so as to remove the atmosphere of fear in which people live, and to offer, young people especially, an alternative livelihood to the army or the mafia'.[15]

The aim of this is what Luc Reychler calls 'sustainable peacebuilding', and it can therefore be said to now be the norm since 1990. Reychler defines this as having as its aim being 'to transform conflicts constructively and to create a sustainable peace environment'. In itself 'it refers to all the efforts required on the way to the creation of a sustainable peace zone: imagining a peaceful future, conducting an overall needs assessment, developing a coherent peace plan, and designing an effective implementation of the plan.'[16]

Both Kaldor and Reychler would quote as very good recent examples East Timor, Bosnia and Kosovo and here some progress can be said to have been made in creating Kaldor's zones of 'civility'. But the problems have of course even wider dimensions than creating such 'zones'. The end of the Cold War has bought a host of states into the reconstruction 'net' that would never have been seen as problems previously. Russia is an obvious example, but we must also cite Iraq as emblematic of the huge problems that are now faced. This has meant the reconstruction of whole societies previously thought of as 'developed', like the former Soviet Union. Large international organizations have been set up for this purpose, like the European Bank for Reconstruction and Development (EBRD).[17] There has also been a growing realization that it encompasses everything from old style reconstruction to election monitoring, the creation of new polities, even societies.[18] Reconstruction has become a global task with complex local implications derided as 'imperialism' by many of its supposed beneficiaries, or subject to great ethical dilemmas when Western public opinion is faced with the sight of starving children and seemingly corrupt local governments. The result is usually that in any given case the ethical dilemma of whether to intervene, and subsequently to 'reconstruct', is based on the political climate of the liberal states towards that case. Hence we will now look at some of the key examples of how those dilemmas have played out in practice.

Post-1990 case studies of reconstruction

Russia post-1990

The response of the international community, and more especially of the West, to the collapse of the Soviet Union has been muddled. Initial hopes of a 'Big Bang', as proposed by the then Finance Minister Anatoli Chubais, were predicated on a massive de-nationalization of Soviet assets. This led to massive factory closures, attendant social problems and a huge drop in overall GDP as the military industrial complex which had provided (by some estimates) over 50 per cent of Soviet production was massively reduced. In Georgia the decline was reported at 77 per cent in the period 1989 to 1994. Think tanks in the West, especially in Washington DC, have expended huge effort in trying to work out what the likely outcome of the collapse was and is likely to be and to try and get some under-standing of what this might mean. The activities of the Carnegie Endowment and of the Kennan Institute are most illuminating for what might be called a liberal reaction.

Liberals naturally welcomed not only the collapse of the Stalinist state but also the collapse of centrally planned economies, to see both replaced hopefully by democracy and the rule of law and by capitalism. Kaldor's model (for example) approximates much of this ambition, as do many of the utterances of the World Bank and IMF in the early 1990s. But they also agree on the links between any such attempts at reconstruction and the economic and even psychological reactions of the Russian economy and people to what they see as intrusive globalization

So even though the Carnegie's Anders Åslund[19] has questioned the extent of the true economic 'collapse', as he sees no reason to believe Soviet statistics upon which the calculations were made, he also believes that the problem with Russia has not been the over-use of a 'Big Bang' but the painfully slow nature of structural reform, which has 'reinforced rent-seeking and prolonged stagna-tion'.[20] Other Carnegie scholars, like Yuri Federov, have pointed to the way in which the pattern of reform has reinforced the role of certain groups in Russian society and see this as the factor that has slowed up democracy and the growth of a real civil society. In order to persuade the Russian population to embrace the idea of democracy Federov believes that it is not so much a question of 'building of appropriate governmental institutions and civil society orga-nizations' as in changing 'cultural attitudes' – what he calls the 'Russian psyche'.[21]

Those who had long observed the workings of the Soviet Union, as in the Kennan Institute, have none the less been very cautious in their judgements about what was likely to be the result of its collapse in 1991. Director Blair Ruble saw 'reason for optimism' in 1991 as 'an authentic sense of communal accom-plishment pervaded the air of Russia's great cities, and new political leaders and institutions gained momentum and legitimacy. The future is unlikely to be the past.' By 1993 Ruble was observing that:

> Russia today is in the throes of reinventing itself as a state. What will the boundaries of this new state be? How democratic will it be? Which social groups or institutional interests will predominate? How centralized will state institutions be? These questions are, of course, unanswerable at this juncture.

Equally, as Ruble reminded us in 1997 'it is extremely misleading to consider post-socialist transitions solely within the experiences of the former Soviet Union. ... The challenge ... is to discern which phenomena are local manifestations of global forces and which are uniquely connected with the peculiar experience of Soviet Power.'[22]

For liberal governments and opinion in the West the problem has been as to whether Russia will be the ultimate proof of the democratic peace theory. One of the reasons that the United States is seen as having neglected to fully address the problems of the break-up of the former Yugoslavia in the early 1990s was because of the sheer importance of the collapse in the former Soviet Union. That this has not had worse consequences for global stability may be said to indicate a much greater success for the West than the initial 'failure' in the Balkans.

In the 1990s a twin, and contradictory, liberal impulse can be said to have been played out. Either, as many scholars and political figures have argued over the last hundred years, we should let Russia develop in its own way, giving credit (in both senses of the term) for a slow but steady transition to capitalism, or we should guide it firmly. The assistance given by such new organizations as the European Bank for Reconstruction and Development (EBRD) has extended the principle of conditionality to include in effect not only the acceptance of capitalism but also Western models of democratization and 'governance'.[23] The reasoning behind the first impulse has always been that Russia cannot just be forced to join the West without creating huge unemployment and cultural dislocation, as Federov indicates. The evidence for this can be seen in popular attitudes across Eastern and Central Europe, where many citizens have seen the rise of political democratization and capitalism more as the advent of 'Burglar Capitalism', not freedom. The reasoning behind the second has again been part of the need for 'value for money' and the need to do the job quickly, as slow development will just not work. We have certainly seen political instability, but was that not inevitable? How can the judgement be made?

In a sense it has always been thus. In Bolshevik times there was a constant debate about whether there could be, in Lloyd George's famous term, 'civilization though trade' leading to diplomatic recognition or President Herbert Hoover's ideal of 'as much trade as we can do with them' but no recognition. After the Second World War this was translated into 'Containment', or 'roll back' or the opposite development of some form of 'detente' such as West Germany's Chancellor Willi Brandt's celebrated *Ostpolitik*. It might be argued that Russia is now different, but many have their doubts. These doubts have led to contradictory signals being given to Russia in terms of economic help and political acceptance.[24] The difficulty of trusting Russia is still there but to ignore it would be suicide. Under President Boris Yeltsin the expansion of capitalism meant the extension of the role of the 'Oligarchs', or even what can collectively be called the *mafiya*. President Putin has expelled one of the most prominent of these, Boris Beresovsky, and jailed another, Mikhail Khodorovsky. If Russia is to be the key test case of the merits of reconstruction for promoting liberalism the jury is still decidedly out.

The European Union and the Balkans

Bosnia

The war in the Former Yugoslavia figures large in the liberal conscience for a number of reasons, many of which are outlined in Chapter 6 (on War Crimes Tribunals). The response of the international community to the horrors of that war, and especially the response of liberal Western European states, was much criticized for being too little, too late. As James Gow put it, this was a 'triumph of the lack of will', or, in the words of Brendan Simms, Britain and Europe's 'unfinest hour' faced with the greatest European conflict since 1945.[25] After the Dayton Agreement of 1995 it was clear that the European Union (EU), in particular, would have to make up for its seeming dilatory caution during the war by doing something after it. From 1991 to the end of 1999 the EU has estimated that it had disbursed almost 4.5 billion euros 'including humanitarian and macro-financial aid' to the Balkan region.[26]

Dayton and the subsequent EU agreement in Rome of February 1996 are constantly evoked in EU documents as representing the 'foundations of financial aid for reconstruction in the former Yugoslavia'. There are also constant references to the belief that 'lasting peace cannot be built by military means alone, but must be founded on a genuine commitment to reconciliation, and supported by effective administration of justice, corresponding public order, economic reconstruction and the creation of democratic societies'.[27] But how was this to be done? The answer on a broader front was the Stability Pact for Southeastern Europe signed in June 1999 at a Cologne meeting of the foreign ministers of the EU and their counterparts from all the Balkan states with the exception of the rump (of the then) Yugoslavia (now known as Serbia and Montenegro). Its origins were also in a liberal think tank, in this case the influential Centre for European Policy Studies in Brussels. It evidently took a hard look at the Marshall Plan, hence the emphasis on 'stability' which one of the Pact's admirers sees as the key result of the Marshall Plan: 'what worked in Western Europe was a system that fostered reconstruction (and then sustained growth), liberalization and integration. It was clear from the beginning that the three should work together.'[28] The basis had to be regional, again a Marshall insight even if, again like with Marshall, the 'Stability and Association Agreements' were bilateral to check that individual states were complying both with technical requirements and with the underlying rationale of the programmes implemented.

An admirer of the Pact, Franz-Lothar Altman, describes it as having as its main rationale a centring

> on economic development aid as the key instrument for diverting people's energies from conflicting interests to reconstruction and social stability in the individual countries as well as throughout the region.

This was a classic attempt at creating a zone of 'Kantian peace' through what Altman approvingly quotes as 'removing the environment in which nationalists and demagogues can thrive'.[29] The emphasis on the liberalization of trade, economic integration and good governance are here seen as classic ingredients in the reconstruction mix. Liberal market reforms and free and fair elections were seen as the twin drivers of this process. So the Pact was clearly liberal in impulse.

Previous to the Stability Pact there were other important EU initiatives linked into the wider EU imperative of 'enlargement', bringing in a number of East European, some of them former Soviet, states (the Baltic Republics) and beginning the idea that the Balkans themselves should be integrated into the expanding European 'zone of peace'.[30] There was constant reference in Commission documents and discussion in the European Parliament during the period of the late 1990s linking the need for economic reconstruction and the need for free and fair elections – none of the plan would work without all of it working was a constant refrain, as was the 'indispensable role of NGOs in building up a civil society in all states of the former Yugoslavia. A widely diffused *Staff Working Paper* of 1997 emphasized this as a way of putting pressure on Balkan states to transform themselves not only economically but also politically. [31]

This was operationalized in a series of initiatives that were summarized in EU actions under various titles: CARA, PHARE and the more appropriately named 'OBNOVA (renewal) Reconstruction Programmes for the Former Yugoslavia'.[32] There is no space here to enter into detail about these but they bear all the hallmarks of the kind of civil society thinking previously discussed in the work of writers like Kaldor. In the enabling Proposal to the EU Council in April 1996 the wording makes clear that the aim of these programmes was:

> to foster reconciliation between the various parties and prevent any resurgence of fighting [and] special attention should be accorded to operations aimed at achieving economic social objectives, in particular employment, the restoration of civil society and the return and reintegration of refugees and displaced persons.[33]

The only other general point we can emphasize about these initiatives by the EU (in the main) has been the persistent use of the carrot of reconstruction to encourage the development of proper democratic activity. In the Dayton Agreement one of the key clauses was that free and fair elections must be held before substantial economic aid was provided.

In Bosnia this has not really worked according to plan, in spite of the guidance and leadership exercised under almost impossible conditions by the OSCE high Commissioner for Bosnia, Lord Paddy Ashdown. The post-Dayton political landscape has seen a hardening of nationalist attitudes, with a virtual 'cantonization' being implemented by the voting populations of the Croat, Muslim and Serb-dominated regions of Bosnia. There is no real central government except the High Commissioner. Ashdown himself has been more sanguine, as he expressed the view in October 2003 that he is 'on the right course' to 'trying to build the checks and balances of a European state'. This speech, records the *Financial Times*, was 'greeted with silence and long faces' from the locals who heard it. The article spells out that even the liberal opposition of the early 1990s in Bosnia is now relegated to a small and ineffectual rump of Bosnian politics.[34] The EU, which took over the running of Bosnian 'protectorate' in 2004, believes that it can successfully integrate Bosnia into a zone of peace.

There are some reasons for optimism. In Croatia the results for a liberal agenda have been spectacularly better as the end of the Franjo Tudjman era in the late 1990s removed the taint of 'war criminal' from Croatia's governing leadership and led to EU cooperation with Croatia in the framework of the Stability Pact.[35] Serbia's democratic future is much more fragile but at the time of writing still not hopeless from a liberal perspective. Bosnia still looks like the hardest liberal nut to crack open with the tools of reconstruction but it would be illiberal to say that this cannot yet happen.

Kosovo

In Kosovo after the debacle of the Rambouillet Conference bombing campaign and subsequent retreat of Yugoslav troops from it in 1999, the paradoxes of trying to head off a humanitarian catastrophe and then to undertake reconstruction became blindingly evident. As Smith and Latawski have pointed out, the mismatch between the political aims (liberate the people of Kosovo) and the military means (bombing above the range of Serb anti-aircraft fire at 30,000 feet) of the chief protagonists were obvious from the outset. For them 'it is ultimately unclear how or why NATO succeeded'.[36] The intervention led to Serbia expelling huge numbers of Kosovars, the United Nations was split, with this being the first intervention after 1990 not justified by a Security Council Resolution. It was then desperately needed for the reconstruction effort; an acceptance embodied in a UN Security Council resolution of 10 June 1999 after the fighting had stopped.

The EU immediately extended its programmes to the Kosovo theatre, taking a 'leading role' in the wider UN effort.[37] A large proportion of this was channelled through the European Community Humanitarian Office (ECHO), disbursing 400 of its roughly 800 million euro budget in Kosovo alone in 2000.[38] The OBNOVA programme was also adapted in November 1999 to focus on Kosovo, with over half of its 284 million euro budget going in that direction. The main aim of this was again democratization. We might question whether the main *result* has rather been to make Kosovo a protectorate of the UN, NATO and the EU?

We cannot claim that so far this has created a self-sustaining peace. Hence, for example, in Bosnia the real task is how to stop fighting re-emerging by bringing communities to transformation. The UN 'blueprint' is for a military component (withdrawal of foreign forces); and a human rights monitoring/enforcement; repatriation; rehabilitation and election component. There have been many examples of this is the 1990s, with the Dayton Agreement of 1995 being the most celebrated to date. The real challenge, say Miall, Ramsbottam and Woodhouse, is how to make it work. How, for example, do you make up the military/security deficit (civil police when the population is heavily armed for example); the 'political/constitutional deficit'; the 'economic/social deficit' and the 'psycho-social deficit'? Is the deployment of IFOR/ SFOR the way to do it? How do you arrest leaders (for war crimes) that you want to cooperate with each other? In other words how to do you get from 'negative' peace to 'positive' peace?[39] Dayton seems to indicate that we have not yet got it right.

Afghanistan and Iraq 2001–3 – the 'inside out solution'?[40]

The cases of Afghanistan and Iraq are two of the best to illustrate the question of 'what happens afterwards' if there is an attempted military solution to a sanguinary dictatorship that is seen as threatening world peace in the post-Cold War period. Both were run by regimes seen as inimical to liberal Western ideas, and indeed to the main norms of human rights and decency that underpin the UN Charter. The problem lay, and lies, in what should be done about such regimes, especially in the aftermath of the attacks on America on 11 September 2001, seemingly backed by either or both of these 'rogue states' as the United States Government refers to them. In both cases there was an eventual American-inspired and executed 'regime change', although in the case of Iraq this had to wait until a President was installed in the White House who believed in American exceptionalism to the point of unilateralism.

From the vantage point of a book like this, one of the key problems has been that the wars of 2001 and 2003 and the subsequent attempts at reconstruction have seen a positively devastating scene of disagreement among the public opinions and the elites of all the liberal states that were involved, especially over Iraq. Only the British Government, as well as small contingents from another few countries, backed the invasion of Iraq in 2003 and then in the teeth of opposition from virtually the entire United Nations and three veto-holders on the Security Council, China, France and Russia. Within Britain, and also, but to a lesser extent, within the United States, few issues have so divided opinion as the conception and execution of this latter war. The following sections will try and draw out what can only at this point (late 2004) be called 'provisional' lessons of this episode in liberal states' attempts at reconstruction.[41]

Iraq 1991–2002

In 1991 the Allied coalition forces that had liberated Kuwait in Operation Desert Storm were ordered to stop at the border with Iraq, the state responsible for the invasion of Kuwait in the first place. This was done for two reasons. First, and perhaps least significantly, there was a feeling that the United Nations resolutions pertinent for the liberation of Kuwait had not included a mandate to overthrow the regime of Saddam Hussein. To do so would be to diminish the credibility of the UN as a legitimizing agent in such operations in the immediate aftermath of wars and in the light of George Bush Senior's 'New World Order' speech of 1990 that had given the UN the final word in what military action could or could not be carried out on its behalf. Second, and more significantly, there was a real fear that the result of an invasion of Iraq would be the break-up of the state of Iraq into Kurdish, Arab and other smaller units, thus destabilizing the whole area. Regime modification or possibly change, not country destruction, was seen as the key to a democratic and peaceful Iraq.

The first event that changed all this were the arrival in the White House of the present President George Bush, carrying a neo-conservative agenda as outlined in Chapter 2. The second was the attack on New York of 11 September 2001 ('9/11') by Islamic fanatics that had been trained in the Islamic fundamentalist country of Afghanistan. For the new American Administration, the UN disarmament and sanctions regimes directed against Afghanistan and Iraq now became increasingly seen as inadequate and a more radical solution of regime change was envisaged by President Bush for both countries, with or without the acquiescence of the UN. The son would deal with the 'unfinished business' of the father.

Afghanistan – 'nation building'

The main activity by the United States in the year of 9/11 consisted of an invasion of Afghanistan, a military campaign that was sanctioned by the UN Security Council, initially with massive air strikes against the Taliban regime, beginning on 7 October 2001. The Taliban collapsed within a very short period of six weeks although 'mopping up' operations have continued ever since, especially in the region next to the Pakistani border. Four years after the invasion the United States is still frequently accused of behaving as if it were in a conquered land. More importantly it is seen as not seeming to understand the land they have conquered, a mistake made by the British (twice) in the nineteenth century. Most serious of all, the world's (and especially its liberal) press has often to be seen accusing the American forces that make up the majority of the international force of not wanting to 'nation build'. Steve Bell drew a celebrated cartoon strip for the *Guardian* during the war in Afghanistan which had B52 bombers dropping huge numbers of bombs, at the end of the strip saying 'We don't do Nation Building.'[42] So a key question has to be whether it is true that nation-building has taken second place in American attentions, or has their principal activity been to 'buy' the warlords of the country with cash and weapons? The military logic of this may be clear – to get their help on the ground to round up remnants of the Taliban and Al-Qaeda. But, as David Blair reported in the *Daily Telegraph* on 8 October 2002: 'if Afghanistan is to be rebuilt as a nation, the war lords must be curbed. One year after their arrival in the country, American troops remain in the business of fighting, not nation building.'[43]

Afghanistan is a country beset with a hugely complicated ethnic tribal structure that has always been legitimized by the use of the *Lloja Djerga*, a gathering where the tribal elders elect a council that then forms the Government, or in previous years advised the King. This met in 2002 and duly elected Hamid Karzai, a leader acceptable to the West and generally to the Afghans themselves. Karzai is a Pushtun (an ethnic grouping which makes up roughly 43 per cent of the Afghan population) but he is kept in power by the Tadhziks (who are a distinct minority and based in the Panshir valley on the Russian border) of the old 'Northern Alliance' that was once organized by Massoud and which helped the Americans take Kabul in 2001. Tadhziks also control the key ministries of defence and education. All the Taliban leaders were Pushtun and it is from this group that the Taliban drew its strength and continues to do so. Added to this there are considerable external alliances, as between Puhstun Taliban and extremists in (Pushtun areas of) Pakistan. One key demonstration of this is that the Northern alliance and Karzai's government finds it relatively easy to have their writ run in the North but hardly at all in the South where fighting is continuous. The implications for humanitarian and UN work are clear – they do not go much into the South where they are arguably most needed. So the key problem has been to expand the zone of peace in which reconstruction can take place.

But this is not to say that reconstruction cannot and does not take place. A huge humanitarian effort has been and continues to be deployed, to build everything from water pumps to providing basic health care. Western universities and NGOs have provided much of this effort.[44] In reply to the accusation that there was no real activity outside Kabul Provincial Reconstruction Teams (PRTs) have been deployed. General F. L. 'Buster' Hagenbeck, then acting commander of US forces in Afghanistan, was quoted in July 2003 as saying that 'PRTs are a means to extend central government authority to the regions, enmesh local government with the central government and help with reconstruction'. PRTs are also planned by the German contingent in Herat and the EU in Jalalabad in the east, with a proposed one in Kandahar in the south. An FCO official was quoted as saying in July 2003 that '[p]rimarilly our objective is to spreaed the good word of outreach of the central government'. As of that date there were three such American PRTs (at Kunduz, Gardez and Bamiyan) with the first British PRT at Mazar-I-Sharif.[45]

Several observations may be made. First, the idea is clearly to expand the role of a central government to help them communicate or even to deal with the warlords and spread the notion of civil society. It might be noted that all four are in the relatively peaceful North or East, none so far in bandit country in the South except the proposed one in Kandahar. The lessons of Yugoslavia are also being used as a model, with the British PRT being led by Colonel Dickie Davis who has had 'experience of similar missions from Yugoslavia to Northern Ireland'.[46]

Other news is also good. There has been a huge educational drive in the North and Kabul in particular to educate women, none of whom were able to go to school when the Taliban ruled.[47] After 23 years of war much of this effort is necessarily symbolic when 4 million women out of a potential 6 million want to learn how to read and write, but any effort is welcome when only 3 per cent of women in general and 30 per cent of urban women are literate. There has also been much effort put into restoring public services. What is really needed is that the World Bank embark on job creation schemes such as those used in other very poor Third World countries. At the time of writing, interviews with UN officials indicated that this would not be able to happen until after the 2004 elections had demonstrated a modicum of political stability. It also depends on who is elected to power, a government acceptable to the West or one that is acceptable to the majority of Afghans, who may prefer the 'stability' of the Taliban or some other 'extremist' Islamic belief system to the liberal democracy of the West. One indication of this was that there was virtually no debate in the *Lloya Djerga* about whether the name of the new state should be the 'Islamic Republic of Afghanistan'.

But the story is far from being entirely rosy. Many civilians had been killed in accidental air strikes, and the initial relief at having rid themselves of the Taliban is being slowly but surely replaced with resentment. There was even a poem published on the anniversary of the attacks on New York by Mariam Nasseri, evoking the Afghan expulsion of the British invaders in the nineteenth century. Now as then the menfolk were 'playing with bracelets in their homes. ... Afghans ... now live with their eyes cast downwards, once lions in their heroism, they are now allowing themselves to be ruled by mere jackals.' Even representatives of Afghan NGOs are quoted as saying that 'We don't need guests in our country. The Panjshiris ["The Northern Alliance" that now dominates Afghanistan] are like the KGB and America wants to keep Afghanistan as the second Israel in the region. We are not Taliban or al-Qaeda; they are finished now.' Why, in other words, do not the new conquerors take the path of their predecessors and leave Afghans in peace to reconstruct their shattered country?[48]

On occasion the story of the post-war reconstruction in Afghanistan has descended into farce, as when the French Government sent philosopher Bernard Henri-Levy (known as 'BHL' in trendy Parisian circles) to Afghanistan to make proposals for France's potential contribution to international efforts. The British press in particular poured heavy scorn on *Le Monde*'s devoting of 3,000 words to the 100 page report bought back by Levy. One commentator derided 'its somewhat surreal proposals includ[ing] training Afghan army officers at St Cyr, the French military academy; the creation of a Afghan *Ecole Nationale d'Administration* to imbue the civil service with Cartesian rationality "We did it in Algeria, why not in Kabul?"'; and the establishment of a French cultural centre in Kabul and the formation of a crack team of 'hussars to spread the values of 1789'.[49] It could be argued that the ideas were not so much impracticable as, in the eyes of many British and American commentators, irredeemably French.

But in the cases of Afghanistan and Iraq there was a clear need to graft democracy on to a local culture. In the case of Afghanistan there was not the split in the UN that was seen over Iraq in 2003 and yet the same problems of a more serious potential lie in the rarely stressed differences that exist between the paradigmatic cases of Germany and Japan and these later exemplars. In both cases there had been some experience of democracy onto which it was not impossible to graft Western institutions.

Iraq 2003 – the present

Much has been written about the 2003 war against the Iraqi regime of Saddam Hussein. The main point of this section is to try and highlight what might be said to be the 'lessons so far' on reconstruction after that war, even if these remarks are by their very nature provisional. Some obvious elements overhang this discussion. The pre-war divisions in the UN for the first time since its creation affected the entire Security Council. The UN weapons inspectors, first sent in 1991, gave ambiguous impressions of the 'threat', and there were huge splits in conservative and liberal opinion in the West.[50]

Stefan Halper and Jonathan Clarke see the 2001 Bush administration's actions in Iraq as the 'operational roll out of the neo-conservative template', the objective 'clarification of America's global objectives and moral obligations'. In other words it was a supremely 'ideological' reasoning that drove events between September 2001 and March 2003. In this scenario the 'discursive construction of reality' required the invention of 'threats', and especially that of the 'weapons of mass destruction' (WMDs). Some even more extreme accounts from within the White House make the astonishing claim that President Bush only invaded as he did out of a personal grudge against Saddam Hussein.[51]

Such thinking has to be put alongside the more than a decade of stand off between the UN and Iraq over WMDs, Iraq's appalling human rights record and its persecution of its population over decades, not to mention its invasion of two states in 20 years (Iran and Kuwait). The boundaries within Western thinking about dislike of and acceptance of the need to topple Saddam Hussein on one hand and a desire to ridicule American President George W. Bush are often blurred and quite unprecedented in the post-Second World War period. Be that as it may, an invasion none the less took place in March 2003 with only Britain, the USA and Australia sending significant detachments. There was a rapid advance and a victory with minimal losses, declared in a matter of weeks.

Our concern is with the process of what happened after the 'war' had 'ended'. Both words are put in inverted commas deliberately. The attack, known as 'shock and awe', is the best example to date of the revolution in military affairs.[52] The war has at the time of writing not ended for all that. Military casualties among the 'coalition' have been higher than they were until victory was declared. The televisions of the world are still (late 2004) full of signs of American troops and other foreign workers being humiliated and, in some cases, executed live on screen. This section has to at least try and ask 'what went wrong?'.

The Bush administration has been widely accused of not foreseeing the course of the war of 2003 and consequently not really planning the post-war reconstruction of Iraq. As in Afghanistan the United States main effort has been military and it was spectacularly successful in that respect, as the vaunted Iraqi army collapsed within a few weeks. Since the end of the war (officially declared by President Bush on 1 May 2003) there have been other major successes with over half of the most wanted 'pack of cards' indicating the most wanted members of Saddam Hussein's former regime being arrested or killed, most notably Hussein's two murderous sons Uday and Qusay on 22 July. Photographs of their bullet-riddled corpses were widely published to prove their deaths. But, as the French Foreign Minister, Dominique de Villepin, was quick to state, this did not help the 'political process' by which he meant both a return of Iraqis to power in their own country or a return to normality or a better and more acceptable role for the United Nations.[53]

Before the conflict began there had been attempts to define what might be the problems that Iraq was likely to face after the war in terms of reconstruction needs. The State Department set up a 'Future of Iraq Project' which held at least the promise of 'post-war planning' of the Second World War era. Presumably this was on the basis apparently expressed by Secretary of State Colin Powell that 'if you break it you own it'. Although it is known to have started meeting in April 2002 (and can even be dated back to meetings at Columbia University in New York the previous year) very few of its substantive findings have ever emerged other than through some State Department briefings and press releases. It seems to have bought together a large number of Iraqi exile groups, much as the Post-War Planning Process did in the 1940s with European exiles.[54] Unfortunately this planning seems to have not been used, or only to a very small extent. The Pentagon seems to have assumed full control of the occupation after the rapid victory of March 2003 and it is to their conceptions which we must now turn.

Two main policies underlay these American plans to reconstruct Iraq after the war of April 2003. The first of these is 'democratic decentralization' a policy that in the case of Iraq was initially given to the 'Triangle' organization based at the University of North Carolina to develop. One obvious problem with such 'democratic decentralization' is that this has been seen as inevitably leading to balkanization. The second is the awarding of the main civil engineering projects that will be necessary to rebuild the Iraqi oil industry and most the country's infrastructure to Bechtel Corp and Halliburton Inc. There has been much worry that this would lead to the United States deciding on who gets what contract and a cutting out of the seemingly neutral broker of the United Nations. A third, and possibly the most important side of this reconstruction effort, was the installation of retired American Lieutenant General Jay Garner as the Director (and British Major General Tim Cross as Deputy Director) of an Office of Reconstruction and Humanitarian Assistance (ORHA). Their aim was the creation of an 'architecture' for reconstruction.

Garner had an impeccable CV for the job, as a former Ambassador and the top State Department expert on counter-terrorism as well as the former Chief Executive of Marsh Inc 'a consultancy which gives advice on how to deal with crises' [*sic!*]. By mid-September 2003 Garner was able to say that 'the Iraqis are extremely grateful' for what the Coalition was doing for them, with an independent Cabinet of Iraqis appointed, an independent judiciary established and 'a lot of progress working on reconstruction projects … 8000 and counting'. The aim he said was to take up the 'legal and moral' obligation pursuant to defeating the Iraqi Government of Saddam Hussein 'to succeed in stabilizing Iraq, giving it a decent government and a decent economy' so as to assure that there was established 'a free, stable country which doesn't have weapons of mass destruction and which does not support terrorism'.[55] Unfortunately he was found wanting and a replaced by a man who is widely held to be much more of 'true believer' in the extreme neo-con views of the President and Vice President, Paul Bremer, in late

2003. He in turn stood down in July 2004 upon the installation of an Iraqi Interim Authority (IAA), which has not seen a reduction in the level of anti-American or other violence. The lessons of that will have to await an updating of this book.

The British Government does not seem to have been any better prepared, The 'first reflections' of the British Ministry of Defence in July 2003, that is to say two months after hostilities had officially 'ended' on 1 May, had very little to say about what needed to be done 'after the conflict'. The majority of the relevant chapter dealt with security, humanitarian assistance and the finding of weapons of mass destruction. Reconstruction got just two paragraphs, one referring to the primary role of ORHA and the other to the 'vital role' that was outlined for the 'UN in the reconstruction of Iraq' in Security Council Resolution 1483 of 22 May 2003, itself a discussion fraught by intra-Western arguments, again mainly between the British and Americans on one side and the French, Germans and Russians on the other. The main elements of this Resolution dealt with winding down the Oil for Food Programme, the need to provide humanitarian assistance, the lifting of sanctions and the 'endorsement of an appropriate post-conflict administration for Iraq'. It also referred to 'UN cover' being provided for 'any state wishing to contribute troops to the stabilization force which the coalition is assembling in Iraq'. All this was with the aim of 'demonstrat[ing] the continued commitment of Security Council members to the future of Iraq and its people and gives the UN the vital role the [British] Government has always envisaged'.[56]

Criticisms by non-Americans have been most severe of the reliance on private firms, and especially those linked to the Bush dynasty.[57] The most glaring example was the lead role given to Halliburton Corp., an oil services firm for the rebuilding of Iraq's oil infrastructure. Vice President Dick Cheney was for many years a senior executive of this firm. More broadly, the evident problem with the awarding of contracts mainly to American firms[58] is that it in effect gives the monopoly over the overall planning, if not the on-the-ground execution of reconstruction to one state. Even Garner had a private sector interest in post-war Iraq through the abovementioned role in Marsh Inc. The Americans have counter-attacked by saying that the French motivations for *not* going to war in Iraq were commercial, which de Villepin dismissed as 'absurd'.[59] It none the less has to be agreed by all concerned that Iraq's possession of the second-greatest reserves of oil make it a vital economic factor in the calculations of any state. There is a slightly hollow ring about those who claim that their intentions are honourable when those of their ideological opponents are not.

The Coalition discovered that it is essential to 'hand Iraq back to the Iraqis' as quickly as possible. President Bush's promise of an early withdrawal and the awful spectre at the feast of the Vietnam syndrome are enough in themselves to ensure that, as is the escalating cost, put at over $100 billion to date. In the context of the huge American fiscal, budget and trade deficits and the Presidential election in November 2004, the importance of this American domestic nexus could be understated. The Democrats had seemingly been slowly but surely rebuilding their opposition to President Bush on the back of accusations that the President lied to Congress over WMDs as a *causus belli* and over the giving of reconstruction contracts to the President's cronies.[60] But the American people still voted for Bush again, which either means that they either agreed with his policy over Iraq, or that other issues were more salient.

The pressure from those outside the United States still smarting under American arrogance in March 2003 has also been unrelenting. The Security Council Resolution of late September 2003 was directed precisely at the terms on which the handover would take place. The French and German governments, as well as most of the rest of the Security Council, wanted this to be quick and complete with the UN there to monitor the handover and provide help. The Russian Government was said to have been using the opportunity to increase American support for its actions in Chechnya with the *quid pro quo* of some troops for Iraq, a classic case of profiting from the Superpower's discomfort.[61] The American and British view was that it should be done in the 'right' way. This 'right' way is to make sure that Iraq is not only handed over to a reasonably democratic government in January 2005 after Elections organized by the IIA. The Coalition's preference was initially for one based on the nucleus of the Iraqi National Council, later known as the 'Coalition Provisional Authority' (CPA) set up in the immediate aftermath of the war and consisting largely of Iraqis returned from exile.

This programme also extends to redeveloping the oil industry, directed by American oil firms like Halliburton, and to reform of the farm sector. The Food and Agriculture Organization (FAO) of the UN estimates that over 7 million Iraqis live directly off the land but the country still imports huge amounts of food, but that only 38 per cent of potential agricultural land is under cultivation, mainly because of problems with irrigation and low prices in Saddam's Iraq after 35 years of subsidies. The CPA declared in September 2003 that it would cut agricultural subsidies to encourage more entrepreneurial agricultural activity. The transition will be very difficult but it is clearly inspired by the reforms that have been used in many other developing countries under the impetus of market-based reforms. In the short run it will inevitably result in more leaving the land but in the long run it is hoped that it will result in a viable agricultural sector.[62]

Much of the criticism of the Coalition's actions and those of its CPA, and now of the IIA, is obviously directed at the logic of using the forces of capitalism to reconstruct a state that was defeated by the armed forces of another. It ill-suited a clash between those who think that reconstruction, indeed world governance more broadly, should be concentrated in the hands of an allegedly impartial international organization, the UN, or in the hands of a clearly partial American state that sponsors liberal capitalist enterprises of which it approves.

There may be some logic in keeping all the levers of patronage in one place and governed by the same norms of corporate (liberal) governance, but it reduces the sense of ownership that is also essential for that same liberal governance structure to operate. People defend what is *theirs*. The American forces that occupied Germany in 1945 were anxious for that reason to pass back effective policing to the German local forces, despite that fact that many of them must have had strong Nazi sympathies. Similarly Coalition forces in Iraq are having to hand over policing power to local Iraqi warlords – they know the local population, understand its culture(s) and are much more light on their feet than a clumsy military machine. The risks of balkanization are again evident, as warlords are the natural controllers of 'their' territory, but what is the alternative?[63]

This has also paradoxically been illustrated by the attacks on the United Nations building in Baghdad on 20 August 2003, when at least 24 people were killed, including the UN Chief Representative in Iraq, Vincente de Mello.[64] When the UN was rumoured to be pulling out there were grave fears among the local population of chaos. One report stated '[i]f the UN goes, it will be as if the Iraqi people lose their father. They are the only ones who can bridge the gap between the people and the soldiers.'[65] The American and Coalition forces in Iraq have not been able to provide proper security for themselves or the other parts of the reconstruction machine – NGOs and the UN itself. It has indeed been widely argued that by tying their reconstruction effort and the personnel involved in it so closely together in both Iraq and Afghanistan that humanitarian workers are increasingly being seen a legitimate targets by those who oppose the 'occupation'. At the time of writing *Medecins sans Frontieres* had already pulled out of Afghanistan and the professional association of the UN has suggested that its personnel should also do the same, especially after the bombing of the HQ and subsequent violence towards foreigners of all persuasions by way of kidnapping and video executions.

The Coalition compounded this tendency to conflate the 'invaders' with the 'helpers' in the mind of the local population both by their precipitate victory and also by their belief in a complete clean slate for the creation of the new Iraqi state, starting with its army. As John Keegan, a firm believer in the attack on Iraq has put it:

> In retrospect the disbandment of the army was a serious mistake, one of several made by the American interim administration in the immediate aftermath of Saddam Hussein's collapse. It released several hundred thousand young men on to the unemployment market, leaving them unpaid and discontented, at precisely the moment when the need became apparent to rebuild ... security forces.[66]

There will never be a true 'end' to this particular way of ending wars. Iraq demonstrates what a long-term process this must be and what a long haul to accomplish it. Even the capture of Saddam Hussein in December 2003, referred to by one newspaper as 'a giant step forward in the rebuilding of Iraq', is so because it shows the need to carry not just the indigenous Iraqi population but also the 'Arab Street'.[67] The battle for hearts and minds is as much influenced by Saddam having being captured with a pistol that had not fired a shot or because he looked so pathetic, old and care-worn. The London based *al-Quds al-Arabi* spoke of a 'New Indignity for the Arabs'.[68] Suspicion about American and British intentions, always strong in the Middle East, was not allayed by this victory for the powers. To reconstruct Iraq is as much about giving Iraqis a sense of dignity as anything else, without which no reconstruction can take place, as Germany and Japan's trajectory can be said to show. Whether this is achieved by finding Saddam in a hole in the ground or not only history will judge. Certainly the bombs let off by his supporters did not end with his arrest.

Conclusions: the politics of reconstruction in the period 1991–2004

The previous chapter pointed to the growing impetus for the notion of reconstruction in the increasingly destructive nature of war in the early twentieth century, a tendency that has grown ever since. Even after 1815 France was not as devastated as Germany and Japan, indeed most of Europe, were after 1945. Neither was France left without bridges, power, or many basic services as Serbia was after the relatively short 1999 NATO bombing campaign. But neither was France 'reconstructed' in the way that was attempted in all these later cases. So what might be said to be some of the main actions taken and lessons learnt in some of these cases? Can a sustainable peace or zones of civility be seen emerging in any of the parts of the world where reconstruction has been attempted since 1991?

One of the key lessons of the period has been that much of the actual business of reconstruction is not done by *states*, but by IGOs like the EU and by private NGOs, often working on behalf of these IGOs. This has given NGOs a political clout not only with the target states but also with the UN and other states. They act as executors. They also act as a 'public conscience' and can raise huge amounts of money. This trend really started before the end of the Cold War with Bob Geldof's activities in raising huge amounts of money for Ethiopia in 1986 with his 'Live Aid' concerts and other activities. He literally called on ordinary people to 'Save the World' and this started a trend towards a personal and individual commitment to reconstruction that would not have been conceivable in 1945.

Equally for liberals like Mary Kaldor all is not lost in spite of 'new wars'. This is well encapsulated in Michael Ignatieff's hope, almost prayer:

> [t]he idea that different races and ethnic groups can co-exist in peace and even good will is not a hopeless illusion. Even the long-standing, apparently adamantine antipathies of the ethnic war zones turn out on closer examination to be expressions of fear created by the collapse of absence of institutions that enable individuals to form civic identities strong enough to counteract their ethnic allegiances. When individuals live in stable states – even poor ones – they do not need to rush to the protection of the group. It is the disintegration of states and the Hobbesian fear that results that produces ethnic fragmentation and war.[69]

The solutions being proposed are twofold. Mary Kaldor has suggested that we must strengthen the state itself. The President of East Timor, Xanana Gusmao, suggested that there could be no reconciliation without reconstruction, which in that case means a large amount of foreign aid and technical assistance. Democracy is the connection that links these ideas in the minds of both Kaldor and Gusmao. But, as both also point out, how can you bring that about when the main problem is one of abject poverty and its attendant handmaidens such as illiteracy, are the reality for a huge proportion of the population? Both also suggest that since the international community makes the rules that community should foot the bill.[70] The key therefore lies in creating a modern, inclusive, democratic state for everyone to live in. It also requires showing the population that an inclusive society is more likely to provide for security and prosperity than an exclusive one. In pushing these solutions the logic is that of the liberal.

Michael Mandelbaum, as we have seen one of the greatest contemporary advocates of both Woodrow Wilson and what he calls the current 'age of reconstruction' as a way of bringing about the liberal desire for 'peace, democracy and free markets', has to say that the reconstructions of Afghanistan and Iraq are to date the 'least successful postwar reconstruction ... after World War I ... that bears the most resemblance to the international order after the end of communism.' The question, left hanging in the air in his first chapter, is why, when the 'establishment and success of liberal values and practices helped to end the Cold War on Western terms'[71] we are now looking at such a negative comparison? Wilson 'failed' but he had a prophetic vision that was followed after the Second World War by his successors, who were able to put flesh on the bare bones of Wilson's ideas. How has it all gone wrong in the aftermath of the Cold War with a so much better base line of liberal success?

A few general points may be made. The first is the problem of having to deal with 'failed' states and having to create what can only be described as unviable states. But should that have been done? The Cold War had propped up a series of regimes in Africa and elsewhere that were patently only kept going by vast instalments of military aid that sufficed only to keep sanguinary dictators in power. With the end of the Cold War these dictators fell and their countries largely fell with them. The 'International Community' (for which read the West) has then proceeded to agree to the establishment of a series of unviable states, in the Balkans, in the Former Soviet Union and elsewhere (we might cite East Timor, Eritrea) that are now in many cases looking as shaky as the 'failed' variety. With hindsight we may ask if it would it not be better to 'give war a chance' *à la* Luttwak, so that failure would be righted by the laws of war?

Or should we indeed have tried to create small democratic states that will then be protected by the EU/West? By 'reconstruction', had we invested properly in it, would we not have much widened the 'zones of peace'? Might it not be argued that this is exactly what we have achieved in Eastern Europe, and other places too? Is it not incumbent on us to deny the atavistic forces of repression and nationalism? Is it not inevitable that full-scale intervention (even if in the name of reconstruction) is the only action that will deter or stop rogue states?

Before the toppling of the Taliban in 2001 Afghanistan refused aid unless subject to strict rules that most NGOs will not respect (treatment of women, etc.).

After the invasion the only parts of the country where the rule of law runs are where Western troops are present in great numbers (essentially Kabul). Linked to this is the problem that it was not realized just how fast these regimes would fall, meaning that proper preparation for the peace has usually not been made. However in all the cases outlined above the end came with bewildering speed, from Russia, through Bosnia, Kosovo, Afghanistan and Iraq. It seems clear that any further reconstruction of 'failed states' must be planned even before the overthrow is contemplated.

Second, these actions are clearly tied into the debate over the both the role of IOs (especially the UN) and the linked problem of war crimes and suchlike. Given the above remarks on the speed of collapse of the failed states of the 1990s it could be argued that there must be a mechanism of last resort to deal with the reconstruction effort in all its variety. If this logic is correct then a coalition of states, or even one major state, must do the reconstruction and that means in practice the United States.

If they are not prepared to do so there is no alternative to the UN. Humanitarian relief has to be built into the battle plan and then protected as part of it. George Soros commented to the BBC after the Iraq war of 2003 that the problems encountered by the United States in rebuilding the country confirm that the UN is indeed vital for picking up the pieces after a war but that the agonizing over the decision to go to war demonstrated that the UN is incapable of taking the really tough decisions. Secretary General Kofi Annan argued in the same programme both that the states of the international system must understand that the United States has to be recognized as a new kind of superpower but also that this same superpower must understand that it also benefits from a rule-based system. The UN is the only organizational structure capable of creating such a rule-based consensus argues the Secretary General. Equally he argued which conflicts should be entered into must be decided by consensus. Otherwise there will be 'orphan conflicts' round the world that cannot be attended to as all the resources and the best troops are sucked into the Iraq quagmire. For him the UN should therefore be supported at all times, as well as bolstered and much better funded.[72] Whether these arguments will end up strengthening the UN or not is still dependent on the attitude that the United States decides to settle upon after the Iraq war. There has always been a huge and genuine liberal dilemma in the United States about trusting an organization that is made up largely of illiberal states.

But it could also be counter-argued that it is the United States that has defined the rules repeatedly over the last hundred years and has always been at the forefront of promoting liberal values and practices. This makes the role of an International Criminal Court (a focus of the next chapter) even more imperative. When the UN tried to introduce a new resolution defining attacks on humanitarian workers as a 'war crime' after the attacks on the UN building in Baghdad in August 2003, the United States threatened to veto it for its mention of the International Criminal Court as the body who would define what a 'war crime was'. Who decides what happens in the international system and order? It might be argued that in these conditions reconstruction through force is essential. But if this is the case then the principle of state sovereignty is clearly subordinate to the wishes of the UN as a whole.

Third, we have to accept that, given the overwhelming power of the United States, reconstruction efforts will always be partly dependent on the exigencies of American foreign and domestic policy. We are currently living though such a debate about Iraq, but all previous reconstruction efforts have been so influenced. In 1999 President Clinton was able to make his claim at the G8 Summit, referring to Kosovo, that the 'most expensive of reconstructions is cheaper than the cheapest of wars' and receive full public recognition for the logic of his remark except from the extreme conservative wing of the Republican Party and the likes of Pat Buchanan, who would oppose any foreign involvement for any reason other than self-defence. In 2002 it was not clear again whether President George W. Bush was happy to get involved in the reconstruction effort in Afghanistan. Once again there was a witch-hunt around the world for sympathizers of the Taliban as there was in 1918–19 for sympathizers with Bolshevism. The same logics are at work over the years. American leadership in such efforts is essential if they are to succeed; this leadership will be resented even if no alternative is presented; the Americans will be accused of arrogance whatever they do and it will lead to what John Dewey had called 'the cult of the irrational' in the United States in 1918.

Criticism of the way the war was inaugurated, fought and how it was ended are still very much debated at the time of writing. The French and German governments fought every inch of the way in the Security Council and with public opinion to stop what they saw as an illegitimate use of force against a country that, in their view, was unlikely to pose a real threat in the future, whatever may have been the case in the past. With hindsight we can perhaps see that the failure to achieve an international consensus in Kosovo reflected a deep split in the international community about how to intervene as well as whether to intervene in wars that we can identify as 'new'.

In the case of Iraq this gap between Security Council members enlarged to a chasm and as a consequence neither of the main groups of protagonists of a war (the United States and Britain) and the opponents of action (the rest of the Security Council) could find a way to allow the UN to participate in the reconstruction efforts as all would have lost face in so doing. The *Financial Times* summed it up in September 2003: 'UN's Big Five agree on end goal for Iraq – but not on the means'. Secretary of State Colin Powell was quoted using yet another historical analogy to justify a present difference of opinion with the Security Council:

> The United States has no desire to remain. Why would we want to? It's costing us a great deal of money, it's tying down a large number of our troops, and we pay an economic as well as a political price. We want to transfer sovereignty from the Coalition Provisional Authority to the Iraqis as fast as we can. . . . [But] we can't leave the country until the country is ready

to assume responsibility. ... America is the same America that liberated Europe, that liberated Japan. It is our goal not to seize anyone's land or to seize anyone's resources, especially oil, but to create partners.[73]

This quote about the Iraq war illustrates that liberal thinking about ending wars in the main liberal states, the United States and Britain, has not really moved far since 1945. As has been noted over and over in this book, the Americans have always distrusted 'multilateral' action when they have seen it as against American interests, however defined. They prefer, in Powell's above quoted phrase, to 'create partners'. It must be noted, as we did in the last chapter, that there have always been large sections of the American political and business elite that have defended the right of small and larger capitalist interests to override the interest of what is euphemistically referred to as the international community. Neither have the majority of other states in the system moved far from the emphasis on multilateral action controlled by the UN that was envisaged in 1945 by most other states in the system. Then they saw the UN as a way of restraining, or at least tying in, the superpowers into a system of mutual self-help. The 'international community' is no such thing. It is perhaps united in terms of the norms of democracy, free enterprise and human rights, but in terms of how to translate these into practice it is far from so agreed when it comes to the concrete problems of reconstruction. By the time the final edit of this book was being made (late 2004) a composite resolution on the role of the UN in Iraq was still causing great problems of agreement among the liberal powers.[74]

So can we blame 'globalization'? Have the forces of the 'market' increasingly forced the hand of the state's advocates as economics renders progressively more irrelevant the demands of politics, and other forces (such as the emergence of TNCs) and where even international institutions and powerful states are no longer in 'control'? Do the 'partners' now have to have capitalist credentials, preferably as businesses? However it is clear that business, and indeed the UN, cannot exist in a security vacuum to do the work of reconstruction. The American army was needed to partner UNRRA in 1944–5, and was needed again in 2003–4 in Iraq. The issue of who was in charge then was an unclear as it is now. The question of who 'partners' whom is therefore now as crucial as it has ever been.

Or has reconstruction simply become a synonym for blackmail, or at least the use of a carrot or a stick to encourage the development of liberal capitalist states? In Autumn 2001 EU Commissioner Patten refused to hold a reconstruction donor conference for Macedonia on the grounds that Macedonia had not done enough to democratise. In the post-Cold War period holding out the possibility of future reconstruction has become a popular way of encouraging the population of a country (Iraq and Serbia are again good examples) to overthrow their rulers in return for which they will get lots of aid, and without which they will only get more destruction. It is a form of economic statecraft. But, as Christopher Cramer has claimed, and Iraq has proved, the fact that 'peace-building exercises are not technical projects but are sharply political' also means that the liberal state that is trying to do the reconstruction 'depend[s] in large measure on what coalition of interest groups succeeds in dominating the peace'. If it is an anti-capitalist coalition the reconstruction process will be severely hampered. The consequential point that Cramer makes is that 'the developmental outcomes of peace settlements depends on whether economic [and he might have added 'political'] policy is a product of ideological fantasy or of a realistic acknowl-edgment of particular economies and of historical experience'.[75] So what if the state being reconstructed has never had much historical experience of democracy and capitalist institutions, like many that are now being so treated?

When this question is put there is a tendency, certainly in Washington, to breeze over the problem as one of it being a 'mopping up operation' against the forces of illiberalism – 'terrorists' and suchlike. There are some signs that differ-ent voices are beginning to be heard, but they are faint as yet. The motivation for such thinking is that it is increasingly being realized that in the drive for the post-modern state we have left many pre-modern ones behind, as Robert Cooper has posited (see Chapter 2). But the pre-modern state is now in many cases the vir-tual 'property' of the post-modern one. The adage that 'if you break it you own it' has accrued a new importance with the creation of the new East Timor, Sierra Leone and Afghanistan, and even more so with Iraq. The United States at least seems to agree, but not by being the government themselves. 'Our goal is to leave as small a "footprint" as possible,' said Paul Wolfowitz in 2001 about Afghanistan.[76]

For the legacy of how the liberal West has dealt with troublesome 'rogue' states there is also a painful possible lesson if they confuse their imperialist urges with the conveying of benefit to those they attack. George Orwell was scathing about what he saw as 'Kipling's jingoism and brutality' but is perspicacious about why Kipling was so wrong about the Boer War as we described in Chapter 2:

> It is notable that Kipling does not seem to realize ... that an Empire is a money-making concern. Imperialism as he sees it is a sort of forcible evan-gelising. You turn a Gatling gun on a mob of unarmed 'natives', and then you establish 'the Law', which includes roads, railways and a court-house. He could not foresee, therefore, that the same motives which bought the Empire into existence would end by destroying it.[77]

We might ask if the reconstruction of Afghanistan or Iraq at the end of the twentieth century is so very different from the Liberal Imperialists at the begin-ning of it? Certainly the 'hyper liberals' (as the French call them) of the 2003 George W. Bush Cabinet have shown the same certitude in their actions, as did Viscount Milner, Cecil Rhodes and Rudyard Kipling in 1900. Such beliefs may well have their justifications in the writings of John Locke and his 'incon-sistencies' but they would also do to remember the dictums of Kant, Mill and Cobden, that freedom cannot be forced on an individual or on a community. They might also reflect on what John Adams said in 1776: 'the business of America with Europe ["the old world"] was commerce, not politics or war'.[78]

6 Retribution – the logics of justice and peace

The next challenge is how to bring about a much deserved execution.
John Keegan about Saddam Hussein, 2003[1]

It goes to show that if you get into a war, it is supremely important to win it. You and I [Ismay, his Chief of Staff] would be in a pretty pickle if we had lost.
Winston Churchill in 1945[2]

Introduction

This chapter, and its sequel, respectively on retribution, reconciliation and resolution, continue our exploration of the fundamental liberal conundrum of how a political and, above all, moral, system of thought can be imposed by one or more (powerful) liberal state(s) on states that are not in that category through a variety of 'legal' approaches to change. The whole idea of imposing liberal standards of justice after wars is based on the idea that this imposition will not only be for the good of the liberal state doing the imposing but also on the illiberal victim. The question for liberals has and will be: can outside (even liberal) forces impose a democratic freedom on peoples that have not previously had it without fundamentally breaching the basis of liberalism itself? Moral autonomy has to be learnt by the individual or the people, says Mill, not imposed. So how can we square that with the use of force to make people free, especially if that results in tribunals that may impose harsh sentences for illiberal acts, up to and including the death penalty?

But we must start by moving to a pre-, or perhaps non-, liberal logic. If you were to be asked 'whom do you hate?' or 'whom do you feel aggrieved by?' most would have an answer either personally or in our family circle. All of us have lost friends/family members/land/property/esteem to another. We have a choice of how we deal with that – we either get our own back; we ignore it or we seek reconciliation by some process of truth seeking and forgiveness. Peoples and states also have the same dilemmas during and after wars but the consequences are in general far more momentous and deeply rooted. As with personal animosities they come back to haunt the future relationship with the party seen as 'guilty' of the action that has engendered hatred, and in the case of people or states that can mean a new war. So grappling with the possibility that retribution or reconciliation may be possible or desirable requires us to look anew at the basic idea that the last war is the cause of the next, unless something is done to break the cycle of humiliation, hatred and revenge.

Two vital sub-divisions of this notion can be detected, one through what might be called 'internal' reconciliation, as has been seen in Chile after the return to democracy in the early 1990s and also in South Africa after the end of Apartheid at the same period. The other is by what might be termed 'external' reconciliation through the use of legal redress in War Crimes Tribunals (WCTs), of which the main ones currently under way are those in The Great Lakes region of Africa and the International Criminal Tribunal for the Former Yugoslavia (ICTFY). This has been termed 'retribution' in that, as Kegley and Raymond point out, it 'lacks the resentful, vindictive spirit of revenge: it avenges a moral transgression dispassionately, without personal rancour. Retributive justice attempts to halt . . . escalatory momentum by taking jural-like activity out of private hands, distinguishing between crimes and their punishment, and placing limits on the penalties wrongdoers pay'.[3] Such would be an example of an ideal modern liberal view of the impartiality of retributive justice. It would not be shared by many of those who have appeared before such tribunals, as is shown by the apoplectic denunciations of the ICTFY by Slobodan Milosevic since the summer of 2001 (still continuing as this is written in the autumn of 2004).

Some very difficult practical and metaphysical questions have to be posed in the course of this and the next chapter. On a practical level, can we put our faith in gestures of retribution or reconciliation to mend the broken polities, bodies and minds of those affected by war? This is an emerging central belief of the liberal agenda to prevent future war and it has all its contradictions. If we want reconciliation can we also have war crimes tribunals, for example, the primary aim of which is retribution and hopefully repentance? Can we expect to pacify the former Yugoslavia and punish 'war criminals', with which we have to talk to make peace? In Chile is General Pinochet a reconciling hero or a war criminal? In Sierra Leone was Foday Sankoh leader of a murderous band known as the Revolutionary United Front or a key player in the peace process? Is, indeed, Gerry Adams of Sinn Fein in Northern Ireland a key and valued member of the Government or a bandit? What dilemmas are posed in the case of South Africa and the Middle East by including former 'terrorists' or 'agents of government-sponsored atrocity' in the same new government?

Hence this and the next chapter will firstly explore the links that have developed since 1918 between the ending of wars and the reconciliation of the peoples that have been involved in war and conflict. As David Whittaker says, a relatively recent development in thinking about war and its aftermath is that we are now thinking much more deeply about the long-term need to rebuild relationships both within and between conflicting parties. So although '[a] great deal has been written about conflict and conflict resolution . . . [l]ess has been written about the cycle of conflict, resolution, reconciliation.' The three elements of this cycle have always been implicitly linked, but only recently explicitly widely formulated in thinking about the aftermath of conflicts. Whittaker's definition of reconciliation is a good starting point: 'reconciliation goes beyond resolution to refer not just to the political arrangements to resolve differences and hostile action but to the psychological process whereby understanding and tolerance lead to readiness to live together in a new framework of peace and well-being'.[4] This chapter will concentrate on the other side of reconciliation – the perceived need for retribution, or justice meted out through the judicial system and is in most cases dispensed through a liberal court system according to liberal precepts and practices.

The logic of peace and the logic of justice

A key element of the seemingly opposed logic of reconciliation and retribution is what Aurelien Colson has called the 'logic of peace and the logic of justice'. For him '[h]ow wars end and when peace starts is the central question in an examination of the links between peace and justice'.[5] Justice might well require that the party that is 'guilty' be identified and punished in some way, either by accepting guilt and giving restitution of some kind, or through being put before and judged by a tribunal. Of course the content of both these logics has changed over the years, as has the relative weight given to each. The difficulty lies in showing how those weights have changed and how this has impacted on the administration of justice in international wars and in domestically generated wars as the opposing ideal of reconciliation has also emerged to complement, or even to challenge justice in the harshest, retributive, sense of the word.

In both the logics of peace and justice the role of law and of its allied instruments such as international tribunals is of crucial importance. However if such thinking is to be generalized then the role of international law is particularly important as a way of setting basic norms and cataloguing precedent in what is often called 'customary' international law. The links between IR and international law have not, as has been noted, always been strong. The input of law into thinking about IR was strong during the early part of the League of Nations period, and also during the early part of the Cold War, when it came to be known as 'World Peace Through Law' under the impulse of thinkers such as Louis Sohn. Why this should be so is partly that the realist tradition that dominated the Cold War period of IR theorizing has always put more emphasis on power and tended to see law as a communitarian construct, enforced only by those who can so enforce it. Law has in other words often been subjugated to 'order' as a primary value.

Memory and the debate about justice

When Kenneth Christie refers to the 'twentieth century [being] the century of the missing and the obliterated'[6] he is tapping into a widespread sense that the dictatorships of the last hundred years, especially those of Nazi Germany and

Soviet Russia, have produced a qualitatively and quantitatively more awful paradigm of suffering. Although he is referring in his wider book to the crimes of *Apartheid*, there is no doubt that the last hundred years have increased the need for reconciliation far beyond what previously existed. It is necessary to go back to the time of Genghiz Khan and Ivan the Terrible to find examples of the deliberate terror that has been a feature of war in recent times. Of course they existed in a pre-modern, and therefore pre-state, period, used the tools of pre-modernism and had a clear if barbaric political intention. What has made the twentieth century worse is that this has happened again in a supposedly enlightened age, one where huge advances in scientific, philosophical and humanistic knowledge has been evident.[7]

Possibly the greatest living voice of moral outrage on the specific horror of the twentieth century is Tzvetan Todorov, whose work has both placed the particular horrors of the Western European civilization in the first half of the twentieth century in its historical context and made us appreciate the internal logic of that civilization's failings. For Todorov the conquest of America in 1492 and all the subsequent horrors of imperial conquest set the stage for the eventual turning in on ourselves in the two World Wars.[8] His view is that what has truly distinguished the twentieth century from all others is the emergence of totalitarianism and the largely successful defence against this put up by liberal democracies, even if for an African the key event would have been first colonization, then decolonization. However, in Africa the same battle between democracy and totalitarianism has been engaged, is far from over and represents the remains of yet another appalling European export.[9]

This leads him directly to the heart of the way in which this essential dialectic can be dealt with. He muses on the role of memory: 'is it always a good thing, and forgetfulness an absolute curse'? For him it must be seen as a Weberian 'ideal type' that must always and everywhere be resisted by judging it against the other 'ideal type', which is liberal democracy. Both of these ideal types existed in an almost symbiotic relationship for decades and the existence of both was dependent on the forces of public opinion. Does this mean that 'the crime ... could ... become legitimate because the people wanted it and the individual has accepted it?' No, he claims, because something stands above both individual and collective will, and that is 'the very idea of justice'.[10] The twentieth, and by extension the twenty-first, centuries have had a far greater feeling of a need for justice, or accountability, precisely because the crimes committed were so, and are still so, done in the name of the people. The people must therefore be purged of those crimes in a very public way. Retribution is thus not a new phenomenon but it has been interpreted in a radically new context, which lauds the 'apotheosis of public opinion' and the emergence of the individual as the key actor in IR.

Guilt, retribution and repentance as emerging norms

The notions of guilt for, and retribution after, wars sit well with older ideas of revenge and also form a conceptual bridge with both the realist idea of reparation and at the same time with the liberal ideal of reconciliation. Of course, there are much older precedents for retribution being tempered by charity, or what we might call a suspension of memory in the interests of drawing a line under a conflict. In the Book of Leviticus the confiscation of land and property from a guilty party in war or in crime was fixed under normal circumstances as being until the 'Jubilee' (or 'jubile' in the St James Version). This was intended to mitigate the overwhelming rights possessed by the Children of Israel over all other groups. The Jubilee would happen however on the 'day of atonement', or forty years after the events concerned.[11] Equally the Book of Isaiah promised the Children of Israel that 'your God will come, he will come with vengeance; with divine retribution he will come to save you. Then will the eyes of the blind be opened and the ears of the deaf unstopped. Then will the lame leap like a deer and the mute shout for joy . . . [and much more in the same vein]'.[12] Retribution in this sense is a liberation as well as a vehicle of vengeance.

These two meanings are reflected and amplified in later (New Testament) Christian ideas of charity to former enemies and those weaker or outcast among us, as well as those who have wronged you with the aim of setting of clear limits to, and reason for, retribution. There are echoes of this in Kant's hope that 'some level of trust in the enemy's way of thinking [*Denkungsart*] must be preserved even in the midst of war, for otherwise no peace can ever be concluded and the hostilities would become a war of extermination'.[13] The contemporary view of retribution that will hopefully lead to reconciliation thus sits alongside the older, what has been termed 'legal', notion.

Both traditions can accept the idea of a basic prerequisite of proving guilt before any further remedial action is taken. 'Guilt' is an idea that has always existed in domestic law; indeed it is the basis of it. But until the idea of an international society of states grew up nations were seen as incapable of guilt in their dealings with each other. To suggest that the Romans should bear some guilt for their treatment of, say, the German tribes, or the Visigoths for their treatment of the Roman Empire, could only be suggested on some abstract moral plane. Even today such films as *Gladiator* seem to encourage a celebration of technologically advanced states punishing 'backward' ones. Western states especially have a long tradition of admiring the warriors of classical antiquity, reflected in a concentration on classical studies until quite recently for the elites. Even liberals like Theodore Mommsen stressed that Rome was a spreader of ideas of 'freedom'[14] as much as a perpetrator of huge atrocities against 'barbarians' in defence of its imperial power. Modern day IR specialists use the term 'Empire' in different ways, sometimes to stress that imperial design can be 'Athenian', though the spreading of ideas as much as 'Roman', through the use of force. Empires could even protect the weak against the strong – who would prefer the era of Yugoslav domination of the Muslims of Bosnia to that by Austria Hungary?[15] We are highly ambivalent about our European imperial past, even if we are liberals.

But in the twentieth century the notion that guilt by a nation or people towards other nations or peoples can not only be ascribed, but the idea that it might lead to restitution or some other form of compensation has grown to the level where the current Queen of England now apologizes retrospectively for the guilt of the British Empire in massacring Indians at Amritsar in 1922 or Boers in the concentration camps of 1899–1902. The Queen was also asked to apologize for the drowning of black prisoners taken by the British during the Napoleonic Wars who drowned in a storm in Dorset in 1797. The United States refused to join the 2001 United Nations World Conference Against Racism in Durban on slavery mentioned in the a previous chapter if the demand on the agenda for compensation for the transatlantic slave trade were not dropped.[16]

Probably even more significantly, in 1997 Swiss banks agreed to recompense those Jewish people who had deposited money in Switzerland before 1939 and had those assets in effect confiscated. It illustrated, as a study of the phenomenon of the 'guilt of nations' by Elazar Barkan points out, that '[t]he surprise is not only that Switzerland rattled the financial markets ... but that moral issues have become so powerful in the international arena they seem to turn even tailored bankers into compassionate radicals'. Even given the tinge of cynical commentary that the author rightly gives to this Swiss decision – 'appearing compassionate and holding the moral high ground has become a good investment' – it is also clear that we are witnessing a development where '[t]he demand that nations act morally and acknowledge their own gross historical injustices is a novel phenomenon'.[17]

Ariel Colomonos suggests that we should look at how norms such as that referred to by Barkan, or the allied one of 'repentance' are disseminated. His premise is that '[t]he diffusion of values and norms, their reformulation, and the birth, or rebirth, of new normative aptitudes [is] the outcomes of political mobilizations within the international arena'.[18] Repentance is thus for him such a currently emerging norm of behaviour, but he is aware that those scholars using historical perspective have always noted the emergence and transformation of rituals such as repentance, or other more issue-focused phenomena as the anti-nuclear movement of the 1960s, or the animal rights movement of the past decade.

If this is a new phenomenon we should therefore ask why repentance and restitution are much older ideas than the date of 1997, and certainly than that of 1945, which was the end date of the primary injustice for which the Swiss Government is atoning. We should also ask what is new about the current breast-beating where one generation seemingly apologizes and gives compensation for crimes of which it could not possibly have been guilty. Barkan justifies his 'new-ness' thesis by saying that although the ideas of repentance, restitution or indeed reparation (he uses the two interchangeably) are older than the last 50 years, what has changed is that what was once a 'legal' concept has now become a 'cultural' one. It is now accepted he says that 'gross historical injustices in both international and domestic conflict resolutions' have to be addressed. He further links this recently acknowledged need for restitution to a much wider debate about 'human rights ... public morality and the augmented efforts to amend past injustices'.

In turn Barkan feels that this is linked both to the Enlightenment view that rights accrue to individuals and to the more modern view that the identities of nations, peoples and other nomenclatures of groups are constantly '(re)nego-tiated'. The implication of this is that we have to constantly acknowledge the wrongs done to each other historically: 'a form of negotiated justice'.[19] It must be said that the 're-negotiation' of a previously accepted historical memory has been a very striking feature of the post-Cold war era. In many Western states there have been historical commissions set up to re-examine key moments of the past – as with the Swiss Commission to review both the question of Nazi gold and also to study the behaviour of the International Committee of the Red Cross (ICRC) during the Second World War. We also have the case of the Finnish Commission to reviews the events of 1918, the Finnish Civil war, and many cases of smaller such bodies being set up in Former Soviet states (Moldova, the Baltic states) to look into Soviet-era deportations to Siberia. This is without counting the Truth and Justice Commissions that will be looked at in the next chapter. These 'his-torical' events are at the very heart of the rethinking of national identity upon which many states are embarking.

Another explanation for the recent development of the phenomenon comes from those writers who have identified changing attitudes to the state. The state has a different ethical status in a globalizing world than was ever the case in the past. It is no longer the dominant ethical point of reference for many, including politicians, as even religious belief has again become global and not national. It might be argued that this is partly attributable the 'neo-Medievalism' to which so many writers now refer, a return to an older form of relationship. The relatively new, and liberal, language of rights has done much to promote this. Nowhere is this clearer than in the allegedly diminishing power of the state. Liberals see the state as a social construct, not as an immutable category. And as David Forsythe, one of the greatest exponents of human rights, has put it,

> Like the concept of human rights itself, the idea of state sovereignty is a claim relating to proper exercise of public authority, a claim to be evaluated by the rest of the international community. Thus state sovereignty is not some immutable principle decreed in fixed form once and for all time, but rather an argument about state authority whose meaning and scope are constantly subject to re-evaluation.[20]

This is the nub of the problem. Liberals believe that the state is being modified in the interest of the individual. Many individuals in Western societies welcome this as a possibility to extend their domain of personal freedom to gain and be accorded respect and make money, to paraphrase Francis Fukuyama.[21] But what about those who do not have states that protect them from the wolves of capit-alism or indeed liberty, and what is to guarantee the very basic framework of civil society and protection that is one of the very reasons for the state's existence? To put it at its most crude: does freedom to make money and exercise individual rights to various kinds of freedom for some, thereby mean that many who cannot or will not ascribe to this dogma be thrown into the dustbin of history? The process of reconciliation (and, in Barkan's use of the term, restitution) is about trying to redefine the parameters of loyalty to the state on one hand and to the concept of a wider global civil society on the other. It is about giving unto Caesar that which Caesar must have, but also acknowledging the need for personal respect, or what we shall see it was called in the Northern Ireland peace process, 'parity of esteem'.

War crimes tribunals

Realist and liberal views on tribunals

The majority of the horrors of the twentieth century have been committed by states either against their own populations or against a generalized population that was deemed to merit persecution (the Jews are the classic example).[22] They have practically all been committed by organized and efficient state structures, not one of which can be termed a liberal state (with the obvious exception of the British state during the Boer War highlighted in Chapter 1). Liberal states won two World Wars and a Cold War against such totalitarian states and their settled norms make up the essential of what passes for rules in the International Community. As was stressed in Chapter 2, since the end of the Cold War the Charter of the United Nations has been increasingly interpreted to implement a norm of humanitarian intervention. This includes the use and extension of the idea of War Crimes Tribunals (WCTs) from their very limited 1945 beginnings to one where now any state or its governing bodies or individuals, including, in theory at least, its Head of State, can be translated before such bodies. Former President Slobodan Milosevic of Serbia is the first of such Heads of Government to appear, in July 2001.

The key purpose of all WCTs is to establish a historical 'truth', to give a basis for remembering that truth and to punish the offenders. It is also to give a basis for reconciliation by clearing the slate of history and allowing for a new beginning. The perceived need for an acceptance of responsibility, for the delivery of a form of apology and a commemoration of the horrors of wartime atrocities has become one of the most enduring themes of the last 50 years. They have gone through a series of normative and procedural periods, which will be examined in the following sections. Some key basic ideas motivate those who agree with them and those that do not.

But as Aleksander Jokic points out there can be said to have been relatively little philosophical linking of war crimes and international justice. The real impetus has come from the inauguration of tribunals in the Former Yugoslavia and Rwanda after the wars there of 1991–5 and 1994–present. Broadly speaking these can be identified as 'realist' and 'liberal'.[23] Gary Jonathan Bass has given us a very useful summary of both.[24] Bass says that 'to realists international moralizing is mystifying', as is the punishing of war criminals. He quotes E. H. Carr in justification of this claim, for 'politics are not a function of ethics, but ethics of politics' – you do whatever is necessary to win. Morality, as Kennan and others have said, is the 'problem' in IR. Mervyn Frost has pointed to no less than ten major 'realist' objections to it, ranging from accusations of it being 'value – ridden' to being 'utopian', in other words being used to hide the 'true' nature of what states really want. Morality is a 'tool of policy' and we have to accept that 'in the actual world there are diverse sovereign states and a multiplicity of moral orders. This in itself rules out the possibility of a universally agreed normative theory of international relations which would in fact require a universal world order by a single all-powerful state.'[25] To put it into more populist language, we could say that if we rely on notions of justice and morality we let in those who have no respect for it – Hitler, Milosevic, Osama bin Laden, *et al.* The key moral test is that which has been stressed by many prosecutors in war crime trials: 'do these charges shock any plain man's conscience?' as British solicitor, General Ernest Pollock put it in 1919 or, as Robert Jackson said at Nuremberg: 'our test of what is legally crime gives recognition to those things which fundamentally outraged the conscience of the American people'.[26]

Frost furthermore denies that what realists are often accused of, an 'amoralist' position, is possible, for he asserts, not without reason, that 'it is not possible to conceive of something of a state independently of its own making and recognizing claims based on some code of right conduct'.[27] So to be human (or the leader of a state) is to recognize the existence of common rules of humanity. The question is what those rules are and here it would be easy to assert that the rules are 'liberal'. The international system and its codes are full of liberal statutes, especially in this century, as we have seen. But, as Bass says, for such liberals it makes a difference who the victors are. As Woodrow Wilson put it: 'we are at the beginning of an age in which it will be insisted that the same standards of conduct and responsibility for wrong shall be observed among nations and their governments that are observed among the individual citizens of civilized states.'[28] We might easily take an opposite, 'realist', view and say that this is not part of being 'civilized', or even 'human', it is merely a recognition that those in power use whatever means at their disposal to keep it, including the evocation of morality.

In that case the use of force to bring the 'guilty' to justice or to destroy their political and military machine in any way is 'morally unproblematic' unless we are worried that any use of force is so problematic.[29] But liberals, as we have seen, are not usually pacifist, they are, in Ceadel's terms 'pacificist', they have no problem with the use of force to uphold what they see as civilization. In this context we can therefore see WCTs and the force that puts them into positions of legal control as the necessary spreading of norms of decent conduct, and those norms are *liberal*. Otherwise, a good liberal would say, Hitler, Milosevic and Osama bin Laden will 'win'.

It should also be noted that *all* War Crimes Tribunals have been instigated by liberal states – Leipzig, Constantinople, Nuremberg, Tokyo and The Hague. In effect the Tribunal has become the ultimate instance of what Gerrit Gong has called the 'standard of civilization',[30] for the person on trial, and by extension for the political system that gave him or her birth and nurture. The parameters for the dispensation of such justice can be seen as quite explicitly those defined by liberal states since the beginning of such trials in the aftermath of the First World War when Wilsonian ideals were first making a real impact on the organization of international society. It is to this development that we must now turn.

War crimes tribunals during and after the First World War[31]

Reconciliation was not a word on many people's lips after the signature of the Treaty of Versailles. As has been stressed the Treaty was a largely vengeful document by the standards that had prevailed before. The only use of the word reconciliation that was mentioned in the literature on the Treaty and its aftermath is in a 'Reconciliation Committee', or *Verstandigungskommission*, set up in Germany to try and bring together German industrialists and miners to try and sort out the mess engendered by the huge demands for coal reparations demanded, so not reconciliation in the contemporary sense at all.[32] Moreover, in Article 231 of the Treaty, the 'War-Guilt Clause', one state was for the first time singled out as being solely responsible for the outbreak of the First World War, and that was Germany. The German Kaiser was the first Head of State ever to be described in advance of any trial as a 'war criminal'. Those who inserted this clause were perfectly aware that this was a 'first' in international relations, for as Foreign Secretary Viscount Curzon boasted in the House of Lords, it 'fundamentally distinguishes the Treaty of Versailles from any previous peace treaty'.

Anthony Lentin has summed up the consequences of this imposition on one party of the responsibility for the war. 'Few sentences in history can have been as fraught with consequences. . . . To Germans of almost every persuasion between the wars ... the war-guilt clause remained the ultimate symbol of unacceptability. . . . Far from reconciling Germany to a sober consciousness of her role in the origins and course of the war, Article 231 helped to nurture all that was worst in the German character, accentuating feelings of self-pity and fostering an exaggerated spirit of aggrieved pugnacity against Versailles and all its works.'[33]

Liberals in Britain largely felt this at the time, and impugned the reputation of those who had suggested it. When Lloyd George suggested the prosecution of the Kaiser on 11 December 1918, as well as 'the punishment of war criminals; Germany to pay the whole cost of the war; Britain for the British; re-habilitation of those whom the war had broken', it is clear that liberals saw the whole package as abhorrent. Gilbert Murray was initially 'bewildered. I did not realize that any one could be, I will not say wicked, but so curiously destitute of generous ambition, so incapable of thinking creatively.' Lloyd George's motives, considered Murray, were purely domestic, 'to crush his old colleagues, and conceivable rivals, entirely out of existence', in other words to get rid of any challenge from former (Liberal) Prime Minister Herbert Asquith, the current (Liberal) Prime Minister Lloyd George was prepared to sell the future of Europe down the river. As Murray commented, '[o]f course he succeeded'.

But the longer term problem, said Murray, was even worse, as the Treaty had 'produced a condition so intolerable that the vanquished must be expected to seize the first favourable opportunity for fighting to free themselves. It has sown the seeds of future war.' This was a complete reversal of what should have been the lessons of even Britain's recent history. The peace settlement in 1906 with the Boers had led to genuine reconciliation after the 1900–2 war, Abraham Lincoln had wanted (although he died before he could get it) 'a peace of reconciliation, entirely different from that which took place when he was gone', even Bismarck had ended the war with Austria in 1866 with reconciliation. Now 'Europe might have had a genuinely Liberal peace' as Wilson had proposed in the Fourteen Points, all Wilson's proclaiming of a need for peace with 'justice' betrayed.[34]

The obvious lack of reconciliation can be seen as an important negative lesson of the perils of ignoring the need to make such processes open and accountable. It is also clear that Germany's historical path was changed forever, and thus that of Europe and the world, by introducing such a concept as 'war guilt'. But having introduced it, we have had to come to accommodate ourselves to it. The implications of this became ever more apparent after the Second World War.

There is just one case from this period that is often overlooked that merits brief consideration, that of the attempted setting up of tribunals to try the perpetrators of the Armenian massacres during the war and the last days of the Ottoman Empire. The most commonly accepted version concerns the forced march of many millions of Armenian men, women and children when they were considered to be a real internal threat to the Ottoman war effort. In these marches up to a million and half people are claimed to have died. The facts of the case are still discussed today with a 'Holocaust denial' industry very active in Turkey that denies both successor responsibility for the massacres and the accusation that took place.[35]

The British Government of Lloyd George nevertheless saw fit to demand that the Ottoman regime identify the alleged perpetrators of the massacres. They were subsequently taken to Malta where legal proceedings were initiated against about 50 defendants. The difficulties of gathering evidence and the paucity of witnesses (many of whom were presumed to in any case to be among the victims) in the confusion of wartime meant that the trials were less than satisfactory, especially as the British insisted on the full panoply of their own justice with a defence and prosecution lawyer and the use of rigorous standards of evidence.[36] The result was a farce in the sense that no prosecutions succeeded but a triumph of a small kind in that individuals were bought to book for the crimes initiated by a government. This was the beginning of the end for the 'I was only obeying orders' defence, one that was formally repudiated at Nuremberg in 1945. It was also, less gloriously, the first time that a government whose nationals had not been affected by the alleged crimes was able to deport suspects to a neutral third territory and not try the 'crimes' under the jurisdiction of either rules of the alleged perpetrating government or that of those of the victim, in this case not yet a 'state', although now with some claims to that status since 1991 and the end of the Soviet Union.

The PCIJ and ICJ after the First World War

Although a 'Permanent' International Court of Justice (PICJ) had been set up as a result of the Hague Treaties of 1899 and 1907, and the ICJ had continued after the First World War (losing its adjective 'permanent' under the League of Nations in 1919), the absence of the United States and Soviet Russia from the League was a major impediment to any idea of a universalizing of the notion of criminal responsibility being imputed to states. Moreover the idea of guilt being imputed to *individuals* went no further until 1945, as will be seen below.

But the idea did have its adherents, even in the United States. In 1929 Henry Stimson, President Herbert Hoover's new Secretary of State, wrote a Memorandum on the possible future involvement of the United States in the ICJ. His views are illuminating as an internationalist member of a Republican administration (and later to serve as the wartime Secretary of State for War under Roosevelt). He recognized that the 'Court is now, and has been for ten years, a going institution. . . . It has evidently come to stay; a permanent institution in the affairs of the world, which is playing a constantly increasing part in promoting peace and stability.' His worry was that 'at present our country has no voice in the enactment of the statutes and rules which govern the existence of the Court'. He wanted that to change through full membership, for the interesting reason that he felt that would lead to 'the acquisition of greater privileges and greater power over the conduct of the Court and greater immunity for ourselves'. Most significantly for Stimson:

> Our nation has been the historic leader in promoting the judicial settlement of international disputes. We have been a leader in our dependence upon judicial methods for the determination of constitutional questions. We have been one of the leaders in our reliance upon our courts to weave the fabric of a wise and flexible criminal law. Along each of these lines the World Court should play an important function in the society of nations, and in each of these lines it will play its part more wisely and effectively if it has behind it the traditions and influence of the American nation.[37]

This bid for world legal leadership saw its high point at Nuremberg in 1945 where the Chief Prosecutor was an American, Robert Jackson. Stimson's view was eminently realist and not liberal in the sense outlined above. He wanted membership to be able to exercise leadership and influence, not to give up American sovereignty, and he felt, as most Americans have since, that America acted out of far nobler and moral impulses in its foreign policy that did, say, Britain, widely discredited after the Boer War and the Treaty of Versailles as liberal 'lead state' in any case in most (including British) eyes.

However Stimson was not the only voice in American Government on such matters before 1945. The United States played a much more important role than is often assumed in the legal processes of the League of Nations and it also played an unofficial role as arbitrator in a number of key cases, perhaps unsurprisingly in South America,[38] but also in the legal disputes over reparations. American policy think tanks like the Carnegie Endowment and the CFR played an important behind the scenes role in drawing up the Optional Protocol that went with the Kellogg Briand Pact to outlaw war. But the United States did not join either the global IO or the World Court until after Pearl Harbor.[39]

During the Second World War

Stimson, whom it has been stressed was a long term advocate of American membership, was again given the job of rethinking the uses to which the World Court could be put even while he was engaged in directing American forces in the Pacific and Normandy at crucial moments of the war. This was not an afterthought for Roosevelt but a central plank of his post-war conception of the international order, his new world order. On 23 October 1944, when victory over Germany at least seemed surer, he recorded a conversation with Averill Harriman, Roosevelt's chief interlocutor with the Russians. They agreed that 'freedom cannot exist in country where the government uses secret police to dominate its citizens, and there is nothing to choose between the Gestapo which the Germans have used and the OGPU ...'. This equation of Nazi Germany and Soviet Russia could not be voiced directly to Roosevelt, but it was felt widely in his Cabinet, and Harriman played a major role in the post-war order under President Truman. On 24 October Stimson met with Assistant Secretary of War John McCloy and assorted generals and a decision was taken to set up WCTs to deal with the Nazis in Germany. It was necessary to get rid of the 'secret police', that had 'depraved' the Germans, and all would be well. On 27 October he developed his idea of a 'big trial for conspiracy involving the leaders and the actors all the way down to who had taken part in the different atrocity camps and mass murder places'. As he told US Ambassador Winant in London, this would be a 'conspiracy charge'.[40]

After the Second World War: Nuremberg[41]

The principle of retribution took a big leap forward after the discovery of the concentration camps and as a reaction to horror about the Nazi regime. The liberal complaints of Gilbert Murray about the treatment of Germany after 1918 were much modified by those discoveries. One explanation of this has to be that there was a feeling of guilt among liberals themselves that they had encouraged appeasement towards Germany. The Germans were not seen as having responded to this generosity of spirit in kind, but rather they had elected an utterly illiberal government. How could Germany be treated with anything other than harshness after what it had collectively done? Her Majesty's Government was of the opinion as late as the London Conference of April 1945 that 'execution without trial is the preferable course' such would be the 'exceedingly long and elaborate nature' of any trials and that they would be open to the accusation of retrospectively made justice. This logic was overruled by that established by Stimson in the United States. As Richard Minear has put it, the American logic was that '[w]ar itself must be eliminated. Since all war begins with aggression, there is always a right and a wrong side. Civilization must mobilize its resources on the side of right.'[42]

In fact after the Second World War far more was done to ensure that stability, or 'order', was a more important consideration than justice. The experiences of a destabilized Germany in the 1920s, the chronic instability of the whole of Central and Eastern Europe in the inter-war period and the corresponding lack of prosperity meant that the United States in particular wanted to bring Germany and Italy back into the 'Comity of Nations' as rapidly as possible.[43] Certain rough justice was permitted in the West of Europe. Hence there was a period of '*épuration*' [cleansing] that probably owed as much to the settling of scores as to justice in France.[44]

None the less at both the Nuremberg and Tokyo trials the numbers of those actually condemned to be executed was small by the standards of the horrors to which people had become inured by 1945, nine at Nuremberg and seven in Tokyo, although others were executed as a result of subsequent prosecutions. As many writers about the WCT phenomenon have pointed out, these prosecutions were based both on 'conventional' war crimes but also on the new ones of crimes 'against peace and against humanity'. They were also retrospective of the legislation of 1945, in that they covered events both during and even before the war.[45] One feature that they expanded on from the earlier trials after the Treaty of Versailles was that they personalized guilt, thus avoiding the blanket guilt dealt out to Germany by the Treaty that many in the United States saw as having given Hitler his excuse for aggression. So for the United States Prosecutor Robert H. Jackson, 'this trial is part of the great effort to keep peace secure. ... This trial, implementing the Kellog-Briand Pact [of 1928, outlawing war] constitutes another step [towards] juridical action of a kind to ensure that those who start a war will pay for it personally.'[46]

The Tokyo trials were and are less controversial to this day. It might be argued that the evidence of Japanese crimes was more apparent, given that the Rape of Nanking in 1937, was, among many other massacres and atrocities, well known before the war in Europe even started. But it more likely that the perceived 'fanaticism' of the Japanese military government and the generalized brutality with which Japanese armed forces treated their captives that was well documented very shortly after the war ended helped to reduce any residual feelings of sympathy that might have existed in Europe or the United States. In particular the treatment of Western POWs rankles even to this day. Equally, most Japanese scholars have, in Minear's words, since 1945 'stayed away from the trial and its verdict. Apparently they fear that denigration of the trial will lead to a positive re-evaluation of Japan's wartime policies and leadership'.[47]

The problems with these trials has been well documented, especially the accusation that they are victor's justice. Linked to this are easy accusations of double-standards. When he heard of the death sentences in Nuremberg sentences, Churchill is said to have commented: 'it goes to show that if you get into a war, it is supremely important to win it. You and I [Viscount Ismay, his Chief of Staff] would be in a pretty pickle if we had lost.' His Majesty's Government's views at the London Conference quoted above are proof positive that the British at least realized the shaky moral and legislative ground on which they stood with the trials. 'Realist' logic at least has the benefit of consistency. That became even more evident once memories had started to fade. Arguably more 'guilty' people were not hanged, but spared and even freed as the Cold War advanced. Even Churchill commented in 1947 that:

> Revenge is of all satisfactions the most costly and long drawn out; retributive persecution is, of all policies, the most pernicious. Our policy ... should henceforth be to draw the sponge across the crimes and horrors of the past, hard as that may be. ... There can be no revival of Europe without the active and loyal aid of the German tribes.

So, as Sellars says, '[p]olitics led the advance to Nuremberg and politics sounded the retreat, with the Cold War killing off enthusiasm for the punishment of their wartime enemies'.[48]

The problem with history is that it has to be constantly re-written. The story of the punishment of Nazi Germany and Imperial Japan for the then new notion of 'war crimes' and 'crimes against humanity' is one such example. As Istvan Deak has pointed out: 'it used to be easy to write contemporary European history. World War II came to an end in 1945, and with it ended a thirty-year crisis. ... In the conventional story as thus told, everything changed after 1945' with the emergence of different spheres in Western and Eastern Europe, and they continued their development in isolation from each other. But 'in the course of the 1990s all of this has changed in ways that now make the post-war historiography of Europe curiously outdated almost before the ink has dried'. There is no longer a post-war order, 'so the history of the post-war era has to be rethought'. For Deak a further result has been the 'revival of memory' and the 'related question of justice – or more accurately, retribution'.

In the longer term that is also the problem of words coming back to haunt their expressers. Minear makes much of Jackson's speeches at Nuremberg criticizing those who start wars of aggression, especially such statements as 'launching a war of aggression is a crime and ... no political or economic situation can justify it' in his condemnation of American activities in Vietnam.[49] What is sauce for the goose is also sauce for the gander.

During the Cold War

As Geoffrey Robertson and others have noted, crimes committed by victorious political elites during the Cold War, as in Kampuchea after 1975, the 'worst atrocity since the Holocaust', were almost impossible to understand or forgive. How can we envisage reconciliation between killers and survivors in such circumstances? His opinion is that since such '[c]rimes against humanity are, by definition, unforgivable', so he makes 'the case for retribution' rather than that for reconciliation, at least at the highest levels of responsibility.[50] The question had to be posed in the case of Kampuchea as to how we should decide what logic should dominate – the need for a peace that would stick which seemed to necessitate a government of old enemies, including the arraigned mass murderers of the Khmer Rouge, or the need for justice, which would have put these same people on trial for genocide. This dilemma has haunted all peace settlements since and into the post-Cold War period.

After the Cold War

The end of the Cold War bought the assumption that we were now all respecters of human rights and in particular of the rights of individuals, and that those who dared to abuse these rights were therefore subject to a new and much more ferocious anathema than before 1990. This has culminated in the setting up of the International Criminal Court (ICC) in 1999, a permanent instance for the judging of human rights abuses. It is, as Judge Gabrielle Kirk McDonald put it, 'recognition by the international community that, at long last, humanitarian norms must be enforced'.[51] The idea is that there will be no more ad-hoc tribunals set up at the behest and with the necessary backing of the Great Powers. Now everyone could be judged. Although we might doubt that this will prove to be the case – how exactly do you punish Russia for massacres in Chechnya or China in Tibet? – we cannot doubt that the principle is now in place. However the ICC is also a body that the United States has conspicuously so far refused to ratify on the grounds that it would most probably make American peace-making efforts open to international scrutiny and lead to unfair accusation of 'war crimes'.[52] The objections that stymied Stimson in the 1920s are now formally in the ascendant again.

The war in the former Yugoslavia

The war in the former Yugoslavia undoubtedly gave the biggest boost to the idea for such a Court. The liberal West had got used to the idea that the Soviet Union behaved in a beastly way and that although the West had on occasion to behave in a similar fashion, this was always an aberration from normal behaviour and deeply regretted. The prospect of democratically-elected *European* politicians or groups behaving in an unacceptable way towards their fellow citizens was one that was simply inconceivable in the post-Cold War era. And yet, in 1991, Europeans were confronted with the spectacle of mass 'ethnic cleansing' (a new and appalling expression), the re-establishment of concentration camps, and the systematic rape of women for political ends. These events unfolded no more than two hundred miles from Vienna and took place on prime time television in villages that could have been practically anywhere in Western Europe. They also took place in Africa (especially in the Great Lakes region) but most people could accommodate that within their usual stereotypical view of Africa as the 'Heart of Darkness', as Joseph Conrad had put it.

It has become almost a commonplace to write, like Bertrand de Rossanet, a commentator on the war in the Former Republic of Yugoslavia (FRY) after 1992, that '[c]onflicts, internal and international, abound in our times'. Surely there have always been conflicts 'abounding'. Yet this commonplace is an essential one with which to grapple as it has a new dimension, for as de Rossanet goes on to say, '[g]enocide and ethnic cleansing enfeeble the efforts of half a century to let a universal culture of human rights take root and blossom'.[53] Geoffrey Robertson expresses a similar despair.[54]

The shock of the generation that saw both Cold War and the wars in the FRY therefore lies at least partly in sense of outraged innocence. We had been born again in 1990, and this was not supposed to happen. The peace dividend was to be replaced with horrors not seen since 1945. The titles of books written about the FRY wars reflect this outrage. David Rieff's *Slaughterhouse: Bosnia and the Failure of the West*, or James Gow's *Triumph of the Lack of Will*, or Brendan Simms' *Unfinest Hour*,[55] are thus not symptoms of an isolated hyperbole, but of a widespread sense of betrayal of liberal principles by the West. The reaction to the wars in the Balkans was originally one of shocked and horrified non-intervention and then one of possibly over-enthusiastic intervention where the whole might of the West was used to crack the relatively tiny armies of the rump of Yugoslavia. Public opinion led the way but where it leads politicians like John Major and Bill Clinton followed with enthusiasm.

In this we should ask whether there is clearly a danger of losing a sense of perspective? First, the wars in the FRY have not come anywhere near the casualty figures of previous wars, or indeed of many contemporary ones. The genocide in Rwanda led to well over a million deaths in a comparable population, whereas claimed figures for the dead in Bosnia do not generally exceed 200,000. Second, there has been a clear rush to blame one party more than the other in this war, and particularly to finger particular individuals.

Probably we should not be too critical of this outrage, or at least we should understand it. The difference between these wars and others is that they have taken place in the full glare of public view, and on the borders of Western Europe (some would claim within it), what might be called a 'good neighbour' argument. The international commissions that have studied the war have roamed the battlefields at the same time as the battles have raged, or only very shortly afterwards. They have accumulated a mass of detail that has no parallel, not even in the Second World War where Hitler's Germany recorded every last horror in a welter of euphemistic hubris. The generations that have been the direct victims of these wars or who have observed them have not themselves, in most cases, any personal knowledge of war, in stark contrast to the two generations before them. Even the main leaders in the war were born too late to have a vivid memory of the Second World War.

The bare bones of the story of the war in the FRY are worth briefly outlining. In December 1990 Slovenia and Croatia announced their intention to secede from Yugoslavia. This unleashed a wave of fear among non-Croats and (less) Slovenes that they would be dispossessed by this, especially among the Serbs of Knin (in the Kraijina part of Croatia). The new Croatian Constitution has been widely criticised since for giving no guarantees of freedom to minorities, a problem that had resulted in the nineteenth and twentieth centuries in inter-ethnic conflict (during the Second World War in particular). Self-determination is thus seen as a threat by minorities across the entire FRY.

Micha Glenny has argued that the Balkans was a powder keg of very different religions and cultures, and that they have developed a historical consciousness at very different rates and in many different ways. In his view Muslims of the region are wedded to the Ottoman idea, the Serbs to Kosovo and mythical greatness, and very different economic and military power distributions. They are all in the 'prisons of history' of whatever era.[56]

In a more venal, and recent, development the personal and nationalist aspirations of Slobodan Milosevic of Serbia and Franjo Tudjman of Croatia built their political appeal and programme on a restoration of pre-Yugoslav entities. There is much actual and anecdotal evidence of this. One particularly intriguing piece is that recounted by (former British Liberal Democrat leader) Lord Paddy Ashdown in his memoirs. In a conversation in a restaurant Tudjman doodled a 'map' of his view of a future post-Yugoslav entity on a paper tablecloth, and explicitly excluded Bosnia from his new design.[57] Both Serbs and Croats believe Bosnia and Serbs parts of 'their' land. So when fighting broke out, Bosnia and bits of Croatia were crushed (as in the Second World War). Bosnia was trapped between the historic nationalisms.

The international reaction was confused. The EU was divided with, broadly speaking, Germany (itself the recent beneficiary of an unexpected reunification) wanted to recognize Croatia, Slovenia, Bosnia on the basis of the principle of self-determination. Again, broadly speaking, the French and UK Governments of President Francois Mitterrand and Prime Minister John Major wanted to let the Yugoslavs work it out for themselves and then (perhaps) recognize a different set of 'states'. President Clinton of the United States wanted a solution to be found by Europeans, and initially refrained from intervention in Bosnia and Croatia while criticizing the EU for its infectiveness in doing anything substantial about the mass killing and ethnic cleansing. Initially Clinton's Secretary of State Lawrence Eagleburger was quoted as saying that the United States 'does not have a dog in this fight'. More concretely, there was widespread reticence in getting involved in a potentially open-ended intervention that might require 300,000 men, a figure largely plucked out of the air and inspired by the memory of Yugoslav resistance to German troops during the Second World War, not a parallel that should have inspired much confidence.[58] The context of the US debacle in Somalia in 1991–2 had much to do with American reticence: the European disunity with the lack of a viable alternative to American power.

Given these clear differences between the Western liberal states a compromise was reached and a peace-keeping force (UNPROFOR) was sent in 1992 to distribute and safeguard humanitarian assistance and stayed until end of 1995. Mediation was tried by various EU and UN mediators (largely unsuccessfully) for three years, with a variety of maps being drawn up that changed with the fighting on the ground.[59] These measures undoubtedly reduced the killing to some degree, but could not stop major attacks continuing with (to pick out but some of the major atrocities) Croat attacks on Krajina (many Serbs expelled), huge numbers of deaths in Sarajevo, and the massacres in the UN 'safe areas' of

Srebrenica in 1995 (now officially called a 'genocide' with over 7,000 men and boys killed), as well as at Zepa and Gorazde.

Eventually the UN mandate was given teeth, and transformed into a heavily armed IFOR, which secured a cease fire in Sarajevo and the Dayton Peace Accords, negotiated in Dayton, Ohio and signed in Paris on 14 December 1995, and brokered by Richard Holbrooke of the US State Department.[60] This set up a 'cantonized' Bosnia and attempted a complete peace settlement that included provisions for election monitoring, police reforms and the sending of the 'war criminals' of all sides to the Hague Tribunal which will be further explored below. Kaldor, among many others, has said that the international community was 'at best confused and sometimes stupid, at worst culpable for what happened'.[61] By the time of Dayton it could be argued that the ethnic cleansing was largely over, and that by involving some of the main war criminals in its design and execution the international community was making peace with war criminals (see below for more discussion of this). But while there has been much criticism of the Dayton Accords, from many different sides, they did have the merit of stopping the fighting and creating at least the blueprint for a solution to the problems of Bosnia.

The international conference on the former Yugoslavia, 1991–5[62]

There was also a wider forum for reflecting on the 'lessons' of the war in the FRY, when the International Conference on the Former Yugoslavia (CFY, to differentiate it from the International Tribunal ICTFY) was set up in August 1992. It laid down principles that were later to be used as a basis for the Dayton agreement in 1995. Among these were a respect for human rights, supposed to be paramount, and the need to rebuild the state, as it was hoped that democracy and rule of law in a rebuilt state would achieve reconciliation, a classically liberal logic.

The CFY provided an essential backdrop to what later became, after Security Council Resolution 827 of 25 May 1993, a classic Nuremberg-style attempt at reconciliation and retribution, the International Criminal Tribunal for the Former Yugoslavia (ICTFY). The CFY was established at the London Conference on the Former Yugoslavia, in August 1992[63], met between August 1992 and January 1996 and was designed to provide a framework for establishing peace in the area, or as Bertrand de Rossanet puts it 'a framework for multi-track efforts to help bring peace with justice and respect for human rights to the former Yugoslavia'.

As such it had an impressive record. It had a 40-strong headquarters in Geneva and it also had a 500-strong international monitoring mission in the field on the River Drina, on the Serbia–Montenegro border and in the Bosnian Serb Republic. It initiated the 'first ever preventative deployment of peace-keeping forces in the FYR of Macedonia – the first ever preventative deployment of United Nations peace-keeping forces' as well as negotiating a number of important specific agreements over its four years of existence.[64] But the lessons that might be usefully learned for this book about the CFY are not really in the area of reconciliation. Most of the actions by the Conference led to extensive and wide-ranging attempts at conflict resolution between the parties and here they achieved heroic things. But the best that can be said for it in the area of this chapter is that the Conference did try and get initial contacts between the parties going, but ultimately during the war, not after it.

One of the key principles that the co-chairs tried to achieve was, as a document of 1993 put it, that 'any solution [for Bosnia] eventually worked out to convey a sense of a functioning state organized around three constituent peoples, the basis for an eventual reconciliation. This was reiterated in every subsequent accord, up to and including Dayton. De Rossanet comments that 'the Constitution of Bosnia and Herzegovina invokes a faith that democratic governmental institutions and fair procedures best produce peaceful relations within a pluralistic society'.[65] In effect it was hoped that democracy and the rule of law would effect eventual reconciliation.

But the main efforts of the Conference had to be concentrated on how to broker an agreement on the ground to stop the ethnic cleansing and the fighting. This was classic mediation and horse-trading. However, one of the lessons of these experiences for the longer-term problem of reconciliation is how, as the war progressed and the atrocities on all sides piled up, a lasting and mutually acceptable peace could be achieved. If there had been a settlement in 1993 then reconciliation might have been easier, that it happened in 1995 made the process much more difficult. As it was, the only other thing the Conference could do was to report details of the many atrocities it knew about to the Commission of Experts for War Crimes, which later informed the ICTFY.

By the time of the Dayton Agreement in 1995, it had come to the point when there could not be a separation of peace and justice. The State Department spokesman, Nicholas Burns, claimed that 'there is no need for a trade-off' between the two. But Roger Cohen of the *New York Times* was surely right when he said that 'by most estimates, no semblance of justice can be done in Bosnia. If peace is now built, it will be on the basis of enormous shifts of population and widespread killing.'[66] Such judgements did not bode well for the future of Bosnian democracy and rule of law, upon which reconciliation had to be based.

They also provided the most stark warning since the 1940s that the 'logic of peace' and the 'logic of justice' might well be in contradiction with one another. As Holbrooke put it after Dayton, when asked about Milosevic's involvement in war crimes, he said 'it's not my role to make a judgement. ... You can't make peace without President Milosevic'.[67] This was flatly contradicted by the then President of the ICTFY, Justice Richard Goldstone, who during the Dayton talks opined that '[t]hese are matters that will not affect the decisions we make. ... We are interested in building a body of legal evidence regardless of the political consequences.'[68] But there did not at the time of Dayton seem to be any choice.

One point widely made in Western, and especially American, circles, was that they were 'all as bad as each other'. The Deputy Commander in Chief of the

United States European Command from 1992–5, General Charles G. Boyd, expressed this common view when he averred that all those in the Balkans were guilty, quoting Rebecca West that everyone is 'eternally the massacree and never the massacrer'. He himself felt that although the Serbs had been responsible for appalling acts:

> [r]egrettably that behaviour is not unprecedented in Balkan conflicts. . . . If one comes into the movie in 1991 or 1992, a case can be made that the Serbs are indeed the villains of the picture, but to ignore the previous reels will, at a minimum, imply divulging the ultimate plot line.

So although the Serbs have behaved badly 'the question is how bad? On what scale? And how unique?' Boyd stated the widely held view in Serb circles that the Bosnian Government itself was itself the imposer of 'some of the city's suffering'. Equally he claimed that the Serb population also suffered whenever armies moved 'with little interest or condemnation by Washington or CNN correspondent Christiane Amanpour'.[69] Boyd's spleen is therefore directed mainly at the Clinton administration's effectively abandoning all of its relative even-handed condemnation of all sides, a feature of the first term, and coming firmly down on the side of the Bosnian Government. This view was held as an almost exact mirror image by Richard Holbrooke who decried what he called 'bad history, or the Rebecca West factor. . . . Yugoslavia's tragedy was not foreordained. It was the product of bad, even criminal, political leaders who encouraged ethnic confrontation for personal, political and financial gain', a view I found confirmed in a number of conversations within the (independent but Federal Government sponsored) United States Institute for Peace in 2001.[70]

So how could a peace that had justice be concluded? De Rossanet gives four main suggestions for a lasting peace. The first of these is that the war must not be allowed to re-start. That had already been breached in Kosovo and in Macedonia as well. Second, there must be negotiation 'in good faith'. That has not proved terribly easy, although with a new and democratic Serbia and Croatia it may prove easier. Third, he suggests studying the 'aspirations, grievances and claims of the different ethnic groups', a key problem in all post-Cold war arguments. Lastly he suggests that 'there w[ould] need to be a catharsis concerning the terrible atrocities which have taken place', and he specifically recommended the 'Truth Commission' route for this purpose, an idea that will be explored in the next chapter.[71]

The International Criminal Tribunal for the Former Yugoslavia (ICTFY)

Nonetheless the main vehicle in the FRY for a post-conflict settlement is the identification of the 'guilty', and their calling to account before the ICTFY. This was set up in principle by Security Council Resolution 770 of 13 August 1992, and by Resolution 771 of the next day holding all combatants 'individually responsible in respect of such breaches [of the Geneva Conventions of 12 August 1949]'. This was followed by Resolution 780 of 6 October 1992, which established a Commission of Experts to examine Human Rights violations in Bosnia. A further Resolution of 6 October, 787, reaffirmed that any territory taken by force would not affect the settlement.

The ICTFY was set up formally by Security Council Resolution 808 of 22 February 1993 by a unanimous vote of the Council. The main categories of charge were: grave breaches of the 1949 Geneva Conventions; violations of the laws or customs of war; genocide or crimes against humanity.[72] Its main aims were threefold; to bring those guilty of war crimes to justice; to help stabilize the peace in the FRY, and; to help effect a reconciliation between the nations engaged in the war. This third option is for the purposes of this chapter the most interesting as it is explicitly linked to the first two. This was a first in international relations, in that the whole international community had voted for its establishment, unlike in 1945. It was also the first tribunal set up *during* a war, as the Tribunal to try the Kaiser and the Nuremberg Tribunal had not been set up until after their respective conflicts. As Pierre Hazan points out, it was also the first truly media-friendly tribunal as the court room was designed to help the cameras, right down to the choice of wall coverings, and the diffusion rights were given to any TV company that wished them. This was truly an attempt by the international community to see justice unfold on a public stage: 'the serene justice of the Hague in contrast to the tumults of the Balkans in the image of a civilization founded on law against hate and barbarism'.[73]

Negative opinions on the ICTFY

There has not been unanimity on the role of the ICTFY. In the region itself there is a feeling that the people of the FRY are all victims, Serbs feeling this very strongly indeed, and that the international community has not been as impartial as might be hoped. One excellent description of this feeling comes in a book by Aleksander Fatic, a Professor of Management in Belgrade. He wrote his book during the NATO raids on Serbia and Kosovo in the spring of 1999 when '[h]uman suffering on both sides in the conflict, Serbian and Albanian, ha[d] reached new heights'. But his main opposition to the trying of the crimes of that war is that 'a justice that is mixed with diplomacy in the sense that it serves the purposes of those who have a greater force at their disposal, would hardly be a justice at all. Yet, many in the region of south-eastern Europe believe that the [ICTFY] administers just such a type of justice.'

Its respectability as a tribunal, writes Fatic, will therefore be:

> decided by its responses to charges of impartiality and judicial consistency. If the [ICTFY] reacts vigorously to defend its independence, and if in its actions after the latest Balkan war it brings forward indictments of all those responsible for civilian deaths and breaches of international humanitarian law, it stands a good chance of becoming the bedrock of an entrenched and

integrated system of international justice for war crimes. If, on the other hand, the actions of the [ICTFY] remain at least perceivably biased and aligned with western diplomacy, then the [ICTFY] may well bury the future of international justice for a long time to come.

Such a test may well prove to be beyond any such tribunal, but Fatic's point has some basic merit. Another of his critiques lies with its origins. If the ICTFY is a 'result of diplomacy ... it depends on diplomacy in the sense that the feasibility of all its actions is conditioned by what international diplomacy can deliver'. But his main point is that 'individual' guilt must be ascribed, not 'collective', because only then can the Tribunal 'hope to facilitate a de-escalation of tensions and animosities between the ethnic collectives, and encourage a rapprochement between the formerly warring nations'. The logic of the Tribunal implicitly accepts this point, in that there is no suggestion of such a collective guilt being ascribed, but Fatic's comments again show that there is widespread perception that this is the case. For him therefore, diplomacy is dispensed not by a global, and therefore inclusive, international community but by 'the world's most powerful countries'.[74] This again chimes with the belief of many who see the global order as being the product of a few states' dominance of the international system. Until that perception is broken or amended there can be no true acceptation of such tribunals and therefore little hope of them bringing about reconciliation.

Others from outside the region, but with some intimate knowledge of it, such as journalists, criticize the ICTFY, or rather its main sponsors, in a different way. Hazan, a journalist with the moderate left French papers *Liberation* and *Le Temps* in Paris, also points out that this was a war in which the media and the NGOs and IOs led the way in revealing the awful truth of what was unfolding, and that the international community followed where they were forced to go by public opinion. Given that when it was set up, up to 70 per cent of Bosnia was already occupied by Serb bandits and 'ethnically cleansed', Hazan asks if the Tribunal was ever more than 'an instrument which allowed Western governments to wash their dirty consciences?'[75]

One of the main accusations that can surely be levelled against the ICTFY and that certainly cannot be directed at the similar Tribunal for Rwanda[76] (see below) is that the international community was forced to negotiate with those who were clearly going to be brought before the Tribunal as prospective war criminals. As we saw above in the discussion of Dayton, Milosevic was seen in 1994 as an essential player in the peace process. Yet many journalistic, if not yet legalistic, accounts of the war in the FRY, such as the BBC's 'The Destruction of Yugoslavia' produced in the late 1990s, have him and his aides at the centre of any suspicion for the way the war unfolded. As Adrian Hyde-Price has recently written, 'the prosecution of those responsible for war crimes by the International Tribunal is an intrinsic part of the search for justice in Bosnia. However, a peace accord could only be achieved by negotiating with some of those responsible for ordering war crimes.'[77]

The apotheosis of the ICTFY – Milosevic goes to The Hague

The recent nature of this conflict and its incomplete resolution undoubtedly means that the debate on the ICTFY and on the war in the FRY more broadly will be difficult to bring down from the emotional plane on to which it has climbed. We are, in terms of comparison, where the West was with Germany in 1946. The Hague Tribunal has only relatively recently started to get its full contingent of prisoners, some of whom are now starting to be arrested or giving themselves up. Milosevic has appeared before it, but Mladic and Karadic may well never be arrested. Milosevic was himself arrested in Serbia at the beginning of April 2001 and on Friday 29 June 2001 was unceremoniously taken from his cell in Belgrade by the Chief Warder, Dane Blanusa, and told, 'Mr Milosevic, you have to go on a trip'. When Milosevic asked where, he was told 'To the Hague', his reply is supposed to have been, 'What, already?' This banal exchange of words between the man the British and other press have dubbed 'the Butcher of the Balkans' marked the most important single step for the idea of external retribution by the International Community since Nuremberg.[78]

The man who authorized his arrest, Serbian Prime Minister Zoran Djindjic, was shot by a Milosevic supporter a year or so later. Milosevic's party was the majority on the Serb Parliament by the time these words were written in late 2004. So it might be surmised that this arrest has not been enough to bring about reconciliation within Serbia, or at least not yet.

Afghanistan and Iraq, 2002–4

At the time of writing (late 2004) there have been no international WCTs of any kind set up to try the war criminals that worked for Saddam Hussein's regime, although there is now, for the man himself, a mechanism of that kind in place that will try him after the much toted January 2005 elections. The charges will boil down to accusations that the regime broke many of the basic rules of international and national law, including the development and use of weapons of mass destruction (chemical and biological); the sequestration and illegal killing and wounding of foreign nationals (in Kuwait in 1991); the invasion of not one but two states in flagrant denial of the Charter of the UN (Iran and Kuwait); not to mention a host of crimes against his own population. The charge list could be one of the longest ever issued by an international or national WCT. British Prime Minister Tony Blair and The British Ambassador in Baghdad both urged that reconciliation and punishment should go hand in hand. Maybe as a consequence of this a domestic tribunal has been decided upon. This is a major advance and possibly shows that the comments of people like Fatic above have finally been heeded. For reconciliation to take place should the main perpetrators not be tried by those they acted against directly, in this case the Iraqi people?

Both President Bush and Prime Minister Blair have also made it very obvious that they were not averse to a death penalty being imposed by a domestic Iraqi Tribunal. Bush is a well-known advocate of the ultimate deterrent in the United

States. But the quote from John Keegan at the head of this chapter – 'the next challenge is how to bring about a much deserved execution'[79] – was largely typical of the widely held desire to make sure that Saddam Hussein got his just deserts. Keegan even suggested that it was a pity that Hussein had not done the honest thing like Hitler and shot himself. The whole process rather implied that he would be 'given a fair trial and then executed' in the best traditions of the Wild West. Vengeance may well be served but would justice? Perhaps the most positive words were uttered by Blair: 'the rebirth of Iraq is the death of their attempt to sell the lie that we are fighting Muslims. Muslims were Saddam's victims. Muslims today are the beneficiaries of his demise.'[80]

In the case of Afghanistan, the rounding up of thousands of foreign and Afghan supporters of the Taliban Government after the war of 2002 and the pursuit of those being harboured by the Taliban, indicted for crimes such as the attacks on New York of 11 September 2001 was much remarked upon. Many were detained by American and local troops in the worst possible conditions (including being put in containers in the heat of the sun where many died of heatstroke) and a small but significant number were sent to the American base in Guantanamo Bay in Cuba where they have been held in a legal limbo not as either Prisoners of War or in the custody of the American penal system. In effect they have no rights other than those accorded them by the American military. Only one of these prisoners, an American national, has so far been brought to trial (in his case in a Federal court on the mainland) and sentenced to prison for aiding the Taliban cause. This may be the first time that this has happened since the example of the accused in the Armenian massacres being taken to Malta by the British authorities in the Ottoman period as described above. But in this most recent case, many feel that, as Bass puts it about previous cases, WCT's are 'punishment, revenge, spectacle, anything but justice'.[81] It is essentially *victors'* justice.

Conclusions: the 'power of selfishness' and the 'power of idealism'

To draw any conclusions about our last case study, that of Iraq, will have to wait for a future edition of this book. Bass stresses that the main obstacle in the way of liberal states bringing war criminals to their Western justice is 'the power of selfishness', to which we could add what Holbrooke calls the 'Vietmalia' syndrome, the fear that Americans will be victims if intervention takes place to bring criminals to justice. There is, in other words, a fear of the criminal. But there is also a disregard for those who are not the direct enemies of liberal states. It could be argued that Hitler threatened liberal states, while the executors of Sierra Leoneians, Bosnians or Tutsis did not. As Bass says, 'it was the great misfortune of Rwandans and Bosnians to be able to make appeals to the West only in moral terms'.[82] It might also be noted that Roosevelt does not seem to have given much attention to Hitler killing German Jews whereas he clearly did to other aspects of the need for justice in 1945. What he centrally objected to was Hitler killing

British people or Americans. The debate about what to do with Bosnia had to be shifted by Western liberal elites from the idea that intervention in Bosnia would be too costly and ineffective to a belief that we could not allow this to go on.

The role of British Prime Minister Tony Blair in this is perhaps crucial. His foreign policy was explicitly based on human rights and liberal beliefs in a way that Cobden or Gladstone would have recognized. Equally Prime Minister Margaret Thatcher is alleged to have persuaded President George Bush Senior in 1990 at Aspen that liberal states should seize the time of the end of the Cold War to assert liberal principles in the Gulf. Noam Chomsky's accusation that there is an Anglo–American liberal conspiracy to create a new world order in their image is not without truth. The only problem is whether one agrees with such a vision. For Bass this 'power of idealism' is a mixture of true idealism based on a belief in universal and inviolable human rights, and a belief in the legalism that has made most western societies liveable and envied places to reside and self-interest; 'liberal states would be better off in a world where aggression and violent bigotry are punished'. The main beneficiaries would be the soldiers who do not have to die to stop such behaviour, the potential hostages who would not have to carry two passports. Bass is surely echoing most liberals when he says the alternative to legalism is not a happy one to contemplate.

As was stated at the outset, the themes of this and the next chapter should be read as two sides of a very complex psychological, cultural and of course political, coin. The line between retribution and reconciliation in international, or indeed personal, politics and behaviour is often very thin indeed. The next chapter will talk about how many would now like to see some process established of forgiveness being succeeded by reconciliation. One of the most interesting authors on forgiveness makes the equation explicit. Michael Henderson quotes Ambassador Joseph Montville, a former State department officer who has done much to promote the idea of 'Second Track Diplomacy', the use of unofficial channels of conflict resolution, a practice that has arguably become a key elements of the liberal arsenal for preventing wars developing, and helping to stop them if they have erupted or even to solve their long term causes. His 'equation' is that there has to be a 'transaction' that involves 'acknowledgement – contrition – forgiveness'.[83] The key point must be to stress the emphasis now being put on individual action for peace, often in spite of or in opposition to the state from where that individual comes. This is not merely a return to older ideas of religious responsibility but further evidence of the declining or changing role of the state.

But when it comes to forgiving a Milosevic, or an Ottoman Commander responsible for massacring Armenians in 1915, or an Adolph Eichmann, the role of the individual in political action has its limits. On a personal level we can all appreciate the usefulness and worth of such an equation and many of use aspire to such behaviour, even if we often do not live up to it. But such attempts can be difficult to square with institutional responses to wrong, such as those of the WCTs outlined in this chapter. Hence one of the main leitmotifs of the next chapter is about the links between acts of forgiveness and reconciliation.

7 Restorative justice, reconciliation and resolution

> The fact that we are around testifies to a lot of conflict resolution capacity. And reconstruction. And reconciliation. How come?
>
> Johan Galtung, 2001[1]

Introduction

The previous chapter explored the liberal and realist dilemmas inherent in the processes of efforts to bring about a lasting peace by the identification of 'guilty' parties, the definition of the 'truth' and the attempted laying to rest of old ghosts in what can be described as a 'legalistic' approach aimed at a retributive justice through War Crimes Tribunals (WCTs). The aim of these tribunals has always been to punish the guilty. However, they have also been presented as being about bringing reconciliation between the community from which the perpetrators of the crime came and those who were wronged. But as we have seen the imposition of what is often called victors' justice means that all externally imposed tribunals are nearly always looked at with suspicion. To extract Milosevic from Serbia and try him in The Hague may look like a good way of showing international approbation for the process of punishment and reconciliation, but it can have the opposite effect. Milosevic is now seen as having stood up to his accusers 'like a true Serb'.

The same phenomenon has been observed by Kirsten Sellars over the Nuremberg trials, held in Germany but legally exterior to it, whatever other political objectives it may have attained for the Allies in showing who was now boss in the international system. As she observes, when *Germans* tried Germans in the next wave of war crimes trials in the 1950s, a very different reaction took place. Germans now felt that they were 'facing up' to their failings in the past, and truly turning a new page in their history.[2] The fact that Saddam Hussein is now going to be tried in Baghdad by Iraqis seems to be an appreciation that this is the best way of bringing about closure for the Iraqi people and for the international community. It is a mark of the growing influence of American liberal individualistic theory and practice that since 1918 the practice of state absolution through the supposed possession of sovereignty has been further modified by the new notion of 'blame' being extended not only to the state but also to individuals within that state.

This chapter thus looks at another series of ways that the past can be laid to rest in what is often termed a turn from 'retributive' to 'restorative' justice and even to 'resolution' of the conflict itself and the 'reconciliation' of the previously warring parties, the linkage that Galtung expressed at the top of this chapter. These are much more internally and personally generated, within populations and between them, often in very informal ways, and in ways that often have little to do with Western liberal legal formulas. They can all be termed as part of a 'people's reconciliation' that often gives the impression to realist and even to Western liberal commentators of being rather weakly based on sentiment and wishful thinking. Yet it would be a mistake to ridicule or minimize the effect of these movements, as they have in many ways set the public tone within which more formal processes can take place.

As was stressed in Chapter 2, a key point about liberal states is that they have to reflect their public opinion in their foreign policy actions, but that people will form pressure groups of various kinds to decide upon and bring about its own forms of 'justice' or 'reconciliation'. This is what has happened on an increasing scale since the end of the First World War and what Wilson called the 'apotheosis of public opinion', even if it was only markedly important in the victor states. Much of the remembering of past wrongs and the movements towards reconciliation has come on a very unofficial level, even if they have also received official backing. The classic example is the remembrance of the war dead, especially of the First World War in the Western European states, but also of the dead and other victims of the Second World War in other parts of the world, for example in Japan, Korea and China. We could argue that some of these are not liberal states in the Western sense, but they do seem to have an increasing propensity to try and use historical memory as a way of working out their differences as Western Europeans have done. We could also point to the 'truth commissions' that have sprung up around the world to bring out the 'facts' of internal wars that wracked many Third World states during and after the Cold War, the classic examples being Argentina, Chile and South Africa, with more to follow in the Balkans and elsewhere. None of these sprang out of official thinking; they were the product of organized public opinion, the strength of democracy incarnate and the bane of its leaders.

Finally this chapter will look, if only briefly, at an 'R' that many think is one too far, the final 'ending' of wars through 'resolution' of the conflict and the establishment of a new way of living in peace together. Departments of Peace Studies the world over have put much emphasis on this need to 'resolve' conflicts since at least the 1950s. Resolution is here taken to mean that a conflict or a war can be said to have fully ended in that the parties to that conflict have transformed their relationship in such a way that future conflict or war between them is now seen as unthinkable. There are real historical precedents for this, of which the most notable is the present relationship between Germany and France (or even France and the UK) after many wars.

However it has to be said that liberal Western governments have not seen the possibility of transferring such examples in quite the same way as some academics. If we contrast the amount of money and effort expended by Federal and unofficial agencies in the United States and the UK on 'security' issues with the amount expended on agencies and organizations dedicated to the peaceful resolution of conflicts we can see that it is really only in the 1980s and 1990s that such ideas have been taken at all seriously.

The most striking development of an 'official' nature in this field was the setting up of the United States Institute for Peace (USIP) in 1984 as an afterthought of the Carter Presidency. Of course the Carnegie Institution has existed since the early part of the twentieth century, but even the Carnegie was not, and is not, entirely wedded to the idea that conflicts could be 'resolved'. The ideal type of a war or conflict that could be definitively said to be over largely remained the domain of hippies and idealists until very recently. What changed this was the waning of Cold War tensions, and the rise of the denizens of the peace movements of the 1970s to positions of power and influence. The 'hippies' are now in academia, Downing Street and the White House (the present incumbent excepted from this accolade!)

What has also happened is that we now have the example given by the relatively peaceful ending of the Cold War, of the war in Northern Ireland (the 'Good Friday Agreement' of 1998) and the Oslo Agreements of 1993–9 to try and change the relationship between Palestine and Israel, as well as the subsequent attempts to bring about a resolution of the seemingly intractable problems of those conflicts. We can also cite the activities of such bodies as the Carter Center and small groups of academics who can be said to have had some success in developing new techniques that do seem to have had some impact on other conflicts in the sense of helping them towards resolution.

But even at their moment of greatest influence such ideas and actions have again been widely rejected, especially in the United States as again missing the fundamental 'truth' that some cultural and political milieus will always 'hate' the West and try and destroy it, the idea so strongly developed by Samuel Huntington in his *Clash of Civilisations* thesis. As we have seen, this tendency has been accentuated by the events of 11 September 2001 and the rise to prominence of the neo-conservatives within the Bush Administration. One such neo-con, Professor Daniel Pipes, was appointed to the USIP Board in August 2003 to howls of dismay from many Democrats in Congress and countless academics. Pipes' 'crime' was to believe that there is:

> a small but significant minority of Muslims, perhaps 10 to 15 percent of the population. Many of them are peaceful in appearance, but they must be considered potential killers. ... We need protection from the ideology that targeted us, both in violent and non-violent ways: Militant Islam. ... If you are looking for supporters of Militant Islam, where are you going to look? By analogy, if you are looking for a rapist, where are you going to look? In the male, or in the female population?

While Pipes' views stated thus seem relatively unexceptional to most of the Bush Administration, they of course carry within them the problem that it is virtually impossible to find *which* '10 to 13 percent' are 'out to get us', thus tarring the entire Muslim community with the brush of extremism. How can such a conflict be 'resolved'?[3] The short answer is that it only can if we look at 'Muslims' not as an out-group, but as a group of individuals like us, a profoundly liberal way of thinking.

This chapter will look at these more unofficial processes and attempt to unravel the principle dilemmas implied in their development. It will further ask what they may be said to have contributed to the practice of IR in general and to the hope for the reduction or further use of war as a way of solving differences within or between states. It is hoped to demonstrate that the internal logic of 'reconciliation' and 'resolution' are much the same, as are the difficulties in the implementation of either.

New wars and old wars?

As we saw in the discussion on the former Yugoslavia in the last two chapters, we are now living with very different kinds of problem than those addressed by WCTs, and arguably because the nature of war itself has changed. WCTs were, and are, intended to bring about closure in wars between states. But what can be hoped for in the ending of wars in parts of the world where the writ of the state no longer runs? It has been argued that in the 'old' days there were wars that merely re-arranged the balance of power (as between 1712–89 in Europe) and those that severely put into question the international order as a whole. These were, according to Miall, Ramsbottam and Woodhouse, 'Clausewitzean' wars, 'fought out by power centres which used organized force against enemy forces in order to break the opponent's will to continue'.[4] We could therefore argue, using a 'Clausewitzian' logic, that the First and Second World Wars and the Cold War were in the order threatening category, and that the wars since 1991 (Former Republic of Yugoslavia, Former Soviet Union, Central Lakes of Africa) are in the balance of power category.

But in the 'new' days that no longer pertains. Advocates of the 'new' war thesis, like Kaldor, would argue that wars are now '"post-Clausewitzean" … involving fragmented decision making and disorganized forces directed against civilian populations'.[5] Kalevi Holsti refers to them as 'wars of the third kind'. His view is that 'our understanding of contemporary wars is not well served by older analytical approaches'.[6] These new war advocates agree that the big change has been bought about by the disintegration of modern state structures, especially where they were controlled by authoritarian regimes. The state hence loses its monopoly on legitimized violence, a kind of privatization of violence by criminal gangs who fill the vacuum left by a vanished political legitimacy. The most obvious places where this has happened are the Former Soviet Union (FSU), the Former Republic of Yugoslavia (FRY) and those states in Africa that have disintegrate as a result of losing their external patronage at the end of the Cold War – Angola, Zaire, etc.

In the way they are fought they are also not 'rational' in any sense that would be understood by a liberal. The aim is not to capture territory as in conventional wars but to control and select the population of a given territory. The strategic goal is thus to expel any 'alien' population 'through various means such as mass killing, forcible resettlement, as well as a range of political, psychological and economic techniques of intimidation.'[7] Holsti points out that this makes 'everyone ... a combatant merely by virtue of their identity' and this means that where as in 'old' wars casualties were experienced in a ratio of one soldier for every eight civilians now the proportions are exactly inversed.[8]

The wars in the FRY, especially Bosnia, where Kaldor first came to this conclusion, as well as in Rwanda and Sierra Leone can be seen as good examples of this development. In the FRY the slow collapse of the economic and political legitimacy of the state started before the end of the Cold War. The demands for independence of its constituent parts in 1991 led to a core of the different ethnic populations rallying to a nationalist identity banner. The leaderships of Serbia and Croatia aided and abetted a descent into ethnic violence that was largely unchecked for several years by the international community. Paramilitary groups carried out most of the really appalling ethnic cleansing[9] with the deliberate intention of making reconciliation after the war more difficult and thus creating a new status quo that would be, its perpetrators hoped, impossible to reverse: As Bennett puts it: '[e]ach death diminishes the prospects of reconciliation and intensifies the desire for revenge'.[10]

So we need to ask what conceptual basis there might be for reconciliation. How can we have any kind of 'closure' in wars where the old rules are seemingly all no longer appropriate? Do we need to despair?

Forgiveness

Arguably, an essential prerequisite for reconciliation could be said to be 'forgiveness', the specific antidote to despair. The idea is deeply embedded within the Judeo-Christian religion from which liberalism takes so many of its major impulses. The Christian sacrament of confession is technically referred to as the 'Ministry of Reconciliation' showing the close links between truth telling and renewal. However, one of the recent collections on the notion of forgiveness, edited by Michael Henderson, gives the clue to why so many, even liberal, intellectuals reach for their revolvers on hearing the word uttered. The 'Preface' starts with a discussion of the editor's Snoopy cartoon, then engages in a disclaimer of the qualification of the same editor for any real qualifications to edit the book, continues with the difficulty of defining what forgiveness is and talks about the near impossibility for most people to countenance it if they have directly suffered the loss of a relative or close friend. The editor ends with the ringing statement that: '[n]either forgiveness not its inverse, repentance, will alone solve the world's problems or bring peace. But without these two elements, it is hard to see how settlements will prevail over time.'[11]

Liberal intellectuals write most of the texts of IR; most do not have religious belief, and most want to see concrete evidence before they will embark on any discussion that would make them look foolish in other intellectuals' eyes. I have myself scoffed publicly at calls for repentance and sneered at the idea 'all you need is love', except on the purely personal level.[12] It is none the less difficult not to be moved by the disarming sincerity of such a series of statements, and far more difficult to ignore the belief of many that such processes are not only possible but also necessary. So we should make the effort and find out where these notions come from and how they might be used in thinking about ending wars. Andrew Rigby posits a spectrum of possibilities to do with forgiveness ranging from amnesia to retribution. The first was seen in the aftermath of the death of Franco in Spain in 1975, the latter in the Nuremberg cases and in the process of 'cleansing' that took place after the Second World War in all the European states.

It is also worth hypothesizing that the First World War and Woodrow Wilson's 'apotheosis of public opinion' created both a major voice for the person in the street but also a liberal impulse for a felt need for revenge or atonement, and certainly for the 'truth' that had not previously existed. Foreign policy has become progressively 'privatized' since 1919, and never more so than since 1990.

Truth, memory and identity

In elucidating some answers as to the (at least theoretical) possibility of reconciliation and resolution, the next set of questions that we could ask circles around the joint problems of 'truth', 'memory' and 'identity'. There has been an enormous amount of interest expressed in recent years about all these phenomena.[13] The most intractable problem lies in defining how the 'truth' can help end a conflict, a claim made by virtually all those who write about forgiveness as an essential prerequisite to peace.

Truth

Truth is obviously at least partly a subjective category; no historian would nowadays claim that history is '*wie es eigentlich gewesen ist*'. Equally finding the truth may lead to retribution and/or forgiveness, but it might not. There are many examples of forgiveness being accorded by victims of terrible crimes and also of much wishful thinking. The recent book on forgiveness edited by Henderson quoted above evokes the comments of a couple present at the re-burial of Russian Czar Nicholas II and his family, butchered at Ekaterinberg in 1919 by Bolshevik troops on Lenin's orders. They described how President Yeltsin 'really spoke from his heart, admitting his own personal wrong and spoke movingly of the need to enter the next century in a spirit of repentance and reconciliation'. A cynic or a non-religious person might not believe that much sincerity was present, but even the most cynical can see the *realpolitik* usefulness of such statements, if they succeed in healing wounds and reintegrating the population into national structures.

Memory

Memory has particular importance in a hundred years that have traumatized whole nations, even continents. War has defined their consciousness and thus the way they remember those experiences has been widely understood to dictate how they will deal with the aftermath of war, even across generations. The wars in the FRY and FSU are particular instances of this being bought to stark public attention. The reason is that the 'identity' of the constituent peoples of the FRY and FSU has conspicuously come to full nationhood in the context of war, as arguably have many nation states in the past two hundred years. Tilly's statement that 'war made the state, and the state made war' has often been quoted in that context. If we are to unravel how to transform that formative experience into a peaceful future coexistence, then the mechanisms of memory and truth and how they link into that of identity are crucial ones to explore.

The idea of forgiveness and reconciliation after wars is one deeply embedded in the religious and moral discourses of peace. Christianity is full of symbols of reconciliation and *not* taking revenge – 'turn the other cheek'; 'love your enemy' and so on. These dictums are all based on the sound idea that we have to live with each other *after* the war. Hence forgiveness can be and has been interpreted in many ways. *Roget's Thesaurus* giving as near equivalents 'pardon, exoneration, absolution, dispensation, acquittal, reprieve, amnesty, mercy, forbearance, grace, exculpation, deliverance, indulgence, clemency, compassion, charity', a roll-call of religious (certainly Christian, Jewish and Islamic) key words.[14] Equally, the idea that we should apologise and then atone for our crimes is also one that is lost in the depths of the great moral and religious traditions. It is arguably one of the bedrocks of all moral conscience and behaviour. It has also always been difficult. One of the difficulties for the application of such a concept in this context is that what may be conceivable in personal religious terms is inevitably more difficult in relations between states or peoples. The latter do not have a collective conscience, so to what can one appeal?

Equally, in all religions, forgiveness is usually preceded by apology, and an apology sincerely felt, as well as a heartfelt promise to change the behaviour that elicited the forgiveness in the first place. Forgiveness therefore equates with a transformation of the relationship between two previously hostile parties, but it does not allow for too many future lapses. An example of the wrath that this might be said to have bought down on the 'forgiven' is the American reaction to Germany in 1945. Woodrow Wilson chastized his allies in 1918 for the harshness with which they had treated Germany; in 1945 it was an American, Henry Morgenthau, who is remembered for his plan to reduce Germany to agricultural servitude. Forgiveness and reconciliation took a great deal more effort in 1945 than they would have done in 1918.

The logic gets more difficult with historical experience of repeated betrayal. In the Middle East, Jews and Arabs will have to do a deal eventually, unless war for the next 50 years is envisaged as a possibility. The histories and mythologies of all states have examples of individuals being made to atone for crimes against

God or against the people and to atone for this in public ways, from execution, to the abasement of self. Ian Baruma suggests that there are cultures that work through shaming (as with the Japanese or Chinese) that would have different perspective on this atonement.[15] As one who comes from Canterbury the obvious example is that of English king Henry the Second who crawled through the streets to apologize at the shrine of Thomas à Beckett for having him put to death.

But we are still stuck with the dilemma about what is remembered and by whom, and also why do certain historical memories get forgotten, while others remain as 'truth'. Why did the Germans 'forget' that they invaded Belgium, but 'remember' that the Treaty of Versailles was 'iniquitous'? Paul Ricoeur sees this as a phenomenological problem, one of how, to uses Husserl's term, we create our *Lebenswelt* and how that relates to what Charles Casey calls 'Remembering'. This in turn is made up of a series of 'mnemonic modes' – 'Reminding, Reminiscing, Recognizing'. 'Reminding' can be as banal as tying a knot in your handkerchief, or not forgetting to give the cat some food; 'Reminiscing', a much more profound form of remembering, is a process of re-living the past which takes place in the writing of volumes of memoirs and the historical archival record; while 'Recognizing' in effect fixes a memory in the mind, individual or collective.[16]

Identity

This phenomenology of memory is one of the great driving forces in the process of changing that memory and making reconcilation possible. It is also one of the great forces for potentially making the opposite happen. The memory machines are constantly at work in Ireland and in the Balkans for example. In Ireland, Alan D. Falconer points out that 'Roman Catholic identity would be affirmed as an identity-in-opposition to Protestants. ... Now to be a Catholic was not to be a Protestant.' This in turn led to the independence of two traditions, and an identification of the 'other' as the basis of two worldviews, or *Lebenswelt*. This in turn led to a constant entrenchment of position based on historical 'truth'.[17]

Joseph Liechty, again talking of forgiveness in Northern Ireland, stresses 'repentance is both personal and corporate'. The argument he puts forward to underline this comes 'from the fact that we are social beings who find our identity in historically rooted communities. ... To the extent that we identify with a particular community, we must be involved in repentance for its sins.' The example he cites, apart from Northern Ireland, is that of the 1945 Stuttgart Confession of Guilt by the German Evangelical Church for their part in Nazi excesses. He also points out that the processes of forgiveness are part of a human need with a moving quote from Hannah Arendt:

> Without being forgiven, released from the consequences of what we have done, our capacity to act would, as it were, be confined to one single deed from which we could never recover; we would remain victims of its consequences forever.

In other words, we could never change or grow as people.[18] Only liberals would ever assume that this was truly possible for most, if not all, people. But equally those who refuse to forgive cannot grow themselves, perhaps the true meaning of 'hell is other people.' Forgiveness for such moral and religious philosophers is thus part of a process that leads to all other forms of development and peace. To reconcile people or to resolve conflicts between them thus has an identical logic that is only acceptable to a liberal mindset.

As to how this might apply to war and peace we all have an intuitive feeling, often based on a certain amount of 'empirical' evidence learnt at a grandparent's knee, that war and memory are linked experiences. As Martin Shaw has put it: '[w]e can hypothesise that tradition, myths, memory and propaganda to do with past wars will be extremely important in our relationships to current conflicts.'[19] Two of the key emotions that this relationship provokes are the twin assertions of guilt and the demand for restitution, whether that is in the form of an apology, a punishment or a payment of some kind. This then contributes to the creation and perpetuation of 'national traditions and myths' that motivate feelings in the next conflict or conflicts.

An obvious and widely quoted example would be British feelings about the Japanese as a result of atrocities committed against prisoners of war in the Pacific theatre. In that case there is an apparent clash between Baruma's 'shaming' culture, one that finds it difficult to admit to past faults without sensing deep humiliation, coming into collision with a Christian culture that sees such admissions as cathartic but essential for all concerned. Hence the importance of small words. Snoopy would not have much sympathy for the idea that 'being Japanese is never having to say you are "sorry"'. The Japanese Emperor's expression of 'deep regret' would be seen by many Japanese as going far more than the extra mile in meeting the pain of those who had suffered on the Burma railway.

There is also the question of when do you have to stop apologizing. When Japanese Premier Junichiro Koizumi, by far the most genuinely popular Premier with the electorate since the Second World War, dared to offer his condolences at the Yasukuni War Shrine in Tokyo the outrage in Korea and China was enormous, a dozen Korean gangsters even lopping off their fingers in public in protest. The anguish was also directed against the Japanese refusal to withdraw school textbooks that minimized the Japanese wartime exploits in China and Korea, including massacres, the setting up of slave brothels and lethal medical experiments on live subjects, but the appearance of Koizumi at the Shrine seemed to give these disquiets official confirmation. President Kim of Korea remarked '[s]ome people in Japan are attempting to distort history, casting dark clouds over Korea–Japan relations again. How can we make good friends with people who try to forget and ignore the many pains they inflicted on us? How can we deal with them in future with any degree of trust?'[20]

Shaw widens that discussion to bring in what we might term 'truth by analogy'. He uses the example of the British memory of the Second World War and their effect on the Gulf War of 1991. He quotes many who equated Saddam Hussein with Hitler and even one man who said you could 'substitute Kurds for

Jews ... Kuwait for Poland and so on'.[21] Memory can therefore create what are self-evidently false analogies that fuel the fires of war; as for example did Anthony Eden's famous, and fatuous, equation of Nasser with Hitler during the Suez crisis of 1956. Such evocation of memories is particularly important when public opinion plays such an important role in war. The fact that Eden's comparison was so evidently absurd for a large part of the British population probably had an influence on his subsequent resignation. It was much easier for Saddam to evoke memories of the British colonial presence in the Gulf to mobilize even sceptical Arab opinion around his appalling regime.

Conflict resolution

Given such renewed and often inspiring thinking about the possibilities of addressing the 'new' conditions of war and peace, how can we try and distil some basic ideas and wisdom out of what has in fact been tried to bring about conflict resolution and, ultimately, reconciliation? It has to be appreciated that the two concepts are intimately linked, as Galtung points out in the quote at the top of this chapter. He would indeed probably argue that you cannot have one without the other. But an academic text has to try and tease out the logics of doing what are two rather different activities, conflict resolution often by small teams of academics or diplomats in either 'first track' (diplomatic) or 'second track' (informal) settings; reconciliation by and between huge numbers of people in truth commissions and other such settings and definitely at a grass roots level. To do this I shall first try to emphasize some of what I believe to be the key insights of those who have written about and practised conflict resolution, of necessity a very small part of a huge and growing field.

What is conflict?

It is generally agreed that conflict can be said to be where there occurs a clash of interests, values or incompatible goals between two or more parties. It is seen as an increasingly complex phenomenon, especially as regards the context of the practice and study of IR. This is because conflict, of which one variant is war, is not just seen as taking place between states, but also within them. We could ask ourselves of course whether this is a real insight or whether it is only one derived from a long rejection of non-realist arguments during the Cold War. But it can be said without much fear of contradiction that the kind of conflict that was the focus of study and action during the Cold War was that of state versus state. And it also can be said that we now talk far more in terms of a global possibility to resolve conflict and of a corresponding fear of 'global chaos'.[22] The language of conflict resolution has thus paradoxically turned, for the optimists, from management to resolution and for others in the obverse direction.

This has led to much more reflection about how conflicts can be predicted and even prevented. Many international organizations, such as the UN and the EU, have set up bodies and structures to try and achieve this aim and the academic discipline of IR has produced many tomes and articles on these efforts and their problems. There is much debate as to whether this is a an 'art' or a 'science'.[23] The central idea of this thinking at both theoretical and institutional level has to do with the prevention of the escalation of potential but not yet serious conflicts into war so as to avoid the prevention of the emergence of future conflicts based on current problems.

What is conflict resolution?

The discipline of conflict analysis has been divided for many years about what theoretical insights can be drawn from a case study of third party activity within conflict situations.[24]

The main relevant body of thought hinges around the definition of what a third party is actually doing by being involved in someone else's conflict. Is the party a 'mediator', a 'problem solver', or an 'arbitrator' for example? Sharp distinctions between these categories of action are often drawn, and many miles of print have been used up on definition. The argument often hinges around the initial 'paradigmatic approach' taken by the theorists of conflict (be they realist, Marxist or liberal/pluralist'), the nature of the actor involved (individual, state, international organization, etc.) and the level of power in the hands of this actor.

It is, however, arguable that the functional result of any such activity is the same, whether it be by an official 'first track' mediator (for example a state or an international organization), or by an unofficial third party actor (often referred to as a 'second track' actor and sometimes as a 'problem solving' track in that it has no inherent power except to persuade). All these third parties are trying:

(a) to complement, or even to constitute, the basis for the negotiation process. They are not likely to be the only party trying to act as a third party;
(b) to both manage (or settle, often by coercive means) and resolve the conflict.

A great deal of the academic debate is about the distinction between these different modes of operation. What is perhaps different about the problem solving approach, which explicitly aims at long-term resolution, as opposed to other forms of mediatory activity, is the emphasis put by its theorists on encouraging a 'dialogue between adversaries' which 'implies acceptance of the other person's fundamental values and the worth of the person him- or her-self', the goal being in Herbert Kelman's words 'to establish working trust'. The aim is thus a transformation of consciousness, so that the adversaries try and work side-by-side, not face to face.

It might be said that this overestimates the desire by most adversaries to try and accommodate the other in some way. But it does have the merit of reflecting the phenomenon of the 'new' war better than that of the 'Clausewitzian' variety. As John Darby and Roger McGinty have put it, in the 'new' conditions, even more than in the 'old':

> Peace Processes do not emerge from a vacuum. They require conscious decisions, initial steps, fresh analyses and risk taking. . . . [They are] necessarily delicate and often proceed against a backdrop of continuing violence and instability.[25]

The reasons for this are complex, but they are surely linked into the changing nature of war itself. As war has become less the exclusive preserve of the Prince and more that of the community and even of the individual, as in Bosnia or much of Africa, the nature of peacemaking has had to adapt too. As war is now far less 'top-down' so peace making has had to become far more 'bottom-up'. Powerful liberal states now trying to democratize the world in their own image have had to get down to the grass roots to do so, and have found their military and diplomatic establishments wanting. They have had to turn to much less conventional methods and personnel for the realization of their peace aims, especially to Non-Governmental Organizations, think tanks like the USIP and academic departments that specialize in dealing with war-torn societies. Liberal states have developed internal mechanisms for the prevention and resolution of conflicts in their own polities. When confronted with the debris of illiberal communities that were once states, as in many parts of the world, there has been a growing attempt to transfer not only democracy and other liberal institutions but also the practices of liberal societies.

That this has seen an explosion since 1990 is clearly linked to the end of the Cold War and the possibility for liberal states and societies to export these practices. It would be wrong to over-state this process, but what has seemingly been happening over the last decade or so has been the 'civilianizing' of peace-making. A question that is still moot is as to whether this very recent development will prove to be the harbinger of future core action by liberal international society and the entities that make it up or a false dawn that will be consigned to oblivion by a renewed presence of the state?

The United States has even avoided recourse to the United Nations as much as possible in its recent pacification of Iraq. But even the United States uses a liberal logic to underpin its actions there, the spread of democracy. The idea of preventive war has taken firm root since the attacks on New York of '9/11'. What is being prevented is allegedly the return of an illiberal regime in Iraq and the export of violence by such a regime to its neighbours or violence being visited upon its domestic population. The best guarantee of this is democracy. The United States Administration can thus with some justification claim that it is pursuing liberal aims using a liberal logic.

However, whereas the terms prevention and resolution have long semantic ancestries, the linking of the two is a phenomenon that can be said to be very recent. Again a central reason can be said to be the increasing liberal-led debate about the nature of the state in a globalizing world and the corresponding belief that there is a normative sea change away from the rights of states and towards those of individuals, the agenda that we can characterize as that of human rights. Neither theorists of IR or even of its sub-sets of normative or ethical thinking in IR or students of human rights were until recently taken seriously *en bloc*. The main reason though is because during the Cold War it was usually taken as a given within IR theory that the motives of Western statesmen and politicians were generally honourable and invested with a natural understanding of ethical values. The 'bad guys', those who systematically abused such rights in the name of democratic centralism or proletarian internationalism, were obviously the Socialist states. After all they had never signed up to the civil and political aspects of the United Nations human rights legislation, they denied in other words the very importance of the individual.

With the end of the Cold War the widespread feeling was that all that had changed. We now all belonged to what the 1990 Charter of Paris called a 'New Era of Democracy, Peace and Unity. . . . Ours [was] a time for fulfilling the hopes and expectations our peoples have cherished for decades.' This was contemporaneous with a large number of new states springing forth from the former Soviet Union in August 1991, and a half dozen largely 'velvet' revolutions liberating the former satellite states of Eastern Europe. As Unto Vesa put it from the standpoint of 2000: '[t]his non-violent transformation of the international system is a truly remarkable achievement.'[26] Much of the activity to bring about conflict resolution, up to and including a belief in the possibility of conflict prevention has fed on this optimism and renewed belief that war can be conquered.

But of course all this congratulation has now turned sour for many of those who first trumpeted the triumph of non-violent change. This has led to some startling contentions from distinguished scholars of peace and war. For example, William Zartman tells us in his 1998 USIP publication, *Peacemaking in International Conflict*, that '[o]n the edge of the millennium, the methods of conflict have been more brutal and the methods of conflict resolution more sophisticated than ever before, leaving a tremendous gap between reality and theory that remains to be filled'.[27] It remains to be proved that wars and conflicts are somehow far more 'brutal' than they were, and it also remains to be tested as to whether the methods to resolve them are far more 'sophisticated'. What is clear however is that liberal beliefs in the tractability of conflict have declined in line with liberal self-belief as the euphoria of 1990 has faded. So why is this?

One answer has to do with the links between the state and conflict. As has been noted in this book and elsewhere there has been much theorizing and empirical observation about how the post-Cold War era might be said to have led, or be leading, to a new negotiation of the state/people/history relationship, with a concomitant interest in questions of identity, and the new ethical position of the state. The main problem, as has also been widely noted, is that worries, as expressed by the 'post-modernists' about a post-territorial state are largely nonsense for those who cannot benefit from non-state phenomena. For many, war still justifies the need for a state and its hoped-for provision of basic human needs. There is therefore a central liberal dilemma in that Western dominated liberal elites and institutions are trying to grapple with both a world that they see as more aspiring to the needs of individual and global forces while many just hanker after strong states or wish to have such an institution to defend them.

The conflicts in the former Soviet Union and former Yugoslavia, it has been argued, are classic examples of this dichotomy of desire and praxis in action. In these cases there is also the problem that their interests are quite simply too difficult to ignore as they are part of a much greater whole. Gail Lapidus has mused on the quasi-impossibility for the rest of the world to do much about, say, the Russians in Chechnya for such actions raise:

> troubling questions about the possibilities and limit of preventative diplomacy when the behaviour of a major power (Russia) is at stake, when the issue is framed as an internal rather than interstate conflict, and when other political priorities take precedence (the wars in Bosnia and Kosovo).[28]

Another observation is to summarize what many see, erroneously in the view of this writer, as a natural progression in the contemplation of conflict by the international community since the Second World War. To enlarge on the comments above about 'management', settlement' and 'resolution', it is certain that the school of thought which has dominated what is known as the 'first track', that is the work of diplomacy and foreign offices in general, has been one of conflict 'management'. According to this version of history the assumption was that it is impossible to actually bring about a transformation of conflict, but rather just to hold a lid on it, or 'manage' it. Some even claim that conflict can only be dealt with by 'settlement', often a euphemism for the use of force. One major liberal dilemma must therefore be why there are so many opportunities for conflict 'resolution' and so few real examples of the idea being taken on board and used by diplomats. One case where it was, in the so-called 'Oslo Process' in the Middle East, has been deemed a failure as peace has certainly not descended on that area, though there is still a 'Quartet' of countries (the United States, Russia, the EU and the UN) engaged in a long term 'first track' enterprise that produced a 'Road Map' for peace, one that has so far led nowhere.

So liberals might claim that since the end of the Cold War we now have a new paradigm of resolution where conflicts are seen as transformable, and where the parties' behaviour and even attitudes can be changed to make conflict a thing of the past, at least in theory. But while there has certainly been an explosion in the *belief* in the possibility of resolution of the type here described, that has most emphatically not replaced the belief in, and the consequent actions of, management and settlement.

Reconciliation

As we have seen, the first essential element of a discussion of retribution and reconciliation is to acknowledge that these are very old ideas and practices. A second essential starting point is that for liberals, interdependence and then globalization means that we have to get on together or there will be endless war among states and peoples who have access to almost unlimited weaponry of destruction of increasing sophistication. In other words liberal ideas about peace and realist ones about the need to regulate violence are now seen as having come together from opposite ends of a spectrum to combine in a sole logic.

Nonetheless, misgivings about peace without real justice continue to concern peacemakers and warriors alike. Can you make peace without satisfying basic needs for justice and esteem? Are those not based not only on an acceptance of the other, but also on a genuine mutual respect? How can this ever be ensured and maintained? To quote a commentator on the Northern Ireland peace process, might you not just end up with a 'bad-tempered peace', not a real one?[29]

The answer to this is often coined in the word reconciliation. However, if resolution has had a hard time getting itself accepted in the corridors of government, no matter how much it has been urged on policy makers by think tanks and academics, the concept of reconciliation has fared little better. But, like conflict resolution, this has not stopped academics and, more importantly, governments in war-torn countries from trying it out.

Truth commissions

There is a growing band of academics and policy makers who have taken to the study of the attempts, started in the mid-1970s, to bring about a new kind of reconciliation that aims at finding out the truth as its primary aim, without the concomitant pair of retribution that is a feature of all war crimes tribunals, through what are usually called truth commissions with the aim of producing a restorative justice. Kenneth Christie defines them as 'mechanisms, amongst other strategies, to consolidate and establish some form of democratic process in a country – usually following a long period of authoritarian or dictatorial rule'.[30] To this could be added, 'usually after a prolonged internal war', or in some cases even an external one, as in the case of Argentina in 1982.

Patricia Hayner and Christie have identified 15 such commissions that were set up between 1974 and 1994, including Argentina, Chile, Uruguay, Bolivia, Zimbabwe, the Philippines, Chad, Germany, El Salvador, Rwanda and Ethiopia, as well as calls for them in Mexico and South Korea. The number has risen since, with Commissions in Sri Lanka, Haiti, Burundi, Nigeria and, most famously, South Africa (1995–2000), 21 in all by 2001.[31] The initial fervour for them arose after the Falklands/Malvinas war of 1982, when the defeated Argentinian Junta was forced to stand down. The newly elected democratic government of Raúl Alfonsín decided that the best way to find out the truth of the disappearances that had taken place under the Junta was to give immunity from prosecution to the offending military and para-military agents of the state.[32]

There is not space here to discuss all of these cases in detail, so an attempt will be made to see what are the wider lessons of a few more recent ones, starting with that of South Africa.

Truth and reconciliation in South Africa

The history of apartheid is only now being fully written. Apartheid literally means 'separation' or 'apartness' and was defined as a 'crime against humanity', almost on a par with genocide in 1961. UN General Assembly Resolution 3068 of 30 November 1973 created an 'International Convention on the Suppression and Punishment of the Crimes of Apartheid'. The preposterous and illogical nature of a policy that believed in the separation of races in education, land and virtually very aspect of life right down to the marriage (or extra-marital) bed should not blind us to its reality for millions of South Africans of all races from 1948 to 1992. *Apartheid* left 4 million people confined forcibly to 13 per cent of South Africa's territory, all in very infertile, desegregated so-called 'homelands'. It was kept going though incredible brutality, 'Pass' laws, massacres like that at Sharpeville in 1960, and a Bureau of State Security. It has no equivalent in the history of the world outside Nazi Germany, except possibly in some aspects of the segregation policies of some states of the Deep South of the United States, whose policies are said to have inspired the National Party politicians of South Africa.[33] But finally *apartheid* proved too difficult to keep going and it collapsed in the 1990s. In 1994 elections were held, and Nelson Mandela was the first properly elected President of a new South Africa.

But one of the key places where the history of *apartheid* was revealed, and arguably the place where it was finally buried, was in the South African 'Truth and Reconciliation Commission' (TRC), set up in 1995.[34] It was of course played out in the shadow of other events around the world. Christie relates how in the early 1990s many in South Africa feared that South Africa might become 'another Bosnia'. The negotiations that took several years and culminated with the release of Mandela, elections and the setting up on new democratic institutions and the TRC were immensely delicate and took place against the background of a white minority that held most of the military cards and yet acknowledged that it would have to share power with the black majority. The testimony that took place over nearly two years was intended to minimize a violent takeover; to promote a democratic climate and institutions and; 'to facilitate reconstruction and development, especially where violence had been particularly acute. The remit of the TRC was to elicit as much of the whole truth about state violence during the apartheid era as possible, in return for which amnesty would be granted. In so doing it was hoped that the TRC would act as a "nation-building" mechanism and reconcile old enemies.'[35]

Its basic principles[36] were: that it was open, that it was not a 'trial', but that in order that a real trial would not follow, those who testified must make full disclosure of their crimes in order to obtain amnesty. Its aims were to tell the truth and heal wounds. This was not to equate forgiveness with reconciliation, and it was accepted that victims may be able to do the second but not the first. Equally there was an expectation that acknowledgement would not be the same as apology without true repentance and forgiveness and that you cannot expect the whole 'truth' – high expectations would make the job very difficult, if not impossible. Finally it had to be accepted that 'justice is a search not a single event', in other words that you cannot stop evil, even if you exorcise it. It was also accepted that although time must be allowed to do its work, with the hope that at least knowing what happened and asking for forgiveness would start a process of reconciliation.

The 'lessons' of the TRC

The literature on the lessons of this and other TRCs is voluminous and we cannot here but scratch the surface. For Christie, the first big problem of the TRC, and one that has enormous resonance for all new democratic states since the end of the Cold War, has been to ask: 'how is legitimacy established' in states after the terror of war or conflict has subsided? As he puts it:

> Should ... a hard line [be taken], attempting to prosecute through their criminal justice system the perpetrators of misdeeds or should they offer unconditional amnesty to the former, a willed amnesia to simply forget the past, let bygones be bygones and plan for the future [?]

This is especially difficult in the 'transitional stage' of a country's history, in this case South Africa, but in general terms when any state is moving towards democracy. Hence 'truth commissions have emerged as a middle ground often trying to avoid either end of the spectrum while coming to terms with the past'. It is nonetheless 'an attempt to clean up the moral and social fabric' or even, in Christie's view, to *create* a social fabric as one did not exist for most of the population before the end of *apartheid*. It was a choice of the new democratic South Africa to try and avoid 'half measures' and the reason for this is because South Africa itself was:

> born out of a series of negotiations in which there were no outright winners and losers. It was also an affirmation that the new South Africa would be a place of 'openness' and 'willingness to face the past', quite unlike the old country which it replaced.[37]

Second, Christie points out that finding the whole truth is almost impossible, but much does in fact come out, about the accusers as much as about the accused. Much is lost through selective memory either because the mind tends to block out horror, or because there has been so much that has intervened since dreadful events happened. However, for the victims the memory is always fresh of dead loved ones or events that were seen as minor by officials that committed them in the course of their 'duty'. In effect, transition must excuse much; many of those interviewed by Christie seem to be saying. Not that it maybe so, but that in many such societies there is not much choice if you want the society to calm down, reassess itself and move on. In South Africa, as in Chile and other cases, there was no clear 'winner' so the winner could not impose the definition of truth. That had to be negotiated. The post-conflict settlement therefore has to be seen as 'therapeutic' not, as after 1945, as settling scores between victim and torturer. Equally there are those, like Archbishop Tutu, who believe in the power of genuine apology that leads to exorcism, forgiveness, and ultimately reconciliation, if not forgetting. On the whole for Tutu and Christie the important thing is not to concentrate on the 'icebergs of resentment' that will always remain, but to concentrate on 'forging shared values and attributes, allowing us to remember and not forget, but of course to learn from memory'.[38]

Getting people to admit their role in crimes of *apartheid* is also difficult. In 1967, 67 per cent of whites voted for the National Party and a survey by the Centre for the Study of Violence and Reconciliation found that even in the immediate post-apartheid era 40 per cent of whites saw the discredited policy as having been a 'good idea, but poorly implemented' and that most whites interviewed 'were unconvinced that they had any role in apartheid abuses'.[39]

The problems are till acute. It is questionable whether 'nation building' has so far been enhanced. The TRC itself has admitted that it is impossible to 'reconcile the nation', although one of its supporters argues that this is because there is a misconception 'that it was called to initiate reconciliation instead of promoting that which already existed'. Perhaps the great achievement was to achieve democracy, 'the enabling act as it were for all future projects with the view to advancing and consolidating reconciliation'.[40] Many believe that such appalling crimes cannot be forgiven or forgotten. Some believe that memory gets in the way of nation building – as Christie quotes Ernst Renan as saying, and noting that the National Party and the Inkhata [Zulu] Party agreed with him.[41] Not all share Tutu's Christian charity, stupendous and impressive though this may be. Much of the violence of *apartheid* South Africa has indeed gone, but it has been replaced by a different kind of violence, much of which may still be fed by racial hatred, and memory of past misdeeds. So the question still remains as to whether the telling of 'truth' will necessarily lead to reconciliation.

Reconciliation as a panacea?

Can reconciliation be a panacea for all crimes committed in the past and all deeply felt historical wrong? Clearly not. As Mick Cox has written [though] all wars run their courses and ultimately come to an end, this does not in itself eradicate the underlying causes of the conflict. Nor does it necessarily lead to reconciliation between the various parties.'[42] The reasons for this are eloquently stated by Robert Rothstein: for 'the psychological traumas of the past are still powerful because the past is neither forgotten nor forgiven what ever the nature of the peace agreement'.[43] The peace is therefore hopefully just the beginning of reconciliation, not the end of it. In some cases, as in 1918, the peace agreement is the beginning of the end for all reconciliation as it has been made abundantly clear to the vanquished parties that they are solely to blame for tall the horrors that have just been endured in the war.

'Peace without reconciliation' – Northern Ireland?

If we take the example of Northern Ireland, it might appear at first sight that there can be examples of 'peace without reconciliation', to use the words of Robin Wilson.[44] As one of the longest and seemingly most intractable conflicts in modern European history, the peace process in Northern Ireland is one of the most interesting to test against the above considerations of reconciliation as policy option in ending wars. The process could be said to have been going on since the time of Cromwell. English rulers have always considered that the whole of Ireland has been their natural fiefdom and it is often claimed that Ireland was the first British colony and the last to be liberated. The above discussion about Irish 'identity' has in turn led to a constant entrenchment of position based on historical 'truth'.[45]

One major problem is one of what are the Irish, or who is being reconciled to whom? There are traditions in Irish life that contradict and therefore have constituted several political realities. The sheer length of the history of the island and its internal relationships as well as those with the mainland of Great Britain mean that historical justification by all sides has been a *sine qua non* for continuing the struggle seen by those sides and the righting of historical wrongs as a key aim of any eventual peace settlement.

The phenomenon of a continual renewal of such demands by successive generations has made the making of peace a very difficult task to undertake. Hence in the Home Rule struggle of the late nineteenth century there was an extreme wing of Irish republicanism that emerged (Sinn Fein) to demand absolute sovereignty; in 1921 there was a breakaway from the Irish Free State under Eamonn De Valera (The Irish Republican Army – IRA) that again demanded full sovereignty. In the 'Troubles' of 1969 there were calls for more civil liberties in the North that soon became demands for a renewed claim to total sovereignty and the IRA split into 'Official' and 'Provisional' wings. Then the Provisional wing itself split over the Good Friday Agreement of 1999 and a new 'Real IRA' emerged. It is legitimate to ask if this cycle of inter-generational conflict can ever be ended.

None the less, serious attempts at a reconciliation of the demand for self-rule by the Irish and the Good Friday agreement in Northern Ireland provides a paradigmatic case of reconciliation being given a good start by the introduction of the notion of parity of esteem. In this way of looking at the peace, the parties are said to accept that there is no blame attributable, just the aspiration for a future balanced and respectful relationship.

Reconciliation in the former Yugoslavia

Quite apart from the legal discussions of the previous chapter we also have the problems that the peoples of the Former Yugoslavia still have to try and live together. Since the Dayton Agreement of 1995 there has been some progress within Bosnia, but this has been painfully slow. At the time of writing there have been dialogue attempts undertaken by a series of NGOs, where there has been little real academic or political interest. The only semi-official attempts at reconciliation have been under the auspices of the 'German Mediator', a body in Bosnia/Herzegovina.[46]

On a practical level there as been much progress between Serbia and Croatia. It is now possible for the first time to take a train between Belgrade and Zagreb, air links have been restored and the flow of populations, even to take up former residences, has accelerated. The first 'official reconciliation visit' since 1995 by the Presidents Stjepan Mesic of Croatia and Svetozar Marovic of Serbia and Montenegro took place on 10 September 2003.[47] The emphasis was on apology, the existence of 'good Serbs' even during the war,[48] and on turning a new page in Balkan history, but the newspaper reports still stressed the security worries of having such a juicy target for Serb nationalists in Belgrade. Serb Prime Minister Zoran Djindjic's assassination in Belgrade by such people in February 2003 underlined the fact that not everyone wanted such a reconciliation to take place. There is also a deal of evidence of a widespread phenomenon of what might be termed 'denial'. Many Serb women simply refuse to believe that their men could behave like that. One source shows that many Serbs refuse to believe the Srebrenica massacres happened at all.[49]

Rwanda and Sierra Leone[50]

Rwanda is a landlocked African state with a population of barely 7 million. Between April and July 1994 one group, the Hutus, massacred approximately 800,000 of their Tutsi co-citizens, about 11 per cent of the total population, or about 8,000 a day for one hundred days.[51] The massacres took place within a civil war, which ended, at least provisionally, when the Tutsi based Rwandan Patriotic Front took over after the massacres. By the end of 2003 there were still 120,000 suspects detained by the Rwandan Government in connection with these crimes, of whom about 40,000 have now been released in an amnesty on the understanding that they admitted to their crimes.[52]

There is general agreement that this ethnic identity divide was largely the invention of the colonial power, Belgium in this case, in order to better control the population by imposing a hitherto non-existent hierarchy, with the Tutsis at the top. This introduced a racial element into a society that had not seen the world in that way before.[53] The colonists left another legacy behind them, that of an organized state system, that was used with dazzling efficiency during the massacres (as it was in Germany between 1933 and 1945). The rate of killing has been calculated at five times that of the Nazi death camps, with 80 per cent of the victims dispatched within six weeks.

Although there is in existence an official WCT to deal with aftermath of the 1994 massacres in Rwanda, it has been largely discredited and has had little effect. The International Criminal Tribunal for Rwanda (ICTR) has thus been complemented by internal processes that have led to overcrowded prisons and mass public executions, as well as the Gacaca courts which resemble far more the workings of the South African TRC. These latter courts are people's courts that operate in a very open way and that attempt to find the truth and to bring about reconciliation between people who wish to resume their former lives in a new way. They are deeply embedded within pre-colonial tribal practice, much as it might be said that the TRC is embedded within South African religious practice.

But there are clear dilemmas both with the ICTR and the domestic processes. It could easily be argued that the crimes committed in Rwanda were indeed ones of one community against another, an idea, as Jackson Maogoto suggests, which is not consonant with the idea of a WCT. These were not, in the words of the resolution setting up the ICTR 'individual violations of international criminal law'. As Maogoto points out the only dissenting voices to the setting up of the ICTR were Rwanda itself which feared the emergence of a 'culture of impunity' if individuals could blame some larger structure and voted against the Tribunal, and the Czech Republic which dissented but still voted for it. This latter, struggling with its own problems of reconciliation thought the ICTR would only be a vehicle for justice, 'but it is hardly designed as a vehicle for reconciliation. ... Reconciliation is a much more complicated process.' Maogoto suggest that the problem lies with its 'actor-oriented' approach.[54]

It remains to be seen if the Gacaca courts can do better. Maogoto considers that what we have seen in practice in Rwanda is the mass punishment of many by the Government, which has in effect ignored the WCTR. While the International instance has 53 indictees, of whom 45 are actually in custody, the Rwandan Government has over 125,000 in custody. This is retribution on a grand scale, not the 'actor-oriented' approach of the liberal WCTR: 'the Tutsis are more focussed on the national trials that will send the guilty to the gallows, not some ritzy international trial that will send the guilty to Europe'.[55] These are not sentiments which fit well with a liberal sensibility, but do have the ring of authenticity.

The same might yet be said of the Special Court for Sierra Leone. This however has the unique characteristic (to date) of being a hybrid of belonging both to the Provisional Government of Sierra Leone and the international community, which has largely organized its implementation. Many of the problems it poses are practical: how can the right mix of local personnel and customs with international practices and norms be achieved?; how can it physically be set up? The latter has been achieved by bringing in 188 Slovenian containers, the former by using international legislation for such crimes as genocide, while using the local code for 'lesser' crimes such as child abuse.[56]

Conclusions

The first series of what must be tentative conclusions have to be about liberal views and practices themselves and their internal contradictions. The foundational problem with a liberal claim to ownership of the rise of reconciliation as a basic ideal to end wars and various types of conflict resolution as mechanisms to help in this aim is that they are not tendencies that can be entirely laid at the feet of liberal ideology. Liberals and realists alike have alternatively turned hot and cold on mechanisms like truth commissions and the use of techniques of conflict resolution as they either seemed to be working or were not.

In the twentieth century it was a liberal coalition of the Allies after 1918 that did much to damage the notions of reconciliation and resolution for the next 20 years after the Treaty of Versailles. But liberals were then among the major advocates of a peace with justice and reconciliation with Germany in the 1930s.

The paradox is that they themselves then became retroactively associated with policies of appeasement that had let the Nazis rise to power. Realists of the 1940s thus claimed that liberalism had proved itself bankrupt on moral as well as political grounds. But liberals can also be said to have reclaimed the mantle after the Second World War by demanding a peace with justice for the oppressed masses of Europe and a reconciliation of the peoples, even if that justice also looked rather like the victors were defining the wrongdoers. It would be absurd to make a moral equation between the bombing of Germany or of Japan, carried out with the clear war aim of shortening the war against aggressive states and therefore the overall level of suffering. But would it be entirely wrong to say that there was guilt on all sides? The Russian army conducted the Katyn massacres of Polish officers in 1941, not the Wehrmacht or the SS war crimes were committed by Allied troops. The Allied bombing campaign of Germany has now been reappraised and not without guilt being attributed to the bombers.

How can this play out in the conditions of 'new' wars alluded to in the first part of this chapter? Undoubtedly the idea of the 'new' war has the ring of truth and the structural problems that many failed states have are largely as Kaldor points out, but this is not the whole story. Wars of the last few years cannot be taken as a huge sample, and many of them are about getting nationhood, so are in line with a much older liberal idea of self-determination, not the more recent one of globalization. The international community does intervene, but that is still largely based on powerful states, as it always has been, and alliances of such states such as in the EU, UN and OSCE.

Cannot we say that 'failed states' can always be taken to have been typical of the majority? And what might be the solutions? Kaldor suggests the spread of a 'cosmopolitan democracy' is the only answer, with a strengthening of the institutions of civil society. The liberal model of parliamentary democracy (free elections, a focus on individual liberties) is the model hitherto pursued (for more on this see Chapter 5 in particular) cannot be said to have worked well in the countries of Africa, and in the FSU and FRY where it has long been touted as the solution.

The argument in favour of spreading the liberal peace through democracy and the growth of civil society also begs the question of whether the supporters of Osama Bin Laden or Milosevic, or the thugs that fight for and against Charles Taylor in West Africa really want this.[57] It also takes for granted that to transfer the ideas of the liberal intelligentsia to the Third World will meet with local or official favour, not necessarily so. It will seemingly have in any case to be imposed by Western power, which like all power (*pace* Mao Tse Tung) 'comes out of the barrel of a gun.'

Even if the hyperbole of Pipes' statements about Muslims earlier in this chapter jar on the liberal conscience, they also contain what a number of experts feel are some difficult truths. Commentators like Paul Wilkinson who have decried the illiberal backlash against civil liberties in the United States as a response to 9/11 also accept that the old responses to terrorism will not work where there is, in theory at least, no possible rapprochement between the demands for a pan-Islamic Caliphate demanded by Osama bin Laden and Western liberal democracy. The former requires a stateless world made up exclusively of Muslim entities, the latter a world based on Kantian democratic nation states open to all manner of 'strangers'. An organization like Al-Qaeda which is prepared to wage war not only on 'infidels' without mercy or quarter for civilians or military forces alike, or even on Muslims if they are considered 'apostate' by the extreme standards set by Al-Qaeda, can have nothing to talk about to liberal democracies. They are quite simply incompatible. Equally you cannot 'talk' to an organization like Aum Shinryiku in Japan that tries out its sarin on the Tokyo underground railway system. But, as Wilkinson has also pointed out, liberal states that respond with extreme measures of their own to such challenges will only give rise to more terrorism.[58]

So within think tanks like the USIP the dominant paradigm is still to look to conflict management – to do otherwise would be to be reproached for neglecting the national interest of the United States, and indeed of the liberal West. The Oslo accords have been seen as a failure by most policy makers in Washington.[59] But we should not overstate the differences between the 'managers' and 'resolvers' of conflicts. In many cases this can turn into a theological argument that has little application in the real world of making peace processes work. Peace processes in all cases require communities to find a way of living with or side by side with each other after a major internal or international war. In Bosnia, for example, there can be a managed peace while the wounds are still fresh, often in different regions of the country, ruled over by the High Commissioner of the OSCE (at the time of writing Lord Paddy Ashdown) or a ongoing process of 'resolution', such as that undertaken by the German Mediator, as outlined very briefly above. One does not negate the other. There is a need, as Ronald Fisher has pointed out, to understand that different levels of conflict treatment are needed, contingent on different levels of conflict, from war to peace.

There is also evidence that the emergence and evolution of the system of international justice, from the early beginnings of the Permanent International Court of Justice, which in effect put states on trial to the process, has seen its recent culmination in the International Criminal Court, one which has the power to put individuals on trial, and is a genuine liberal achievement. The international tribunals in Rwanda and the former Yugoslavia are also a reflection of what are seen by liberals as universally applicable rules of justice. The 'international community is invoked in all these cases as the legitimizing agent. But is the appeal of these bodies truly universal or does it rather again shows that the power of those that can exercise it has a tendency to overcome the objections of those that cannot?

We also need to ask a whole series of questions about the tensions between retribution and reconciliation. Do War Crimes Tribunals do the same thing as TRCs? In the Argentinian, Northern Ireland and South African cases the parties essentially reconciled themselves, even if third parties did play some role. In the case of Nuremberg/Rwanda/FRY the international community has done it – so the question is whether this is a good idea or not? Maybe we can only have closure, as has been argued in the Rwandan case, with 'justice'. But where does that justice stop, and where does the need for peace begin?

Christie also notes the difficulty of comparison, and the absence of studies of TRCs. His study of South Africa is explicitly an attempt to do this, but in fact it serves to underline the problems that are faced. Many states now face democratization and transition, most if not all face problems of eliminating political violence and all need to 'facilitate reconstruction and development'. So is the only logic that of the use of external or internal pressure, as in the Former Yugoslavia or Germany in 1945 or in Rwanda where the Hutu majority was finally routed so when there is an overwhelming military advantage for the international community – the logic of the winners? Conversely where there is no clear military victor or where there is an overwhelming need to negotiate an internal peace, as in South Africa or Argentina we might argue that TRCs are a *pis aller*, the only alternative to civil war and chaos.

If that is the case then the arguments of President Kostunica that Serbs needed to try Milosevic, not the Hague Tribunal, has much to recommend it. A successful attempt to extradite Milosevic, who was a democratically elected ruler in Serbia, would only have served to underline the collective guilt of Serbs, while not helping to solve democratic transition that the international community so desires. As with Germany in 1945, we would be left with the choice – peace or justice or rather peace and partial justice. It is surely better that Milosevic be tried in his own country and that this helps the internal reconciliation of Serbs than that we have the spectacle of justice (for he can scarcely have an unbiased trial) that then makes internal Serb reconciliation impossible. However where does that leave all the non-Serbs for whose suffering and deaths Milosevic is (allegedly) responsible? The analogy might be made that it was better to jail Al Capone for tax fraud when that was the least of his crimes – the very fact that he was shown to be sometimes subject to the law was better than he should be seen to be always above it.

There is also the problem evoked earlier of memory and historical understanding. One way of doing this is to return to the insight highlighted by Martin Shaw in his discussion of how wars create and perpetuate 'national traditions and myths'. In the British context one could also quote the counter-point of initial British reactions to the war in the FRY. A widespread claim, bolstered by Fitzroy MacLean who had acted as a liaison officer with the Partisans in the Second World War, was that military intervention would be impossible because 'Tito held down 300,000 German troops' and the same would happen again, another example perhaps of American envoy to the FRY, Richard Holbrooke's 'Rebecca West syndrome' quoted in the last chapter. But equally there was widespread confusion in Western Europe because the 'plucky Serbs' of 1914 and 1941 now seemed to be acting as if they were themselves the SS. There is an evident replaying of this in the accusations of many in Britain and elsewhere that the Serbs were the main culprits for the atrocities committed in the wars in the FRY, and that they should therefore pay a correspondingly higher price in terms of guilt and restitution.

The final comment comes as a reaction to the extremely provoking thoughts of Elazar Barkan. His conclusions are grouped around the idea that restitution for past crimes has now become a norm because the simple liberal idea of the individual has for him, in our 'post-Enlightenment' new phase or 'synthesis . . . supplemented by sociological insights about the place of the community and specific identity in the life of people'. This posits that we have become both global (through a shared acceptance of the importance of human rights) and local, so that we have to negotiate settlements locally 'among social movements with political identities. Thus any settlement is a social treaty' and it is specific to each case. He further argues that this system that leads to restitution as well as reconciliation, is different because 'both sides enter voluntarily into negotiations and agreements, they are not imposed by the winner upon the loser or by a third party'. This he argues is part of a growing culture, world wide, where restitution has become an important element of a 'moral economy' of restitution, most notably in Europe (as with the Germans and the Swiss) and in Northern America.[60]

Perhaps the key problem with what is an extremely moving and illuminating book that takes in the Holocaust, the crimes committed by the Soviet Union against Eastern Europe, and the mistreatment of colonial peoples is its very all-encompassing nature. He leaves the question of what actually constitutes an 'historical injustice' somewhat unresolved, leaving a sense with the reader that all victims of war are subject to such injustice, Germans, Jews, British, Americans, Poles, etc. The list can never end. Are we then all victims of historical injustice? Furthermore, as he himself states, this is a 'trend . . . still in its formative phases in international relations. . . . But such a standard is of a very provisional nature and if history teaches us anything, future circumstances will most likely shift notions of morality.' However, what is clear is that the phenomenon that he describes is very new and as yet undigested.

Lastly, and to return to the first premise of these concluding remarks, it could be argued that the idea of the dispensing of justice by the international community is still a very Western liberal idea. There is not much sign that the idea has caught on outside the narrow confines of Western states and liberal governments. The view amongst most Yugoslavs, of all ethnic groups, is that they are as much victimized as victimizers. There is no real willingness to accept global guilt and to make restitution. On the other hand there is the willingness, and much more widely than in the West, for reconciliation. Perhaps Barkan is thus embarking us on a route of conceptual confusion. What has happened in South Africa and in the Former Yugoslavia disproves at least some of his points. For one thing in South Africa and Northern Ireland there is no real talk of restitution, only the need for knowledge and truth. In the former Yugoslavia the reconciliation is externally imposed and reluctantly accepted because the powerful states of the system say it must be, through the Hague Tribunal.

Ultimately whether we believe in the power of forgiveness and the possibility or reconciliation, and though that peace, depends on our personal and collective *Lebenswelt* and *Weltanschauung.* A person of religious beliefs may have as much difficulty in this as an agnostic moral philosopher. Being a Christian did not help many 'ordinary' Germans, to use Daniel Goldhagen's phrase, from joining the more or less enthusiastic extermination of Jews on the Eastern Front.[61] Neither did it prevent many millions of Americans from hoping that the top, and many lesser, Nazis and Japanese would be tortured, slowly, before they were executed after 1945.[62]

Conclusion

Do liberal dilemmas disable all liberal solutions to war?

It is impossible for a foreigner to run another people of their own free will indefinitely.

T. E. Lawrence ('of Arabia'), 1918[1]

The war is not ended. It may be only at the beginning of the end of the first phase.

Tony Blair, 5 March 2004[2]

A war without an ending in sight.

John Kerry, 21 September 2004[3]

As this book is being finished the United States and the United Kingdom and a few other, mainly Western, states find themselves embroiled in an attempt to 'liberalize' and reconstruct Iraq after a spectacularly successful military intervention in March–April 2003. The reasons for getting involved in this war, especially the non-agreement of the United Nations Security Council and the reasoning invoked for it (the need to eradicate weapons of mass destruction) has become a vital part of the national politics of much of the West, and a source of much anger and disquiet in the Third World and Middle East. What has attracted even more attention however are the constant attempts to end it. The number of American battle casualties incurred in the post-war pacification of Iraq has been much greater than those who died in combat during it. The Iraqi opposition has caused constant mayhem not only among the American consultants and soldiers trying to impose order and rebuild infrastructure, but also to ordinary Iraqis who have tried to sign up for the few precious jobs that are being offered on reconstruction contracts or in the revamped Iraqi police and armed forces. The shock waves have spread much further than Iraq. On 10 March 2004 a series of bombs clearly linked to Spanish involvement in the Iraq reconstruction process ripped through trains in Madrid and killed at least 201 people. The effect was at least partly to ensure the election of a government against Spanish involvement in Iraq. The new Spanish Prime Minister declared that the 'war was a disaster. The reconstruction is a disaster.'[4] The 'apotheosis of public opinion' in that case led to the defeat of a liberal government that had got the country into a war and into the rebuilding after it.

There has also been much discussion of the intentions of the United States in dealing with future threats to its national interest (the so called rogue states) and even accusations of the creation of a new American Empire.[5] We have to ask if we can really say that liberal states, of which the United States is now by far the most powerful, have found a way to deal with the challenges of 'new' wars and terrorist wars that now confront the international system. The evidence is that in the wake of the re-election of President George W. Bush in November 2004 the United States, and whatever 'coalition of the willing' it can put together, will continue to spread the notion of the superiority of Western liberal democratic practices, by force if necessary. The President was quite explicit in his acceptance speech that this would be the case. His Secretary of State, Colin Powell announced that in his second term 'the President is not going to trim his sails or pull back ... It's a continuation of his principles, his policies, his beliefs'. This policy would be 'aggressive' but also 'multilateral in nature' though 'the US would act alone when necessary'.[6] Although the French President has led a counter-coalition in Europe against an expanded or continued American interventionism other states seem to agree with the American position, again with the British leading the way. The British Defence Minster was quoted as saying on the day of the election that 'I suspect that all sophisticated countries with significant military [*sic*] are going to be involved in these kinds of operations for the foreseeable future.'[7]

So in these few concluding pages there will be an attempt to suggest what the future might hold in the light of the discussion in this book about liberal attitudes to wars and trying to draw general conclusions across them. Much of the discussion in this book has been about drawing on historical analogy to get such-and-such a policy approach used in a situation then being faced.

The lessons of history revisited

After the victory of the Allies in 1918 it was hoped by many liberals that there could be a different way to end wars. Had not Lloyd George pronounced that this was to be the 'war to end all wars'? But the disappointment consequent to the actual implementation of the Treaty of Versailles (described in Chapter 3) and the recourse to 'reparations' led to huge disillusionment and, perhaps not at all coincidentally, to a renewed attack on the 'hypocrisy' or 'weakness' of liberalism. Its revitalization came about to a great extent, if by no means totally, as a result of the liberal powers victory in 1945 and the very successful reconstruction of Germany, Japan and wide swathes of Western Europe.

Liberal aspirations then managed to hold their tenuous hold on our consciousness until the massive victory of the Cold War. Since then we have been on a roller-coaster of largely self-imposed anguish about whether liberal states have done the 'right thing' in rebuilding the world after the fall of the Soviet Bloc in order to capitalize on our collective liberal victory, with each minor or major glitch in this process being greeted with howls of derision or despair. The great culmination of this was to be seen in the aftermath of 11 September 2001 – which could be termed the 'why do they hate us so much?' syndrome. Can we therefore possibly say that liberal solutions to war are better than previously seen alternatives? My one word answer would be a resounding 'yes', but, being a good liberal, not without many reservations.

As the material reviewed in this book hopefully shows, the musings of political commentators and historians about how wars can be brought to a successful (liberal) conclusion has a long pedigree. For Thomson, Meyer and Briggs writing in 1946 it was a question of bringing about 'a fusion of power and purpose', but 'most important of all is the relation between ends and means' – so war has to have a purpose, but also be a harmony between 'desirable ends and available means'.[8] Their inspiration for this is not idealist; these writers were in line with much thinking at the end of the Second World War. For a realist like E. H. Carr or Reinhold Niebuhr Hitler had shown the negative proof of the relationship between power and purpose in his *Neueordnung* – the desire to destroy bourgeois capitalist Europe; as had Lenin:

> The idealists were inclined to believe that power is immoral in itself, and that in any case history was in the process of gradually eliminating all power from politics ... [and] regarded its use as a temporary expedient

as Reinhold Niebuhr put it in June 1945.[9] As Thomson *et al.* commented '[i]nstead they [the idealists] merely left power in the hands of the unscrupulous, and allowed purpose to wither and die in face [*sic*] of strong men armed ... Such a fusion of power and purpose can be achieved solely against a historical setting' as peacemaking must grow out of 'past patterns', so must it grow out of 'several complex parallelograms of forces' – governments, statesmen, world conditions, desires of peoples, pressure groups 'will probably be the most decisive'.[10] This is also the logic used by a later liberal, Zaki Laidi, in 1990, and one used against all of the liberal West's enemies ever since.[11] It shows up the hollowness of the liberal–realist dichotomy. Liberals, as has been repeatedly stressed, have no problem with waging war, even if they do find it illogical.

An attack by Islamic fanatics on New York can have no possible moral justification for any liberal, but neither can that same liberal entirely justify the disproportionate use of force against two of the weakest states in the world. There was clearly no real contest possible between the finest and most technologically equipped military machine in the history of the world and the armed forces of the Taliban and Saddam Hussein. Kabul in 2002 and Baghdad in 2003 fell so fast that even commentators, like John Keegan, that were in favour of both actions, had to opine that 'Saddam was easily defeated – which is why the war goes on'. The argument goes that the rapid defeat of the Iraqi army and of Ba'athism will only encourage 'outrage' at the 'unbelievers' material superiority' and lead Iraqis opposed to the West to resort to ever more terror in the pursuit 'of novel and alternative methods of resistance to the unbelievers' power'. In other words it will not persuade them to adopt liberal belief systems or practices. But we can also point to the hubris attendant on such easy victories. The logic of liberal victory, in 2003 as in 1918 and 1945 dictates that the enemy has not only to be defeated but also convinced of the rightness of the liberals state(s)' intentions.

For John Keegan, 'Western civilisation, rooted in the idea that the improvement of the human lot lies in material advance and the enlargement of individual opportunity, is ill-equipped to engage with a creed that deplores materialism and rejects the concept of individuality, particularly individual freedom.'[12] But what cannot be ignored by sympathizers and detractors alike of the state that is now carrying out this task, the United States, is that we now have one power that can assert itself in ways that have never before been possible. The United States since 1990 sees many more places than it would have done as both in its 'interest' and responding to a global need for peace and security 'beyond containment'.[13] Not since Britannia ruled the waves has there been such a conflation of power and purpose. What may be said to be most interesting is that Britain is the greatest supporter of this new American hegemonic thrust. This is truly war in the service of a *liberal* world order.

It is an oft-quoted banality that war is a terrible thing. It matters little whether it is being waged by Nazis or liberals, many people will inevitably be killed, maimed and morally incapacitated. The aftermath of war is similarly terrible whosoever perpetrates it. Germans and Japanese suffered cruelly after the wars that they lost to liberal states. It is well documented how about 15 million Germans were expelled after 1945 from Eastern parts of Germany and Poland and the Sudetenland. Most of these crimes were committed by the Russians or other Western allies but they were aided and abetted by liberal states. The controversy over who was to blame for the sending back of many Yugoslav prisoners to their deaths after 1945 by British troops cannot ever entirely exculpate those who carried out the policy.[14] In truth we were all responsible. Liberals have to accept a moral conscience comes with the territory of being a liberal. Each war brings with it new practical and moral challenges that are inescapable for a self-reflexive ideology like liberalism. We are incapable of forgetting about others' crimes and we should therefore be so incapable of ignoring our own.

The paradoxes raised by liberal thought and practice are very deeply embedded. For many liberals, of which a very small sample would include Kant, Mill and Walzer, there is no possibility of forcing people in the singular or in the collective to be free. Yet like John Locke, a host of American Presidents professing liberal credentials such as Woodrow Wilson, Franklin Delano Roosevelt, William Clinton and both George Bushes have seen the export of 'freedom' as a moral imperative for liberal peoples and states. The implications of this for the key doctrine of non-intervention in the practice and theory of international relations are immense. An international system underpinned by liberal states during most of the nineteenth and much of the twentieth century has felt that it can, at will, act in a way that can only be described as 'liberal imperialist'. Is there such a wide difference between the statement by liberal imperialist Cecil Rhodes in 1901 that 'the absorption of the greater part of the world under our

[British] rule simply means the end of all wars' and the American belief that the only way to end wars is for an American-imposed 'democratic peace' to prevail?

The post-Cold War period has seen an increasingly self-confident extreme, even 'militant', liberalism emerge in the United States. The neo-conservative (or 'neo-con') domination of policy making in the first and second Bush Administrations has demonstrated the possibilities and limits of this newly militant liberal internationalism. There are widespread fears that the successful attacks on Afghanistan in 2002 and Iraq in 2003–4 will whet the appetite for a much wider interventionism where ever democracy is flouted, what neo-cons refer to as 'draining the swamp'. Even generals are worried about the implications of this. General Wesley Clark, the architect of the successful Kosovo campaign of 1999 argues in his book *Winning Modern Wars*[15] that Bush has the intention of finishing off his entire 'axis of evil' – 'Syria, Lebanon, Libya, Iran, Somalia and Sudan' make up the full list according to Clark. He claims that this is what he has been told by Pentagon officials. If this were to come from a dissident pacifist it would be easy to ignore, coming from General Clark it is not.[16]

Other scrupulous supporters of the general aims of Western policy about democracy, 'freedom' and other liberal values are also uneasy. The British Ambassador to Rome was widely reported as saying that President Bush is 'al-Qaeda's best recruiting sergeant'. Defeated Democratic challenger, John Kerry, pinned much of this foreign policy criticism of the President on his belief that the war in Iraq and the wider 'war on terror' was a conflict 'without an end in sight'. The *International Herald Tribune* even reported him as saying that this could lead to a 'war without end' (I prefer the credibility of the *Financial Times* version which refers to a 'war without ending in sight').[17]

Yet others have suggested that the United States *should* become an imperial power and that such an imperialism would be infinitely better than the alternative possibilities of illiberal mayhem that currently assails much of the Third World. Philip Bobbitt is the key example of this tendency from what we might categorize as the liberal 'right'. Bobbitt derides those of the liberal 'left' like Noam Chomsky who preach that the United States is acting like any old fashioned imperial power, out for its national interest and the securing of markets and sources of raw materials. For Bobbitt, the necessity is to create a 'society of market states',[18] in effect an upgraded version of the democratic peace principle. But demands for intervention also come from the liberal 'left' in the United States. A much commented upon contribution from Samantha Power, suggests that the Superpower should intervene not 'whenever it feels like it' but 'when there is badness on the face of the earth', by which she means the existence of genocide. In her reasoning the time to have intervened in Iraq should have been in 1988 when Saddam Hussein's regime gassed the Kurds of Halabja, not in 2003 more than ten years later.[19] Many neo-cons in the United States talk openly of Islamo-fascism. The liberal left in Britain has generally been against the war in Iraq but there are some voices, such as that of Nick Cohen in the *New Statesman*, who do go along with the war as a way of fighting the conspiratorial anti-democratic theories and practices of Al-Qaeda and its ilk.[20]

This reasoning goes much further than that of Michael Walzer in the 1992 Preface to his classic *Just and Unjust Wars*, which suggests, inspired by Mill, that intervention should be principally to 'restore' regimes that have been unlawfully destabilized (like that of Kuwait in 1990), and be 'limited' and 'proportional'. Walzer will admit to the waiving of the general norm of non-intervention 'only in cases of massacre or politically induced famine and epidemic, when the costs are unbearable' as he seems to be saying they were in Iraq in the civil war that erupted in the Kurdish and Shia areas after the repulsing of the Iraqi army from Kuwait in 1991.[21] Samantha Power's feeling is perhaps stronger than Walzer's as a result of her experiences in Bosnia and her observations of the non-intervention in Rwanda in 1994, by suggesting that intervention should take place when genocide has taken, or is taking, place.

We might argue that to hesitate is wrong, but to use such genocidal actions as post-facto justifications (as Bush and Blair did in 2003) is also wrong. It might also be said that only the United States has even thought it *could* draw up such lists of illiberal states and then actually make them disappear. We have seen such ambitious programmes by the United States three times in the last 100 years, in the First and Second World Wars and the Cold War, and on each occasion they have been realized. General Clark's annoyance with Bush is not so much over his ambitions (after all he helped the previous President take out a minor 'evil state' himself) but in the fact that he has ignored the much greater potential threat of Saudi Arabia and Pakistan who harbour terrorists but are supposed to be 'friends'.

It is always invidious to select one episode in any historical period for particular consideration but the current invasion of Iraq by a force made up largely of the forces of the 'Anglo-Saxon' liberal states (the United States, the UK and Australia prominent among them) has the potential to mark a turning point in the way that the world thinks about not just liberal states but also war itself. So while some on the left and even on the right have proclaimed and lamented the advent of a much more aggressive imperial America, with the more thoughtful pointing out that the last time a great republic acted this way it turned into Imperial Rome, others truly believe, as a United States soldier in Iraq was quoted as saying that 'we have freed a society'. For such people the war in Iraq is the latest round of a war between liberty and justice on one hand and tyranny on the other.[22]

The echoes of this debate have been seen in all the chapters in this book and at the time of writing (November 2004) the consequences have yet to be fully played out. It is already clear however that the word 'reconstruction' will never be seen in the same light again, for example. Equally, as we saw in the chapters on retribution and reconciliation, we have had to ask repeatedly since the end of the Cold War if outside liberal forces can impose a democratic freedom on peoples that have not previously had it without fundamentally breaching the basis of liberalism itself? Moral autonomy has to be learnt by the individual or the people, says Mill, not imposed.

Woodrow Wilson was aware of this problem as well. He saw democracy as 'a stage of development . . . built by slow habit. Its process is experience.' As Wilson's biographer Thomas Knock interpreted this, what Wilson meant was that 'in order to put down firm roots, democracy required a well-educated and enlightened people, wide public debate, a citizenry with a common purpose and, 'not the habit of revolution, but the habit of resolution.' Other countries, therefore could attain democracy only by steps, 'through a period of political tutelage', before their people would be ready to 'take entire control over their affairs'.[23]

Wilson thus re-interpreted Mill and set the stage for a century of American attempts at such 'political tutelage'. To that extent the 'neo-cons' are right to see themselves as the inheritors of the Wilsonian tradition and not in that which eschews 'all entangling alliances' and advocates non-intervention.

The dangers of historical analogy

They are of course not alone in this feeling either. Many commentators have been scathing about the inadequacy of the European, indeed the Western, response to recent wars, with the war in Bosnia as a seminal example. Richard Holbrooke has argued that it was '[t]he greatest collective security failure of the West since the 1930s' with particular opprobrium being heaped on the European Union. James Gow refers to that as the 'triumph of the lack of will' commenting that 'the international community generally reacted to events in Bosnia rather than anticipating them', and then with 'bad timing, inappropriate measures, incoherence and a lack of political resolve'.[24] In the case of Bosnia as in many others of the past and future, there will be a conscious, if often erroneous use of historical analogy. Holbrooke called it 'bad history or the Rebecca West factor' after the famous pro-Serb book by West in 1941, *Black Lamb and Grey Falcon*, which he says has been imbibed in full by other writers who then dissuaded the first Clinton Administration to take no action to end the Bosnian war, like Robert Kaplan in *Balkan Ghosts*.[25] The fear of becoming embroiled in civil wars that are imbued with 'ancient hatreds' is a real one nonetheless. All the force of the RMA cannot stop a militiaman who is unafraid to die knocking out hi-tech Humvee vehicles or even tanks with a point blank shot from a rocket-propelled grenade.

As the current war in Iraq has shown there is a real difficulty of false historical analogy in more than one direction. In that war it seems reasonably clear that President Bush believed that his forces would be welcomed with open arms as liberators at best or at worst in a spirit of resigned acceptance like in Germany in 1945. One famous speech on Iraq went as follows:

Rebuilding Iraq will require a sustained commitment from many nations, including our own: we will remain in Iraq as long as necessary, and not a day more. America has made and kept this kind of commitment before – in the peace that followed a world war. After defeating enemies, we did not leave behind occupying armies, we left constitutions and parliaments. We established an atmosphere of safety, in which responsible, reform-minded local leaders could build lasting institutions of freedom. In societies that once bred fascism and militarism, liberty found a permanent home. There was a time when many said that the cultures of Japan and Germany were incapable of sustaining democratic values. Well, they were wrong. Some say the same of Iraq today. They are mistaken.[26]

It has not turned out quite like that. As a direct result, others have immediately jumped up to cite other historical 'parallels'. The problems that the British encountered in Iraq in 1920 were evoked by the distinguished, if controversial, historian, Niall Ferguson, who trumpeted that 'this Vietnam generation of Americans have not learnt the lessons of history'. The gist of Ferguson's argument was that the Americans were so tied up in their own 'exceptionalism', as not to see that they were repeating the imperial mistakes of their forerunners in Iraq, the British. Mark Steyn immediately riposted that 'liberty and imperialism don't mix', that it was a nonsense to say the Americans were historical 'ignoramus'. Had he not seen ordinary GIs in Iraq with copies, on the passenger seats of their vehicles, of 'Karsh's *Empires of the Sand* and David Franklin's *A Peace to End All Peace*? "That's a great book" he [the American sergeant driving him] said of the latter.' For Steyn the historical lesson that had been learnt is not to placate the French (as he says Britain did in 1920), not giving 'excessive deference to the modish international umbrella of the day' and that America was 'spending a lot of time mopping up the failures of British imperialism. The lessons of the 1920s are as pertinent for *Guardian*esque transnationalists as for Rumsfeldian neocons.'[27]

It could also be observed that when the American forces responded to one particular crisis with characteristic force, but then seemed to be effective, as in the attack by Moqtada al-Sadr's 'Mahdi militia' in early April 2004 the comments can themselves change. The newspapers veered from saying that the Americans should have listened to the British example before assuming Shias and Sunnis could be divided and therefore treat such people with consideration and restraint, to saying that they had been right to act with such heavy-handed tactics once al-Sadr was forced to back off by his own Shia leadership. Then the 'lesson' was that

> 'Iraq's Shia establishment has bitter memories of previous uprisings that bought disaster on their followers. The Shia revolts against Saddam Hussein in 1991 and the British in 1920 were both defeated, resulting in Iraq being dominated by the Sunni minority for the whole of the 20th century.'[28]

All of these lessons have their points to make, but they are all equally misleading as well. There is never an exact historical analogy that can be drawn, even if that is the best we have.

Are liberal beliefs now dominant?

Michael Mandelbaum has been cited as believing that Wilson's views of 1918 were not the naive 'utopian' nonsense denounced by E. H. Carr in the *Twenty Year's Crisis*. They were rather the 'ideas that conquered the world'. Is this so wrong-headed? Are not the principles of liberal democracy, capitalism and human rights indeed such ideas? What can challenge them in global terms? What military power can effectively rebut them? Others have asserted that neo-conservatives have in effect hijacked this Wilsonian project for their own ends, a view one that one commentator on the internet claimed was even endorsed by Wilson's biographer, N. Gordon Levin, in his allusion to Wilson's 'rationalizing and pacifying [of] the political universe'.[29]

Much of this book has been about the possibility of a transformation of a 'state of war', in which Locke says illiberal states exist, into a 'state of nature' for all. Is the 'democratic peace theory' thus generated any more true in the past 100 years as in the 100 after Kant first declared its possibility? When Germany and Japan became liberal (as opposed to Listian) trading nations post-Second World War they became both democratic and peaceful. The EU project is posited on the idea that by expanding the zone of democracy we will expand the zone of peaceful 'civilian powers'.

But it might also be questioned whether democracy is a category that all states can accept. In the case of Japan, there is some doubt that the standards of its democracy are ones that would be recognized by any British or American liberal. One cornerstone of the Japanese liberal constitution of 1945 was that the Emperor should no longer be seen as a deity and that Japan should no longer be seen as 'a divine nation with the Emperor at its core'. There are now many nationalist voices raised to revoke this clause. There have also been, as was noted in the last chapter, visits by Prime Minister Junichiro Koizumi to the Yakasuni Shrine, which celebrates not only Japan's war dead but also those hanged as war criminals by the Tokyo War Crimes Tribunals after the Second World War. Japan has refused to face up to many aspects of its non-democratic past, its school books still largely ignore atrocities committed in Korea and Japan's part in the 'Greater East-Asia Co-Prosperity Sphere'. Liberalism is not fully embedded in the Japanese cultural mentality, however much it may exist on paper. If such a modern, indeed post-modern, 'democratic' state can be seen thus, what chance is there for 'pre-modern' equivalents to do likewise?[30]

Earlier on in the book Richard Bellamy was quoted as having written that

> [t]oday all major groupings employ the liberal language of rights, freedom and equality to express and legitimize their views and demonstrate a corresponding general acceptance of liberal conceptions of democracy and the market. From new right conservatives to democratic socialists, it seems we are all liberals now.

This was because 'liberal ideas and politics fashioned the states and social and economic systems of the nineteenth century, creating the institutional framework and the values which most of us in the West continue to live and to think.'

Might we not also argue that for most of those that suffer, those that cannot rely on their states to defend them as the states are their primary oppressors, that the West has the obligation to come to their aid and to 'nation-build'? Might it not be argued that poor people in what are (very) euphemistically deemed 'developing' countries want to be global liberals but are not allowed to by their local oppressors? If they feel betrayed therefore it is because liberals do *not* come to their aid unless it is seen to be in the interests of global liberal powers (like the USA or the UK). Might it not equally be argued that there is no alternative to the political agenda of liberalism? This agenda is essentially that of the new world order of Wilson, Roosevelt and Bush – the self-determination of individuals, the appropriate use of global organizations, and global capitalism, tempered by tolerance, openness, and charity. Or, do we not fool ourselves into thinking that we are being liberal when in effect we are being imperialists – a repetition of the idea that the 'Orientals' are children that need to be looked after by their liberal modern state counterparts; taught the benefits of capitalism and democracy? This is the view developed by Noam Chomsky in a whole series of books attacking liberalism.[31] It is also an idea that would have been familiar to Cobden or Mill. War is often declared in the name of liberty or liberal values, which in effect hides a much more venal notion of self-interest.

Liberalism and the 'war against terror'

It is clear from all the above that liberals themselves feel very uneasy about the way that the liberal West has seemingly been exporting such beliefs by force of arms, especially since '9/11'. As has been made clear by Bellamy, talking of the early 1990s, but it would be true of virtually any era, liberals have often complained that they '[f]eel badly let down by the historical process as a number of their core assumptions were called into question by the further development of the very social order that they had helped to create.' We can see this in the way that many Liberals became Labour Party members after the First World War, or many Liberals became Communists in the 1930s, or how many liberals attack liberalism in its impact on the Third World now. Bellamy goes further and says that we now see liberalism's transformation [or] 'mutation from ideology to meta-ideology [as] indicative of its current theoretical and political bankruptcy'.[32] Perhaps liberals are doomed to always feel this?

But this unease spreads further when we consider how liberal societies now feel about the kind of war that we are now waging against terror. Maybe this one is a war that cannot be won, a war that has no ending? Specialists on terrorism like Walter Laqueur do not take this view but they give plenty of good reasons why it might be so. As Laqueur points out, '[t]errorism, like revolutions, occurs not when the situation is disastrously bad but when various political, economic and social trends coincide'. We now have a situation in the Muslim world in particular where poverty, political and religious discontent and the rise of a huge educated elite has fed the rise of Islamic 'fundamentalism'. The rallying cry is often anti-Israeli, ironic given that Israel is the only liberal democracy in the Middle East, but one that has ignored UN Security Council Resolutions and committed a fair number of other breaches of diplomatic etiquette. As Laqueur points out, it should have given up the territories occupied in 1967 'long ago, for its own sake, not to pacify the outside world. No democratic country can rule in the long run so many hostile subjects and retain its democratic character.'[33] This is a direct echo of T. E. Lawrence's injunction of 1918 about the Middle East quoted at the head of this chapter: 'It is impossible for a foreigner to run another people of their own free will indefinitely.'

So how do or can liberals live up to their ideals and thus hopefully bring about an end to war? First we have to accept that liberals are not plaster saints – they break their own rules constantly. As has been made clear in previous chapters, liberals and liberal societies have by no means always been against war or even against inflicting suffering on others if it was felt that this was a 'necessity'. The majority of the British population was in favour of the Boer War, many liberals shared quasi-racist beliefs in the nineteenth century – America was (what we now call) ethnically cleansed by liberals of Native Americans. Max Weber agreed with German nationalist views on the 'pollution' by Slavs of their Eastern areas (although on social and economic, not political grounds).[34] Many British liberals hailed the outbreak of the First World War with great enthusiasm. The explanation lies partly with what Martin Ceadel calls pacificism, the feeling that liberalism had to be fully supported by force of arms once a certain threshold of attack had become obvious, as with Chamberlain's decision to declare war on Germany in 1939 over the invasion of Poland. Liberalism had to eradicate militarism by force because reason had not worked in 1914 or 1919. A world based on *race* could not be tenable to a liberal, nor could any other form of universalism that did not embrace the freedom of market and politics – so Nazis and, later, Communists could not be allowed to dominate the international system and had to go.

Second, we have to accept that liberalism is a doctrine that both encourages and discourages intervention. But this inevitably has always led to questions as to where do the limits of such action lie? Early liberal thinkers (Cobden, Mill) were clearly *against* intervention under nearly all circumstances. Woodrow Wilson developed the idea that it is the right and even duty of the liberal states to intervene against violent states, a principle that is incorporated as the idea of Collective Security in the Covenant of the League and the UN Charter. Humanitarian Intervention takes the idea even further in the 1990s. But as Alan Kuperman has pointed out, and against his earlier condemnation of Western inaction in the Rwandan massacres of 1994, there is little that any liberal state or states can do to stop indiscriminate slaughter if it is well enough planned.[35]

This liberal debate on intervention has been rumbling on since the early 1800s at least. Tony Blair recently suggested that all of the above mentioned landmarks in international humanitarian legislation needed major shocks to the system to implement. The *Daily Telegraph* quoted him as saying that:

> even before September 11 [the attacks on New York of 2001], he had been reaching for a 'different philosophy' in international relations that had held sway since the Treaty of Westphalia in 1648. This ended the Thirty Years' war with a declaration that a country's internal affairs were for it 'and you don't interfere unless it threatens you, or breaches a treaty, or triggers an obligation of alliance'. . . . Under international law a regime could systematically

brutalise and oppress its people, and there was nothing anyone else could do, unless it came within the definition of a humanitarian catastrophe. 'This may be the law, but should it be?', he said. This necessitated a reform of the UN's Security Council so that it 'represents 21st century reality'.[36]

The speech also held the line '[t]he war is not ended. It may only be at the beginning of the first phase.' Blair feels that we are now in a 'new kind of war', one that is a 'risk to our security and way of life'. There are many occasions when this could have been said to have been the case, it is unlikely to be true now. But this Churchillian invocation has much in common with Bush's obsession with Churchillian imagery.[37] One way of understanding the Anglo–American alliance over most of the interventions since 1991 is to see it as a continuation of the Anglo-American pursuit of militant liberalism and the rolling back of the forces of 'darkness', whatever form they may take. The neo-con agenda in this sense has much in common with Wilsonian thinking, and it is seen as a 'hijacking' of the ideas by those who believe that they, not Blair or Bush, are the true believers in, and holders of, the Wilsonian and wider liberal flame. They therefore most resent what they see as the Prime Minister's and American President's occupation of their own high moral ground more than they resent the target of Blair and Bush's actions, the regime of Saddam Hussein. To read the dismay of the liberal wing of the anti-war-in-Iraq movement is to feel that it would have been better to have Bath'ists in Iraq than the Argyll and Sutherland Highlanders or the Black Watch in Basra.

Interestingly, the Conservative Party gave its full agreement to Blair's suggestion, the Liberal Democrats warned against a 'doctrine of pre-emptive strikes' while a member of Blair's own party, Tam Dalyell, called Blair's comments 'passionate, self-justifying drivel', condemned the Iraq war as illegal and said Blair was 'in the position of a war criminal'.[38] Of course Blair is wrong that the doctrine of non-intervention has remained unchanged since 1648. It has been in constant mutation as international instruments have weakened the basic Westphalian idea of non-intervention, one that had always been respected more in the breach than in the respect for it. It was indeed breached a few years after 1648 by those who had signed up to it. Powerful states, including liberal ones, have always felt they could intervene when their moral outrage sufficiently matched their national interest.

What has not changed is the debate itself. Locke, Cobden, Bright and Mill would have recognized the anguished discussion over whether or not to intervene against a brutal dictator, as would the liberals who championed or condemned the Boer War, or were in favour or not of 'appeasing' Hitler, 'containing' the Soviet Union, 'liberating' Kuwait or indeed Kosovo. The only difference is that now the debate is much more played out in a liberal press that has flourished enormously over the last 200 years, in the United Nations and other international organizations that are the product of liberal victories over the past 80 years or so and in the liberal think tanks which have sprung up over the same period. As far as the content of the debate goes, *plus ca change plus c'est la meme chose.*

But Bush and Blair have only themselves to blame for not understanding the profound splits that they have caused in liberal opinion in the West by refusing from the outset to allow the UN to provide the fig leaf of global legitimacy for what would inevitably in any case be an Anglo-American military operation in essence, as it had been in 1990–91. Then, no one complained because they felt that they had been consulted and accepted as part of a 'coalition'. Practically the two cases are no different. Ideologically they differ enormously, and the fault lies with those who were too impatient or too arrogant to understand the need of liberal world leaders to carefully nourish and promote a global coalition of like-minded democratic states. In that sense Blair and Bush are to blame for the deaths of many young Muslims in Iraq who have taken on the practically invincible American army equipped with their own courage and a few sticks of explosive, as well as for the deaths of the equally blameless young American and British soldiers who have paid the price of neo-con hubris.[39]

In the light of all of the above can we say that liberal attitudes to war and to ending them are coherent? A true believer in liberal values would argue that the reason for such internal contradiction is that liberalism is a self-reflective ideology, constantly carping about itself and ready to change. Liberals attacked the British conduct of the Boer War and the two World Wars while they were happening while not in any way condoning the forces that were being fought. Liberals like me can inhabit American and European universities and universities in other liberally minded states and criticize and check the behaviour of their governments. They can even agree to let their own state's behaviour be subject to the scrutiny of regional or international criminal courts. And yet, liberals are confused about their own destiny, deeply worried by criticism, as troubled as any Reformation cleric that their God is not, perhaps, on their side or looking with approval at their actions. It is this auto-ambivalence that gives realists and Marxists such an open target with liberals but also what makes liberalism such a vibrant and adaptable ideology.

Or maybe the Bush Administration has done much to put a brake on liberal impulses to 'bottom-up' solutions to wars. How long that influence will last depends on how far the current fear of terrorism is allowed to run in the United States. Maybe, like Mrs Thatcher and the National Union of Mine Workers leader Arthur Scargill during the Miners' strike of 1984, the 'extremes' will continue to crush the liberal centre of Western politics.

Notes

Introduction

1   J. Charmley, *Churchill's Grand Alliance: The Anglo-American Special Relationship, 1940–57*, London: John Curtis/Hodder and Stoughton, 1995, p. 5.
2   Palmerston quoted by J. Rosenberg, *The Empire of Civil Society: A Critique of the Realist Theory of International Relations*, London: Verso, 1994, pp. 150–1.
3   P. Berman, *Terror and Liberalism*, New York: W. W. Norton, 2003, p. 4.
4   M. Ledeen, 'America's Revenge: To Turn Tyrannies into Democracies', *Daily Telegraph*, 11 September 2002.
5   A. C. Grayling, *The Meaning of Things: Applying Philosophy to Life*, London: Phoenix, 2002, p. 153.
6   The expression is one coined by A. George in A. M. Kacowicz, Y. Bar-Simon-Tov, O. Elgstrom and M. Jerneck (eds), *Stable Peace Among Nations*, London: Rowan and Littlefield, 2000, p. xiii.
7   M. Mandelbaum, *The Ideas that Conquered the World; Peace, Democracy and Free Markets*, New York: PublicAffairs, 2002. The most recent review of this literature that I have seen has come from K. Allerfeldt, 'Wilsonian Pragmatism? Woodrow Wilson, Japanese Immigration and the Paris Peace Conference', *Diplomacy and Statecraft*, Vol. 15, No. 3, September 2004, pp. 545–72
8   T. J. Knock, *To End All Wars: Woodrow Wilson and the Search for a New World Order*, New York: Oxford University Press, 1992, p. 11.
9   Lloyd-George to the War Cabinet, March 1917, quoted by G. J. Ikenberry, *After Victory: Institutions, Strategic Restraint and the Rebuilding of Order after Major Wars*, Princeton: Princeton University Press, 2001, p. 130
10   Charmley, *Churchill's Grand Alliance*, p. 5.
11   Charmley, *op.cit.*, p. 35.
12   For other recent literature on the Special Relationship see: D. Reynolds, *The Creation of the Anglo American Alliance, 1937–41*, London: Europe, 1981 and *Britannia Overruled: British Policy and World Power in the Twentieth Century*, London: Longman, 1991; B. J. C. McKercher, *Transition of Power: Britain's Loss of Global Pre-Eminence to the United States, 1930–1945*, Cambridge: Cambridge University Press, 1999; R. Skidelsky, *John Maynard Keynes: Fighting for Britain, 1937–1946*, London: Macmillan, 2000; A. Williams, 'Before the Special Relationship: The Council on Foreign Relations, The Carnegie Foundation and the Rumour of a Anglo-American War', *Journal of Transatlantic Studies*, Vol. 1, No. 2, Autumn 2003, pp. 233–251.
13   Berman, *Terror and Liberalism*, pp. 4–6.
14   Chris Brown, *Sovereignty, Rights and Justice*, Cambridge: Polity, 2002, p. 58.
15   The edition of Kant that will be used in this book is: *Immanuel Kant, Perpetual Peace and Other Essays*, Indianapolis: Hackett, 1983.

16 As expressed by E. G. Yesson in his interpretation of Kantian thought, quoted by Alexander George in A. M. Kacowicz *et al.*, *Stable Peace Among Nations*, London: Rowan and Littlefield, 2000.

17 A. Williams, *Failed Imagination? New World Orders of the Twentieth Century*, Manchester: Manchester University Press, 1998. For a sympathetic review of the historical approach used, see J. –A. Pemberton, 'Towards a New World Order; A Twentieth Century Story', *Review of International Studies*, 2001, Volume 27, April 2001, pp. 265–72. See also Edward Newman's review of the same book, *International Peacekeeping*, Vol. 7, No. 2, Summer 2000.

18 I would like to thank Peter Wilson of the London School of Economics for pointing out the logic of this in a review of my last book that he wrote for the *International History Review*, 2001.

19 N. M. Naimark, *Fires of Hatred: Ethnic Cleansing in Twentieth Century Europe*, Cambridge, MA: Harvard University Press, 2001, p. 2

20 Of which some of the most significant for me have been: F. C. Ikle, *Every War Must End*, New York Columbia University Press, 1991; W. B. Gallie, *Philosophers of Peace and War*, Cambridge: Cambridge University Press, 1978; M. Doyle, *Ways of War and Peace: Realism, Liberalism and Socialism*, New York: Norton, 1997; C. Kegley and G. A. Raymond, *How Nations Make Peace*, New York: St Martin's Worth, 2000; M. Howard, *The Invention of Peace: Reflections on War and International Order*, New Haven, CT: Yale University Press, 2000; J. MacMillan, *On Liberal Peace: Democracy, War and the International Order*, London: Tauris, 1998; and D. Thomson, E. Mayer and A. Briggs *Patterns of Peacemaking*, London: Kegan, Paul, Trench, Trubner and Co, 1945, which I think must be the oldest, and still one of the best, of the genre.

21 K. van der Pijl, *Transnational Classes and International Relations*, London: Routledge, 1998; I. Parmar, 'CFR–RIIA Interconnections: A Nascent Transnational Ruling Class, Liberal Atlantic Community, or Anglo-American Establishment?', *Think Tanks and Power in Foreign Policy: A Comparative Study of the Role and Influence of the Council on Foreign Relations and the Royal Institute of International Affairs, 1939–1945*, London: Palgrave Macmillan.

22 For a full view of S. Gill's work see his: *American Hegemony and the Trilateral Commission*, Cambridge: Cambridge University Press, 1990, and *Gramsci, Historical Materialism and International Relations*, Cambridge: Cambridge University Press, 1993.

23 A good recent example of this phenomenon can be found in the sneering at the success of A. de Botton, often dismissed by jealous 'serious' writers.

24 A recent author suggests that it in fact never took place but has been used in a post-facto justification of the claim that the 'first great debate' in IR was between these two groups. See L. M. Ashworth, 'Did the Realist-Idealist debate ever happen? A Revisionist History of International Relations', *International Relations*, vol. 16, No. 1, April 2002. See also: D. Long and P. Wilson (eds) *Thinkers of the Twenty Years Crisis*, Oxford: Clarendon Press, 1995.

Chapter 1: The roots of liberalism and the first great liberal century

1 J. Milton, 'To the Parliament of England', *Doctrine and Discipline of Divorce*, 1643, quoted in the *Oxford Concise Dictionary of Quotations*, Oxford: Oxford University Press, p. 230.

2 Oliver Wendell Holmes, letter to Harold Laski, 24 October 1930, quoted in Louis Menand, *The Metaphysical Club: A Story of Ideas in America*, London: Flamingo/HarperCollins, 2001, p. 62.

3 C. Brown, *International Theory: New Normative Approaches*, Brighton: Harvester, 1992, p. 11.

4 For a contemporary view that advocates intervention see M. Ignatieff, *The Warrior's Honour: Ethnic War and the Modern Conscience*, London: Vintage, 1999. A prominent advocate of the 'communitarian' view might currently also be said to be C. Brown, whose *Sovereignty, Rights and Justice: International Political Theory Today*, Cambridge:

Polity, 2002, is critical of Mervyn Frost, a prominent cosmopolitan liberal who believes in the emergence of a global civil society. As Brown points out, Frost's cosmopolitan view is based on Hegelian premises, and Hegel was the most prominent defender of the state, so such a distinction has to be taken with care. For details see Brown, pp. 82–4.

5 D. Dunne, *The Invention of International Society: A History of the English School*, London: Macmillan, 1988. See also G. Gong, *The Standard of Civilisation in International Society*, Oxford: Clarendon Press, 1984.

6 T. Eagleton, 'Jacques Derrida', *New Statesman*, 14 July 2003, p. 31.

7 For example J. Reid in his PhD thesis 'Wars without Ends: Power, Modernity and Counter-Strategy', University of Lancaster, 2004. My thanks to Julian for pointing it out to me.

8 One of the best expositions of this process can be found in H. Joas, *War and Modernity*, Cambridge: Polity, 2003.

9 Doyle, *Ways of War and Peace, op. cit.*

10 J. M. Welsh, *Edmund Burke and International Relations*, London, Macmillan, 1995.

11 Ikenberry, *After Victory, op. cit.*

12 J. Gray, *Liberalism*, Milton Keynes: Open University Press, 1986, p. 10.

13 R. Bellamy, *Liberalism and Modern Society: A Historical Argument*, Pennsylvania: The Pennsylvania State University Press, 1992, pp. 2–3.

14 J. A. Hall, 'In Search of Civil Society', in Hall (ed.), *Civil Society: Theory, History, Comparison*, Oxford: Polity, 1995. My thanks to Jeremy Worthen for pointing this out to me.

15 J. Dos Passos, quoted by M. Baker in the *Daily Telegraph*, 25 October 2003. The author of the article commented that 'J. P. Morgan was the original target of the Fat Cat syndrome'.

16 Bellamy, *Liberalism and Modern Society*, pp. 3–4, 47–57. The end of the nineteenth century and the beginning of the twentieth saw the development in Britain of what is called the 'new liberalism', with T. H. Green and L. T. Hobhouse as its main publicists.

17 R. Bellamy, *Rethinking Liberalism*, London: Continuum, 2000, p. ix.

18 Menand, *The Metaphysical Club*, pp. 236–7.

19 P. Gay, *The Bourgeois Experience, Victoria to Freud*, Vol. 1, *Education of the Senses*, Oxford: Oxford University Press, 1984, pp. 40–1.

20 D. Williams, 'Liberal Theory and Liberal Practice in International Politics', paper given to the ECPR Conference, Canterbury, UK, 2001.

21 Doyle, *Ways of War and Peace*, p. 205.

22 Doyle, *Ways of War and Peace*, p. 208.

23 A.C. Grayling, *The Meaning of Things: Applying Philosophy to Life*, London: Weidenfield and Nicholson, 2001. See also N. Malcolm's critique of Grayling's book in the *Daily Telegraph* of 12 August 2001. He criticizes Grayling for using 'Aunt Sally technique[s], which involves setting up an unworkable definition of a term, knocking it down, and then triumphantly concluding that the term has no meaning at all'. The terms include 'nation', 'patriotism' and 'loyalty to one's own community'.

24 The classic statement in recent years was of course: K. Popper, *The Open Society and its Enemies*, 2 vols, Princeton NJ: Princeton University Press, 1971.

25 I. Kant, *Perpetual Peace and Other Essays*, p. 110 (first section of Kant's 1795 work).

26 A. de Botton, *The Consolations of Philosophy*, London: Penguin, 2000, p. 83.

27 Review of J. Gray, *Straw Dogs: Thoughts on Humans and Other Animals*, London: Granta, 2002, by E. Skidelsky in the *New Statesman*, 2 September 2002.

28 As Menand shows in 'The Metaphysical Club', the effect of the Civil War on a whole host of key American liberals of the nineteenth and twentieth centuries, including Holmes, William James, Charles S. Pierce and John Dewey, was immense.

29 G. Murray, *The Problem of Foreign Policy*, London: George Allen and Unwin, 1921, pp. 5–6.

30 M. Caedel, *Pacifism in Britain, 1914–1945*, Oxford, Clarendon Press, 1980, p. 24.

31 G. Gong, *The Standard of 'Civilisation' in International Society*, Oxford: Clarendon Press, 1984, pp. 14–15.

32 The three paragraphs above are modified from my *Failed Imagination: New World Orders of the Twentieth Century*, Manchester University Press, 1998, pp. 181–2, and Chapter 6, *passim*.

33 Again see: Grayling, *The Meaning of Things, op. cit.*

34 D. Long, 'J. A. Hobson and Economic Internationalism' in D. Long and P. Wilson, *Thinkers of the Twenty Years' Crisis*, Oxford: Clarendon Press, 1995, p. 160.

35 My thanks to Jarrod Wiener for this quote by Mill.

36 Doyle, *Ways of War and Peace*, pp. 213–19.

37 Menand, *Metaphysical Society*, p. 244 and pp. 423–30. Menand points out that it was not until 1925 that the United States Supreme Court fully recognized the right to free speech but the Patriot Act in effect has temporarily restricted that, as did legislation during the First and Second World Wars. Once again the United States believes itself to be 'at war'.

38 Doyle, *Ways of War and Peace*, p. 220–5.

39 D. Williams, 'Liberal Theory and Liberal Practice', *op. cit.* pp. 7–11.

40 M. Walzer, *Just and Unjust Wars: A Moral Argument with Historical Illustrations*, New York: Basic Books, 2nd edn, 1992, p. 209.

41 This section was inspired mostly by W. B. Gallie and Chris Brown.

42 C. Brown, *International Theory: New Normative Approaches*, pp. 14 and 29–30.

43 Brown, *International Theory*, quoting Kant, pp. 30–1.

44 Brown, *International Theory*, p. 33.

45 Gallie, *Philosophers of Peace and War*, p. 9.

46 A point that Brown makes, *International Theory*, p. 37.

47 cf. Doyle, *Ways of War and Peace*, pp. 241–6.

48 F. H. Hinsley, *Power and the Pursuit of Peace*, Cambridge: Cambridge University Press, 1963, p. 81.

49 A. Osiander, *The States System of Europe, 1640–1990: Peacemaking and the Conditions of International Stability*, Oxford: Clarendon Press, 1994, p. 3.

50 T. Paine, *The Rights of Man*, 1791, quoted by Hinsley, *Power and the Pursuit of Peace*, p. 92.

51 Walzer, *Just and Unjust Wars*, p. 87.

52 K. Marx and F. Engels, *The Communist Manifesto*, Harmondsworth: Penguin. See also F. Wheen, *Karl Marx*, London: Fourth Estate, 1999, Chapter 5, for the most refreshing re-examination of Marx's works in recent years.

53 For details see Hinsley, *Power and the Pursuit of Peace*, Chapters 6 and 7.

54 O. Anderson, *A Liberal State at War: English Politics and Economics During the Crimean War*, London: Macmillan, 1997, pp. 1–6.

55 Anderson, *A Liberal State at War, op. cit.*, p. 12.

56 J. A. Hobson, *Richard Cobden: the International Man*, London: T. Fisher Unwin , 1919, pp. 18–22.

57 Hinsley, *Power and the Pursuit of Peace*, p. 81.

58 Walzer interpreting Mill, *Just and Unjust Wars*, pp. 87–8

59 W.H. Dawson, *Richard Cobden and Foreign Policy*, London, George Allen and Unwin, 1926, Chapter 1, 'The Man'.

60 Dawson, *Richard Cobden*, pp. 57–58.

61 Hobson, *Richard Cobden*, pp. 138–40.

62 Walzer, *Just and Unjust Wars*, p. 90.

63 M. Ceadel, *Thinking about Peace and War*, Oxford: Oxford University Press, 1987, p.10, quoting F. H. Hinsley, 'Reflections on the Debate about Nuclear Weapons' in D. Martin and P. Mullen (eds), *Unholy Warfare: The Church and the Bomb*, Oxford: Blackwell, 1983, p. 57.

64   E. Hobsbawm, *Industry and Empire*, London: Penguin, 1969, p. 41; and K. E. Born, *International Banking in the 19th and Twentieth Centuries*, Oxford: Berg, 1977, p. 38.

65   N. Angell, *The Great Illusion: A Study of the Relation of Military Power to National Advantage*, London: William Heinemann, 1910.

66   For a detailed exposition of Milner's views see C. Headlam (ed.), *The Milner Papers, 1897–1905*, London: Cassell, 1931–3, 2 vols (documents); T. H. O'Brien, *Milner*, London: Constable, 1979; For contemporary, largely approbatory accounts, see C. P. Lucas, 'Lord Milner', *United Empire*, vol. 6, 1925, pp. 347–9; W. B. Worsfold, *Lord Milner's Work in South Africa, 1897 to the Peace of Vereeniging, 1902*, London: Murray, 1906, and: *The Reconstruction of the New Colonies under Lord Milner*, London: K. Paul, Trench, Trübner, 2 vols, 1913; L. Curtis, *With Milner in South Africa*, Oxford: Basil Blackwell, 1951 [his diary of the period]. This is also a good account of what came to be known as Milner's 'Kindergarten', the brilliant young men who went to South Africa to serve under him; See also Chapter 4 of this book.

67   For a survey of some aspects of Anglo–German relations and the Boer War see: J. MacMillan, *On Liberal Peace: Democracy, War and the International Order*, London: Tauris, 1998, pp. 174–235 and 236–71.

68   R. Evans, *The Coming of the Third Reich*, London: Allen Lane, 2003.

69   Take for example Hardy's 'Drummer Hodge': 'They throw in Drummer Hodge, to rest/Uncoffined – just as found:/His landmark is a kopje-crest/That breaks the veldt around;/And foreign constellations west/each night above his mound.': *Selected Shorter Poems of Thomas Hardy*, London: Macmillan, 1966, p. 11.

70   B. Stuchtey, 'The International of Critics, German and British Scholars during the South African War (1899–1902)', unpublished manuscript, 1999. Stucktey quotes Bryce, himself one of the greatest liberal thinkers and activists Britain has ever produced, saying that Mommsen was the 'patriarch of European science, the first among living intellectuals.'

71   I am indebted to William Fortescue, an expert on late nineteenth century French history, for this information. Some of the documents have been reproduced in his: *The Third Republic and France, 1870–1940: Conflicts and Continuities*, London, Routledge, 2000, Document 3.11 (The Boer War) (October 1899–May 1902). The Third Republic of France, 1870–1940: Conflicts and Contradictions, London: Routledge, 2000.

72   D. Gilmour, *The Long Recessional: The Imperial Life of Rudyard Kipling*, London: John Murray, 2002, pp. 124–6.

73   D. Judd and K. Surridge, *The Boer War*, London: John Murray, 2002, reviewed by Piers Brendon in *The Independent*, August 2002.

74   K. G. Robbins, 'Lord Bryce and the First World War', *The Historical Journal*, Vol. X, No. 2, 1967, pp. 255–77, p. 255.

75   Headlam, *The Milner Papers*, Vol. II, pp. 242–3. The statement was in a letter by Milner to Major Hanbury Williams of the Colonial Office, 27 December 1900.

76   Gilmour, *The Long Recessional*, pp. 138–9.

77   Gilmour, *The Long Recessional*, p. 137.

78   J. Marlowe, *Milner: Apostle of Empire*, London, Hamish Hamilton, 1976, pp. 5–8.

79   Marlowe, *Milner: Apostle of Empire*.

80   Marlowe, *Milner: Apostle of Empire*, pp. 179–83. The 'Co-efficients' included the Webbs as well as Milner, the 'Compatriots' included Leo Amery (later Colonial Secretary under Chamberlain and Churchill), Sir Halford MacKinder, J. L. Garvin, (Editor of *The Times*), John Buchan and other Imperial luminaries such as F. S. Oliver.

81   Menand, *The Metaphysical Club*, p. 62.

82   Bellamy does not see a clear distinction between these two forces but many others do, including Karl Popper in the next century; cf. Bellamy, *Rethinking Liberalism*, Chapter 1.

83   For a definition of this dilemma see Z. Laïdi, *A World Without Meaning?* London: Routledge, 1998.

Chapter 2: Twentieth century liberalism and thinking about war and peace, 1918 to the present

1   S. Sassoon 'Absolution', in 'War Poems, 1915–1917', *Collected Poems, 1908–1956*, 1942, p. 11.

2   J.A. Hobson *Richard Cobden: the International Man*, London: T. Fisher Unwin, 1919, p. 402.

3   A small collection of recent books on the history of the twentieth century would have to include: E. Hobsbawm, *The Age of Extremes: The Short Twentieth Century, 1914–1991*, London: Michael Joseph, 1994; P. M. H. Bell, *The World Since 1945: An International History*, London: Arnold, 2001; P. Brendon, *Dark Valley: A Panorama of the 1930s*, London: Jonathan Cape, 2000; M. Mazower, *Dark Continent: Europe's Twentieth Century*, London: Penguin, 1998; J. M. Roberts, *Twentieth Century: A History of the World 1901 to the Present*, London: Penguin, 1999. All of them in one way or another see the history of the century as one of competing ideologies and social forces.

4   R. Vinen, *A History in Fragments: Europe in the Twentieth Century*, London: Abacus, 2002, p. 4.

5   S. Sassoon, *The Weald of Youth*, London: Faber and Faber, 1942, pp. 27–74; G. Dangerfield, *The Strange Death of Liberal England*, London: Grenada Publishing, 1970 (first published 1935), R. Fussell, *The Great War and Modern Memory*, Oxford: Oxford University Press, p. 8.

6   Polk to Jusserand, MAE 13/218, Ministry of Foreign Affairs, Paris. [n.d. 1921].

7   Report on the speeches by President Bush and S/G Annan to the General Assembly, *Financial Times*, 22 September 2004.

8   A. M. Kacowicz *et al.*, *Stable Peace among Nations*, Lanha, Boulder: Rowman and Littlefield, 2000, p. xiii.

9   Howard, *Invention of Peace*, p. 2.

10 J. Goodby, 'Stable Peace in Europe' in: Kacowicz *et al.*, *Stable Peace among Nations*, p. 239.

11 M. Hankey, quoting Burke in *The Supreme Control at the Paris Peace Conference*, London: G. Allen and Unwin, 1963, p. 11.

12 There have been several recent publications on think tanks in general. See, for example, I. Parmar, *Think Tanks and Power in Foreign Policy*, London: Palgrave, 2004, and D. Stone, *Think Tanks across Nations*, Manchester: Manchester University Press, 1998.

13 W. Bagehot, *The English Constitution*, 1867, Chapter on the 'House of Lords', quoted in *the Oxford Dictionary of Quotations*, 1997, p. 26.

14 The best introduction to the *Round Table* can be found in: A. May, 'The Round Table, 1910–66', D.Phil, Oxford, 1995.

15 See: I. Parmar, 'Anglo-American Elites in the Interwar Years: Idealism and Power in the Intellectual Roots of Chatham, House and the Council for Foreign Relations', *International Relations*, Vol. 16, No. 1, April 2002, pp. 53–76.

16 Parmar, 'Lord Lothian's Moment: The Anglo-American Establishment and the Saving of Britain, 1939–1941', paper presented at the University of Edinburgh, May 2001, pp. 6–7.

17 For a fascinating recent account of the intellectual climate of the inter-war years see: D. Edmunds and J. Eidinow, *Wittgenstein's Poker: The Story of a Ten-Minute Argument Between Two Great Philosophers*, London: Faber and Faber, 2001.

18 J. Kampfner, *Blair's Wars*, London: Free Press, 2nd edn, 2004, p. 3.

19 N. Chomsky, *World Orders, Old and New*, London: Pluto, 1994; also *Hegemony or Survival: America's Quest for World Dominance*, London: Penguin, 2003.

20 See my 'Before the Special Relationship: The Council on Foreign Relations, The Carnegie Foundation and the Rumour of an Anglo-American War', *Journal of Transatlantic Studies*, Vol. 1, No. 2, 2003, pp. 233–51. See also Fiona Venn '"A Futile Paper Chase": Anglo-American Relations and Middle East Oil, 1918–1934',

Diplomacy and Statecraft, Vol. 1 No. 2, July 1990, pp. 165–84, here p. 167 and p. 172. See also N. Cull, 'Selling Peace: The Origins, Promotion and Fate of the Anglo–American New Order during the Second World War', *Diplomacy and Statecraft*, Vol. 7, No. 1, March 1996, pp. 1–28.

21 'Report of the International Commission To Inquire into the Causes and Conduct of the Balkan Wars, 1913', republished by the Carnegie Endowment as: *The Other Balkan Wars: A 1913 Carnegie Endowment Inquiry in Retrospect with a New Introduction and Reflections on the Present Conflict* by George F. Kennan, Washington Carnegie Endowment for International Peace, 1993. Hereafter: *Carnegie, The Balkans.*

22 *Carnegie, The Balkans*, p. 313, Appendix C. Another letter reads: 'This war has been very painful. We have burnt all the villages abandoned by the Bulgarians. They burn the Greek villages and we the Bulgarian. They massacre, we massacre, and against all those of that dishonest nation, who fell into our hands, the Mannlicher rifle has done its work. Of the 1,200 prisoners we took at Nigrita, only forty-one remain in the prisons, and everywhere we have been, we have not left a single root of this race. I embrace you tenderly, also your brother, and your wife, Spiliotopoulos Philippos', pp. 307–308.

23 *Carnegie, The Balkans*, p. 11.

24 *Carnegie, The Balkans*, pp. 16 and 19.

25 MAE, SDN 1, (Commission de la SDN), Séance d'ouverture, 1918, Ministry of Foreign Affairs Archives, Quai d'Orsay, Paris.

26 One interesting statement of this can be found in A. Hopkinson, *Rebuilding Britain: A Survey of Problems of Reconstruction after the World War*, London: Cassell and Co., 1918.

27 H. G. Wells, *War and the Future: Italy, France and Britain at War*, London, Cassell and Co. Ltd, 1917, pp 8 and 127–8

28 Howard, *War and the Liberal Conscience*, p. 9.

29 Menand, *The Metaphysical Society*, p. 404.

30 T. J. Knock *To End All Wars: Woodrow Wilson and the Search for a New World Order.* New York, Oxford University Press, 1992, p. 52 and *passim.*

31 M. Ceadel, *Thinking About Peace and War*, pp. 9–11.

32 Hobson, *Richard Cobden*, pp. 402 –7.

33 For a near contemporary view of the sudden decline of the Liberal Party just before and during the First World War, see Dangerfield, *The Strange Death of Liberal England.* See also M. Bentley, *The Liberal Mind, 1914–1929*, Cambridge University Press, 1977, and; *The Climax of Liberal Politics*, London, Edward Arnold, 1987.

34 For a detailed analysis of Wilson's political thinking see T. J. Knock, *To End All Wars: Woodrow Wilson and the Quest for a New World Order*, Oxford: Oxford University Press, 1992.

35 Knock, *To End All Wars*, pp. 4–5.

36 For more discussion of this see: Williams, *Failed Imagination?* esp. pp. 217–21.

37 E. D. Morel, 'Original Introduction' of 1912 to *Ten Years of Secret Diplomacy: An Unheeded Warning*, London: National Labour Press, 1915, pp. xvii–xix.

38 Review by G. H Perris of Murray's *The Foreign Policy of Sir Edward Grey, 1906–1915*, Oxford: Clarendon Press, 1915, in *The Daily Chronicle*, 4 August, 1915.

39 M. Mandelbaum, *The Ideas that Conquered the World: Peace, Democracy and Free Markets in the Twentieth Century*, Washington, Public Affairs, 2003.

40 H. Kissinger, *Diplomacy*, New York: Simon & Schuster, 1994.

41 L. Gelfand, *The Inquiry: American Preparations for Peace, 1917–1919*, New Haven: Yale University Press, 1963, pp. 81–4; A. Walworth, *America's Moment: 1918*, New York: Norton and Co., 1963.

42 E. Goldstein, *Winning the Peace: British Diplomatic Strategy and the Paris Peace Conference, 1916–1920*, Oxford: Clarendon Press, 1991. See also Williams, *Failed Imagination?*, Chapters 1 and 2.

43 For details on Post-War Planning during the Second World War see: *Failed Imagination?*, Ch. 5 and 6.

44 M. G. Fry, *Lloyd George and Foreign Policy, 1890–1916*, Vol. I, Montreal: McGill University Press, 1977, pp. 22–5.

45 M. Macmillan, *Peacemakers: The Paris Conference of 1919 and Its Attempt to End War*, London: John Murray, 2001, p. 23.

46 Williams, *Failed Imagination?*, Chapters 1, 2 and 8.

47 Macmillan, *Peacemakers*, p. 66.

48 First Meeting off the 'Armaments' Group of the CFR, 8 February 1940, Armstrong papers, Box 72, Seeley Mudd Library, Princeton.

49 For a sophisticated view of this distinction see Brown, *Understanding International Relations*, pp. 26–34. See also D. Long and P. Wilson, *Thinkers of the Twenty Years' Crisis: Inter-War Idealism Reassessed*, Oxford: Clarendon Press, 1995.

50 A. Sweetzer, 'Foreword' to H. Aufricht, *A Guide to League of Nations Publications, 1920–47*, New York: Columbia University Press, 1951, pp. v–vi.

51 Sweetzer, 'Foreword', p. vi.

52 I. Brownlie recently reiterated this idea, first stated in *International Law and the Use of Force*, 1963, in a talk to the Graduate Institute of International Studies, Geneva, *HEIecho*, No. 20, Spring 2001.

53 K. Polanyi, *The Great Transformation: The Political and Economic Origins of Our Time*, New York: Beacon, 1939.

54 W. Rappard, *Uniting Europe*, New Haven: Yale University Press, 1930, pp. 7–8 and 104.

55 Bellamy, *Rethinking Liberalism*, pp. ix and x.

56 G. Kennan, *American Diplomacy*, Chicago: Chicago University Press,1984.

57 C. Brown, *Understanding International Relations*, pp. 30–32. The italics are his.

58 N. Angell, *The Steep Places*, London: Hamish Hamilton, 1947, p. 103.

59 Review of: E. D. Weitz, *A Century of Genocide: Utopias of Race and Nation*, Princeton: Princeton University Press, 2003, by B. Simms, in *The Higher*, 2 January 2004.

60 R. Bellamy, in R. Eatwell and A. Wright, (eds), *Contemporary Political Ideologies*, London: Continuum, 2nd edition, 1999, p. 41.

61 F. Hayek, 'The Intellectuals and Socialism', *University of Chicago Law Review*, vol. 16, no. 3, Spring 1949, republished under the same title by the Institute of Economic Affairs, London, 1998.

62 A. Applebaum, *Gulag: A History of the Soviet Camps*, London: Allen Lane, Penguin, 2003; S. S. Montefiore, *Stalin: The Court of the Red Czar*, London: Wiedenfield and Nicholson, 2003; D. Rayfield, *Stalin and His Hangmen*, London: Viking, 2004.

63 Krasner, 'Rethinking the Sovereign State Model', p. 40.

64 Sir John Colville, entry for 13 March 1944, Colville Diaries, 1/6, December 1943–May 1944.

65 General Jan Smuts to Colville, 29 April 1944, Colville MS Diary 1/6.

66 J. G. Ruggie, 'International Regimes, Transaction and Change: Embedded Liberalism in the Postwar Economic Order', *International Organization*, vol. 36, pp. 379–415 (1982).

67 P. Hindess and G. Thompson *Globalization in Question: The International Economy and the Possibilities of Governance*, London: Routledge, 1996.

68 R. Skidelsky, *John Maynard Keynes: Fighting for Britain, 1937–1946*, London: Macmillan, 2000.

69 *The New Republic*, 1 January 1945.

70 V. M. Dene, 'What do we want in Europe?' *The New Republic*, 22 January 1945.

71 The most complete history of the High Authority can be found in: D. R. Spierenberg and R. Poidevin, *Histoire de la Haute Authorité de la Communauté Européene du Charbon et de l'Acier: Une Experience Supranationale*, Brussels: Bruylant, 1999 (English translation Weidenfield and Nicholson).

72 P.V. H.A. CECA, 11 August 1952, First Meeting, Box 1, Archives of the High Authority, Brussels.

73 *ibid*, my translation.

74 J. Monnet, Memoirs, London: Collins, 1978.

75 M. J. Dedman, *The Origins and Development of the European Union, 1945–95*, London: Routledge, 1996, pp. 10–11. The most quoted book by Lipgens is: *A History of European Integration, 1945–47*, Vol. 1, Oxford: Clarendon Press, 1982.

76 For the influence of American federal ideas on European theories of integration see: J. Pinder, *Federal Union*, London: Macmillan, 1990. The classic American tract of the period on European Union is C. Streit, *Union Now*, London: Jonathan Cape, 1939.

77 D. Mitrany, *A Working Peace System* [1943] Reprinted with an Introduction by H. Morgenthau, Chicago: Quadrangle Books, 1966; C. Brown *Understanding International Relations*, [1997 edition], page 129–33. See also D. Mitrany and P. Taylor, *The Functional Theory of Politics*, London: Martin Robertson, 1975.

78 Murray to Cecil, 3 July 1944, Cecil to Murray 4 July 1944, Murray Papers, Box 130.

79 Cecil to Murray, 23 December 1946 and 2 February 1947, Murray Papers Box 130.

80 J. L. Harper, *American Visions of Europe: Franklin D. Roosevelt, George F. Kennan and Dean G. Acheson*, Cambridge: Cambridge University Press, 1996, pp. 1–2.

81 Geir Lundestad, *Empire through Integration: The United States and European Integration, 1945–1997*, Oxford University Press, 1998, Introduction.

82 The term 'civilian power' was coined in the 1970s by Duchene and has been much developed since by EU specialists like Karen Smith, Christopher Hill and Ian Manners.

83 For the implications for the conduct of warfare see Chapter 1.

84 R. Cooper, *The Postmodern State and the World Order*, London: Demos, The Foreign Policy Centre, London, 1996, 1998, 'Introduction'.

85 Cooper, *op. cit.*, p. 11.

86 F. Fukuyama, 'The End of History and the Last Man', *The National Interest*, Summer 1989, p. 3, quoted by Bellamy, in Eatwell and Wright, *Contemporary Political Ideologies*, p. 23.

87 J. Rosenberg, *The Empire of Civil Society: A Critique of the Realist Theory of International Relations*, London: Verso, 1994, esp. Ch. 5.

88 P. Mandaville and A. Williams, *Meaning and International Relations*, London: Routledge, 2003; Z. Laidi, *A World Without Meaning*, London: Routledge, 1998.

89 F. Fukuyama, *Trust*, New York: The Free Press, 1995 and; *The End of Order*, London: The Social Market Foundation, 1997.

90 N. Wheeler, *Saving Strangers: Humanitarian Intervention in International Society*, Oxford: Oxford University Press, 2000. See also J. L. Holzgrefe and R. O. Keohane (eds), *Humanitarian Intervention: Ethical, Legal and Political Dilemmas*, Cambridge: Cambridge University Press, 2003.

91 I am here using the 1992 edition but assuming that this was written earlier.

92 Walzer, *Just and Unjust Wars*, pp. 101 and 107 and 'Preface to the 2nd Edition'.

93 J. Pilger, *New Statesman*, 28 June 1999.

94 Miall, Ramsbottam and Woodhouse, 1999.

95 M. Kaldor, *New and Old Wars: Organized Violence in a Global Era*, Cambridge: Polity Press, 1999, pp. 1–3. See also M. Kaldor and B. Vashee (eds), *Restructuring the Global Military Sector, Volume 1: New Wars*, London: Cassell/Pinter, 1997.

96 S. Chesterman, *Just War or Just Peace?: International Law and Humanitarian Intervention*, Oxford: Oxford University Press, 2001.

97 R. N. Haass, *Intervention: The Use of American Military Force in the Post Cold War World*, Washington DC: Brookings/Carnegie, 1999.

98 H.W. Brands, *The Strange Death of American Liberalism*, London: Zed Books, 2003.

99 'Fighting Talk from the Prince of "Neo-cons"', interview by Alec Russell, *Daily Telegraph*, 17 November 2003.

100 A. Callinicos, *The New Mandarins of American Power*, Oxford: Polity, 2004.

101 *Daily Telegraph*, 10 November 2004.

Chapter 3: Reparations

1 Some of the early part of this chapter has been adapted from: A. Williams, 'Sir John Bradbury and the Reparations Commission, 1920–1925', *Diplomacy and Statecraft*, September 2002, Vol. 13, No. 3, pp. 81–102.

2 We might also mention academic fashion, with the Thirty Year Rule's emergence in the 1970s removing the incentive for many young scholars to study the dusty depths of the 1920s when the 1950s offered such richer pickings, (an insight I owe to a conversation with Richard Langhorne in 1998).

3 See for example D. Long and P. Wilson, *Thinkers of the Twenty Years' Crisis*, Oxford: Clarendon Press, 1995.

4 I. Brownlie, *System of the Law of Nations: State Responsibility*, Part 1, Oxford: Clarendon Press, 1983, p. 5.

5 Brownlie, *State Responsibility*, pp. 31 and 199.

6 A. G. Mayer, *Politics and Diplomacy of Peacemaking: Containment and Counterrevolution at Versailles, 1918–1919*, New York: Alfred A. Knopf, 1967, pp. 55–62.

7 My thanks to Anthony Lentin for pointing this out to me at a conference in Nottingham in September 2003.

8 O. W. Knauth, *The Nation*, 10 May 1919 – Report.

9 The most complete printed account of the debt and reparations questions after the Treaty of Versailles is P. M. Burnett, *Reparation at the Paris Peace Conference From the Standpoint of the American Delegation*, 2 vols, New York: Columbia University Press, 1940. Some of the best books on the subject are: M. Trachtenberg, *Reparations in World Politics: France and Economic Diplomacy, 1916–1923*, New York: Columbia University Press, 1980; B. Kent, *The Spoils of War: The Politics, Economics and Diplomacy of Reparations, 1918–1922*, Oxford: Clarendon Press, 1989; E. Weill-Raynal, *Les reparations allemandes at la France, 1918–1936*, Paris: Nouvelles éditions latines, 1947. Contemporary accounts include B. M. Baruch, *The Making of the Reparation and Economic Sections of the Treaty*, New York: Harper and Brothers, 1920. The best defence in English of the French viewpoint on reparations can be found in S. A. Schuker, *The End of French Predominance in Europe: The Financial Crisis of 1924 and the Adoption of the Dawes Plan*, Chapel Hill: University of North Carolina Press, 1976.

10 D. Lloyd George *The Truth About the Peace Treaties*, London: Gollancz, 1938, pp. 436–7.

11 D. Lloyd George, *The Truth About the Peace Treaties*, pp. 439–44.

12 A. Williams 'Sir John Bradbury and the Reparations Commission', pp. 84–5.

13 L. Gelfand (ed.), *The Inquiry: American Preparation for Peace, 1917–1919*, New Haven: Yale University Press, 1963 E. Goldstein, *Winning the Peace: British Diplomatic Strategy, Peace Planning, and the Paris Peace Conference, 1916–1920*, Oxford: Clarendon Press, 1991. See also my: *Failed Imagination? New World Orders of the Twentieth Century*, Manchester: Manchester University Press, 1998, Chapters 1 and 2.

14 D. Lloyd George, *The Truth about the Peace Treaties* , p. 436.

15 A. Lentin, 'Lord Cunliffe, Lloyd George, Reparations and Reputations at the Paris Peace Conference, 1919', *Diplomacy and Statecraft*, March 1999, Vol. 10, No. 1, pp. 50–86, pp. 50–1.

16 For Lloyd George's foreign policy predilections see M. Fry, *Lloyd George and Foreign Policy, 1890–1916*, Vol. 1, Montreal: McGill University Press, 1977.

17 'Reparation: Not Indemnities', *New Republic* 23 November 1918.

18 J. M. Keynes, *The Economic Consequences of the Peace*, London: Macmillan, 1920, and *A Revision of the Treaty*, London: Macmillan, 1921.

19 See for example: D. Artaud, *La question des dettes interalliés et la reconstruction de l'Europe, 1917–1929*, Lille and Paris: Honoré Champion, 1978.

20 S. Marks, *Innocent Abroad, Belgium at the Peace Conference*, Chapel Hill, NC: University of North Carolina Press.

21   A. L. Bowley, *Some Economic Consequences of the Great War*, London: Thornton Butterworth Ltd, 1930, pp. 222–4.

22   D. Lloyd George, *The Truth About the Peace Treaties*, p. 465.

23   Keynes to Bradbury, 21 October 1918, Keynes Papers, King's College Cambridge, T/32/2–9.

24   Keynes to Bradbury, 14 January 1919, Keynes Papers, RT/1/32–5.

25   Keynes to Blackett, 30 January 1918, Keynes Papers T/1/59–63.

26   For a clear statement of this see P. A Cravath, 'Suggestions Regarding Indemnities', 1 January 1920, but in essence a statement that he made in December 1918, Keynes Papers PT/13/4–18.

27   Cravath to Keynes, annotated by Keynes, 12 December 1918, Keynes Papers RT/1/3.

28   J. F. Dulles, 'Reparation Commission. Statement on behalf of the American Delegates', 13 February 1919, Dulles Papers, J. Seeley Mudd Library, Princeton, Box 2, 1918–19.

29   Amos T. Crosby, Special US Commissioner of Finance in Europe to Keynes, 7 January 1919, Keynes Papers RT/1/24.

30   Bradbury to Keynes, 22 May 1919, RT/1/111–2 and Chamberlain to Keynes, 21 May 1919 RT/1/100–1, both Keynes Papers.

31   Schuker, *The End of French Predominance*, pp. 8 (fn.6) and 9.

32   Poincaré in the *Revue des Deux Mondes*, 15 May 1921.

33   Keynes, *A Revision of the Treaty*, p. 119.

34   Keynes, *A Revision of the Treaty*, p. 120; D. Lloyd George, *The Truth about Reparations and War Debts*, London: William Heinemann, 1932, p. 58.

35   David Hubback, *Letters from Paris: Reparations and the Ruhr Crisis of 1923*, photocopied edition, Papers in the possession of Ms. Jennifer Hart, p. 6. The letters are from Fischer Williams to Lady Courtney, the older sister of Beatrice Webb.

36   Bradbury to Horne, 22 September 1922, Bradbury Papers.

37   'Statement by the British Delegate on the urgent situation created by a further fall of the mark' Annex No. 1614, Reparation Commission, 6 October 1922, Bradbury Papers 'Swan Song and Bombshell'.

38   Bradbury to Chamberlain, 24 May 1923, Bradbury Papers.

39   Ibid.

40   Quoted by S. Osborne, *The Saar Question*, London: Allen & Unwin, 1923, pp. 23–2.

41   For an analysis of the internal German political scene around this time see C. S. Maier, *Recasting Bourgeois Europe: Stabilization in France, Germany and Italy in the Decade after World War One*, Princeton: Princeton University Press, 1975, especially 'The Politics of Reparation'.

42   M. Hogan, *The Marshall Plan: America, Britain and the Reconstruction of Western Europe, 1947–1952*, Cambridge: Cambridge University Press, 1987, pp. 5–9.

43   Maier, *Recasting Bourgeois Europe*, p. 304.

44   Hogan, *Marshall Plan*, pp. 12–19.

45   *The Times*, 12 December 1924; likewise the *Daily News* of the same date. Sir William Goode was described in the *Daily News* as 'one of the three men in the country who alone understood indemnities and reparation' and that Bradbury had 'originated . . . the whole idea of the Dawes Plan'.

46   B. Kuklick, *American Policy and the Division of Germany: The Clash with Russia over Reparations*, New York: Cornell University Press, 1972.

47   Hogan, *Marshall Plan*, Chapter 1, and pp. 20–2.

48   Hogan, *Marshall Plan*, p. 427.

49   Williams, *Failed Imagination?*, pp. 68–70.

50   Oscar Cox, 'Memorandum for Harry L. Hopkins. Subject: Commitment to Use Force to Secure the Peace', 16 August 1944, and accompanying memo from Cox to Hopkins, 11 January 1945, Hopkins Papers, Roosevelt Library, Box 329.

51 Herbert Hoover and Hugh Gibson in *Collier's Magazine*, 26 June 1943, quoted in a State Department memo entitled 'Settlement of Political Disputes' Leo Pasvolsky Papers, 'Permanent International Organization', file dated 24 July 1943, Box 4, Library of Congress, Washington DC. See also another article [also in *Collier's*] – 'Problems of a Lasting Peace', [n.d. probably 1944].

52 Hoover in 'The Promotion of Economic and Social Welfare', loc.cit., p. 9.

53 Cf. same document, pp. 15–16, International Organization Subcommittee of Congress.

54 'Post-War Problems – Plan of Work', 1941, Pasvolsky papers.

55 CFR, Hamilton Fish Armstrong Papers, n.d., probably 1942; 'Digest of Preliminary Views Regarding the Peace Aims of European Nations', 15 December 1941.

56 Ibid, p. 17.

57 Dalton was both a prominent socialist member of the Labour Party and certainly one of the Labour ministers who had the most impact on foreign policy and the conduct of the war in general. He was in charge of the Special Operations Executive during 1940–2, and President of the Board of Trade, 1942. See B. Pimlott, *Hugh Dalton: A Biography*, London: Pan Macmillan, 1985.

58 B. Pimlott (ed.), *The Second World War Diary of Hugh Dalton, 1940–45*, London: Jonathan Cape, 1986, pp. xxix–xxx.

59 R. Skidelsky, *John Maynard Keynes: Fighting for Britain, 1937–1946*, London: Macmillan, 2000, p. 362.

60 Skidelsky, *Keynes: Fighting for Britain, 1937 – 1946*, p. 363.

61 Memo numbered H-5000, 13 July 1943, Adolf Berle Papers, Box 65, Roosevelt Memorial Library. See also Chapter 4.

62 'The Crimean Conference', *New Republic*, 19 February 1945.

63 Informal Minutes of Meeting of the Joint Steering Committee, Dumbarton Oaks, 25 August 1944, present were Lord Cadogan, Gladwyn Jebb, Gromyko, Edward Stettinius, Leo Pasvolsky and Alger Hiss, Pasvolsky Papers, Box 3.

64 M. Trachtenberg, *A Constructed Peace: The Making of the European Settlement, 1945–1963*, Princeton: Princeton University Press, 1999, p. 3.

65 Trachtenberg, *Constructed Peace*, pp. 8–9.

66 Williams, *Failed Imagination*, Chapter 5; Trachtenberg, *Constructed Peace*, pp. 10–13.

67 A. Gromyko, *Memoirs*, New York: Doubleday, 1989, pp. 87–8.

68 J. L. Gaddis, *The United States and the Origins of the Cold War, 1941–47*, New York: Columbia University Press, 1972.

69 Hogan, *Marshall Plan*, pp. 29–31.

70 For details see: J. Bacque, *Crimes and Mercies: The Fate of German Civilians Under Allied Occupation, 1944–1950*, London: TimeWarner, 1997. He does not spare the Western allies from approbation but it seems clear that the fate of civilians under Soviet rule was far worse than in the Western zones.

71 Trachtenberg, *Constructed Peace*, p. 23.

72 Bacque, *Crimes and Mercies*, p. 176–7. One of his sources is J. Gimbel, *Science, Technology and Reparations: Exploitation and Plunder in Post-War Germany*, Stanford: Stanford University Press, 1990. Bacque also claims that 'the Americans took from Germany at least twenty times the amount the Germans retained under the Marshall Plan', p. 177. These figures seem highly implausible.

73 Trachtenberg makes it clear that he believes that Byrnes and Truman were in effect by the time of Potsdam prepared to accept a *de facto* division of Germany and that a 'clean separation was the best solution'. The Russians were, in Truman's words, '"natural looters". . ., but given what Germany had done to them, one could "hardly blame them for their attitude"'. Trachtenberg, *Constructed Peace*, pp. 27–31 and 37.

74 Trachtenberg, *Constructed Peace*, pp. 39–41.

75 Trachtenberg, *Constructed Peace*, p. 47. For details see his Chapter 2.

76 A. S. Milward, *The Reconstruction of Western Europe, 1945–51*, London: Routledge, 1984, p. 35.

77   Hogan, *Marshall Plan*, pp. 31–3.
78   See for example, Georges Bidault (then French Foreign Minister) to the French Ambassador in London, 19 April 1948, Vincent Auriol Papers 552 AP 71dr2, Archives Nationales, Paris.
79   Truman Papers, OF, 1947, folder, 950-B, quoted by Hogan, *Marshall Plan*, p. 13.
80   Hogan, *Marshall Plan*, pp. 34–5.
81   Hogan, *Marshall Plan*, pp 35–41.
82   Bidault to the French Ambassador in London, 19 April 1948, Vincent Auriol Papers 552 AP 71dr2, document cited above.
83   Hogan, *Marshall Plan*, pp. 26–7.
84   'Haiti seeks change of fortune by suing Paris', *Daily Telegraph*, 3 January 2004.
85   E. Barkan, *The Guilt of Nations: Restitution and Negotiating Historical Injustices*, New York: W.W. Norton, 2000, p. xxii.
86   A. Lentin, 'Lord Cunliffe, Lloyd George, Reparations and Reputations at the Paris Peace Conference', *Diplomacy and Statecraft*, Vol. 17, No. 1, March, 1959, pp. 54–72.
87   Bradbury, 'Notes on the Reparation Settlement', Keynes Papers, FI/9/11.

Chapter 4: Reconstruction until the Marshall Plan

1   CFR Peace Aims Group: memo from Crane Brinton, 'the Political Outlook and the Possibility of Collaborating with Democratic Groups in France and Belgium', 4 November 1942 and 'French Peace Aims', 8 February 1943, Hamilton Fish Armstrong Papers, Box 73, Seeley H. Mudd Memorial Library, Princeton University.
2   Oscar Cox to Harry Hopkins, 31 December 1942, on arguments used against American aid to Europe in 1919, Hopkins papers, Roosevelt Library, Box 329.
3   C. Cramer, 'The Great Post-Conflict Makeover Fantasy', paper presented to the Conference, 'Making Peace Work, UNU – WIDER', Helsinki June 2004, p. 5. See also E. Foner, *Reconstruction: America's Unfinished Revolution, 1863 – 1877*, New York: HarperCollins, 1989; P. O'Brien, *The Economic Effects of the American Civil War*, Basingstoke: Macmillan, 1988 and R. L. Heilbronner, *The Economic Transformation of America*, New York: Harcourt Brace Jovanovich, 1977.
4   Cramer, 'The Great Post-Conflict Makeover Fantasy', p. 5.
5   For an overview of these efforts see D. Armstrong, L. Lloyd and J. Redmond, *From Versailles to Maastricht: International Organisation in the Twentieth Century*, London: Macmillan, 1996, especially Chapter 1.
6   Anderson, *A Liberal State at War*, p. 271, and Chapter 8 on 'War Trade and Trade War'.
7   Dawson, *Richard Cobden and Foreign Policy*, Chapter 1, 'The Man' and Chapter V, 'The Case Against War'; Ceadel, *Thinking about Peace and War*. For the wider liberal debate about peace and war in the nineteenth century see Hinsley, *Power and the Pursuit of Peace*, especially Parts I and II.
8   Again, Gallie's *Philosophers of Peace and War* is a foundational text for explaining the nineteenth-century evolution of this kind of thinking.
9   Dawson, *Richard Cobden*, Chapter XI 'The Friend of America', p. 231.
10   Angell, *The Great Illusion*. The quotations here are from the 2nd edition of 1912, pp. v–xi.
11   There is a famous cartoon in *Punch* of the 1890s illustrating this 'dropping of the pilot'.
12   For a brilliant exposition of this see: F. Stern, *Einstein's German World*, Princeton: Princeton University Press, 1999.
13   J. Marlowe, *Milner: Apostle of Empire*, London: Hamish Hamilton, 1976.
14   J. Dewey, 'The Cult of Irrationality', *New Republic*, 9 November 1919.
15   See A. Williams, *Trading with the Bolsheviks: The Politics of East-West Trade, 1920–1939*, Manchester: Manchester University Press, 1992, esp. Chapter 1.

16 *The New Republic*, 9 November 1918.

17 N. Hapgood, 'A Program of Reconstruction', *New Republic*, 16 November 1918.

18 *New Republic*, 14 December 1918.

19 Stern, *Einstein's German World*, Chapter 3 on Haber and Einstein.

20 A 'Reconstruction Committee' was set up by Prime Minister Herbert Asquith on 2 December 1916 and produced five reports until it was abolished in 1919. Its agenda was mainly limited to the problems of demobilization and resettlement and the post-war resumption of trade. From July 1917 there was a Minister for Reconstruction. See P. B. Johnson, *Land Fit for Heroes: The Planning of British Reconstruction, 1916–1919*, Chicago: University of Chicago Press, 1968.

21 R. Cecil, *A Great Experiment*, London: Jonathan Cape, 1941, p. 102.

22 O. W. Knauth, report on the 1919 meeting of the American Academy of Political and Social Sciences, *The Nation*, 10 May 1919.

23 *The Nation*, 20 September 1919.

24 *Ibid.* The review was of seven books, including: C. F. Lowell, *Reconstruction and National Life*, New York: The Macmillan Company, 1919; I. Lippin, *Problems of Reconstruction*, New York: Macmillan Company, 1919; A. M. Symons, *The Vision for Which We Fought: A Study in Reconstruction*, New York: The Macmillan Company, 1919; H. Mackinder, *Democratic Ideals and Reality: A Study in the Politics of Reconstruction*, London: Henry Holt and Co., 1919; T. Barclay, *Collapse and Reconstruction: European Conditions and American Principles*, Boston: Little, Brown and Co, 1919.

25 Polanyi, *The Great Transformation, op. cit.*

26 H. MacMillan, *Reconstruction: A Plea for a National Policy*, London: Macmillan, 1933.

27 The papers of the PEP can be found in the BLPES, London School of Economics. See also A. Briggs, 'The World Economy: Interdependence and Planning', *New Cambridge Modern History*, Vol. XII, Cambridge: Cambridge University Press, 1968.

28 C. Kindleberger, *The World In Depression, 1929–1939*, London: Allen Lane, 1973.

29 R. Skidelsky, *John Maynard Keynes: the Economist as Saviour, 1920–1937*, London: Macmillan, 1992 and; *John Maynard Keynes: Fighting for Britain, 1937–1946*, London: Macmillan, 2000.

30 Memo prepared for the CFR Hamilton Fish Armstrong Papers, Princeton University Library Box 72, 7 November 1928.

31 Ibid. 'Freedom of the Seas' topped the agenda. Other topics involved the limitation of armaments, treaties of conciliation and inquiry, economic competition and joint action in particular areas, especially China.

32 James Byrne to Hamilton Fish Armstrong, 11 August 1928, Armstrong Papers, Box 72.

33 A. L. Bowley, *Some Economic Consequences of the Great War*, London: Thornton Butterworth Ltd, 1930, p. 224.

34 F. W. O'Brien (ed.), *Two Peacemakers in Paris: The Hoover-Wilson Post-Armistice Letters, 1918–1920*, Texas: A and M University Press, 1978.

35 S. Baker, *Wilson and the World Settlement*, 3 Volumes, New York: Doubleday, 1922–3, this quote from Volume 2, p. 335.

36 *New Republic*, 11 January 1919.

37 Hoover, 1919, quoted in O'Brien, *op. cit.*, p. xxix.

38 T. A. Bailey, *Woodrow Wilson and the Lost Peace*, New York: Macmillan, 1944, p. 134.

39 This version of the SEC Minutes is from the French Archives in the MAE, SDN 1158, notes of 6 February 1920.

40 'Questions d'ordre economique a etudier par le service francais de la SDN' and: de la Baumelle to Clauges, letter of 10 February 1920, MAE, SDN 1158.

41 A. Williams, *Trading with the Bolsheviks: The Politics of East–West Trade, 1920–1939*, Manchester: Manchester University Press, 1992, especially Chapter 1. See also M. J. Hogan, *Informal Entente: the Private Structure of Cooperation in Anglo-American Economic*

Diplomacy, Columbia: University of Missouri Press, 1977. On Hoover see E. Hawley (ed.) *Herbert Hoover as Secretary of Commerce: Studies in New Era Thought and Practice*, Iowa City: University of Iowa Press, 1981; L. Nash (ed.) *Understanding Herbert Hoover: Ten Perspectives*, Stanford: Hoover Institution, 1987 and: J. Hoff Wilson, *Ideology and Economics: US Relations with the Soviet Union, 1918–1933*, Columbia: University of Missouri Press, 1974.

42 'Note au sujet de la sitution économique de l'Europe', 1 March 1920, 29 pages, MAE SDN 1158.

43 *The Nation*, 20 September 1919.

44 Williams, *Trading with the Bolsheviks*, pp. 34–6.

45 For more details see A. Williams, 'Before the Special Relationship: The Council on Foreign Relations, The Carnegie Foundation and the Rumour of a Anglo-American War', *Journal of Transatlantic Studies*, Volume 1, Number 2, Autumn 2003, pp. 233–51.

46 For a more detailed discussion of Genoa see C. Fink, *The Genoa Conference*, Chapel Hill: University of Northern Carolina Press, 1984; S. White, *The Origins of Detente: the Genoa Conference and Soviet–Western Relations, 1920–1924*, Cambridge: Cambridge University Press, 1985 and C. Fink, A. Frohn and J. Heideking (eds), *Genoa, Rapallo and European Reconstruction in 1922*, Cambridge: Cambridge University Press, 1991.

47 Philip Noel Baker, Lecture Notes for 1924/25, NBKR 4/33.

48 M. Petriciolli (ed.), *A Missed Opportunity? 1922: The Reconstruction of Europe*, Bern: Peter Lang, 1995.

49 Cecil, *Great Experiment*, pp. 136–7.

50 *Financial Reconstruction of Austria: Report of the Financial Committee of the Council*, Geneva: League of Nations, 1921 [L.N.II.1921.2] The Conference was held from 12–17 March 1921.

51 *Austria . . . Report of the Financial Committee*, pp. 7–9.

52 P. Noel Baker, *The Financial Reconstruction of Europe*, Geneva: League of Nations, 1922.

53 League of Nations, 'The Settlement of Greek Refugees: Scheme for an International Loan', Geneva 10 October 1924, Doc. C.524.M.187.1924.II.

54 League of Nations, *Greek Refugee Settlement*, Geneva, LON, 1926, page xv. It is worth noting that some Bulgarian refugees: Legaue of Nations C.522.M. 204. 1926. II, 7 September 1926.

55 C. Levy and M Roseman (ed.), *Three Postwar Eras in Comparison: Western Europe, 1918-1945-1989*, London: Palgrave, 2002 .

56 Morgenthau Presidential Diary, 15 May 1942, memo to the President, Vol. 5, 1 January 1942 – 11 April 1945, Fiche 14, Roosevelt Presidential Library.

57 *New Republic*, March 1945 (Editorial).

58 Henry Stimson Diary, entry for 17 November 1942. Stimson Diary, Yale University Library, reel 8. Hull had expressed his fear 'with fire and brimstone' to Stimson that '"the starry eyed" members of the President's entourage, whom he described as young communists . . . [could cause] a complete swing back to reactionary-ism such as the Harding regime after the last war'.

59 See for example the *New Republic*, 26 March and 2 April 1945 on the 'Anglo–American Future'. The signature of the Bretton Woods accords dominated the economic pages of all American and British liberal journals at this period.

60 A. Williams, 'France and the New World Order, 1940–1947' *Modern and Contemporary France*, Vol. 8, No. 2, May 2000, pp. 191–202.

61 CFR Peace Aims Group: memo from Crane Brinton, 'the Political Outlook and the Possibility of Collaborating with Democratic Groups in France and Belgium', 4 November 1942 and 'French Peace Aims', 8 February 1943, Hamilton Fish Armstrong Papers, Box 73, Seeley H. Mudd Memorial Library, Princeton University.

62   See for example E. Penrose, *Economic Planning for the Peace*, Princeton: Princeton University Press, 1953.

63   Brinton, 'The Political Outlook . . .', 1942.

64   Oscar Cox to Harry Hopkins, 31 December 1942, on arguments used against American aid to Europe in 1919, Hopkins Papers, Roosevelt, Library, Box 329.

65   'Notes of a Meeting held April 10, 1943' Lehman Papers, C47/64 'Diary, London, April 1943', pp. 14–15 and War Cabinet Committee on Post-War Commodity Policy and Relief, 14 April 1943, Lehman Papers C47/64, 'Diary, London, April 1943', p. 56.

66   Lehman, Diary of Visits to London and Paris, October–November 1944, Lehman Papers C47/65, pp. 26–7.

67   One important source for Lehman on this was the Department of World Jewish affairs of the American Jewish Corps and other American Jewish philanthropic organizations like the American Joint Distribution Committee. Lehman Papers, Special files, UNRRA Personal and General C46–48.

68   Moses A. Leavitt (American–Jewish Joint Distribution Committee) to Lehman, 14 September 1945 in a long 'Statement on UNRRA', Lehman papers UNRRA, Personal and General, C46–1.

69   There were full-scale missions in Byelorussia, Ukraine, China, Czechoslovakia, Greece, Italy, Poland, Yugoslavia and smaller ones in the Dodecanese islands, Ethiopia, Finland, Hungary, San Marino, Korea and the Philippine Republic. Source Lehman Papers, File 46 – 2 [Personal correspondence and General Files: Administration and Budget].

70   Leavitt to Lehman, 14 September 1945, Lehman papers UNRRA, Personal and General, C46–1.

71   Lehman Papers, loc.cit., 46–2, p. 77.

72   There is a wealth of documentary evidence for this. See Cabinet papers, CAB/60 and /107 Post War Economic Problems and Anglo-American Cooperation and CAB/165 Post War Settlement, Public Record Office. See also B. W. E. Alford, R. Lowe and N. Rollings, *Economic Planning: A Guide to Documents in the PRO*, London: PRO, 1992.

73   My thanks to Ann Stevens for this insight.

74   W. Beveridge *The Price of Peace*, London: Pilot Press, 1945, p. vii. Here he is quoting from his previous work, viz. Report on Social Insurance and Allied Services of November 1942 and his Report on Full Employment in a Free Society of November 1944.

75   War Cabinet Committee on Post-War Commodity Policy and Relief, 14 April 1943, Lehman Papers C47/64, 'Diary, London, April 1943', p. 55.

76   'Notes of a Meeting held April 10, 1943' Lehman Papers, C47/64 in 'Diary, London, April 1943', p. 18.

77   'Notes of a Meeting held April 10, 1943' Lehman Papers, C47/64 'Diary, London, April 1943', p. 12.

78   For some details of this see Williams, *Failed Imagination*, pp. 161–5.

79   War Cabinet Committee on Post-War Commodity Policy and Relief, 14 April 1943, Lehman Papers C47/64, 'Diary, London, April 1943', p. 57.

80   'Notes of a Meeting held April 17, 1943' in 'Diary, London, April 1943?, pp. 107–8. The meeting was with G.S. Dunnet of the Treasury. Lehman Papers, C47/64.

81   'Notes of a Meeting held April 13, 1943' in 'Diary, London, April 1943', Lehman Papers, C47/64, p. 31.

82   The Director of the Board of Trade's Post-War Commodity Policy and Relief Department who led most of the British civilian delegation in talks with Lehman in April 1943 and the Autumn of 1944.

83   Lehman, Diary of Visits to London and Paris, October–November 1944, Lehman Papers C47/65, pp. 33–7.

84   Meeting of April 17 (at 12.30 after the Treasury), ibid., p. 109.

85   Meeting of April 17 (at 12.30 after the Treasury), ibid., p. 111.

86   Lehman, 'Diary of Visits to London and Paris, October–November 1944', Lehman
     Papers C47/65, pp. 27–9.

87   'Notes of a Meeting held April 13, 1943' 'Diary, London, April 1943', Lehman
     Papers, C47/64, p. 33.

88   Lehman, 'Diary of Visits to London and Paris', October–November 1944, Lehman
     Papers C47/65, pp. 12–13.

89   *New Republic*, 19 February 1945.

90   *New Republic*, Review of the 'Road to Serfdom', 1 April 1945.

91   Dewey Anderson to Lehman, 23 March 1945. Anderson was the Executive Secretary
     of the US Senate Special Committee to Study the Problems of Small Businesses,
     Lehman Papers, Letters, File 420.

92   Bevin to Lehman, 24 December 1947, Lehman Papers, Letters, File 420a.

93   J. Plano and R. E. Riggs, *Forging World Order: The Politics of International Organization*,
     New York: Macmillan, 1967, p. 401.

94   W. D. Philips (UNRRA staffer) to Lehman, 20 September 1943, Lehman Papers
     C46–5.

95   J. Ikenberry, 'A World Economy Restored: Expert consensus and the Anglo-American
     postwar Settlement', *International Organization*, Vol. 46, No. 1, Winter 1992, pp. 289–322.

96   M. Hogan, *The Marshall Plan: America, Britain and the Reconstruction of Western Europe*,
     Cambridge: Cambridge University Press, 1987, pp. 42–4.

97   Williams, *Failed Imagination?*, Ch. 3 and 4.

98   *New Republic*, 12 February 1945.

99   'United States Memoranda', Foreign Research and Press Service of the Royal
     Institute of International affairs, 25 February 1943, No. 158, 'The Great Debate on
     Peace Aims', Noel Baker Papers, NBKR 4/381.

100 A. Grünbacher, *Reconstruction and Cold War in Germany: The Kreditanstalt für Wieder-
     aufbau*, Aldershot: Ashgate, 2004.

101 Lehman to Sir Robert Jackson (Under Secretary General at the UN and a great
     friend of Lehman's from UNRRA days), 22 January 1948, Lehman Papers 420A.

102 S. Abouzahr, 'The Tangled Web: America, France and Indochina, 1947–50', *History
     Today*, Vol. 54, No. 10, October 2004, pp 49–55.

103 Cecil to Gilbert Murray, 2 February and 26 March 1947, Murray Papers Box 130.

104 M. M. Narinskii 'The Soviet Union and the Marshall Plan', in A. Varsari and
     E. Calandri *The Failure of Peace in Europe, 1943–1948*, London: Palgrave 2002,
     p. 275.

105 M. Mazower, *Dark Continent: Europe's Twentieth Century*, London: Penguin, pp. x–xi.

106 Editorial, *New Republic*, 23 November 1918.

107 Cramer, 'The Great Post-Conflict Makeover Fantasy', pp. 7–10.

108 Oscar Cox to Harry Hopkins, 31 December 1942, Hopkins Papers, Roosevelt,
     Library, Box 329.

Chapter 5: Reconstruction after the Marshall Plan

1   M. Mandelbaum, *The Ideas that Conquered the World: Peace, Democracy and Free Markets in
    the Twenty-First Century*, Oxford: Public Affairs Ltd., 2002, p. 19.

2   E. Cohen, 'Kosovo and the New American way of War', in A. J. Bacevich and E.
    Cohen (eds), *War over Kosovo: Politics and Strategy in a Global Age*, New York: Columbia
    University Press, 2001, pp. 48–9.

3   J. Dempsey, interview with Patten, 'Patten's Philosophy of the World', *Financial Times*,
    23 May 2001, p. 25.

4   M. Beschloss, *The Conquerors: Roosevelt, Truman and the Destruction of Hitler's Germany,
    1941–1945*, New York: Simon and Schuster, 2002. The President's reading habits
    were reported in a BBC Radio Report of 26 August 2003.

5 See for example letter to the *Financial Times* (to which I was a signatory) of 8/9 March 2003.

6 R. McGinty, 'The Pre-War Reconstruction of Post-War Iraq', *Third World Quarterly*, Vol. 24, No. 4, 2003, pp. 601–17, this quote from p. 604. His longer definition reads 'reconstruction is taken as a range of physical, economic, social, political and psychological activities aimed at catalysing and sustaining long-term human development', p. 604.

7 McGinty, 'Pre-War Reconstruction . . .', pp. 602–3.

8 McGinty, 'Pre-War Reconstruction . . .' p. 603. He is quoting the report by the United Nations Development Programme (Ahmed *et al.*), *Lessons Learned in Crises and Post-Conflict Situations*, UNDP, 2002, p. 115.

9 T. Eagleton 'Rediscover a Common Cause or Die', *New Statesman*, 28 July 2004, p. 19.

10 T. Addison, 'Introduction' to T. Addison (ed), *From Conflict to Recovery in Africa*, Oxford: Oxford University Press/UNU, 2003, p. 8.

11 Addison, 'Introduction', p. 9.

12 P. J. O'Rourke, *Holidays in Hell*, New York: Grove Books, 1988.

13 S. Forman and S. Patrick (eds), *Good Intentions: Pledges for Postconflict Recovery*, London: Lynne Reinner, 2000.

14 J. Rosenau, *Turbulence in World Politics: A Theory of Change and Continuity*, Princeton University Press, 1990.

15 M. Kaldor, *New and Old Wars: Organized Violence in a Global Era*, Cambridge: Polity, 1999, pp. 133–5.

16 L. Reychler and T. Paffenholz, *Peacebuilding: A Field Guide*, London: Lynne Rienner, 2001, p. 12.

17 A. Bronstone, *The European Bank for Reconstruction and Development: The Building of a Bank for East Central Europe*, Manchester: Manchester University Press, 1999.

18 K. Kumar (ed.), *Postconflict Elections, Democratization and International Assistance*, London: Lynne Reinner, 1998.

19 Co-Director of the Carnegie's 'Post-Soviet Economies in Transition' project.

20 A. Åslund, 'The Myth of Output Collapse after Communism', Carnegie Endowment for International Peace, *Working Papers*, Post-Soviet Economies Project, No. 18, March 2001, p. iii.

21 Y. Federov, 'Democratization and Globalization: the Case of Russia', Carnegie Endowment for International Peace, *Working Papers*, Democracy and Rule of Law Project, No. 13, May 2000, 'Foreword'.

22 Kennan Institute, *Kennan Institute: The First Twenty-Five Years, 1974–1999*, Washington DC, 1999, pp. 19–23.

23 Bronstone, *The European Bank for Reconstruction and Development*, 1999.

24 See: A. Williams, *Trading with the Bolsheviks: The Politics of East–West Trade, 1920–1939*, Manchester: Manchester University Press, 1992 and; M. Mastanduno, *Economic Containment: CoCom and the Politics of East–West Trade*, Ithaca, NY: Cornell University Press, 1992.

25 J. Gow, *Triumph of the Lack of Will*, London: Hurst, 1996, or B. Simms, *Unfinest Hour: Britain and the Destruction of Bosnia*, London: Allen Lane, 2001.

26 *Communication from the Commission to the Council and European Parliament*, European Commission, 8 December 1999.

27 See, for example, EU *Official Journal* C 198, 8 July 1996, p. 195 and idem, 'Resolution of the Commission's Communication on the Reconstruction in the FRY Resolution in the European Parliament', p. 191.

28 T. Veremis and D. Dainanu (eds), *Balkan Reconstruction*, London: Frank Cass, 2001, especially Vladimir Grigorov 'Notes on the Stability Pact', pp. 12–19.

29 Veremis and Dainanu, *Balkan Reconstruction*, p. 115. Altman is quoting Patrick Moore in the *Balkan Report* on RFE/RL in December 1999.

30 See for example 'The Commission's Work Programme for 1996', *Official Journal* C282, 26 September 1996.

31 See for example: 'Resolution on the situation in the Former Yugoslavia', *Official Journal* C 096, 1 April 1996, p. 297: 'this plan cannot succeed in reality unless every aspect of the Dayton Accords [are] complied with . . .', and; *Official Journal* C141, 13 May 1996, p. 216. The *Staff Working Paper* prepared by the Commission Secretariat and dated 3 October 1997 was presented to the Council. Its key emphases were on 'Democratic Principles; Human rights and the protection of minorities' as well as 'Market Economy Reform, Regional Cooperation and the need for compliance with obligations under the Dayton agreement'. I was given this document under Chatham House Rules and asked not to quote further from it.

32 These programmes produce roughly bi-annual reports on progress and implementation published by Directorate General 1A of the Commission. I have seen those for December 1998, 1 April 1999, June 1999 and January 2000.

33 *Official Journal* C 179, 22 June 1996.

34 J.-P. Flintoff, 'Bridge Builder' [a portrait of Ashdown], *Financial Times*, 25 October 2003. See also 'Bosnia's Nationalist Governments: Paddy Ashdown and the Paradoxes of State Building, International Crisis Group Report', Sarajevo, Brussels, 22 July 2003.

35 See for example 'Report from the Commission on the Feasibility of Negotiating a Stabilisation and Assistance Agreement with the Republic Of Croatia', European Commission, 24 May 2000.

36 P. Latawski and M. A. Smith, *The Kosovo Crisis and the Evolution of post-Cold War European Security*, Manchester: Manchester University Press, 2003. See also A. J. Bacevich and E. A. Cohen (eds), *War over Kosovo: Politics and Strategy in a Global Age*, New York: Columbia University Press, 2001.

37 *Official Journal* C 021 E 25 January 2000 [submitted by the EU Commissions on 7 July 1999].

38 *Report from the Commission – Annual Report on Humanitarian Aid, 1999*, European Commission, 1 December 2000.

39 Miall, Ramsbottam and Woodhouse, pp. 202–8.

40 The expression is taken from an article by R. Cornwell in *The Independent*, 30 July 2002, 'The "inside-out" solution to the problem of Saddam'.

41 For a taste of this debate within Britain see (for the war) J. Keegan, *The Iraq War*, London: Hutchinson, 2004 and (against the war) J. Kampfner, *Blair's Wars*, London: Free Press, 2004.

42 Cartoon, Steve Bell, *The Guardian*, n.d. 2000.

43 D. Blair, 'America Tries to Buy Off Warlords', *Daily Telegraph*, 8 October 2002.

44 For a thorough study of the technical problems of reconstruction in Afghanistan see S. Barakat (ed.) *Reconstructing War-Torn Societies: Afghanistan*, London, Palgrave, 2004. See also: International Crisis Group, Peacebuilding in Afghanistan, *International Crisis Group Report*, Brussels, ICG, 29 September 2003.

45 'Army is aiming at Afghan rebuilding', *Daily Telegraph*, 26 July 2003.

46 *Ibid.*

47 I am grateful to my friend (and ex-Kent student) Ben Perks of UNICEF for helping me to this understanding of the present situation.

48 L. Morgan Edwards 'Afghan Men are Lions Ruled by Jackals Says Poet', *Daily Telegraph*, 8 October 2002.

49 'The Fame Game', *Financial Times*, 23 August 2003.

50 The definitive account of the search for weapons of mass destruction will probably be H. Blix, *Disarming Iraq: The Search for Weapons of Mass Destruction*, London, Bloomsbury, 2004. Blix had no real qualms about the need for a war to ensure that Iraq had no such weapons, but about the timing of the war that happened. His view is that he would have probably amassed enough evidence by the summer of 2003 to justify a Security Council authorized invasion instead of the Anglo-American one that happened, thus seriously damaging the UN itself.

51 Halper and Clarke, *America Alone*, Chapter 7, 'Iraq: The False Pretenses', and R. A. Clarke (counter terrorism 'tsar' under both Presidents Clinton and Bush), *Against All Enemies: Inside America's War on Terror*, New York: Free Press, 2004.

52 S. Biddle, 'Land Warfare: Theory and Practice', in J. Baylis, J. Wirtz, E. Cohen and C. Gray, *Strategy in the Contemporary World*, Oxford: Oxford University Press, 2002, pp. 104–7.

53 *Financial Times*, 25 July 2003.

54 See for example P. Slevin, 'On the Outside, Planning a New Nation', *Washington Post*, 11 October 2002 and the Centre for Media and Democracy Website: http://www.disinfopedia.org/wiki.phtml?title=Future _of _Iraq

55 'Iraqis are Extremely Grateful, Civilian Head Says', *Daily Telegraph*, 19 September 2003.

56 Ministry of Defence, *Operations in Iraq: First Reflections*, London: Directorate of Corporate Communications, July 2003.

57 One such accusation links Neil Bush, the President's brother, to contracts awarded to companies called New Bridge and Crest Investment Co. cf. *Financial Times*, 12 December 2003.

58 At the time of writing very few had been awarded to others, one notable exception being the rumour that an Iraqi national, Mark Asmar, who had left in 1968, was to be awarded an Iraqi cell-phone contact: 'Asmar family hopes to profit by its close Iraqi connections', *Financial Times*, 12 September 2003.

59 De Villepin claimed that France's only interest in Iraq was to uphold the 'principle of responsibility': *Daily Telegraph*, 11 September 2003.

60 Take for example: 'Democrats Warn of "Profiteering" in Reconstruction Contracts', *Independent on Sunday*, 5 October 2003; 'Bush Should Face an Inquiry Over Iraq War, Says General [Wesley Clark]', *Daily Telegraph*, 4 October 2003.

61 'US pushes for Iraqis to resume control', *Daily Telegraph*, 27 September 2003.

62 'Iraq Embarks on Sweeping Shake-up of Farm Sector', *Financial Times*, 27/28 September 2003.

63 'Powerless to Halt the Cycle of Killing, the US Turns to Tribal Leaders to Restore Order', *Financial Times*, 20/21 September 2001.

64 De Mello had previously been in charge of the post-war operation in East Timor and had recently been the UN High Commissioner for Human Rights. He was truly one of the best and the brightest of UN staff.

65 'Fear of Chaos if Aid Staff Pull Out After Bombing', *Daily Telegraph* 22 August 2003.

66 Keegan, J. *The Iraq War*, London: Hutchinson, 2004.

67 'A Giant Step Forward in the Rebuilding of Iraq', editorial, *Daily Telegraph*, 15 December 2003.

68 Report in the *Daily Telegraph* on Arab opinion about the capture of Saddam Hussein, 16 December 2003.

69 M. Ignatieff, *The Warrior's Honour: Ethnic War and the Modern Conscience*, London: Vintage, 1999.

70 My notes of a speech given by President Gusmao at a meeting held at Chatham House November 2003 'How to Build a Nation in the Modern World' The comments are my interpretation not his words under Chatham House Rules. On Iraq see 'The Way Out', Mark Kaldor, *New Statesman*, December 2003.

71 Mandelbaum, *The Ideas that Conquered the World*, pp. 20 and 375.

72 BBC Radio 4 series of programmes on the UN, presented by Edward Stearton, 5 October 2004.

73 'UN's Big Five agree on end goal for Iraq – but not on the means', *Financial Times* 13/14 September 2003.

74 The debate on the role of the UN in Iraq is complex and convoluted and would require a chapter in itself. Suffice it to say that the sending of Ambassador Lakhdar Brahimi by Secretary General Kofi Annan has done much to symbolize a return to prominence of those who believe that the UN should have a greater role. Blair has

been widely credited for making Bush realize the importance of a UN role, one that Republicans in Congress have always (as we have seen) resented.

75   Cramer, 'The Great Post-Conflict Makeover Fantasy', p. 1.
76   'We Want bin Laden … *Daily Telegraph*, 28 November 2001.
77   G. Orwell, 'Introduction' [first published in *Horizon*, February 1942] in *The Works of Rudyard Kipling*, Ware, The Wordsworth Poetry Library, 1994, pp. xviii–xix.
78   MacMillan, *On Liberal Peace*, p. 41.

Chapter 6: Retribution – The Logics of Justice and Peace

 1   J. Keegan, *Daily Telegraph*, 15 December 2003.
 2   K. Sellars, *The Rise and Rise of Human Rights*, Stroud: Sutton Publishing, 2002, p. 37.
 3   Kegley and Raymond, *How Nations Make Peace*, p. 236. Another definition of retribution is 'vengeance curbed by the intervention of someone other than the victim and by principles of proportionality and individual rights. Retribution motivates punishment out of fairness to those who have been wronged and reflects a belief that wrongdoers deserve blame and punishment in direct proportion to the harm inflicted'. M. Minow, *Between Vengeance and Forgiveness: Facing History after Genocide and Mass Violence*, Boston: Beacon Press, 1998, p. 12.
 4   D. J. Whittaker, *Conflict and Reconciliation in the Contemporary World*, London: Routledge, 1999, p. 1.
 5   A. J. Colson, 'The Logic of Peace and the Logic of Justice', *International Relations*, Vol. XV, No. 1, April 2000, p. 51.
 6   K. Christie, *The South African Truth Commission*, London: Macmillan, 2000, p. 5.
 7   H. Arendt *Origin of Totalitarianism*, New York: Harcourt Brace Jovanovitch, 1973.
 8   T. Todorov, *Facing the Extreme: Moral Life in the Concentration Camps*, London: Weidenfield and Nicholson, 1999.
 9   T. Todorov, *Mémoire du mal: Tentation du bien: Enquete sur le siècle*, Paris: Robert Laffont, 2000.
10   Todorov, *Mémoire du mal*, pp. 10–11 and 18–20. The translations are mine.
11   *Book of Leviticus*, Chapter 25, 'The Sabbatical Year. The Year of Jubilee'. See also J. R. Dummelow (ed.), *A Commentary on the Holy Bible*, London: Macmillan, 1913, p. 99.
12   *Isaiah* 35, v. 4 – 7.
13   I. Kant, *Perpetual Peace and Other Essays*, Indianapolis: Hackett, 1983, p. 110.
14   Entry on Mommsen in W. W. Briggs and W. M. Calder III (eds), *Classical Scholarship*, London: Garland, 1990, pp. 285–309, referred to in: B. Stuchtey, 'The International of Critics, German and British Scholars during the South African War (1899–1902)', manuscript, 1999, p. 4, fn. 9.
15   Lundestad '*Empire' by Integration*. For a fond recollection of the Austro–Hungarian and Ottoman Empires see: D. Lieven, *Empires*, London: John Murray , 2000.
16   'White House Threatens to Boycott UN Racism Talks', *Financial Times*, 28/29 July 2001.
17   E. Barkan, *The Guilt of Nations: Restitution and Negotiating Historical Injustices*, New York: W. W. Norton, 2000, pp. xv–xvi.
18   A. Colomonos, 'Understanding Global Repentance: Hypotheses and Frameworks for Research', presented to the International Studies Association Conference, February 1999.
19   Barkan, *Guilt of Nations*, pp. xxi–ii.
20   D. Forsythe, *Human Rights in International Relations*, Cambridge: Cambridge University Press, 2000, p. 20.
21   F. Fukuyama, *The End of History*.
22   See N. M. Naimark, *Fires of Hatred: Ethnic Cleansing in Twentieth Century Europe*, Cambridge, MA: Harvard University Press, 2001.

23   A. Jokic, *War Crimes and Collective Wrongdoing*, Oxford: Blackwell, 2001, p. 1.

24   G. J. Bass, *Stay The Hand of Vengeance: The Politics of War Crimes Tribunals*, Princeton: Princeton University Press, 2000. See also H. Ball, *Prosecuting War Crimes and Genocide: The Twentieth Century Experience*, Lawrence, KS: University Press of Kansas, 1999; R. J. Goldstone, 'Bringing War Criminals to Justice', in J. Moore (ed.), *Hard Choices: Moral Dilemmas in Humanitarian Intervention*, Lanham, ML: Rowman and Littlefield, 1998.

25   M. Frost, *Ethics in International Relations: A Constitutive Theory*, Cambridge: Cambridge University Press, 1996, pp. 42–3.

26   Bass, *Stay the Hand of Vengeance: The Politics of War Crimes Tribunals*, pp. 19 and 21.

27   Frost, *Ethics in International Relations*, p. 47.

28   Bass, *op.cit.*, pp. 18–19.

29   For an excellent discussion of this see Brown, *Sovereignty, Rights and Justice*, pp. 99–101.

30   G. Gong, *The 'Standard of Civilization' in International Society*, Oxford: Oxford University Press, 1984.

31   For more detail on the prosecution of war criminals after the First World War see J. F. Willis, *The Politics and Diplomacy of Punishing War Criminals of the First World War*, Westport, CT: Greenwood Press, 1982. More generally see Sellars, *The Rise and Rise of Human Rights*, and: Bass, *Stay the Hand of Vengeance*.

32   C. Maier, *Recasting Bourgeois Europe: Stabilization in France, Germany and Italy in the Decade after World War I*, Princeton: Princeton University Press, 1975, pp. 221–4.

33   A. Lentin, *Guilt at Versailles: Lloyd George and the Pre-History of Appeasement*, London: Methuen, 1985, p. xi.

34   Murray, *The Problem of Foreign Policy*, pp. 12 and 21–30. He added to this tirade: 'I hope I have put this statement forward without any malice or party feeling'!

35   See, for example K. Gürün, *The Armenian File: The Myth of Innocence Exposed*, Nicosia: Rutum, 2001 (first pub. 1983).

36   Bass, *Stay the Hand of Vengeance*, p. 000.

37   H. Stimson, 'Memorandum on the World Court', dated 1929, Stimson Papers, Library of Congress, reel 126.

38   Frances White to Stimson, July 16 1927, Stimson Papers, Reel 72.

39   A. Williams, 'Before the Special Relationship: The Council on Foreign Relations, The Carnegie Foundation and the Rumour of a Anglo-American War', *Journal of Transatlantic Studies*, Vol. 1, No. 2, Autumn 2003, pp. 233–51.

40   Stimson Diary, entries for 23, 24 and 27 October 1944, Stimson Papers, reel 9.

41   A good summary of the trials can be found in G. Robertson, *Crimes Against Humanity*, London: Allen Lane, 1999, Ch. 6, 'An End to Impunity'.

42   R. H. Minear, *Victor's Justice: The Tokyo War Crimes Trial*, Princeton: Princeton University Press, 1971, pp. 9–11.

43   C. Levy and M. Roseman, *Three Postwar Eras in Comparison: Western Europe, 1918–1945–1989*, London: Palgrave, 2002. The use of the word 'stability' is one of the leitmotifs of the book for the period after 1945.

44   A. Shennan, *Rethinking France: Plans for Renewal, 1940–1946*, Oxford: Clarendon Press, 1989.

45   According to Minear '5,700 Japanese were tried on conventional war crimes charges, and 920 of these men were executed' Minear, p. 6.

46   Minear, *Victor's Justice*, p. 12.

47   Minear, *Victor's Justice*, p. ix.

48   Sellars, *The Rise and Rise of Human Rights* pp. 37–9.

49   Minear, op.cit., especially his comments in the 'Preface'.

50   Robertson, *Crimes Against Humanity*, Ch. 7, 'Slouching Towards Nemesis'.

51   'Remarks made by Judge Gabrielle Kirk McDonald, President of the International Criminal Tribunal for the Former Yugoslavia, To the Preparatory Commission for the International Criminal Court', New York, 30 July 1999, Press Release,

The Hague 30 July, 199, JL/P.I.S./425-E, http://www.un.org/icty/pressreal/p425-c.htm

52   The best source on the origins of this can be found in: W. A. Schabas, *An Introduction to the International Criminal Court*, Cambridge: Cambridge University Press, 2001.

53   B. de Rossanet, *War and Peace in the Former Yugoslavia*, The Hague: Kluwer Law International, 1997, p. 163.

54   Robertson, *Crimes Against Humanity*, Ch. 8, 'The Balkan Trials'.

55   D. Rieff, *Slaughterhouse: Bosnia and the Failure of the West*, New York: Simon & Schuster, 1995, or J. Gow's *Triumph of the Lack of Will*, London: Hurst, 1996; B. Simms' *Unfinest Hour: Britain and the Destruction of Bosnia*, London: Allen Lane, 2001.

56   M. Glenny, *The Death of Yugoslavia*, London: Penguin, 1992 and *The Balkans: Nationalism, War and The Great Powers, 1804–1999*, London: Granta, 1999.

57   P. Ashdown, *The Ashdown Diaries*, London: Penguin, 2000.

58   One of the best accounts of this early period can be found in A. Danchev and T. Halberson (eds), *International Perspectives on the Yugoslav Conflict*, London: Macmillan, 1996.

59   Possibly the best account of this period is by one of the unfortunate mediators, D. Owen, *Balkan Odyssey*, London: Indigo Press, 1995. See also Gow, *Triumph of the Lack of Will*, New York: Columbia University Press, 1997.

60   Holbrooke's account of this and his subsequent activities in the FRY is described in *To End a War*, New York: The Modern Library, 1998.

61   Kaldor, *New and Old Wars*, p. 32.

62   The published papers of CFY have been gathered in two very useful volumes by B. G. Ramcharan (ed.), *The International Conference on the Former Yugoslavia: Official Papers*, The Hague: Kluwer Law International, 1997, Two Volumes. Hereafter: 'Ramcharan, *CFY*'.

63   For details of the London Conference see Ramcharan, *CFY*, pp. 29–158.

64   de Rossanet, *War and Peace*, p. 1.

65   Meeting between Presidents Milosevic of Serbia and Tudjman of Croatia, Geneva, 17 July 1993, in de Rossanet, *War and Peace*, pp. 50 and 139–40.

66   R. Cohen, quoting Nicholas Burns and commenting in 'When the Price of Peace is Injustice', *New York Times*, 12 November 1995, quoted by de Rossanet, *War and Peace*, pp. 135–6.

67   Holbrooke, in the *Financial Times* of 2 November 1995, quoted by de Rossanet, *War and Peace*, p. 175.

68   Goldstone, quoted in the *International Herald Tribune* of 9 November 1995, quoted (very unfavourably) by de Rossanet, *War and Peace*, p. 179.

69   C. G. Boyd, 'Making Peace with the Guilty', *Foreign Affairs*, Sept/Oct. 1995, Vol. 74, No. 5, pp. 22–38.

70   R. West, *Black Lamb and Grey Falcon*, New York: Penguin, 1982 (first pub. 1941) Holbrooke, *To End a War*, pp. 22–23. Interviews conducted by the author. I found this confirmed largely in interviews at the Carnegie Foundation and elsewhere in Washington DC at this period.

71   de Rossanet, *War and Peace in the Former Yugoslavia*, p. 183.

72   International Criminal Tribunal for the Former Yugoslavia, 'Fact Sheet', http://www.un.org/icty/glance/fact.htm, in this case dated 25 January 2000, Doc. PIS/FS-60.

73   F. Hazan, *La justice face a la guerre: De Nuremberg a La Haye*, Paris: Stock, 2000, p. 17–21.

74   Fatic, *Reconciliation via the War Crimes Tribunal*, pp. vii–viii and 2–3.

75   Hazan, *La justice face a la guerre*, p. 20.

76   Set up by Security Council Resolution 955 of 8 November 1994.

77   A. Hyde-Price, *Germany and European Order: Enlarging NATO and the EU*, Manchester: Manchester University Press, 2000, pp. 54–5.

78   *Independent*, 30 June 2001.

79 *Daily Telegraph*, 15 December 2003.
80 *Daily Telegraph*, 15 December 2003.
81 Bass, *Stay the Hand of Vengeance*, pp. 9–11.
82 Bass, *Stay the Hand of Vengeance*, pp. 276 –8.
83 M. Henderson, *Forgiveness: Breaking the Chain of Hate*, Wilsonville, OR: BookPartners Inc., 1999, p. 13.

Chapter 7: Restorative justice, reconciliation and resolution

1 Galtung quoted by W. J. Long and P. Brecke, *War and Reconciliation: Reason and Emotion in Conflict Resolution*, Cambridge, MA: MIT Press, 2003, p. 1.
2 Sellars, *The Rise and Rise of Human Rights*, pp. 45–46
3 'Fury Over Us Post for Islamic Scholar', *Daily Telegraph*, 22 August 2003.
4 Miall, Ramsbottam and Woodhouse, *Contemporary Conflict Resolution*, p. 16.
5 Miall, Ramsbottam and Woodhouse, *Contemporary Conflict Resolution*, p. 16
6 K. J. Holsti, *The State, War and the State of War*, Cambridge: Cambridge University Press, 1998, p. xi. M. Van Creveld, *The Rise and Decline of the State*, Cambridge: Cambridge University Press, 1999, uses a similar language.
7 Kaldor, *New and Old Wars*, p. 8.
8 Holsti, *The State, War and the State of War*, p. 8.
9 The UN Commission of Experts identified 56 Serb groups, 13 Croat, and 14 Bosnian, of which the most notorious were Arkan's Tigers and Seselj's White Eagles, who would embark on systematic terrorizing of the local population, and the setting of neighbour against neighbour. They also identified 715 detention centres, better described as 'concentration camps', across the FRY, which were the constant scene of mass executions, torture and rape, this latter used as way of permanently scarring the female and male populations and making reconciliation that bit more difficult *Final Report of the UN Experts on the Former Yugoslavia*, May 1994, http://www.his.com/~twarrick/commxyu1.htm. In only one major case that I have come across in Croatia was this resisted successfully by the local population, which still lives in multiethnic peace and harmony, Vrbovsko in eastern Croatia (visited by me in March 2000).
10 C. Bennett, *Yugoslavia's Bloody Collapse*, London, 1995, p. 222.
11 Henderson, *Forgiveness: Breaking the Chain of Hate*, p. xvi.
12 I am a practising Anglican.
13 M. Evans and K. Lunn (eds), *War and Memory in the Twentieth Century*, Oxford: Berg, 1997; J. Winter, *Sites of Memory, Sites of Mourning: The Great War in European Cultural History*, Cambridge: Cambridge University Press, 1995; P. Ricoeur, *La memoire, l'histoire, l'oubli*, Paris: Editions du Seuil, 2000.
14 Henderson, *Forgiveness*, p. 2.
15 I. Baruma, *The Wages of Guilt: Memories of War in Germany and Japan*, London: Jonathan Cape, 1994.
16 A magisterial discussion of this can be found in Ricoeur, *La memoire, l'histoire, l'oubli*, pp. 44–8.
17 A. D. Falconer , 'Remembering' in: A. D. Falconer and J. Liechty, (eds) *Reconciling Memories*, Dublin, The Columba Press, 1998, pp. 14–15.
18 Liechty, 'Repentance and Peace: A Challenge to the Churches', in Falconer and Liechty, *Reconciling Memories*, pp. 262–3.
19 M. Shaw, 'Past Wars and Present Conflicts: From the Second World War to the Gulf?', in Evans and Lunn, *War and Memory in the Twentieth Century*, p. 191.
20 'Tokyo Hopes to Repair Ties with South Korea', *Financial Times*, 16 August 2001.
21 Shaw, *ibid*.
22 One seminal example is the USIP publication: C. Crocker (ed.), *Managing Global Chaos*, Washington, USIP, 1996, and C. Crocker (ed.), *Herding Cats: Multiparty Mediation in a Complex World*, Washington: USIP, 1999.

23   L. Reychler, 'The Art of Conflict Prevention' in W. Bauwens and L. Reychler, *The Art of Conflict Prevention*, London: Brassey's, 1994.

24   For a brief overview see K. Webb, 'Third Party Intervention and the Ending of Wars: A Preliminary Appraisal', *Paradigms*, Winter 1995.

25   J. Darby and R. McGinty, *Contemporary Peacemaking: Conflict Violence and Peace Processes*, London: Palgrave Macmillan 2003, p. 7.

26   U. Vesa (Tampere Peace Research Institute) writing in the *EuPRA Newsletter*, EuPRA photocopy, November 2000, p. 3. It is interesting to note that the European Peace Research Association (EuPRA) was founded in 1990 'in this historical and social context' and is now struggling to keep its activities alive and its members motivated.

27   I. W. Zartman, 'Towards the Resolution of International Conflicts', in I. W. Zartman and J. L. Rasmussen (eds), *Peacemaking in International Conflict: Methods and Techniques*, Washington: USIP, 1997, p. 3.

28   G. W. Lapidus, 'The War in Chechnya: Opportunities Missed, Lessons to be Learned', in B. Jentelson (ed.), *Opportunities Missed: Opportunities Seized*, New York: Carnegie Corp, Rowman and Littlefield, 2000, p. 39.

29   The expression was used in a discussion between Nick Palmer and Andrew Hunter about the Northern Ireland Peace Process on BBC Radio 4's *Newsnight* programme, 6 March 2001.

30   Christie, *The South African Truth Commission*, London: Macmillan, 2000, pp. 37–8.

31   P. B. Hayner, *Unspeakable Truths: Facing the Challenge of Truth Commissions*, New York: Routledge, 2002, esp. Chapter 2 and Appendix 1.

32   Christie. *op.cit.*, p. 37, Hayner, *Unspeakable Truths*, pp. 33–4.

33   For some details on the absurd but enforced policies of apartheid see Christie, *op. cit.*, pages 19–27.

34   For a general introduction to the theme of reconciliation in South Africa, see: K. Christie, *The South African Truth Commission*, London: Macmillan, 2000; D. Tutu, *No Future Without Forgiveness*, London: Rider, 1999; W. James and L. van de Vijver, *After the TRC: Reflections of Truth and Reconciliation in South Africa*, Athens, OH: Ohio University Press, 2000.

35   Hayner, *Unspeakable Truths*, pp. 40–54; Christie, *The South African Truth Commission*, pp. 69–71 and 121–41.

36   C. Scott, in J. Callies (ed.), *Agenda for Peace: Reconciliation*, Loccum: Evangelische Akademie Loccum (Loccumer Protokolle 55/98), 1998.

37   Christie, *The South African Truth Commission*, pp. 173–5 The 'amnesia' point is also one bought out well by A. Rigby, *Justice and Reconciliation: After the Violence*, London: Lynne Reinner, 2001, Ch. 1.

38   Christie, *The South African Truth Commission*, pp. 182–7.

39   Christie, *The South African Truth Commission*, p. 114. Unfortunately he does not give a date for the survey, but by implication it was about 1995.

40   J. Durand, review of: C. Villa and W. Verwoerd (eds), *Looking Back, Reaching Forward: Reflections on the Truth and Reconciliation Commission of South Africa*, Cape Town: University of Cape Town Press and London: Zed Books, 2000, in *African Journal of Conflict Resolution*, Vol. 1, No. 2, 2000, p. 110.

41   Christie, *The South African Truth Commission*, pp. 115–16.

42   M. Cox, '"Cinderella at the Ball": Explaining the End of the Conflict in Northern Ireland', *Millennium*, Vol. 27, No. 2, 1998, pp. 325–42, here p. 341.

43   R. L. Rothstein, p. 239.

44   R. Wilson, 'Peace without Reconciliation?' in Callies (ed.), *Agenda for Peace: Reconciliation*.

45   A. D. Falconer , 'Remembering', in A. D. Falconer and J. Liechty, (eds) *Reconciling Memories*, pp. 14–15.

46   K. Miyamoto, 'Peace from Below: Developing Inter-ethnic Dialogue Amongst Citizens for Bottom-up Conflict Transformation in Bosnia', PhD, University of Kent, 2004.

My thanks go to Dr Juan Diaz for talking to me about his experiences working with the German Mediator over several years in Bosnia.

47 'Balkan Leaders Apologise for Carnage', *Daily Telegraph*, 11 September 2003.

48 Kaldor reports the UN Commission on Human Rights 'consistently notes the action of brave Serbs who tried to protect their Muslim and Croat neighbours', Kaldor, *New Wars*, p. 57.

49 D. Rohde, quoted in Y. Beigbeder, *Judging War Criminals – The Politics of International Justice*, London: Palgrave Macmillan, 1999.

50 Literature on the Rwandan massacres includes: G. Prunier, *The Rwandan Crisis: History of a Genocide*, London: Hurst, 2002; Human Rights Watch; *Leave None to Tell the Story*, New York: HRW, 1999; S. M. Khan, *The Shallow Graves of Rwanda*, London: Pluto, 2002; *The Danida Report: The International Responses to the Conflict and Genocide: Lessons from the Rwanda Experience*, www.um.dk/danida/evalueringsrapporter/ 1997_rwanda/b4/pre.asp

51 As ever, figures quoted by different sides are at variance. The Rwandan Government claims a death toll of 1,074,017: www.rwanda1.com/government/011101genocide week5.htm

52 J. Carlin, 'Could You Share a Pint With a Man Who Killed Your Family?', *New Statesman*, 15 September 2003. See also P. Gourevitch, *We Wish To Inform You that Tomorrow We Will Be Killed With Our Families; Stories From Rwanda*, New York: Farrar, Strauss and Giroux, 1995.

53 A. Destexhje, *Rwanda and Genocide in the Twentieth Century*, London: Pluto, 1995.

54 J. N. Maogoto, 'The International Criminal Tribunal for Rwanda: A Distorting Mirror; Casting Doubt on Its Actor-oriented Approach in Addressing the Rwanda Genocide', *African Journal on Conflict Resolution*, Vol. 3, No 1, 2003, pp. 55–97, p. 58.

55 Maogoto, pp. 79–80.

56 'Ramshackle Huts in Africa Offer Clue to How Justice May Be Done', *Daily Telegraph*, 16 December 2003.

57 M. Kaldor, *Global Civil Society: An Answer to War*, Cambridge: Polity, 2003.

58 Talk by Paul Wilkinson, BISA, Birmingham, December 2003 Statement to House of Commons Select Committee

59 A generalization I am aware, but based on a series of interviews in 2002 in prominent think tanks and US Government agencies.

60 Barkan, *Guilt of Nations*, 'Conclusion: Towards a Theory of Restitution', especially pp. 318–22.

61 D. J. Goldhagen, *Hitler's Willing Executioners: Ordinary Germans and the Holocaust*, London: Abacus, 1997.

62 Bass, *Stay the Hand of Vengeance*, pp. 160–1.

Conclusion: do liberal dilemmas disable all liberal solutions to war

1 T. E. Lawrence to Clayton, PRO, FO882/4 [in Syria, c. 11 February 1918] quoted by M. Asher, *Lawrence, The Uncrowned King of Arabia*, London: Penguin, 1999, p. 306.

2 'Blair Confronts War Critics: I was Right, and I Still Am', *The Independent*, 6 March 2004.

3 *Financial Times*, 21 September 2004.

4 *Financial Times*, 11 March 2004.

5 Probably the best known advocate of the 'United States as Imperial Power' thesis is N. Chomsky. See, for example his *Pirates and Emperors, Old and New: International terrorism in the Real World*, London: Pluto Press, 2002. This is itself the 5th edition of such a work, each time with additions and a new title, dating back to 1986. See also W. Blum, *Rogue States: A Guide to the World's Only Superpower*, London: Zed Books, 2nd edition, 2002; A. Callinicos, *The New Mandarins of American Power*, Oxford: Polity,

2004. In a more neutral vein see: I. H. Daalder and J. M. Lindsay, *America Unbound: the Bush Revolution in Foreign Policy*, Washington: Brookings, 2003.

6   'Bush Has Mandate to Continue Pursuing "aggressive" Foreign Policy, Says Powell', *Financial Times*, 9 November 2004.

7   J. Kampfner, 'Interview Geoff Hoon', *New Statesman*, 4 November 2004.

8   Thomson, Mayer and Briggs, *Patterns of Peacemaking*, pp. 6 and 9–10.

9   BBC radio broadcast, *Listener*, 24 June 1943.

10   Thomson, Mayer and Briggs, *Patterns of Peacemaking*, pp. 7–9.

11   Z. Laidi (ed.), *Power and Purpose after the Cold War*, Oxford: Berg, 1994.

12   J. Keegan, 'Saddam was Easily Defeated – Which is Why the War Goes On', *Daily Telegraph*, 4 June 2003.

13   A useful insight into this new thinking can be found in The Institute for National Defense Studies Special Report *Beyond Containment: Defending US Interests in the Persian Gulf*, Washington, DC: National Defense University, September 2002, p. 8.

14   See for example, J. Bacque, *Crimes and Mercies: The Fate of German Civilians Under Allied Occupation, 1944–1950*, London: TimeWarner, 1997.

15   W. K. Clark, *Winning Modern Wars: Iraq, Terrorism and the American Empire*, New York: Public Affairs, 2003. It has to be remembered that Clark was about to announce his candidacy on the Democratic ticket for the United States 2004 Presidency at the time of this book's publication.

16   'Bush Should Face an Inquiry Over Iraq War, Says General', *Daily Telegraph*, 4 October 2003.

17   Both reports were in the *Financial Times* and *International Herald Tribune*, 21 September 2004.

18   P. Bobbitt, *The Shield of Achilles*, New York: Knopf, 2002. See also Bobbitt, 'Tough Love. One Year On: Why the US Is Good for the World', *FT Magazine*, 13 March 2004, pp. 16–24.

19   S. Power, *A Problem from Hell: America and the Age of Genocide*, New York: HarperCollins, 2002. See also P. Williams, 'Play It Again, Sam', *FT Magazine*, 13 March 2004, pp. 14–15.

20   Cohen argues that the bad odour in which Israel is held has helped to prevent Islamic groups from being tainted with the 'fascist' brush, but that does not diminish the similarity of Al-Qaeda's views to fascism 'Is fascism Behind the Terror?, *New Statesman*, 12 April 2004.

21   M. Walzer, *Just and Unjust Wars: A Moral Argument with Historical Illustrations*, New York: Basic Books, 2nd Edition, 1992, 'Preface to 2nd Edition', p. xviii.

22   'Troops Mark Anniversary [of September 11 2001] and Reflect on Why They Are in Iraq', *Daily Telegraph*, 11 September 2003.

23   T. J. Knock, *To End All Wars: Woodrow Wilson and the Quest for a New World Order*, Oxford: Oxford University Press, 1992, p. 6.

24   R. Holbrooke, *To End a War*, New York: The Modern Library, 1998, esp. pp. 21–33; J. Gow, *Triumph of the Lack of Will: International Diplomacy and the Yugoslav War*, London: Hurst and Co, 1997, pp. 299–300..

25   West, *Black Lamb and Grey Falcon*, R. D. Kaplan, *Balkan Ghosts: A Journey Through History*, New York: Vintage, 1994, 1996.

26   President George Bush's speech to the Enterprise Institute, Washington, 26 February 2003.

27   N. Ferguson, 'This Vietnam Generation of Americans Have Not Learnt the Lessons of History', *Daily Telegraph*, 10 April 2004; reply by M. Steyn, 'Liberty and Imperialism Don't Mix', *Daily Telegraph*, 13 April 2004.

28   'US Tanks Give Radical Shia Leader Last Chance to End Revolt.' *Daily Telegraph*, 14 April 2004.

29   N. G. Levin, *Woodrow Wilson and World Politics: America's Response to War and Revolution*, Lexington, MA: Heath, 1972, quoted by Karen de Coster (a 'paleolibertarian

freelance writer'), 'Neo-Wilsonianism as a Great-Granddaddy of Neo-conservatism': http//www.lewrockwell.com/decoster/decoster91.html.

30 'Japan's Revisionists Turn Emperor into a God Once More' *The Guardian*, 21 August 2002. See also P. Duss, 'Imperialism Without Colonies: The Vision of a Greater East Asia Co-Prosperity Sphere', *Diplomacy and Statecraft*, Vol. 7, No. 1, March 1996, pp. 54–72.

31 N. Chomsky, *World Orders, Old and New*, London: Pluto, 1994; *Pirates and Emperors, Old and New*, London: Pluto, 2002.

32 R. Bellamy, *Liberalism and Modern Society*, University Park, PA: The Pennsylvania State University Press, 1992.

33 W. Laqueur, *No End to War: Terrorism in the Twentieth Century*, New York: Continuum, 2003, pp. 18–21.

34 cf. Coker, *War and the Illiberal Conscience*, pp. 96–101.

35 A. J. Kuperman, *The Limits of Humanitarian Intervention: Genocide in Rwanda*, Washington: Brookings, 2001.

36 'New Blair Philosophy on War?', *Daily Telegraph*, 6 March 2004.

37 It is said that he has a bust of the Great Man in the Oval Office and regularly consults him.

38 *Daily Telegraph* and *The Independent*, 6 March 2004.

39 See for example, 'Rage at US Spurs Calls for Jihad in Europe', *New York Times*, 29 April 2004.

Select bibliography

Archival sources

Official

Archives of the High Authority, European Coal and Steel Community, Brussels.
Cabinet and Foreign Office, National Archives, London (PRO).
French Ministry of Foreign Affairs, Paris.
League of Nations Papers, BLPES, London.

Official published

Ministry of Defence (2003) *Operations in Iraq: First Reflections*, London, Directorate of Corporate Communications, July.
European Commission, Official Publications (*Official Journal*, etc.).
International Criminal Tribunal for the Former Yugoslavia, ('*Fact Sheets*', etc.).
Ramcharan, Bertram G. (ed.) (1997) *The International Conference on the Former Yugoslavia: Official Papers*, The Hague, Kluwer Law International, Two Volumes.

Personal papers (a selection of those used)

Adolf Berle, Roosevelt Memorial Library.
Hamilton Fish, Armstrong, Seeley H. Mudd Library, Princeton University.
Vincent Auriol, *Archives Nationales*, Paris.
Philip Noel Baker, Churchill College, Cambridge.
John Bradbury, Private Collection.
John Foster Dulles, Seeley H. Mudd Library, Princeton.
Harry L. Hopkins, Roosevelt Presidential Library.
David Hubback, Private Collection.
John Maynard Keynes, King's College Cambridge.
Herbert P. Lehman, Columbia University Library, New York.
Henry Morgenthau, Roosevelt Presidential Library.
Gilbert Murray, Bodleian Library, Oxford.
Leo Pasvolsky, Library of Congress, Washington DC.
Henry Stimson Diary, Yale University Library (and Library of Congress).

Books

Addison, Tony (ed.) (2003) *From Conflict to Recovery in Africa*, Oxford: Oxford University Press/UNU.

Anderson, Olive (1967) *A Liberal State at War: English Politics and Economics During the Crimean War*, London: Macmillan.

Angell, Norman (1910) *The Great Illusion: A Study of the Relation of Military Power to National Advantage*, London: William Heinemann.

—— (1947) *The Steep Places*, London: Hamish Hamilton.

Applebaum, Anne (2003) *Gulag: A History of the Soviet Camps*: London, Allen Lane: The Penguin Press.

Armstrong, David, Lloyd, Lorna and Redmond, John (1996) *From Versailles to Maastricht: International Organisation in the Twentieth Century*, London: Macmillan.

Artaud, Denise (1978) *La question des dettes interalliés et la reconstruction de l'Europe, 1917–1929*, Lille and Paris: Honoré Champion.

Asher, Michael (1999) *Lawrence, The Uncrowned King of Arabia*, London: Penguin.

Aufricht, Hans (1951) *A Guide to League of Nations Publications, 1920–47*, New York: Columbia University Press.

Bacevich, Andrew J. and Cohen, Eliot A. (eds) (2001) *War over Kosovo: Politics and Strategy in a Global Age*, New York: Columbia University Press.

Ball, Harold (1999), *Prosecuting War Crimes and Genocide: The Twentieth Century Experience*, Lawrence, KS: University Press of Kansas.

Barkan, Elazar (2000) *The Guilt of Nations: Restitution and Negotiating Historical Injustices*, New York: W. W. Norton.

Bacque, James (1997) *Crimes and Mercies: The Fate of German Civilians Under Allied Occupation, 1944–1950*, London: TimeWarner.

Bailey, Thomas A. (1944) *Woodrow Wilson and the Lost Peace*, New York: Macmillan.

Baker, Mary Stannard (1922–3) *Woodrow Wilson and the World Settlement*, 3 volumes, New York: Doubleday.

Barakat, Sultan (ed.) (2004) *Reconstructing War-Torn Societies: Afghanistan*, London: Palgrave.

Baruma, Ian (1994) *The Wages of Guilt: Memories of War in Germany and Japan*, London: Jonathan Cape.

Baylis, John, Wirtz, James, Cohen, Eliot and Gray, Colin (2002) *Strategy in the Contemporary World*, Oxford:Oxford University Press.

Baruch, Bernard M. (1920) *The Making of the Reparation and Economic Sections of the Treaty*, New York: Harper and Brothers.

Bass, Gary J. (2000) *Stay The Hand of Vengeance: The Politics of War Crimes Tribunals*, Princeton, NJ: Princeton University Press.

Bell, Philip M. H. (2001) *The World Since 1945: An International History*, London: Arnold.

Bellamy, Richard (1992) *Liberalism and Modern Society: A Historical Argument*: Pennsylvania, The Pennsylvania State University Press.

Bellamy, Richard (2000) *Rethinking Liberalism*, London: Continuum.

Bentley, Michael (1977) *The Liberal Mind, 1914–1929*, Cambridge: Cambridge University Press.

Bentley, Michael (1987) *The Climax of Liberal Politics*, London: Edward Arnold

Berman, Paul (2003) *Terror and Liberalism*, New York: W. W. Norton.

Beschloss, Michael (2002) *The Conquerors: Roosevelt, Truman and the Destruction of Hitler's Germany, 1941–1945*, New York: Simon and Schuster.

Beveridge, William (1945) *The Price of Peace*: London: Pilot Press.

Blix, Hans (2004) *Disarming Iraq: The Search for Weapons of Mass Destruction*, London: Bloomsbury.

Blum, William (2002) *Rogue States: A Guide to the World's Only Superpower*, London: Zed Books, 2nd edition.

Bobbitt, Philip, C. (2002) *The Shield of Achilles: War, Peace and the Course of History*, New York: Knopf.

Botton, Alain de (2000) *The Consolations of Philosophy*, London: Penguin.

Bowley, Arthur L. (1930) *Some Economic Consequences of the Great War*, London: Thornton Butterworth Ltd.

Brendon, Piers (2000) *Dark Valley: A Panorama of the 1930s*, London: Jonathan Cape.

Briggs, Asa (1968) 'The World Economy: Interdependence and Planning', *New Cambridge Modern History*, vol. XII, Cambridge: Cambridge University Press.

Brinton, Crane (1938) *Anatomy of a Revolution*, Englewood Cliffs, NJ: Prentice Hall.

Bronstone, Adam (1999) *The European Bank for Reconstruction and Development: The Building of a Bank for East Central* Europe, Manchester: Manchester University Press.

Brown, Chris (1992) *International Theory: New Normative Approaches*, Brighton: Harvester.

—— (2001) *Understanding International Relations*, London: Palgrave.

—— (2002) *Sovereignty, Rights and Justice*, Cambridge: Polity.

Brownlie, Ian (1983) *System of the Law of Nations: State Responsibility*, Part 1, Oxford: Clarendon Press.

Burnett, Philip M. (1940) *Reparation at the Paris Peace Conference from the Standpoint of the American Delegation*, 2 vols, New York: Columbia University Press.

Callies, Jorg (ed.) (1998) *Agenda for Peace: Reconciliation*, Loccum, Evangelische Akademie Loccum (Loccumer Protokolle 55/98).

Callinicos, Alex (2004) *The New Mandarins of American Power*, Oxford: Polity.

Camus, Albert (1951) *The Rebel*, Paris: Gallimard.

Carnegie Endowment (1993) *The Other Balkan Wars: A 1913 Carnegie Endowment Inquiry in Retrospect with a New Introduction and Reflections on the Present Conflict by George F. Kennan*, Washington: Carnegie Endowment for International Peace.

Carr, E. H. (2001 [1939]) *The Twenty Years' Crisis*, Basingstoke and New York: Palgrave.

Ceadel, Martin (1980) *Pacifism in Britain, 1914–1945*, Oxford, Clarendon Press.

—— (1987) *Thinking about Peace and War*, Oxford: Oxford University Press.

Cecil, Robert (1941) *A Great Experiment*, London: Jonathan Cape.

Charmley, John (1995) *Churchill's Grand Alliance: The Anglo-American Special Relationship, 1940 – 57*, London: John Curtis/ Hodder and Stoughton.

Chesterman, Simon (2001) *Just War or Just Peace?: International Law and Humanitarian Intervention*, Oxford: Oxford University Press.

Chomsky, Noam (1994) *World Orders, Old and New*, London: Pluto Press.

—— (2002) *Pirates and Emperors, Old and New: International terrorism in the Real World*, London: Pluto Press.

—— (2003) *Hegemony or Survival: America's Quest for World Dominance*, London: Penguin.

Christie, Kenneth (2000) *The South African Truth Commission*, London: Macmillan.

Clark, Wesley K. (2003) *Winning Modern Wars: Iraq, Terrorism and the American Empire*, New York: Public Affairs.

Clarke, Roger A. (2004) *Against All Enemies: Inside America's War on Terror*, New York: Free Press.

Cooper, Robert (1998) *The Postmodern State and the World Order*, London: Demos, The Foreign Policy Centre.

Creveld, Martin van (1999) *The Rise and Decline of the State*, Cambridge: Cambridge University Press.

Crocker, Chester and Hampson, Fen Osler (eds) (1996) *Managing Global Chaos*, Washington: USIP.

—— (eds) (1999) *Herding Cats: Multiparty Mediation in a Complex World*, Washington: USIP.

Crossman, Richard (1949) *The God That Failed*, London: Hamilton.

Curtis, Lionel (1951) *With Milner in South Africa*, Oxford: Basil Blackwell.

Daalder Ivo H. and Lindsay, James M. (2003) *America Unbound: the Bush Revolution in Foreign Policy*, Washington: Brookings.

Danchev, Alex and Halberson, Thomas (eds) (1996) *International Perspectives on the Yugoslav Conflict*, London: Macmillan.

Dangerfield, George (1970) *The Strange Death of Liberal England*, London: Grenada.

Dawson, William Harbutt (1926) *Richard Cobden and Foreign Policy*, London: George Allen and Unwin.

Dedman, Martin J. (1996) *The Development of the European Union, 1945–95*, London: Routledge.

Doyle, Michael (1997) *Ways of War and Peace: Realism, Liberalism and Socialism*, New York: Norton.

Dunne, Tim (1998) *Inventing International Society: A History of the English School*, Houndmills: Macmillan.

Eatwell, Roger and Wright, Andrew (1999) *Contemporary Political Ideologies*, London: Continuum, 2nd edition.

Edmunds David and Eidinow, John (2001) *Wittgenstein's Poker: The Story of a Ten-Minute Argument Between Two Great Philosophers*, London: Faber and Faber.

Evans, Martin and Lunn, Kenneth (eds) (1997) *War and Memory in the Twentieth Century*, Oxford: Berg.

Evans, Richard (2003) *The Coming of the Third Reich*, London: Allen Lane.

Falconer A. D. and Liechty, Joseph (eds) (1998) *Reconciling Memories*, Dublin: The Columba Press.

Fink, Carole (1984) *The Genoa Conference*, Chapel Hill: University of Northern Carolina Press.

Fink, Carole, Frohn, Axel and Heideking, Juergen (eds) (1991) *Genoa, Rapallo and European Reconstruction in 1922*, Cambridge: Cambridge University Press.

Foner, Eric (1989) *Reconstruction: America's Unfinished Revolution, 1863–1877*, New York: HarperCollins.

—— (1990) *A Short History of Reconstruction, 1863–1877*, New York: Harper and Row.

Forman, Shephard and Patrick, Stewart (eds) (2000) *Good Intentions: Pledges for Postconflict Recovery*, London: Lynne Reinner.

Forsythe, David (2000) *Human Rights in International Relations*, Cambridge: Cambridge University Press.

Frost, Mervyn (1996) *Ethics in International Relations: A Constitutive Theory*, Cambridge: Cambridge University Press.

Fry, Michael G. (1977) *Lloyd George and Foreign Policy, Vol. I, 1890–1916*, Montreal: McGill University Press.

Fukuyama, Francis (1992) *The End of History and the Last Man*, New York, The Free Press.

—— (1995) *Trust*, New York: The Free Press.

—— (1997) *The End of Order*, London: The Social Market Foundation.

Fussell, Robert (1975) *The Great War and Modern Memory*, Oxford: Oxford University Press.

Gallie, W. B. (1978) *Philosophers of Peace and War*, Cambridge: Cambridge University Press.

Gay, Peter (1984) *The Bourgeois Experience, Victoria to Freud, Volume 1, Education of the Senses*, Oxford: Oxford University Press..

Gelfand, Lawrence (1963) *The Inquiry: American Preparations for Peace, 1917–1919*, New Haven: Yale Universsity Press.

Gill, Stephen (1990) *American Hegemony and the Trilateral Commission*, Cambridge: Cambridge University Press.

—— (1993) *Gramsci, Historical Materialism and International Relations*, Cambridge: Cambridge University Press.

Gilmour, David (2002) *The Long Recessional: The Imperial Life of Rudyard Kipling*, London: John Murray.

Glenny, Micha (1992) *The Death of Yugoslavia*, London: Penguin.

—— (1999) *The Balkans: Nationalism, War and The Great Powers, 1804–1999*, London: Granta.

Goldhagen, Daniel J. (1997) *Hitler's Willing Executioners: Ordinary Germans and the Holocaust*, London: Abacus.

Goldstein, Eric (1991) *Winning the Peace: British Diplomatic Strategy and the Paris Peace Conference, 1916–1920*, Oxford: Clarendon Press.

Gong, Gerrit (1984) *The Standard of Civilisation in International Society*, Oxford: Clarendon Press.

Gourevitch, Philip (1995) *We Wish To Inform You that Tomorrow We Will Be Killed With Our Families: Stories From Rwanda*, New York: Farrar, Strauss and Giroux.

Gow, James (1996) *Triumph of the Lack of Will*, London: Hurst.

Gray, John (1986) *Liberalism*, Milton Keynes: Open University Press.

—— (2002) *Straw Dogs: Thoughts on Humans and Other Animals*, London: Granta.

Grayling, A. C. (2002) *The Meaning of Things: Applying Philosophy to Life*, London: Phoenix.

Gromyko, Andrei (1989) *Memoirs*, New York: Doubleday.

Haass, Richard N. (1999) *Intervention: The Use of American Military Force in the Post Cold War World*, Washington DC: Brookings/Carnegie.

Hall, John (ed.) (1995) *Civil Society: Theory, History, Comparison*, Oxford: Polity.

Hankey, Maurice (1963) *The Supreme Control at the Paris Peace Conference*, London: G. Allen and Unwin.

Hardy, Thomas (1966) *Selected Shorter Poems of Thomas Hardy*, London: Macmillan.

Harper, John Lamberton (1996) *American Visions of Europe: Franklin D. Roosevelt, George F. Kennan and Dean G. Acheson*, Cambridge: Cambridge University Press.

Hawley, Eliot (ed.) (1981) *Herbert Hoover as Secretary of Commerce: Studies in New Era Thought and Practice*, Iowa City: University of Iowa Press.

Hayek, F. A. (1944) *The Road to Serfdom*, Chicago: University of Chicago Press.

Hayner, Patricia (2002) *Unspeakable Truths: Facing the Challenge of Truth Commissions*, New York: Routledge.

Hazan, Pierre (2000) *La justice face a la guerre: De Nuremberg a La Haye*, Paris: Stock.

Headlam Charles (ed.) (1931–3) *The Milner Papers, 1897–1905*, London: Cassell, 2 vols.

Heilbronner, Robert L. (1977) *The Economic Transformation of America*, New York: Harcourt Brace Jovanovich.

Henderson, Michael (1999) *Forgiveness: Breaking the Chain of Hate*, Wilsonville, Oregon: BookPartners Inc.

Hinsley, F. H. (1963) *Power and the Pursuit of Peace*, Cambridge: Cambridge University Press.

Hobson, J. A. (1919) *Richard Cobden: the International Man*, London: T. Fisher Unwin.

Hobsbawm, Eric (1969) *Industry and Empire*, London: Penguin.

—— (1994) *The Age of Extremes: The Short Twentieth Century, 1914–1991*, London: Michael Joseph.

Hogan, Michael (1977) *Informal Entente: the Private Structure of Cooperation in Anglo-American Economic Diplomacy*, Columbia: University of Missouri Press.

—— (1987) *The Marshall Plan: America, Britain and the Reconstruction of Western Europe: 1947–1952*, Cambridge: Cambridge University Press.

Hoff Wilson, Joan (1974) *Ideology and Economics: US Relations with the Soviet Union, 1918–1933*, Columbia: University of Missouri Press.

Holbrooke, Richard (1998) *To End a War*, New York: The Modern Library.

Holsti, Kal J. (1998) *The State, War and the State of War*, Cambridge: Cambridge University Press.

Holzgrefe J. L. and Keohane Robert O. (eds) (2003) *Humanitarian Intervention: Ethical, Legal and Political Dilemmas*, Cambridge: Cambridge University Press.

Hopkinson, A. (1918) *Rebuilding Britain: A Survey of Problems of Reconstruction after the World War*, London: Cassell and Co.

Howard, Michael (2000) *The Invention of Peace: Reflections on War and International Order*, New Haven: Yale University Press.

Human Rights Watch (1999) *Leave None to Tell the Story*, New York: Human Rights Watch.

Huntingdon, Samuel (1996) *Clash of Civilisation: and the Remaking of World Order*, New York: Simon & Schuster.

Hyde-Price, Adrian (2000) *Germany and European Order: Enlarging NATO and the EU*, Manchester: Manchester University Press.

Ignatieff, Michael (1999) *The Warrior's Honour: Ethnic War and the Modern Conscience*, London: Vintage.

Ikenberry, G. John (2001) *After Victory: Institutions, Strategic Restraint and the Rebuilding of Order after Major Wars*, Princeton: Princeton University Press.

Ikle, Fred C. (1991) *Every War Must End*, New York: Columbia University Press.

Joas, Hans (2003) *War and Modernity*, Cambridge: Polity.

James, Willmot and van de Vijver, Linda (2000) *After the TRC: Reflections of Truth and Reconciliation in South Africa*, Athens, OH: Ohio University Press.

Jokic, Alexander (2001) *War Crimes and Collective Wrongdoing*, Oxford: Blackwell.

Judd, Denis and Surridge, Kenneth (2002) *The Boer War*, London: John Murray.

Kacowicz, Arie M., Bar-Siman-Tov, Yaacov, Elgstrom, Ole and Jerneck, Magnus (eds) (2000) *Stable Peace Among Nations*, London: Rowan and Littlefield.

Kaldor, Mary (1999) *New and Old Wars: Organized Violence in a Global Era*, Cambridge: Polity Press.

—— (2003) *Global Civil Society: An Answer to War*, Cambridge: Polity.

Kaldor, Mary and Vashee, Baskar (eds) (1997) *Restructuring the Global Military Sector: Volume 1: New Wars*, London: Cassell/Pinter.

Kampfner, John (2003, 2004) *Blair's Wars*, London: Free Press.

Kant, Immanuel (1983) *Perpetual Peace and Other Essays*, Indianapolis: Hackett.

Kaplan, Robert D. (1994, 1996) *Balkan Ghosts: A Journey Through History*, New York: Vintage.

Keegan, John (2004) *The Iraq War*, London: Hutchinson.

Kegley, Charles and Raymond, Gregory A. (2000) *How Nations Make Peace*, New York: St Martin's/Worth.

Kennan, George (1984) *American Diplomacy*, Chicago: University of Chicago Press.

Kent, Bruce (1989) *The Spoils of War: The Politics, Economics and Diplomacy of Reparations, 1918–1922*, Oxford: Clarendon Press.

Keynes, John Maynard (1920) *The Economic Consequences of the Peace*, London: Macmillan.

—— (1921) *A Revision of the Treaty*, London: Macmillan.

Khan, S. M. (2002) *The Shallow Graves of Rwanda*, London: Pluto.

Kindleberger, Charles (1973) *The World In Depression, 1929–1939*, London: Allen Lane.

Kipling, Rudyard (1994) *The Works of Rudyard Kipling*, Ware: The Wordsworth Poetry Library.

Kissinger, Henry (1994) *Diplomacy*, New York: Simon & Schuster.

Knock, Thomas J. (1992) *To End All Wars: Woodrow Wilson and the Search for a New World Order*, New York, Oxford University Press.

Kuklick, Bruce (1972) *American Policy and the Division of Germany: the Clash with Russia over Reparations*, New York: Cornell University Press.

Kumar, Krishna (ed.) (1998) *Postconflict Elections, Democratization and International Assistance*, London: Lynne Reinner.

Laïdi, Zaki (ed.) (1994) *Power and Purpose after the Cold War*, Oxford: Berg.

—— (1998) *A World Without Meaning?* London: Routledge.

Laqueur, Walter (2003) *No End to War: Terrorism in the Twentieth Century*, New York: Continuum.

Latawski, Paul and Smith, Martin A. (2003) *The Kosovo Crisis and the Evolution of post-Cold War European Security*, Manchester: Manchester University Press.

Lentin, Anthony (1985) *Guilt at Versailles: Lloyd George and the Pre-History of Appeasement*, London: Methuen.

Levy, Carl and Roseman, Mark (ed.) (2002) *Three Postwar Eras in Comparison: Western Europe, 1918-1945-1989*, London: Palgrave.

Lieven, Dominic (2000) *Empires*, London: John Murray.

Lipgens, Walter (1982) *A History of European Integration, Vol. 1, 1945–47*, Oxford: Clarendon Press.

Lloyd George, David (1932) *The Truth about Reparations and War Debts*, London: William Heinemann.

—— (1938) *The Truth About the Peace Treaties*, London: Gollancz.

Long, David and Wilson, Peter (eds) (1995) *Thinkers of the Twenty Years Crisis*, Oxford: Clarendon Press.

Lucas, C. P. (1913), *The Reconstruction of the New Colonies under Lord Milner*, London, 2 volumes.

McKercher, B. J. C. (1999) *Transition of Power: Britain's Loss of Global Pre-Eminence to the United States, 1930–1945*, Cambridge: Cambridge University Press.

MacMillan, John (1998) *On Liberal Peace: Democracy, War and the International Order*, London: Tauris.

MacMillan, Harold (1933) *Reconstruction: A Plea for a National Policy*, London: Macmillan.

Macmillan, Margaret (2001) *Peacemakers: The Paris Conference of 1919 and Its Attempt to End War*, London: John Murray.

Maier, Charles S. (1975) *Recasting Bourgeois Europe: Stabilization in France, Germany and Italy in the Decade after World War One*, Princeton: Princeton University Press.

Mandaville, Peter and Williams, Andrew (2003) *Meaning and International Relations*, London: Routledge.

Mandelbaum, Michael (2002) *The Ideas that Conquered the World; Peace, Democracy and Free Markets in the Twenty-First Century*, Oxford: Public Affairs Ltd.

Marks, Sally (1982) *Innocent Abroad, Belgium at the Peace Conference*, Chapel Hill, NC: University of North Carolina Press.

Marlowe, John (1976) *Milner: Apostle of Empire*, London: Hamish Hamilton.

Marx, Karl and Engels, Friedrich (1848) *The Communist Manifesto*, Harmondsworth: Penguin.

Mastanduno, Michael (1992) *Economic Containment: CoCom and the Politics of East-West Trade*, Ithaca, NY: Cornell University Press.

Mayer, A. G. (1967) *Politics and Diplomacy of Peacemaking: Containment and Counterrevolution at Versailles, 1918–1919*, New York: Alfred A. Knopf.

Mayne, Richard, Pinder, John, Roberts, John C. De V. (1990) *Federal Union: The Pioneers: A History of Federal Union*, London: Macmillan.

Mazower, Mark, (1998) *Dark Continent: Europe's Twentieth Century*, London: Penguin.

Menand, Louis (2001) *The Metaphysical Club: A Story of Ideas in America*, London: Flamingo/HarperCollins.

Miall, Hugh, Ramsbottam, Oliver and Woodhouse, Tom (1999) *Contemporary Conflict Resolution: The Prevention, Management and Transformation of Deadly Conflicts*, Cambridge: Polity.

Milward, Alan S. (1984) *The Reconstruction of Western Europe, 1945–51*, London: Routledge.

Minear, Richard H. (1971) *Victor's Justice: The Tokyo War Crimes Trial*, Princeton: Princeton University Press.

Minow, Martha (1998) *Between Vengeance and Forgiveness: Facing History after Genocide and Mass Violence*, Boston: Beacon Press.

Mitrany, David (1966 [1943]) *A Working Peace System*, Reprinted with an Introduction by Hans Morgenthau, Chicago: Quadrangle Books.

Mitrany, David and Taylor, Paul (1975) *The Functional Theory of Politics*, London: Martin Robertson.

Monnet, Jean (1976) *Mémoires*, Paris: Fayard.

Montefiore, Simon Sebag (2003) *Stalin: The Court of the Red Czar*, London: Wiedenfield and Nicholson.

Moore Jonathan (ed.) (1998) *Hard Choices: Moral Dilemmas in Humanitarian Intervention*, Lanham: MD, Rowman and Littlefield.

Morel, E. D. (1915) *Ten Years of Secret Diplomacy: An Unheeded Warning*, London: National Labour Press.

Murray, Gilbert (1921) *The Problem of Foreign Policy*, London: George Allen and Unwin.

Naimark, Norman. M. (2001) *Fires of Hatred: Ethnic Cleansing in Twentieth Century Europe*, Cambridge, MA: Harvard University Press.

Noel Baker, Philip (1922) *The Financial Reconstruction of Europe*, Geneva: League of Nations.

Nash, Lee (ed.) (1987) *Understanding Herbert Hoover: Ten Perspectives*, Stanford: Hoover Institution.

O'Brien, Francis William (ed.) (1978) *Two Peacemakers in Paris: The Hoover–Wilson Post-Armistice Letters, 1918–1920*, College Station: Texas A&M, University Press.

O'Brien, Patrick Carl (1988) *The Economic Effects of the American Civil War*, Basingstoke: Macmillan.

Orwell, George (1990 [1949]) *Nineteen-eighty Four*, Harmondsworth: Penguin.

Osiander, Andreas (1994) *The States System of Europe, 1640–1990: Peacemaking and the Conditions of International Stability*, Oxford: Clarendon Press.

Owen, David (1995) *Balkan Odyssey*, London: Indigo Press.

Parmar, Inderjeet (2004) *Think Tanks and Power in Foreign Policy*, London: Palgrave.

Petriciolli, Marta (ed.) (1995) *A Missed Opportunity? 1922: The Reconstruction of Europe*, Bern: Peter Lang.

Pijl, Kees van der (1998) *Transnational Classes and International Relations*, London: Routledge.

Pimlott, Ben (1985) *Hugh Dalton A Biography*, London: Jonathan Cape.

—— (1986) (ed.) *The Second World War Diary of Hugh Dalton, 1940–45*, London: Jonathan Cape.

Plano, Jack and Riggs, Robert E. (1967) *Forging World Order: The Politics of International Organization*, New York: Macmillan.

Polanyi, Karl (1939) *The Great Transformation: The Political and Economic Origins of Our Time*, New York: Beacon.

Popper, Karl (1971) *The Open Society and its Enemies*, Princeton: Princeton University Press.

Power, Samantha (2002) *A Problem from Hell: America and the Age of Genocide*, New York: HarperCollins.

Prunier, Gerard (2002) *The Rwandan Crisis: History of a Genocide*, London: Hurst.

Rappard, William (1930) *Uniting Europe*, New Haven: Yale University Press.

Rawls, John (1971) *A Theory of Justice*, Oxford: Oxford University Press.

Rayfield, Donald (2004) *Stalin and His Hangmen*, London: Viking.

Reychler, Luc and Paffenholz, Thania (2001) *Peacebuilding: A Field Guide*, London: Lynne Rienner.

Reynolds, David (1981) *The Creation of the Anglo–American Alliance, 1937–41*, London: Europe.

Reynolds, David (1991) *Britannia Overruled: British Policy and World Power in the Twentieth Century*, London: Longman.

Ricoeur, Paul (2000) *La memoire, l'histoire, l'oubli*, Paris: Editions du Seuil.

Rieff, David (1995) *Slaughterhouse: Bosnia and the Failure of the West*, New York: Simon & Schuster.

Rigby, Andrew (2001) *Justice and Reconciliation: After the Violence*, London: Lynne Reinner.

Roberts, John M. (1999) *Twentieth Century: A History of the World 1901 to the Present*, London: Penguin.

Robertson, Geoffrey (1999) *Crimes Against Humanity: The Struggle for Global Justice*, London: Allen Lane.

Rossanet, Bertrand de (1997) *War and Peace in the Former Yugoslavia*, The Hague: Kluwer Law International.

Rosenberg, Justin (1994) *The Empire of Civil Society: A Critique of the Realist Theory of International Relations*, London: Verso.

Sassoon, Siegfried (1942) *The Weald of Youth*, London: Faber and Faber.

Schabas, William A. (2001) *An Introduction to the International Criminal Court*, Cambridge: Cambridge University Press.

Schuker, Stephen A. (1976) *The End of French Predominance in Europe: The Financial Crisis of 1924 and the Adoption of the Dawes Plan*, Chapel Hill: University of North Carolina Press.

Schumpeter, Joseph (1919) 'The Sociology of Imperialism', in J. Schumpeter, *Imperialism and Social Classes*, Cleveland: World Publishing.

Schumpeter, Joseph (1950) *Capitalism, Socialism and Democracy*, New York: Harper and Row.

Sellars, Kirsten (2002) *The Rise and Rise of Human Rights*, Stroud: Sutton Publishing.

Shennan, Andrew (1989) *Rethinking France: Plans for Renewal, 1940–1946*, Oxford: Clarendon Press.

Simms, Brendan (2001) *Unfinest Hour: Britain and the Destruction of Bosnia*, London: Allen Lane.

Skidelsky, Robert (1992) *John Maynard Keynes: the Economist as Saviour, 1920–1937*, London: Macmillan.

Skidelsky, Robert (2000) *John Maynard Keynes: Fighting for Britain, 1937–1946*, London: Macmillan.

Spierenberg D. R. and Poidevin, Raymond (1999) *Histoire de la Haute Authorité de la Communauté Européene du Charbon et de l'Acier: Une Experience Supranationale*, Brussels: Bruylant (English translation Weidenfield and Nicholson).

Stern, Fritz (1999) *Einstein's German World*, Princeton, Princeton University Press.

Streit, Clarence (1939) *Union Now*, London: Jonathan Cape.

Talmon, J. L. (1970) *Origins of Totalitarian Democracy*, New York, W. W. Norton.

Thomson, David, Mayer E. and Briggs, Asa (1945) *Patterns of Peacemaking*, London: Kegan, Paul, Trench, Trubner and Co.

Todorov, Tzvetan (1999) *Facing the Extreme: Moral Life in the Concentration Camps*, London: Weidenfield and Nicholson.

Todorov, Tzvetan (2000) *Mémoire du mal: Tentation du bien: Enquete sur le siècle*, Paris: Robert Laffont.

Trachtenberg, Mark (1980) *Reparations in World Politics: France and Economic Diplomacy, 1916–1923*, New York: Columbia University Press.

Trachtenberg, Mark (1999) *A Constructed Peace: The Making of the European Settlement, 1945–1963*, Princeton: Princeton University Press.

Tutu, Desmond (1999) *No Future Without Forgiveness*, London: Rider.

Vanderlip, Frank, A. (1920) *What Next in Europe*, New York: Harcourt Brace.

Varsari Antonio and Calandri Elena (2002) *The Failure of Peace in Europe, 1943–1948*, London: Palgrave.

Veremis Thanos and Dainanu Daniel (eds) (2001) *Balkan Reconstruction*, London: Frank Cass.

Vinen, Richard (2002) *A History in Fragments: Europe in the Twentieth Century*: London, Abacus.

Walzer, Michael (1992) *Just and Unjust Wars: A Moral Argument with Historical Illustrations* (2nd edn), New York: Basic Books.

Weill-Raynal, Etienne (1947) *Les reparations allemandes at la France, 1918–1936*, Paris: Nouvelles éditions latines.

Wells, Herbert George (1917) *War and the Future: Italy, France and Britain at War*, London: Cassell and Co. Ltd.

Welsh, Jennifer M. (1995) *Edmund Burke and International Relations*, London: Macmillan.

West, Rebecca (1982 [1941]) *Black Lamb and Grey Falcon*, New York: Penguin.

Wheeler, Nicholas (2000) *Saving Strangers: Humanitarian Intervention in International Society*, Oxford: Oxford University Press.

Wheen, Francis (1999) *Karl Marx*, London: Fourth Estate.

White, Stephen (1985) *The Origins of Detente: the Genoa Conference and Soviet–Western Relations, 1920–1924*, Cambridge: Cambridge University Press.

Whittaker, Derek J. (1999) *Conflict and Reconciliation in the Contemporary World*, London: Routledge.

Williams, Andrew (1992) *Trading with the Bolsheviks: The Politics of East–West Trade, 1920–1939*, Manchester: Manchester University Press.

—— (1998) *Failed Imagination? New World Orders of the Twentieth Century*, Manchester: Manchester University Press.

Willis, James F. (1982) *The Politics and Diplomacy of Punishing War Criminals of the First World War*, Westport, CT: Greenwood Press.

Winter, Jay (1995) *Sites of Memory, Sites of Mourning: The Great War in European Cultural History*, Cambridge: Cambridge University Press.

Worsfold, W. B. (1906) *Lord Milner's Work in South Africa, 1897 to the Peace of Vereeniging, 1902*, London: Murray.

Zartman, William (1998) *Peacemaking and International Conflict*, Washington, DC: United States Institute of Peace Press.

ARTICLES (and unpublished conference papers)

Abouzahr, Sami (2004) 'The Tangled Web: America, France and Indochina, 1947–50', *History Today*, 54(10), 49–55.

Allerfeldt, K. (2004) 'Wilsonian Pragmatism? Woodrow Wilson, Japanese Immigration and the Paris Peace Conference', *Diplomacy and Statecraft*, 15(3), 545–72.

Ashworth, Lucian M. (2002) 'Did the Realist-Idealist debate ever happen? A Revisionist History of International Relations', *International Relations*, 16(1), 33–51.

Boyd, Charles G. (1995) 'Making Peace with the Guilty', *Foreign Affairs*, 74(5), 22–38.

Colomonos, Ariel (1999) 'Understanding Global Repentance: Hypotheses and Frameworks for Research', presented to the International Studies Association Conference, February.

Colson, Aurelien (2000) 'The Logic of Peace and the Logic of Justice', *International Relations*, XV(1), 51–62.

Cox, Mick (1998) '"Cinderella at the Ball": Explaining the End of the Conflict in Northern Ireland', *Millennium*, 27(2), 325–42.

Cramer, Christopher (2004) 'The Great Post-Conflict Makeover Fantasy', paper presented to the Conference 'Making Peace Work', UNU–WIDER, Helsinki, June.

Cull, Nicholas (1996) 'Selling Peace: The Origins, Promotion and Fate of the Anglo–American New Order during the Second World War', *Diplomacy and Statecraft*, 7(1), 1–28.

Duss, P. (1996) 'Imperialism Without Colonies: The Vision of a Greater East Asia Co-Prosperity Sphere', *Diplomacy and Statecraft*, 7(1), 54–72.

Fukuyama, Francis (1989) 'The End of History and the Last Man', *The National Interest*, Summer.

Hayek, Friedrich, (1949) 'The Intellectuals and Socialism', *University of Chicago Law Review*, 16(3), 417–33, republished under the same title by the Institute of Economic Affairs, London, 1998.

Ikenberry, John (1992) 'A World Economy Restored: Expert Consensus and the Anglo–American Postwar Settlement', *International Organization*, 46(1), 289–322.

Lentin, Anthony (1999) 'Lord Cunliffe, Lloyd George, Reparations and Reputations at the Paris Peace Conference, 1919', *Diplomacy and Statecraft*, March.

McGinty, Roger (2003) 'The Pre-War Reconstruction of Post-War Iraq', *Third World Quarterly*, 24(4), 601–17.

Maogoto, Jackson Nyamuya (2003) 'The International Criminal Tribunal for Rwanda: A Distorting Mirror; Casting doubt on its actor-oriented approach in addressing the Rwanda genocide', *African Journal on Conflict Resolution*, 3(1).

Parmar, Inderjeet (n.d.) 'CFR–RIIA Interconnections: A Nascent Transnational Ruling Class, Liberal Atlantic Community, or Anglo-American Establishment?'.

Parmar, Inderjeet (2001) 'Lord Lothian's Moment: The Anglo-American Establishment and the Saving of Britain, 1939–1941', paper presented at the University of Edinburgh, May, pp. 6–7.

—— (2002) 'Anglo-American Elites in the Interwar Years: Idealism and Power in the Intellectual Roots of Chatham, House and the Council for Foreign Relations', *International Relations*, 169(1), 53–76.

Pemberton, Jo-Anne (2001), 'Towards a New World Order; A Twentieth Century Story, *Review of International Studies*, 27, 265–72

Robbins, Keith (1967) 'Lord Bryce and the First World War', *The Historical Journal*, X(2), 255–77.

Ruggie, John Gerald, (1982) 'International Regimes, Transaction and Change: Embedded Liberalism in the Postwar Economic Order', *International Organization*, 36, 379–415.

Stuchtey, Benedict (1999) 'The International of Critics, German and British Scholars during the South African War (1899–1902)', unpublished manuscript.

Venn, Fiona (1990) '"A Futile Paper Chase": Anglo-American Relations and Middle East Oil, 1918–1934' in *Diplomacy and Statecraft*, 1(2), 165–84.

Webb, Keith (1995) 'Third Party Intervention and the Ending of Wars: A Preliminary Appraisal', *Paradigms*, Winter.

Williams, Andrew (2000) 'France and the New World Order, 1940–1947', *Modern and Contemporary France*, 8(2), 191–202.

Williams, Andrew (2002) 'Sir John Bradbury and the Reparations Commission, 1920 – 1925', *Diplomacy and Statecraft*, 13(3), 81–102.

Williams, Andrew (2003) 'Before the Special Relationship: The Council on Foreign Relations, The Carnegie Foundation and the Rumour of a Anglo-American War', *Journal of Transatlantic Studies*, 1(2), 233–51.

Williams, David (2001) 'Liberal Theory and Liberal Practice in International Politics', paper given to the ECPR Conference, Canterbury, UK.

Unpublished theses

May, Alex (1995) *The Round Table, 191–66*, D.Phil, Oxford.

Miyamoto, Kiyoko (2004) 'Peace from Below: Developing Inter-ethnic Dialogue Amongst Citizens for Bottom-up Conflict Transformation in Bosnia, PhD, University of Kent.

Index

Printed in Great Britain
by Amazon.co.uk, Ltd.,
Marston Gate.